THE ART OF *Baby* NAMEOLOGY

Explore the Deeper Meaning of Names for Your Baby

NORMA J. WATTS

SOURCEBOOKS, INC.
NAPERVILLE, ILLINOIS

Published by Sourcebooks, Inc.
P.O. Box 4410, Naperville, Illinois 60567–4410
(630) 961–3900
Fax: (630) 961–2168
www.sourcebooks.com

Originally published in 2006 by Champion Press, as *The Art of Nameology*.

Library of Congress Cataloging-in-Publication Data

Watts, Norma J.
  The art of baby nameology : explore the deeper meaning of names for your baby / Norma J. Watts.
      p. cm.
  1. Fortune-telling by names. 2. Names, Personal—Dictionaries. 3. Numerology. I. Title.
  BF1891.N3.W38 2008
  133.3'3–dc22

2008018047

Printed and bound in the United States of America.
DR 10 9 8 7 6 5 4 3 2 1

DEDICATION

To children (of all ages), may we live on the positive side of our names.

ACKNOWLEDGMENTS

I want to thank my teachers and guides in Spirit for helping me with this project. Without all their Divine help and inspiration, it would not have come to fruition.

I would also like to thank my friend Elizabeth for some wonderful names to put in my book. Liz was so supportive with her Aries positive enthusiasm. She was probably one of the only people on earth that seemed to know what I was really trying to accomplish.

Six years ago my daughter Kelly mentioned a baby name book to me. I couldn't get the idea of a name book out of my head. A few days later I was struck with divine inspiration on how to write this name book. Thanks, Kelly, for planting the seed.

My daughter Kim gave me the motivation to reach this goal, as with the accomplishment of getting this book published, I will be able to see my three beautiful grandchildren. Thanks for the motivation, Hon!

My daughter Mecauley helped me prove the theory that this book was easy enough for a twelve-year-old to understand. Shortly after her twelfth birthday she read the first three chapters for me and understood it perfectly. It also helped her understand one of her friends better.

Just before the deadline of getting the final draft to the publisher, my son George never said a word about the Christmas tree still being up in February. He didn't complain once about the dust mites or my lack of housekeeping, bless his heart.

My younger siste, Nita, generously helped me as she has in the past with suggestions, thoughts, ideas, and all her positive energy. She's a force of nature.

Although my Dad doesn't really understand my passion for this project, he loves me anyway and calls me every Friday to see how I'm doing. Thanks, Dad!

Last but not least, my Mom is always there for me—morally, financially, emotionally, and otherwise. She never stopped believing in me, not once. Thanks, Mom!

CONTENTS

Nameology is the study of names based on the Pythagorean Method of numerology. Pythagoras, one of the most famous and controversial ancient Greek mathematicians, found that numbers exist everywhere—even in names. Although the concept of associating names and numbers has been around for over 2,500 years, it has been hidden under the guise of numerology. Numerology focuses on numbers—numbers found in our birthday and numbers found in our whole birth name. Numerology looks at the numbers in our addresses, phone numbers, and all the numbers around us, even our checking account numbers. Pythagoras was called "the father of all numbers" for this reason. Each numerology book primarily agrees on the basic concepts, but authors have their own slants on the subject, just as I do. As I wrote this book, I realized I was not just writing about numerology; rather, I was writing about a unique subset of numerology, which deserved its own title. Appropriately, I started calling it "Nameology." In reality, nameology has always been a part of numerology; it just hasn't always been discussed separately.

While most numerology books devote a chapter or two on how numbers can be derived from names, we will give all of our focus to that here and then analyze the implications of those numbers. When looking at the letters and vowels of your name, you will see that intensity and power numbers say quite a bit. You'll also find out the importance of "hidden numbers," which are unique to Nameology. They aren't in your average numerology book because I discovered them during my studies. I want to share the concept of "hidden numbers" here, as they have demonstrated keen validity time and again.

Nameology can be a valuable tool. Every letter in your name says something about who you are, what you most like to do, the people you get along with best, the skills you exceed in, and more. Learning about the letters in your name can give you a greater understanding of yourself and others. Who would have thought it could be so easy to get to know someone just by knowing their first name?

Of course, all this means that choosing a name for someone else is a very important task! This book can be your guide to selecting the best name for your baby. You'll be able to preview the personality of names you are considering in several ways. You can quickly reference the meaning of a name, and you can also break each name down yourself by letter. Furthermore, you will see how to interpret unusual names or names not found in this book, or continue to research on your own.

Why is it so important to think about the letters of the name you're choosing? Test out Nameology for yourself and see. The accuracy of the characteristics associated with each name may surprise you, and you may want to give careful consideration to what attributes correspond to your baby's name.

Whether you are searching for personality insight, reading for fun, or looking for the right name for your new bundle of joy, this book lends a unique yet age-old way of understanding others through the science of numbers.

The easiest way to use this book is to look up a name in the quick reference. Looking up a name will give a brief description of various aspects of that personality; sometimes this is all we need. The number after the name in the quick reference section is called the "power number," or PN. The power number is the sum total of all the numbers in a person's name. It shows the strength of the name and overall capabilities associated with it. Information about the power number can be found in Chapter Two, "Converting a Name to a Number." The definitions found in the "PNs in a Nutshell" section of that chapter are brief (page 22). For a more thorough interpretation of each number, look in Chapter One, the "Numbers" chapter.

If a person has several letters ruled by one number, this is called an "intensity" number. For example: Anne = A-1, N-5, N-5, E-5. Anne's first letter is ruled by the number 1. Three out of four letters of her name are ruled by the number 5. So Anne would have an intensity number of 5. This number strongly influences her personality. Therefore, to better understand Anne, look up number 5 under "intensity numbers" in Chapter Two. This number is intensely inside her. It heavily influences her. Even two letters ruled by the same number are worth looking up, because that number influences a name more than the rest.

Another way to use this book is to look up the meaning of each letter in a name at the beginning of each quick reference section, so you can amalgamate your own meaning for that name. Each letter of a person's name reveals an aspect of their personality. The quick reference is a short summary; looking up each letter gives a better understanding of that person all together. It explains the different aspects of their personality. The first letter in a name is called the "cornerstone." This letter describes a person's basic personality. It's similar to a rising sign or ascendant. The cornerstone shows how a person approaches opportunities and obstacles, or how they are on the outside. Next, look up the first vowel in the name. This is the "heart's desire" letter. It is the way this person will always feel, which reveals part of a person's deeper nature, or how they are on the inside. The last letter of a person's name is called the "capstone." This reveals a person's ability and attitude toward finishing what he started.

You can continue with looking up the other letters,, each number yielding another hidden personality aspect. These are called "hidden numbers," the underlying influence in this person's personality. Sometimes the accuracy of hidden numbers is surprising.

Let's take JOHN and interpret this name using the cornerstone, heart's desire, capstone, and hidden numbers. First, his cornerstone letter starts with a clever and talented J. J is ruled by the independent number I and likes to please everyone. It's an intelligent letter and shows how he approaches new opportunities and obstacles. The cornerstone and capstone letters are the legs he stands on—they support him. Or better yet, they support his name, so they are strong in his personality. At first sight, John will most likely impress others with his intelligence and leadership skills. His first vowel, or "heart's desire" letter, is O. The number 6 rules O and rules love.

Sometimes as we get to know someone better, we "see how they really are." Well, when we get to know John better, we find out about the O and H influence in his name. These aspects of his personality are not quite so out in the open as his cornerstone and capstone letters, which shield the real John. But we cannot simply focus on the cornerstone and capstone; all of the letters in John's name are him. We don't get to meet some letters until we get past the first letter, as is the case here with the O and H. The O is nurturing. Early in life John should have a pet or younger siblings to love. If he doesn't, he will probably boss his parents around or try to take care of them. It's best to allow John to have someone or something to love. Along the same lines, people with O as their first vowels make great parents; they are magnetic and are natural counselors and healers. John will give great advice to family members in need. However, he may live on the negative side of his O and become meddling. Some Os can be moody.

His next letter is an H. There's a little corporate executive in him. H is ruled by the number 8 and is comfortable in the money market industry. H is a very Scorpio-like letter; they can be controlling. I know a John that makes extra money at the casinos. He knows when to hold 'em, and he knows when to fold 'em. H people enjoy competition and rivalry. This you'll discover after you get to know John a little bit better.

John's capstone, or last letter, is the romantic yet opinionated N. This letter shows that John finishes what he starts. It also communicates how he leaves a situation. N is ruled by number 5, which rules change. Often change is beneficial to those with this number in their name. Since this 5-ruled letter of change is his capstone letter, John most likely makes changes on his way to completing each situation. He may end each chapter of his life with a bit of excitement and adventure. He seeks freedom upon closure. Numbers 1, 5, and 7 are the intelligent numbers. His cornerstone and capstone letters are both ruled by cerebral letters. John shields the more vulnerable part of his personality with intelligence.

Let's figure out the hidden numbers for John. Since J is a 1 and O is a 6, if we add them together we find one hidden number, 7. Look up number 7 in the numbers section. John may be spiritual. If he doesn't have a strong spiritual base, then he might be egotistical or prone to escapist tendencies. At any rate, there is some 7 in his personality. It's not obvious, but he doesn't like it when people lie to him. People ruled by 7 are into the truth and usually abhor lying. Only those who know John well know this about him. The 7 is a part of John even though it is not obvious. When we add his hidden number 7 (the first two letters) to the next letter, H-8, it equals 15. This condenses down to a 6, since 1 + 5 = 6. John has two 6s in his name. His first vowel is a 6 and he has a hidden 6. John is a nurturer, but may not want everyone to see this aspect of his personality since it's his "heart's desire" and a hidden number. If John was not taught good moral values at an early age, he may take what does not belong to him. Or, if brought up with good moral values, he may have strong religious convictions, like John the Baptist.

Last, we add 15 to the letter N-5, to figure out John's power number. (Using a calculator will ensure accuracy in the power number.) That would equal 20. The number 2 rules partnership, and 0 rules assistance from God. His name sums up to having partnership or social situations being all or nothing at times. John's 1-ruled J and 8-ruled H make half his name independent and of somewhat strong character, yet he has a soft loving, nurturing side he doesn't readily let others see. His feelings could be easily hurt with a power number 20. In fact with the Scorpio-like H and freedom-loving N at the end of his name, he may go out of his way to be sure others don't know this about him. Most of the numbers in his name are fixed or stubborn, so he's most likely stubborn as well. John is no softy by any means with a 1 and an 8 in his name, but remember the hidden 6 and 7 when interpreting his name. The hidden numbers make the picture complete. They fill in the whole name and help us to understand the whole person. When painting a picture, we need to fill in the details. The "art" of interpreting a name takes a little practice. A successful Nameologist will blend the numbers one by one, filling in the whole personality. Personalities are not cut-and-dried, nor black and white. We are multifaceted. Blending the different numbers gives us depth and color. The "Numbers" chapter may serve as a study guide to improve the beginning Nameologist's ability to interpret names.

Note:

It's important to use a calculator when adding up the numbers in a name. As we added John's name, although we figured the 15 to be a 6 because 1 + 5 = 6, showing a hidden 6 in his name, we need to continue with the 15 until all the letters are added in his name. If we decreased the 15 to a 6 then added 6 to his last letter 5 it would equal 11, which is a master number. In reality his name equaled 20, not 11. The master number 11 never condenses to a 2. Although 20 can be condensed down to a 2, take into consideration the 0, which means assistance from God. When a zero is in a name anywhere, God is close by to offer assistance whenever needed for these individuals.

If interested in learning how to add up names, or convert names to numbers for names not mentioned in this book; read Chapter Two. This chapter teaches simplified basic knowledge about the numerology of names.

CHAPTER 1: *Numbers*

The number after each name in the quick reference section is the sum total of all the letters in the name added up together. Numerologists call this the "power number." The power number shows the strength of a name. It gives more information about that person. As the number pertains to only a first name, it should be read lightly. Adding all the letters of a person's entire name would be a more accurate description of his or her personality. Still, a first name alone can be telling. If you are interested in learning more about a name, you may want to read the number descriptions below in addition to the descriptions in the quick reference section.

The following number descriptions should also be read if a name has several letters (or even two) ruled by that number. When several letters are ruled by the same number, that number is called an "intensity number." For example, Jason would have a 1 intensity number, since three out of five letters are ruled by 1 (J-1, A-1, S-1, O-6, N-5). This number is called an intensity number because it is intensely inside that person. Please refer to the conversion chart in Chapter Two, in the "Converting a Name to a Number" section, to find out the intensity number of a name, if any. Rock stars and other celebrities often have a 5 intensity number. Not all with a 5 intensity number will be as wild, but may have "shocking" moments as did 5 intensity number Jennifer Lopez with her famous Oscar dress. The letters E and N are ruled by 5, so half of Jennifer's name has a letter ruled by the number 5. This means all Jennifers have a 5 intensity number.

One of the most important numbers to study, however, is the number that rules the first vowel of the name. The first vowel represents the "heart's desire." The heart's desire number reveals a person's deeper self, something that person will always feel. It's a small window into people's hearts they may or may not want others to see. If Patricia goes by Trish, then she may not want others to see her A heart's desire influence. Although she has two Is in her name, giving others the feeling of being safe around her humanitarian personality, she may not want others to see the true leader she really is for some reason. Also, the T in Trish is partnership-oriented. Those whose names contain B and T prefer to stand behind their partner instead of enjoying the direct limelight. It's best to read both a given name and a nickname to remove any doubt as to which name describes the person best. Most likely both names will fit a personality.

Also it might help to get acquainted with the first letter of a name. As we already know, it's referred to as the "cornerstone." This is similar to an astrological rising sign or ascendant. It's the beginning of a person's personality, or what they wear up front for the world to see. A cornerstone is what a person is and can't help being. The first letter shows how someone approaches new situations.

Hidden numbers can also influence the personality of a name. Adding the first letter to the second letter of a name will give a "hidden number." Then add the third letter; this tells more about that person. And so on and so forth…each addition of a letter gives another hidden number. Hidden means "not obvious." A hidden number reveals a little facet of ourselves, and we usually have many facets. Similar to a diamond, some angles are hidden from view, unintentionally, and only noticed when turned to a certain angle. Not secretive, just hidden, but bright as the rest of our assets. Close friends and family members have probably seen all of our hidden numbers—and we have seen theirs.

1 OR 10 — THE LEADER

Rules letters A, J, and S: This person is independent and self-motivated. Ones are critical of themselves and others. They have the tools to become original with a creative approach to problem solving. Ones have a competitive spirit and like to win. They have a bully in their head that continually pushes them to do better. As soon as they finish one task they are on to the next. Ones should try to rely on their wit and intelligence to avoid arguments and resentfulness. This number most closely resembles the Aries personality. A lot of I letters in a name can make the bearer a little harsh. Names with many I letters have an abundance of energy. This energy needs to be directed or they could become volatile. This number needs validation or approval now and then. They need to keep their egos in check. Ones have the ability to influence the opinions of others. A healthy I is independent, self-motivated, a hard worker, very intelligent, and superman-like. Ones living on the right side of their vibration will have their egos in tact. An unhealthy I has issues with self-esteem and not being good enough. They may show a rebellious nature. They can also suffer egotism and false pride. Ones living on the wrong side of their vibration will have a tendency to be dependent. All I-ruled people need to stand on their own two feet and learn not to depend or lean on others—even when the opportunity presents itself. Ones are happiest when they are independent.

2 OR 20 — THE MEDIATOR

Rules letters B, K, and T: This person wants peace and harmony. They are excellent mediators because they don't like conflict. This is one of the numbers that does well in business. The 2 vibration makes them dependent upon others. They are social by nature, and the sweetheart of numbers. The number 2 rules partnership; this is the most supportive number for partners. They are affectionate and need lots of hugs. Twos have refined taste in food, music, art, and clothes. Twos come in two personalities: Libra and Taurus. Both are affectionate. The Libra type is more intelligent, but temperamental; the Taurus type is more practical, but stubborn. It's best if this number learns not to take things personally, even if something was meant to be personal, as 2s can be overly sensitive. Similar to Libra, the scales, this number can be thrown off balance by an unkind word or look. Some 2s are easily offended. Those with many 2-ruled letters in their name can be overly emotional. They can be as temperamental as a two-year-old child when they feel threatened or pushed up against a wall. A healthy 2 is a true diplomat and peacemaker, loving and harmonious. They've got built-in radar. Some are very interested in the scientific art studies such as Numerology, Astrology, the Tarot, etc.

They can be psychic. They don't get bored easily. Twos are compassionate and care deeply about others. They can be friends with their children. An unhealthy 2 may experience nervous tension or emotional extremes, including depression. Some can cling to ideas long after they have outlived their usefulness.

3 OR 30 — THE COMMUNICATOR

Rules letters C, L, and U: This person possesses creative skills, mostly in the areas of writing, speaking, acting, or theater; typically the 3 has above-average ability in some art form. They are warm and friendly and make good conversationalists. Threes are animated and have a great sense of humor. They are natural comedians. This number most closely resembles the Gemini personality. They are as youthful and flirtatious as a teenager. An intensity number 3 can make for a nonstop talker. Threes are generally slow to make decisions. The number 3 rules balance. Meditation is beneficial to anyone with a lot of this number in their name as it helps them achieve balance. Threes manage to cope with life's many setbacks and bounce back for more. They are well-mannered and conscious of other people's feelings. They make excellent salespeople; if they believe in a product, they'll have no problem selling it. Threes are fiercely loyal—they don't get over others easily. After a breakup, for example, 3s will be upset if they check their answering machine and there's no message. They have many financial ups and downs and tend to be lucky! Threes are physically and mentally well-adjusted. They often have a lighter skin color, and there is something about their mouths. They are either too big for their face, or there is a noticeable space between the teeth, or a lisp. There is just something about their mouth. They are the spice of life and bring flavor to a bland world. A healthy 3 is cheerful, enthusiastic, optimistic, romantic, and upbeat. They're creative, happy, and inspired. An unhealthy 3 can be an outright liar, someone who enjoys making things up as they go along. They may be so delighted with living that life becomes frivolous and superficial. They may lack discipline and order in their lives. The unhealthy 3 can be overly dramatic if they have no outlet for their creativity.

4 or 40 — The Teacher

Rules letters D, M, and V: This person is a natural teacher and is extremely logical. They don't like to look naïve, so when they learn a skill they tend to become an expert, which is why they make excellent teachers. They are similar to the astrological sign of Cancer, the fourth sign of the Zodiac, and need to feel financially secure. They're not gold diggers; it's just that the sound of rustling currency calms their nerves. This is a very domestic number; work and family is what they're about. They are honest and direct by nature and don't like flashy or flamboyant people. Fours are very down-to-earth and practical. They are the ones who wear glasses. Usually they have darker skin coloring. Most people with 4-ruled letters in their names are excellent cooks. They are the most faithful of all the numbers. Most are task-oriented and don't mind hard work like gardening, cleaning, or paying bills. They are "the terminator" of numbers. They'll go in, assess a situation, then get to work on what needs to be done, methodically, systematically, and in an organized manner. Many 4 letters in a name could make the bearer a little cold or harsh, especially if the person had a difficult childhood. This number also has a bully in their heads. Some consume alcohol to escape the bully. People with 4s in their names will typically say they don't want to argue during a fight, but an hour later they are still arguing. A healthy 4 wants to teach others. They are domestic and family-oriented, hardworking and faithful. They're also logical. An unhealthy 4 might be so interested in preparing for their future that they forget about enjoying today. They can start too many tasks and barely finish anything. An unhealthy 4 will be overly stubborn and rigid.

5 or 50 — The Free Spirit

Rules letters E, N, and W: This person is truly a free spirit. Fives love meeting new people. They love change, excitement, and adventure. Freedom is the nucleus around which their lives evolve. All of life is a playground for their senses. Fives are capable of doing almost anything. Some enjoy going around shocking people. Rock stars usually have some 5 letters in their name. They're extremely adaptable; in fact, change is a blessing for them—5s could die of boredom in a humdrum routine. Any sort of boundary could blind them to their natural limits. This may cause overindulgence in food or sweets. They want to try everything at least once. Fives can be gamblers and often play for high stakes. They fall in and out of love, especially early in life. This number most resembles the sign of Leo. They usually have a flair for decorating. This number is very opinionated! Fives can liven a dull party. The drawback to a 5's overindulgence is that they can get "burned out." Sometimes they will get burned out on driving, throwing parties, relationships, or a demanding job. If they are overdoing it, there is a danger of the burn-out syndrome. A healthy 5 celebrates life and has a sparkling emotional outlook. They manage to attain a sense of freedom and responsibility. They are a social delight and mix well with people of all social standing. An unhealthy 5's life will be unorganized and scattered. They can be shallow and superficial. Overindulgence and escapism are the 5's worst enemies.

6 OR 60 — THE NURTURER

Rules letters F, O, and X: This person puts the needs of others before him or herself. That's why they make natural parents. If they can't have children, they will treat their employees like children. Or they will dress up their pets like children. Their lessons have much to do with love. This number is similar to the sign Virgo. A person with a 6 anywhere in their name will have a well-stocked medicine cabinet. This number likes to shop at warehouse stores to get more for their money. They aren't spendthrifts. A man with this number will attract women who are damsels in distress. A woman with this number who can't have children will often attract men who are little boys. They have to have someone to love and care for. Sixes have a natural gift with flowers, gardens, and animals. Why, the very shape of 6 looks pregnant with love. Although they are natural counselors and healers, they need to be careful not to interfere with the freedom of others. They can be meddlesome, insisting on having their own way in family quarrels. Sixes are magnetic. When they walk into a room, people stop dead in their tracks. Sure, they can be attractive, but it's more than that. They have a way about them that just can't be ignored. Sixes can't work for others; they need to run their own companies. They are all about duty. They make good managers; they don't like to take advantage of others. A healthy 6 has good moral standards, and is loving, nurturing, and responsible. An unhealthy 6 has a problem letting their children grow up. They can be meddlesome and jealous. Their moods can affect everyone around them.

7 OR 70—THE FAITH SEEKER

Rules letters G, P, and Y: This person needs to learn to have faith. They can't really be happy unless they have faith. If a 7 has faith, they tend to be very spiritual and we can learn from them. If not, they can be exhausting to be around, with their constant bragging and boasting. The 7s with little faith tend to have an overly inflated opinion of themselves. They have a brilliant mind and are driven by the desire for knowledge and truth. Sevens are very direct. They tell the truth. If they don't like someone, it's obvious. Their tongue can cut like a sword. Sevens operate on a rather different wavelength. Many of their friends may not really know them very well. This number has a Pisces personality. Those with a heavy abundance of 7 in their names look as if they are swimming when they walk across a room. They can end up in the movie industry or on television. They tend to be psychic and they can also be overly secretive. Sevens are loners. The typical 7 neither shows nor understands emotions very well. It's almost as if they are from another planet. They seem to like technical fields, such as computers, science, and modern technology. Sevens like to discover things. It's been said that "Genius is 1 percent inspiration and 99 percent perspiration." Our 7 friends receive more inspiration than any other number. They are opportunists and "think tank" people. Yet, if they don't take the idea and run with it, it just sits in their heads and dies. A healthy 7 has a strong faith base, untiringly seeks the truth, and follows their inspirations. An unhealthy 7 is highly introverted, self-centered, egotistical, overly critical, and intolerant. They can be prone to escapism through drugs or alcohol. They can dream their life away.

8 OR 80 — THE EXECUTIVE

Rules letters H, Q, and Z: This person is well-equipped in a managerial sense. They have outstanding organizational and administrative capabilities. Eights have the power and potential to achieve great things. They make great leaders and are outstanding judges of character. This number most resembles the personality of Scorpio. Eights can read people like a book—don't try to pull anything over on them, they'll know. They like to control relationships; it's over when they say it's over, not before. Eights can be very stubborn. They can be demanding of those who work for them, often putting things in no uncertain terms: Do it my way or don't do it at all! They won't hesitate, however, to reward the faithful and hard-working employee. Eights go after their goals with courage and tenacity. They enjoy rivalry and challenge. They understand the larger picture, see the broader challenges. Eights are here to learn that obstacles are merely opportunities to find out how to use their power and authority. Most 8 types have to learn things the hard way. Often 8s adopt the saying, "He who dies with the most toys wins!" They are most eager to get all they can out of the material world. If they use their power for selfish means, however, it could backfire disastrously. Negative 8s are too preoccupied with other people's possessions. This is a highly karmic number. It's crucial for an 8's success that they balance the material and the spiritual, give and take, reward and punishment, action and reaction. It's a good luck/bad luck number that gives out exactly what the bearer karmically deserves. Despite the obstacles, they are true survivors. A healthy 8 manages to use their power in a positive way, only giving out what they want to get back. An unhealthy 8 uses their power for selfish means. They can be harsh and overly materialistic.

9 OR 90 — THE HUMANITARIAN

Rules letters I and R: This number usually produces persons that are very trustworthy and honorable and unlikely to harbor any sort of prejudice.

It's a pretty tall order, but 9s feel very deeply for individuals less fortunate than themselves. The number 9 is the highest of the single digit numbers and holds certain responsibilities. Judges, spiritual leaders, educators, and healers often have a 9 somewhere in their name. Nines tend to do their jobs, and everyone else's too, with little or no thanks from those they help. Although material gains are not overly important to the typical 9, they are blessed in some ways. This number is similar to the astrological sign Sagittarius. The 9 has three 3s in it, so balance is a major lesson for them. They are often born into money, inherit it, marry it, or win it. People tend to assume 9s know everything. Some people will walk up to a 9 in a supermarket and ask if they know where an item is, assuming they are the manager. If they are in a classroom, children will approach them thinking they are the teacher. They just look as if they have all the answers. An abundance of this number (or if it rules the first vowel or consonant), can make the person very artistic. In a spiritual sense, they are quite evolved—angels on earth it seems. They can be naughty though. People tend to follow them whether they are right or wrong. Bill Clinton, Michael Jackson, and Britney Spears all have first vowels ruled by 9. Despite all the bad publicity, people still follow them or put them on a pedestal. Nines typically have old family pain that haunts them. Many have "father issues." They can achieve happiness if they forgive and forget those that hurt them in the past. A healthy 9 personality is compassionate, generous, and a humanitarian. An unhealthy 9 needs to speak up when they want something—we can't read their minds. They need to get over their past hurts. Some can be intimidating bullies, using their power the wrong way.

11 — THE LIGHTNING ROD

Rules the letter K: Number 11 is one of two master numbers. This number is the most highly charged of all. Whoever bears this number in their name can be a little high-strung. They can be too exacting. They are a lightning rod, attracting powerful intuitions, ideas, even psychic information, like unpredictable bolts of lightning. They are a channel for higher vibrations. In order to be emotionally and psychologically at peace, they must learn to control that flow of energy. This double 1 energy gives them ambition and the need to succeed. They will achieve excellence. With double 1s they can really beat themselves up, thinking they are never good enough. This number has Aquarian qualities. Aquarius is the eleventh sign of the Zodiac. Others can learn from them; that's why it's a master number. They work well with others because they know how to use persuasion rather than force. The number 11 has all the aspects of the number 2, enhanced and charged with charisma, leadership, and inspiration. They have good analytical minds, but may not be comfortable in the business world. Lightning rods are definitely creative. A healthy 11 manages to ground their energies and use them for the benefit of mankind. They also make wonderful teachers. An unhealthy 11 can be thrown about by emotional turmoil and nervous tensions. They can be more dreamers than doers—beating themselves up all the while for not doing something with their special talents.

22 — THE MASTER BUILDER

Rules the letter V: Number 22 is the other master number. Those born with master number 22 in their name tend to be intuitive and psychic. They are natural teachers with lots of knowledge. They could never be like everyone else. They are here to make an impact in a positive way. If they don't use their power, they can end up in torment and depression. Master builders dream big; all of their goals are enormous in scope. They want to change history, make their marks on human civilization, and create something that will last for centuries. There is no limit to what they are capable of doing. Of all the numbers, 22 possesses the greatest potential for accomplishment. They refuse to back down in the face of a challenge. They like to work in large enterprises on an international scale. They see themselves as world citizens playing on this planet, and refuse to be limited by other people's boundaries. Twenty-twos should marry someone who does not depend on them for entertainment. Instead, they need a partner who is willing to work with them toward their goals. In choosing a career, there are no real limitations. The field is wide open to them. A healthy 22 strives to make their mark on the world, making it a better place, and uses their gift to help humanity. An unhealthy 22, well, the worst they can do is to just be an ordinary 4. It's their choice whether they use their gift or not.

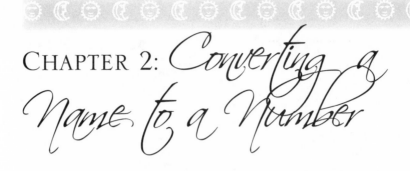

CHAPTER 2: Converting a Name to a Number

This part of the book shows how to convert the letters of a name into numbers by slowly adding them up. This calculation helps us to understand the basic personality traits of each letter or number that rules it. Memorizing these meanings helps us interpret the personality of each name more easily.

Each letter of a name from beginning to end has a number assigned to it. For easy calculations, refer to the "Conversion Chart" below. It's important to use a calculator so as not to overlook *hidden numbers, master numbers,* and *numbers ending with zero.*

General meaning of numbers:
1 – Beginnings
2 – Partnership
3 – Balance
4 – Work/Family
5 – Change
6 – Love
7 – Spiritual/Religion
8 – Reward/Punishment
9 – Completions
0 – Assistance from God

Creative: 3, 6, and 9
3 – socially
6 – service
9 – humanity
Business: 2, 4, and 8
2 – partner
4 – work/family
8 – corporate
Intelligent: 1, 5, and 7
I – personally
5 – groups
7 – spiritually
Master: 11 and 22
II – intuitive
22 – global

Conversion Chart Pythagorean Method

I	2	3	4	5	6	7	8	9
A	B	C	D	E	F	G	H	I
J	K	L	M	N	O	P	Q	R
S	T	U	V	W	X	Y	Z	

Example:

B	R	I	A	N	
2 +	9 +	9 +	I +	5	= 26

The two numbers of the sum are then added together to get a one digit number (unless the sum is one of the master numbers, 11 or 22). The number 26 becomes $2 + 6 = 8$.

Using a calculator:

Add $2 + 9$ (B + R) = 11, then add 9 (I) = 20, then add 1 (A) = 21, then add 5 (N) = 26. Then add those two digits together to get one digit, $2 + 6 = 8$.

Each letter of Brian's name means something. Each letter paints another stroke in the portrait of Brian. The B, ruled by the number 2, at the beginning or the front of his name, is similar to a rising sign. This first letter shows us how Brian first appears. Because the B is ruled by the sensitive number 2, Brian gives the first impression that he is understanding and insightful.

Then add the 9-ruled letter R and we have the number 11. The R is a bit of a bully in the family of alphabets. Although Brian is a sensitive fellow, he does have an ability to intimidate. R is ruled by the number 9 which is ruled by Jupiter, the largest planet. People with the letter R anywhere in their name are big in some way. They are prone to making sweeping gestures and accidentally knocking over the salt shaker. Since the B is a consonant and conjuncts another consonant, the second consonant colors or flavors the first. So we have someone who is sensitive and shy, but not afraid. The 11 is also a master number. His first two letters, or hidden number, add up to a master number. This master number paints its portrait as either a dreamer or a doer. Those ruled by 11 are often visionaries and dramatic. They are "the lightning rod," and often rank as genius, if stubborn enough to see their ideas through. Sometimes they are overwhelmed or a bit high-strung. The 9 and 11 influence could make for an absentminded professor type. In fact, Rs in a name often make a person forgetful, misplacing or losing items.

Then we add another 9-ruled letter, I, which sums up to the hidden number 20. The number 20 is partnership and assistance from God. At some point in Brian's life, probably in the middle of his life, he will be involved with partnership and the social aspects of life. It will be all or nothing as the 0 in the 20 lends weight. The third letter of his name is a vowel. This is called his "heart's desire" letter. Since the I is artistic, philosophical, and creative, Brian most likely is too. Two 9-ruled letters in a row means he will need to learn balance. People will tend to follow him right or wrong with an I first vowel. He may have old family pain that haunts him.

To his 20 we add 1 because A is ruled by the number 1. The number 21 adds together to 3 (2 + 1 = 3), so again balance is something he must learn. The hidden 3 in his name makes him a little bit lucky. He is cheerful and easy to get along with. As this is a hidden number, only those who know him well know this about him. He may have hidden writing talents. But first vowel I conjuncts another vowel, A, so he could be a bit hard on himself, or a bit of a perfectionist. He's more ambitious than the typical first vowel I usually is.

Last but not least, to his 21 we add the last letter N, which is ruled by 5. That would add up to 26 or 2 + 6 = 8. As the 26 he is learning partnership and love. Then after he learns about partnership and love, his name totals the number 8. This sum total is his power number and gives him Scorpio-like tendencies. He learns lessons having to do with joint finances and other people's money. The material lessons of life are the main theme for him in this lifetime. Sometimes lessons are learned the hard way, as this is a karmic-debt number. This could also mean a lifetime of rich rewards.

As you can see, many numerological factors exist in the name Brian, although it only has five letters. The portrait of this person becomes clear only after many brush strokes and much consideration.

POWER NUMBERS

In the quick reference, the number you see after each name is called the "power number," or PN. It is the sum total of letters converted to numbers, condensed down to a single digit. What gives the power number its power is that it shows the strength of a name, the sum total of its personality.

NOTE:

The numbers 11 and 22 never condense to 2 or 4, as they are master numbers. Names with master numbers as their power numbers are here to accomplish something worthwhile. Also listed are power numbers ending in zero. Names with power numbers ending in 10, 20, or 30 have the ability to motivate, uplift, and inspire others through the number before it.

The following are brief definitions of the power number behind each name. If you are interested in knowing more about power numbers, read Chapter One, "Numbers."

PNs IN A NUTSHELL

1—Self-sufficient, dominant, a leader, stubborn. Rules letters A, J, and S.

2—Understanding, insightful, often shy or hesitant. Rules letters B, K, and T.

3—Versatile, playful, a communicator or storyteller. Rules letters C, L, and U.

4—Productive, domestic, traditional, limited thinking. Rules letters D, M, and V.

5—Influential, progressive, entertaining, self-indulgent. Rules letters E, N, and W.

6—Responsible, care-giving, anxious, and guilt-ridden. Rules letters F, O, and X.

7—Seeks truth and knowledge, distant, narrow-minded. Rules letters G, P, and Y.

8—Successful, materialistic, sometimes ruthless. Rules letters H, Q, and Z.

9—Philosophical, intuitive, has a tendency to drift. Rules letters I and R.

11—Visionary, dramatic, nervous, overwhelmed. Rules letter K (co-ruled by 2).

22—Attuned to higher realms, global, fears limitations. Rules letter V (co-ruled by 4).

10—Beginning, plus assistance from God. Rules letter J (co-ruled by 1).

20—Partnership, plus assistance from God. Rules letter T (co-ruled by 2).

30—Balance, plus assistance from God. (co-ruled by 3).

Those with an 11 power number are here to achieve excellence. They are the lightning rod. They need to exercise their bodies to keep their fine minds in tune with the universe. They are creative and inspired.

Those with a 22 power number are intuitive and psychic. They are the master builders. This number indicates a natural teacher and an extremely knowledgeable person. They have no boundaries.

Those with 10, 20, or 30 as a power number have the ability to assist others:

- The 10 power number helps others through personal encouragement and mentoring.

- The 20 power number helps others through love, support and partnership.

- The 30 power number helps others through communicating, counseling and advice.

INTENSITY NUMBERS

When a name has two or more letters in it ruled by the same number, that number is called the "intensity number," or IN. The number is "intensely" inside this person. The intensity number reveals which characteristics a certain personality leans towards. The following shows how each intensity number influences a name. It is an intensity number if there is an abundance of the same number.

Examples: JASON, J-1, A-1, S-1, O-6, N-5. Jason has three letters ruled by number 1. Jason has an "intensity number 1" in his name.

BETTY, B-2, E-5, T-2, T-2, Y-7. Betty has three letters ruled by the number 2. Betty has an "intensity number 2" in her name.

The following are brief definitions of the intensity number (if any) of a name. To learn more about each number, read Chapter One, "Numbers."

INS IN A NUTSHELL

1—(A, J, and S): Independent, natural leader, risk taker; pride and ego are only downfall.

2—(B, K, and T): Socially refined, excellent mediator, intuitive, a bit overly sensitive.

3—(C, L, and U): Cheerful, positive, lucky and charming, undisciplined, talkative, lies.

4—(D, M, and V): Methodical, disciplined, reliable, responsible, can be narrow-minded.

5—(E, N, and W): A free spirit, needs change and variety, overindulgent.

6—(F, O, and X): Natural healer, service-oriented, self-sacrificing, can be meddlesome.

7—(G, P, and Y): Spiritual, scientific, seeks the truth, egotistical, sometimes cruel.

8—(H, Q, and Z): Enjoys rivalry and delegating authority, successful, a bit ruthless.

9—(I and R): Idealistic, compassionate, hard worker, lacks concern for money.

Also:

The 1 intensity has a strong will, competitive spirit, and desire to succeed.

The 2 intensity has a need for partnership, psychic abilities, and a need for love.

The 3 intensity is an excellent talker, has a great sense of humor, and is socially adept.

The 4 intensity is a natural teacher. They seek truth and can be opinionated.

The 5 intensity is passionate. They're romantic and love adventure.

The 6 intensity is magnetic, service- and task-oriented, nurturing and loving.

The 7 intensity is secretive and mysterious. They need their sleep and solitude.

The 8 intensity is successful and business-minded. They can be workaholics.

The 9 intensity is a humanitarian. They work hard for the good of the whole.

CHAPTER 3: *Naming Baby*

Deciding upon the right name for a baby can be a little scary. The name we choose will stay with the child for the rest of his or her life. So much pressure! Many new parents wait until after their baby is born before making a final decision. It could be the hair color, temperament, or overall appearance that helps make the final decision. A suggestion from a family member or birth on a special event or day could help us with the difficult task.

Many people have asked me, can we give someone a personality by naming them a certain name? Our names are subconsciously attracted to us at birth. The vowels are soft (say them out loud), A-E-I-O-U. Consonants are hard, with a different vibration. Each vibration has an aspect that describes a personality. Even psychologists will agree that much of a personality is already formed at birth. Some babies have a temper, some smile easily. When our child is born we sound out a name. If it hits our ear funny, or doesn't quite sound right, we keep sounding out names until we choose the name that best suits that child. That would be their "destiny" name.

Something else that's interesting is that our names often forecast our coloring. It seems the number 3 and the 3-ruled letters, C, L, and U, tend to be in the names of those with a lighter skin, hair, and eye color. The number 4 and the 4-ruled letters, D, M, and V, tend to have darker skin, eyes, and hair. The intelligent numbers 1, 5, and 7, and letters ruled by them, tend to have both light and dark mixed features, such as dark hair and light eyes or reversed. Or these numbers have medium coloring all the way around—not too dark, not too light.

As children get older, they may adopt nicknames that seem to fit their personalities better. When a child is named after someone, such as a parent, movie star, or friend, the child often exhibits aspects of the personality of their namesake. People may think that they share the same characteristics. It's not because they were named after that person. With the principles of Nameology, we understand that since they share the same letters in their name, they will have similar personalities.

With that in mind, when choosing a name for baby, if we like a person with a certain name, we most likely will approve of the child's personality if given the same name. If we don't want our baby to turn out just like daddy, then we shouldn't name the child the same exact name, or most assuredly their personalities will be similar. If the child named after daddy is not likewise the same in personality, the child will most likely adopt a name that fits his or her personality. Someone, probably a family member, will start calling the child a name that "sticks." This is the name that best fits the child's personality.

The birth name is a "destiny" name. It is similar to a natal chart that astrologers read to interpret a person's personality. The nickname or name that the child ends up going by most of the time is a "solar" name. Solar means sun and the sun reflects the personality that shines through. It's similar to a solar chart astrologers read to help understand others. Both charts are accurate, but sometimes the natal chart is more accurate and sometimes the solar is more accurate. Many will want to argue this point, but both give information about a person. The destiny name, or birth name, is accurate. The solar name, or nickname, is also accurate. Each gives us more information about that person. When in doubt, read both. It is my inclination to give the most weight to the name a person goes by most often. A friend of mine has the first name of William, but his close friends call him Bill. When first meeting someone he prefers the new acquaintance to call him William. Those whose names start with W like to meet new people. Sometimes they can be superficial. B people are more sensitive and personal, more easily hurt. They can be shy at first. My friend Bill has a Cancer rising so the sensitive and shy B name does fit his personality better. The fact that he protects his identity by having new acquaintances call him William also gives me reason to believe his solar name fits him better.

When choosing a name, it's best to consider using some of the letters in the parent's first names for compatibility. Besides, we know the child will inherit certain qualities anyway. Why not choose the qualities we like best about ourselves? If the child is adopted, it becomes even more important to share similar letters or compatible letters. It is in our power to choose a name that has the qualities we most desire. We seem to be more compatible with those who share letters ruled by the same number. For example, a father's name is David and his son's name is Matthew. The letters D, M, and V (Dept. of Motor Vehicles) are all ruled by the number 4 vibration. Father and son will be similar in personality with the first letter of their names ruled by the number 4. They are both systematic and organized; both are ambitious and desire financial security. Both may have excellent teaching skills. Both have the letter A as the first vowel in their names. They have a bully in their heads driving them to do better. With these similarities, father and son will most likely have a lot in common. Ideally, when a father shares similar personality traits to his son, the father can help his son through some of their shared weaknesses. The son can forgive his father some of his faults as he's a chip off the ol' block. They may share the same goals, or at least share a basic understanding of one another.

Having some different letters from each other will allow each of them their own personality. Letters that share the same qualities, such as the letters of business, ruled by the numbers 2, 4, and 8, can compliment one another. Letters ruled by the numbers 3 and 5 tend to compliment one another also. As a rule, odd numbers tend to go well together and even numbers tend to be compatible with each other. In astrology, the fire signs tend to be more compatible with the air and other fire signs. The earth signs tend to be more compatible with the water and other earth signs. Even numbers are similar to water and earth signs; odd numbers are similar to fire and air signs.

Letters L, U, and C (LUCK) are ruled by the lucky number 3. They are cheerful and bright—the happiest of all the letters. Lucille Ball had an intensity 3 in her name. She was a natural comedian and performed well onstage. Letters N, E, and W (NEW) are ruled by the number 5 and love meeting new people; they are the entertainers and party people.

The letters ruled by 3 and 5 tend to be sharp dressers and do well out in public and on stage. The letters ruled by 1, 5, and 7 are complimentary to each other as these numbers in a name show a degree of intelligence. The letters ruled by the number 7 are G, P, and Y (GYPSY). These letters like their solitude. Similar to gypsies, the 7-ruled letters can be psychic. Although these letters are compatible with letters ruled by the numbers 3 and 5 on the level of intelligence, 3 and 5 letters like to party and 7-ruled letters prefer to be alone more often than not.

Letters ruled by 7 tend to be more compatible with letters ruled by 1 and 9. A, J, and S are all ruled by the number 1. Number 1-ruled letters tend to be very independent. Only two letters are ruled by the number 9; they are letters I and R. Letters ruled by number 9 tend to be similar to the 7-ruled. They are both more spiritual and closer to God than the rest of the letters. Letters ruled by the number 1 tend to be compatible with 7 for intellectual reasons.

B, K, and T (BUCKET) are the more emotional letters. They can produce a bucket of tears. These letters need and give lots of hugs. If affection and sensitivity are desirable, name the child with a B, K, or T in the beginning of their name. K is ruled by the master number 11, and although it can be overly emotional, the K can also be a bit high-strung. K people can either be dreamers or will be very successful in life. Even if the K doesn't exercise its full potential, it will be emotional and sensitive at times. Again, heredity and upbringing is a factor, as in all the letters.

Our names have a beginning, middle, and end. The letters in our names bring us through a complete cycle of each experience again and again. For example, Joan will be independent at the beginning of each new situation. She will then tend to be nurturing in that situation. With O, she's the boss type. Then she will want to be independent and exhibit her leadership skills. Then she will opt for change and want freedom. This cycle will repeat itself for Joan in every new situation with every person she meets and every job she takes on. Each letter is responsible for providing a lesson for her. Her name is her evolution through life. She travels the way the letters take her. Take into consideration the hidden numbers as they also figure into our travel through each situation.

That in mind, when children are named with double letters in their names, they will have to repeat certain lessons. They will spend more time learning about the lessons brought about by these letters. If we name a child Kelly, he or she will begin every new situation in a sensitive yet ambitious way. The K makes her friendly, and socially adept at first, yet this letter has a strong desire to succeed. Then she will learn the lessons of the E which are change, variety, excitement, new situations, meeting new people. Then she will learn lessons in communication and transportation. She may drive a lot or talk a lot at this point of her development. Then she will have more of the lesson from the letter L because of the second L—more driving, more talking. People with two Ls in their names have to endure financial ups and downs as well. They tend to make many short trips around town, and their housing may be temporary. They need to communicate a lot, twice as much in fact. Two Ls give the bearer of the name a youthful personality, and that person tends to recuperate from illness faster. But does that person really need to repeat certain lessons? The child could learn just as easily with one letter, then move on to the next lesson or begin a new lesson or learning in life. Most numerologists will agree that whenever possible, it is best not have double letters in a name for the simple reason of not making people have to repeat lessons. That said, those with double letters in their names have a certain character about them that most don't have. The intensity of the number that vibrates through their double letters indeed creates a unique personality.

The amount of letters in a name also influence the personality. Seldom do we find a name with just one letter. However if such a name existed, the letter of the single-lettered name would give much weight in the overall personality. The fact that it would only be one letter would make the child independent, a leader, ambitious, and bolder than the rest. Two letters in a name, such as Al or Ed, makes a child more partnership-oriented. Three letters in a name, such as Gil or Kim, give the child more than an average ability to communicate and get along with others. Four letters in a name, such as Doug or Beth, make the child more down-to-earth and practical. Five letters in a name, such as Tracy or Steve, gives the child more of a desire for freedom. This child will adapt to change easier. Six letters in a name, such as Ronald or Janice, make for a more nurturing personality. This child will make a good boss. Seven letters in a name, such as Melissa or Gilbert, can give the child spiritual leanings. They will have lessons in faith. Eight letters in a name, such as Penelope or Clifford, give the child a more than average ability to master the material world. Nine letters in a name, such as Gabrielle or Alexander, give the child a more blessed life. This child will have humanitarian leanings; they may be artistic as well.

NAMES MOST LIKELY...

to be successful: names with letters A, D, H, J, K, M, S, and V.

to fall in and out of love: names with letters E, N, and W.

to nurture children, pets, or plants: names with letters F, O, and X.

to support their partner: names with letters B, K, and T.

to make a great boss: O first vowels, F first letters.

to be young and sexy: names that have CH or QU in them.

to be a flirt: names with first vowels E and U, or letters C, L, and N.

to be affectionate: names with letters B, K, and T.

to be artistic: names with I first vowels, or letters R or X.

to entertain well: names with letters C, L, U, E, N, and W.

to be religious leaders: names with O first vowels and R first letters.

to overindulge: names with E first vowels and letters N, W , and X.

to be scientific and philosophical: names with letters G, P, and Y.

to be hard workers: names with letters I, R, D, or M.

to lie or make things up: names with letters C, L, U, or number 3.

to teach: names with letters D, M, or V or power number 4.

to beat themselves up: names with letters A, J, S, and also D and M.

to be egotistical: names with letters G, P, Y, and number 7 or I.

to be domestic and duty-bound: names with letters D, M, F, and first vowel O.

to cheat on their partner: names with E first vowels, or letters N, W , or number 5.

to be faithful partners: names with letters D, M, V, or number 4.

to get good grades: names with vowels A, E, and Y, or letters J and S.

to be competitive: names with letters A, J, S, H, Q, and Z.

to own their own business: names with first vowel A or O or numbers I or 6.

to be lucky: names with letters C, L, U, or number 3.

to get depressed: names with letters D, M, V, or number 4.

to be musically inclined: names with letters F, O, B, K, and T.

to be talkative: names with U first vowels or letters C and L.

to be tight with money: names with letters H, D, M, and O first vowel.

to be selfish: names with first vowel U, or number 3.

to keep a list: names with first vowel A, letters D, M, V, or number 4.

to have financial ups and downs: names with letters ruled by numbers 3, 5, and 8.

to be a rock star: names with letters N, E, W , or intensity number 5.

$\mathcal{A}$

If a name begins with A, has A as the first vowel, has more than one A, or ends with an A, this person is ambitious, independent, energetic and self-motivated.

Since A is the first letter of the alphabet, A is ruled by the number 1. They're here to brave the new frontier. A-named people are natural leaders who want to lead the way. It all comes from that number 1 vibration. It's a "me first" letter. A types are the "Supermen" of letters and are almost perfect. Like Superman, they're hard on themselves for not being perfect. It's as if a bully was inside their head driving them to succeed. They beat themselves up all the time. A-named people are harder on themselves than anyone else could ever be, except another A type, that is. Like the song goes, "One is the loneliest number." The vibration of the first letter of the alphabet is to stand alone, independent—or the lessons to be learned from the 1 vibration will not be learned. In other words, a person with several As in their name (or other letters ruled by 1) needs to not lean on others. Although the opportunity and temptation will be there, it is imperative they learn to stand on their own two feet. A types will usually admit to being happiest when they are independent or not depending on others.

They make excellent teachers, critics, engineers, and entrepreneurs. People with A names are confident and successful businesspeople. They are great at independently managing or owning a business. Inventors, activists, and politicians also come from A type personalities. Race car drivers and daredevils alike have a touch of that 1 vibration somewhere.

They can be stubborn and willful, but obstinately adhering to their path is what makes the A personality successful. They are born achievers. They won't let others talk them out of doing what they know will work. Strength, perseverance, and willpower are paramount to their accomplishments. If they walk through life with blinders on, however, their stubbornness could lead to complications. The really stubborn A types need to work on seeing all sides more often. They should strive to keep an open mind, so they don't trip or fall over the perfect idea or solution to a problem. Also, A types complain a lot. We can recognize an A person by the amount of complaining they do.

A-named people make good partners, as long as they can be independent within the relationship. They need to follow their own drummer. Support their dreams and goals and you'll have a happy A. They actually don't *need* your support to reach their goals. They have enough energy and drive on their own; however, giving validation periodically will enhance a relationship with the A type. This is also true of the letters J and S, since they too are ruled by the number I vibration.

A or I types are similar in personality to the astrological sign of Aries the ram, which coincidently also begins with A. Aries is ruled by Mars which rules the head. This type of personality is known to jump into things head first. A and I rule beginnings. A is the baby of the letters. When a baby cries or yells they usually get taken care of right away. A or I type personalities operate in a similar manner.

Remember Sally Field's famous speech upon accepting her second Oscar? With tears in her eyes, she said, "You like me, you really like me!" Sally has two I vibration letters at the beginning of her name. As or Is are hard on themselves and try to be perfect. People with two or three I-ruled letters are good; they just don't *know* how good they are. Sally's reaction that night showed everyone she didn't know how good she was. Jason, Sarah, Sam, and Janice can be awfully critical of themselves. It's best to give a little word of support or encouragement from time to time. A complement can go a long way. Laugh at their jokes, but be sincere. They are very intelligent and can usually detect insincerity right away. In fact, A names need to find the humor in situations a little more and get angry a little less. An A personality that can laugh at him or herself is a relief. Some are almost as intense as R names. Sometimes it's hard for them to lighten up.

A or I types need to get out of their heads from time to time. They enjoy watching people win at football, baseball, soccer, drag racing, boxing, wrestling, rodeo, or game shows—anything that involves competition. It helps get our critical friends out of their heads. This provides much needed relief to those with As in their names from beating themselves up. If they don't have a healthy form of escapism, they sometimes turn to other alternatives, such as alcohol or drugs. Awareness of this tendency could help our I-ruled friends make better decisions.

What do Arnold and Ronald have in common? These names have the same letters in them, just arranged differently. Interestingly enough, both Ronald Reagan and Arnold Schwarzenegger had successful careers in Hollywood before running for Governor of California. The R in their names gives them both the ability to somehow intimidate their opponents. The A in their names makes them leaders in whatever field they choose. Since Arnold wears his heart's desire letter (first vowel) up front, he is not afraid to let the world see his true heart's desires. Any man whose name starts with an A and has an R right next to it is no "girly man." Ronald's R up front, a humanitarian letter, next to his nurturing O first vowel, made him strong in a different way. The D in their names gives them the ability to assess any situation in a systematic, almost "terminator" fashion. It also helps them to maintain a disciplined effort toward goals. The O gives them the ability to counsel and a tendency to take on the responsibility of others. The L is great for communication, as both men seem to have no problem getting their message across. The N makes them original, unconventional, and romantic. Since both have D at the end, they clean up in the end. They do the job no one else can. The difference is the first letter. Arnold comes across immediately as a leader because his A is up front. Ronald came across as gentle, kind, and hardworking. However, no one wanted to test him, since he was intimidating with his R up front. Arnold's R conjuncts, or flavors, his first letter, so he's also a little intimidating. Because their letters are arranged differently they have different hidden numbers; however, they still have many of the same personality traits because of the same letters and power number. The wild card in their names is the letter N. All that strength in their letters plus the intelligent, yet unpredictable N is what keeps their opponents at bay. They like to keep everyone guessing.

Some other famous A names: Angelina Jolie, Abraham Lincoln, Andy Richter, Aaron Carter, Ashley Olsen, Andy Rooney, Audrey Hepburn, Albert Schweitzer, Aristotle Onassis, Anton Chekhov, Adlai Stevenson, Al Capone, Alan Alda, Amy Irving, Antonio Banderas, Aretha Franklin, Adam Sandler, Alfred Hitchcock, Andy Griffith, Ashley Judd, Alec Baldwin, Arsenio Hall, Alicia Silverstone, Anita Baker, Art Linkletter, Avril Lavigne, Alanis Morissette, Alexis Bledel, Andy Milonakis, Ashton Kutcher, Ashanti, Anthony Perkins, Anthony Hopkins, and Al Pacino.

QUICK REFERENCE OF "A" NAMES

Aaron, 22: Ambitious leader, great vision. Resolute and purposeful. Gentle, kind, hard worker. Natural counselor and healer. Intuitive and creative.

Abbott, 6: Reads people easily. Friendly, but shy. Affectionate and social. Natural counselor and healer. Dynamic, busy lifestyle. Sensitive and easily hurt.

Abby, 3: Expresses thoughts readily. Loyal and understanding. Emotional and sensitive. Needs a lot of freedom.

Abel, 11: Ambitious leader, great vision. Good business partner. Keenly perceptive. Strong verbal skills.

Abigail, 5: Bold, courageous, adventuresome. Sparkling emotional outlook. Blessed in some ways. Scientific and philosophical. Not easily influenced. Artistic, having good taste. Frequent traveler.

Abimael, 7: Not easily influenced. Friendly, but shy. Idealistic and humanitarian. Domestic, hardworking. Bold, courageous, a bit stubborn. A free spirit, very adaptable. Strong verbal skills.

Abraham, 8: Resolute and purposeful. An excellent mediator. Gentle, kind, a hard worker. Bold, courageous, a bit stubborn. Great judge of character. Pioneer and risk taker. Systematic and organized.

Abu, 6: Pioneer and risk taker. Creative in a practical way. Attractive and charming.

Ace, 9: Hardworking and helpful. Self-expressive, cheerful. A free spirit, very adaptable.

Adam, 10: Independent, critical of self and others. Reliable, responsible. Bold, courageous, a bit stubborn. Domestic, hardworking.

Adel, 4: Natural teaching ability. Down-to-earth, faithful. Loves adventure and excitement. Strong verbal skills.

Adele, 9: Hardworking and helpful. Reliable and responsible. Likes to entertain. Communicates skillfully. Physical and passionate.

Adrian, 11: Ambitious leader, great vision. Natural authority. Strives to improve humanity. Blessed in some ways. Bold, courageous, a bit stubborn. Original and unconventional.

Adriana, 30: Expresses thoughts readily. Reliable, responsible. Optimistic and very kind. Blessed in some ways. Bold, courageous, a bit stubborn. Romantic, sensual. Pioneer and risk taker.

Adrienne, 7: Not easily influenced. Problem solver. Gentle, kind, a hard worker. Blessed in some ways. A free spirit, very adaptable. Original and unconventional. Creative, opinionated. Physical, passionate.

Aeolabi, 9: Hardworking and helpful. Loves adventure and excitement. Natural counselor and healer. Strong verbal skills. Bold, courageous, a bit stubborn. Loyal, understanding. Blessed in some ways.

Aeyoung, 7: Not easily influenced. Likes change and variety. Needs a lot of freedom. Natural counselor and healer. Attractive and charming. Original and unconventional. Scientific and philosophical.

Agatha, 11: Ambitious leader, great vision. Scientific, philosophical. Bold, courageous, a bit stubborn. Dynamic, busy lifestyle. Great judge of character. Pioneer and risk taker.

Agnes, 10: Independent, critical of self and others. Extremely intelligent. Creative and opinionated. A free spirit, very adaptable. Charming and devoted.

Agustin, 10: Independent, critical of self and others. An opportunist. Very lucky. Charming and devoted. Dynamic, busy lifestyle. Blessed in some ways. Original and unconventional.

Ahmed, 22: Ambitious leader, great vision. Self-reliant, successful. Domestic, hardworking. Likes change and variety. A natural authority.

Akai, 4: Natural teaching ability. Strong desire to succeed. Resolute and purposeful. Blessed in some ways.

Aki, 3: Expresses thoughts readily. Enthusiastic, quick-witted. Communicates understanding.

Al, 4: Natural teaching ability. Intellectually sound. Domestic, down-to-earth.

Alan, 10: Independent, critical of self and others. Frequent traveler. Bold, courageous, a bit stubborn. Original and unconventional.

Alanis, 20: Reads people easily, perceptive. Communicates skillfully. Independent, critical of self and others. Opinionated, romantic. Blessed in some ways. Charming and devoted.

Alann, 6: Pioneer, risk taker. Easygoing attitude. Bold, courageous, a bit stubborn. Original and opinionated. Romantic, sensual.

Alannah, 6: Pioneer, risk taker. Strong verbal skills. Independent, critical of self and others. Original and opinionated. Romantic, sensual. Not easily influenced. Enjoys competition.

Albert, 4: Natural teaching ability. Frequent traveler. Friendly, but shy. A free spirit, very adaptable. Gentle, kind, a hard worker. Dynamic, very busy lifestyle.

Aleisha, 10: Independent, critical of self and others. Strong verbal skills. Physical and passionate. Blessed in some ways. Charming and devoted. Enjoys competition. Bold, courageous, a bit stubborn.

Alejandro, 8: Resolute and purposeful. Recuperates quickly. Physical and passionate. Clever and talented. Bold, courageous, a bit stubborn. Original and unconventional. Reliable, responsible. Gentle, kind, a hard worker. Natural counselor and healer.

Alessandra, 4: Natural teaching ability. Strong verbal skills. A free spirit, very adaptable. Charming and devoted. Many mood swings. Bold, courageous, a bit stubborn. Original and unconventional. Reliable, responsible. Gentle, kind, a hard worker. Independent, critical of self and others.

Alex, 6: Pioneer and risk taker. Frequent traveler. Creative in service. Artistic, sensual, very perceptive.

Alexa, 7: Not easily influenced. Strong verbal skills. Likes change and variety. Artistic, sensual, very perceptive. Bold, courageous, a bit stubborn.

Alexander, 3: Expresses thoughts readily. Slow to make decisions. A free spirit, very adaptable. Artistic, sensual, very perceptive. Bold, courageous, a bit stubborn. Original, unconventional. Reliable, responsible. Loves adventure and excitement. Gentle, kind, hard worker.

Alexei, 11: Ambitious leader, great vision. Travels frequently. A free spirit, very adaptable. Artistic, sensual, perceptive. Physical and passionate. Blessed in some ways.

Alexia, 7: Not easily influenced. Intellectually sound. Likes change and variety. Artistic, sensual, perceptive. Blessed in some ways. Independent, critical of self and others.

Alexis, 7: Not easily influenced. Communicates skillfully. Loves adventure and excitement. Artistic, sensual, perceptive. Blessed in some ways. Charming and devoted.

Alfred, 10: Independent, critical of self and others. Strong verbal skills. Nurturing, loving. Gentle, kind, hard worker. A free spirit, very adaptable. Down-to-earth, faithful.

Ali, 4: Natural teaching ability. Strong verbal skills. Idealistic and humanitarian.

Alia, 5: Bold, courageous, a bit stubborn. Frequent traveler. Idealistic and humanitarian. Independent, critical of self and others.

Alice, 3: Expresses thoughts readily. Slow to make decisions. Artistic, having good taste. Great sense of humor. A free spirit, very adaptable.

Alicia, 8: Resolute and purposeful. Recuperates quickly. Idealistic and humanitarian. Optimistic and outspoken. Blessed in some ways. Not easily influenced.

Alife, 6: Pioneer and risk taker. Frequent traveler. Artistic, having good taste. Self-sacrificing, loving. A free spirit, very adaptable.

Alison, 7: Not easily influenced. Strong verbal skills. Blessed in some ways. Charming and devoted. Natural counselor and healer. Original and unconventional.

Allan, 4: Natural teaching ability. Ups and downs financially. Frequent traveler. Independent, critical of self and others. Original and unconventional.

Allen, 8: Resolute and purposeful. Ups and downs financially. Recuperates quickly. Physical and passionate. Creative and opinionated.

Allison, 10: Independent, critical of self and others. Strong verbal skills. Frequent traveler. Blessed in some ways. Charming and devoted. Natural counselor and healer. Original and unconventional.

Aloha, 10: Independent, critical of self and others. Strong verbal skills. Natural counselor and healer. Self-reliant, successful. Bold, courageous, a bit stubborn.

Alton, 8: Resolute and purposeful. Ups and downs financially. Dynamic, busy lifestyle. Natural counselor and healer. Romantic, sensual.

Alvin, 4: Natural teaching ability. Strong verbal skills. Intuitive and inspired. Blessed in some ways. Original and unconventional.

Alyce, 10: Independent, critical of self and others. Frequent traveler. Dislikes limitations. Effective speaker. A free spirit, adaptable to change.

Alysha, 3: Expresses thoughts readily. Slow to make decisions. Needs a lot of freedom. Charming and devoted. Great judge of character. Bold, courageous, a bit stubborn.

Amanda, 7: Not easily influenced. Desires financial security. Bold, courageous, a bit stubborn. Original and unconventional. Workaholic, shrewd and determined. Independent, critical of self and others.

Amando, 3: Expresses thoughts readily. Family communicator. Bold, courageous, a bit stubborn. Original and unconventional. Serious, yet fun-loving. Natural counselor and healer.

Amber, 3: Expresses thoughts readily. Systematic, organized. Affectionate, social. Loves adventure and excitement. Gentle, kind, a hard worker.

Amelia, 5: Bold, courageous, adventuresome. Domestic, hardworking. Physical and passionate. Slow to make decisions. Blessed in some ways. Pioneer and risk taker.

Amir, 5: Bold, courageous, adventuresome. Systematic, organized. Blessed in some ways. Gentle, kind, a hard worker.

Amos, 3: Expresses thoughts readily. Domestic, hardworking. A natural counselor and healer. Charming and devoted.

Amy, 3: Expresses thoughts readily. Family communicator. Needs a lot of freedom.

Ana, 7: Not easily influenced. Creative and opinionated. Bold, courageous, extremely intelligent.

Anabelle, 7: Not easily influenced. Creative and opinionated. Bold, courageous, a bit stubborn. Anticipates next move. Physical, passionate. Strong verbal skills. Ups and downs financially. Loves adventure and excitement.

Anastasia, 4: Natural teaching ability. Original, unconventional. Bold, courageous, a bit stubborn. Charming and devoted. Dynamic, busy lifestyle. Pioneer and risk taker. Impulsive and extreme. Blessed in some ways. Independent, critical of self and others.

Andora, 8: Resolute and purposeful. Original and unconventional. Reliable and responsible. Natural counselor and healer. Intense inner power. Bold, courageous, a bit stubborn.

Andre, 6: Pioneer and risk taker. Creative, opinionated. Domestic, hardworking. Gentle, kind, diligent. Physical and passionate.

Andrea, 7: Not easily influenced. Original and unconventional. Reliable and responsible. Gentle, kind, hard worker. Physical and passionate. Independent, critical of self and others.

Andrew, 11: Ambitious leader, great vision. Creates group harmony. Natural authority. Gentle, kind, and hard worker. Physical and passionate. Likes to meet new people.

Andris, 11: Ambitious leader, great vision. Original and unconventional. Natural authority. Gentle, kind, a hard worker. Blessed in some ways. Charming and devoted.

Andy, 8: Resolute and purposeful. Romantic, opinionated. Creative problem solver. Needs a lot of freedom.

Anette, 20: Reads people easily, perceptive. Socially exciting. Physical and passionate. Dynamic, very busy lifestyle. Sensitive and easily hurt. Loves adventure and excitement.

Angel, 3: Expresses thoughts readily. Creative, opinionated. Scientific and philosophical. A free spirit, very adaptable. Slow to make decisions.

Angela, 22: Ambitious leader, great vision. Original and unconventional. Has willpower, determined. A free spirit, very adaptable. Strong verbal skills. Bold, courageous, a bit stubborn.

Angelica, 7: Not easily influenced. Enjoys the mysteries of life. Extremely intelligent. A free spirit, very adaptable. Communicates skillfully. Blessed in some ways. Optimistic, outspoken. Independent, critical of self and others.

Angelina, 9: Hardworking and helpful. Sometimes naive. Scientific and philosophical. Physical and passionate. Strong verbal skills. Blessed in some ways. Creative, opinionated. Bold, courageous, a bit stubborn.

Angelo, 9: Hardworking and helpful. Creative, opinionated. An opportunist. Physical and passionate. Strong verbal skills. Natural counselor and healer.

Angie, 9: Hardworking and helpful. Original and unconventional. Scientific and philosophical. Artistic, having good taste. Physical and passionate.

Angus, 8: Resolute and purposeful. Creative, opinionated. Extremely intelligent. Attractive and charming. Impulsive and extreme.

Anita, 9: Hardworking and helpful. Original and romantic. Blessed in some ways. Dynamic, busy lifestyle. Independent, critical of self and others.

Ann, 11: Ambitious leader, great vision. Intuitive and creative. Romantic and sensual.

Anna, 3: Expresses thoughts readily. Creative, opinionated. Romantic and sensual. Pioneer and risk taker.

Annalicia, 10: Independent, critical of self and others. Original, opinionated. Romantic and sensual. Bold, courageous, a bit stubborn. Strong verbal skills. Idealistic and humanitarian. Great sense of humor. Blessed in some ways. Pioneer and risk taker.

Anne, 7: Not easily influenced. Creative, opinionated. Original and unconventional. Physical and passionate.

Annette, 7: Not easily influenced. Enjoys the mysteries of life. Creative, opinionated. A free spirit, very adaptable. Dynamic, very busy lifestyle. Sensitive and easily hurt. Physical and passionate.

Ansel, 6: Pioneer and risk taker. Creative and opinionated. Charming and devoted. Physical and passionate. Strong verbal skills.

Anthony, 7: Not easily influenced. Original and unconventional. Dynamic, very busy lifestyle. Self-reliant, successful. Natural counselor and healer. Romantic and sensual. Needs a lot of freedom.

Antoine, 6: Pioneer and risk taker. Puts needs of others first. An excellent mediator. Natural counselor and healer. Artistic, having good taste. Original, creative. Physical and passionate.

Antoinette, 6: Pioneer and risk taker. Creative, opinionated. Dynamic, busy lifestyle. Natural counselor and healer. Artistic, having good taste. Original, unconventional. Physical and passionate. Very protective. Sensitive and easily hurt. Loves adventure and excitement.

Anton, 10: Independent, critical of self and others. Original and unconventional. Dynamic, very busy lifestyle. Natural counselor and healer. Romantic and sensual.

Antony, 8: Resolute and purposeful. Original and unconventional. An excellent mediator. Natural counselor and healer. Romantic and sensual. Needs a lot of freedom.

Anya, 5: Bold, courageous, adventuresome. Opinionated and unconventional. Needs a lot of freedom. Independent, critical of self and others.

Apolonio, 7: Not easily influenced. Intelligent and knowledgeable. Natural counselor and healer. Frequent traveler. Sometimes meddling. Creative, perceptive. Blessed in some ways. Open to opportunities.

Apple, 5: Bold, courageous, adventuresome. Intelligent and knowledgeable. Maintains a high dream. Strong verbal skills. Likes change, very adaptable.

April, 11: Ambitious leader, great vision. Intelligent and knowledgeable. Gentle, kind, a hard worker. Blessed in some ways. Strong verbal skills.

Araceli, 4: Natural teaching ability. Strong and healthy. Independent, critical of self and others. Self-expressive, cheerful. A free spirit, very adaptable. Strong verbal skills. Blessed in some ways.

Aracely, 11: Ambitious leader, great vision. Diligent, helpful. Independent, critical of self and others. Inspiring and highly creative. A free spirit, very adaptable. Strong verbal skills. Needs a lot of freedom.

Archer, 8: Resolute and purposeful. Gentle, kind, a hard worker. Optimistic, outspoken. A great judge of character. Physical and passionate. Intense inner power.

Archibald, 22: Ambitious leader, great vision. Strives to improve humanity. Inspiring, highly creative. Self-reliant, successful. Blessed in some ways. Friendly, but shy. Bold, courageous, a bit stubborn. Strong verbal skills. Down-to-earth, faithful.

Archie, 8: Resolute and purposeful. Intense inner power. Optimistic, outspoken. A great judge of character. Blessed in some ways. Physical and passionate.

Ardasher, 11: Ambitious leader, great vision. Strives to improve humanity. Reliable, responsible. Independent, critical of self and others. Charming and devoted. Great judge of character. A free spirit, very adaptable. Tendency to lose items.

Ariel, 9: Hardworking and helpful. Sometimes naive. Artistic, may have good taste. A free spirit, very adaptable. Strong verbal skills.

Arjana, 9: Hardworking and helpful. Intense inner power. Clever and talented. Resolute and purposeful. Original and unconventional. Bold, courageous, a bit stubborn.

Arjane, 22: Ambitious leader, great vision. Strives to improve humanity. Clever and talented. Resolute and purposeful. Original and unconventional. A free spirit, very adaptable.

Arleen, 10: Independent, critical of self and others. Gentle, kind, a hard worker. Strong verbal skills. A free spirit, very adaptable. Tendency to overindulge. Romantic, sensual.

Arlene, 10: (Same as Arleen.)

Arlie, 9: Hardworking and helpful. Intense inner power. Strong verbal skills. Blessed in some ways. A free spirit, very adaptable.

Arlo, 10- Independent, critical of self and others. Intense inner power. Frequent traveler. Natural counselor and healer.

Armand, 6: Pioneer and risk taker. Diligent, helpful. Systematic, organized. Bold, courageous, a bit stubborn. Original and unconventional. Reliable and responsible.

Armando, 30: Expresses thoughts readily. Optimistic, very kind. Systematic, organized. Bold, courageous, a bit stubborn. Original and unconventional. Reliable and responsible. Natural counselor and healer.

Armani, 11: Ambitious leader, great vision. Intense inner power. Systematic, organized. Pioneer and risk taker. Original and unconventional. Artistic, having good taste.

Armen, 6: Pioneer and risk taker. Diligent, helpful. Systematic, organized. Physical and passionate. Original and creative.

Arnie, 11: Ambitious leader, great vision. Intense inner power. Original and unconventional. Blessed in some ways. A free spirit, adaptable to change.

Arnold, 10: Independent, critical of self and others. Gentle, kind, a hard worker. Original and unconventional. Natural counselor and healer. Strong verbal skills. Down-to-earth, faithful.

Arsenio, 9: Hardworking and helpful. Gentle, kind, and diligent. Charming and devoted. A free spirit, very adaptable. Original and unconventional. Blessed in some ways. A natural counselor and healer.

Art, 3: Expresses thoughts readily. Optimistic, very kind. Dynamic, busy lifestyle.

Arthur, 5: Bold, courageous, adventuresome. Intense inner power. Dynamic, busy lifestyle. Self-reliant, successful. Attractive and lucky. Could be forgetful.

Artie, 8: Resolute and purposeful. Intense inner power. Dynamic, busy lifestyle. Blessed in some ways. Physical and passionate.

Arturo, 30: Expresses thoughts readily. Optimistic, very kind. Dynamic, busy lifestyle. Attractive and charming. Intense inner power. Natural counselor and healer.

Aryana, 6: Pioneer and risk taker. Gentle, kind, a hard worker. Needs a lot of freedom. Bold, courageous, a bit stubborn. Original and unconventional. Independent, critical of self and others.

Aryeh, 30: Expresses thoughts readily. Optimistic, very kind. Needs a lot of freedom. Loves adventure and excitement. Great judge of character.

Ash, 10: Independent, critical of self and others. Very charismatic. Self-reliant, successful.

Ashanti, 9: Hardworking and helpful. Intense and extreme. Self-reliant, successful. Independent, critical of self and others. Original, romantic. Dynamic, busy lifestyle. Blessed in some ways.

Ashby, 10: Independent, critical of self and others. Very charismatic. Self-reliant, successful. Friendly, but shy. Needs a lot of freedom.

Ashley, 7: Not easily influenced. Charming and devoted. Self-reliant, successful. Strong verbal skills. A free spirit, very adaptable. Highly perceptive.

Ashok, 9: Hardworking and helpful. Intense and extreme. Great judge of character. Natural counselor and healer. Strong desire to succeed.

Asia, 3: Expresses thoughts readily. Charming and devoted. Blessed in some ways. Bold, courageous, a bit stubborn.

Athena, 4: Natural teaching ability. Dynamic, very busy lifestyle. Great judge of character. A free spirit, very adaptable. Creative and opinionated. Bold, courageous, a bit stubborn.

Aubrey, 9: Hardworking and helpful. Attractive and charming. Friendly, but shy. Gentle, kind, diligent. A free spirit, very adaptable. Dislikes limitations.

Audrey, 11: Ambitious leader, great vision. Creative and inspiring. Reliable and responsible. Gentle, kind, a hard worker. A free spirit, very adaptable. Dislikes limitations.

Augustine, 9: Hardworking and helpful. Go with the flow attitude. Scientific and philosophical. Difficulty making decisions. Charming and devoted. Dynamic, busy lifestyle. Blessed in some ways. Original and unconventional. A free spirit, very adaptable.

Aurelia, 4: Natural teaching ability. Slow to make decisions. Gentle, kind, a hard worker. Likes to entertain. Communicates skillfully. Artistic, having good taste. Not easily influenced.

Aureliano, 6: Pioneer and risk taker. Attractive and charming. Diligent, helpful. Likes to entertain. Frequent traveler. Artistic, having good taste. Not easily influenced. Creative, opinionated. Natural counselor and healer.

Aurielle, 11: Ambitious leader, great vision. Very charismatic. Strives to improve humanity. Blessed in some ways. A free spirit, very adaptable. Strong verbal skills. Ups and downs financially. Loves adventure and excitement.

Aurora, 11: Ambitious leader, great vision. Creative and inspiring. Gentle, kind, a hard worker. Natural counselor and healer. Intense inner power. Bold, courageous, a bit stubborn.

Austin, 3: Expresses thoughts readily. Attractive and charming. Impulsive and extreme. Dynamic, busy lifestyle. Blessed in some ways. Original and unconventional.

Ava, 6: Pioneer and risk taker. Intuitive and inspired. Strong leadership qualities.

Avi, 5: Bold, courageous, adventuresome. Intuitive and inspired. Blessed in some ways.

Avril, 8: Resolute and purposeful. Strong imagination. Intense inner power. Blessed in some ways. Slow to make decisions.

Axel, 6: Pioneer and risk taker. Artistic, sensual, perceptive. A free spirit, very adaptable. Strong verbal skills.

A-young, 11: Ambitious leader, great vision. Needs a lot of freedom. Natural counselor and healer. Very charismatic. Original and unconventional. Scientific and philosophical.

Azura, 4: Natural teaching ability. Great mediator, successful. Attractive and charming. Gentle, kind, hard worker. Bold, courageous, a bit stubborn.

B

If a name begins with B, or the name has more than one B, or the name ends with a B, then this person is partnership-oriented, sensitive, and emotional.

B-named people are friendly and social, but shy. They can be timid. They can also get themselves in trouble by jumping in to help others out. B types are so caring that sometimes they don't think first before jumping in. Then both are stuck down there. B names are intelligent, but their concern for others sometimes blinds their best judgment. Their emotions are what make them most vulnerable. B names are tactful and refined. Because they are so sensitive to the needs of others, B names make excellent counselors. They often use their keen intuition to guide them through their sessions.

B is the second letter of the alphabet and therefore ruled by the number 2 vibration. In numerology, 2 rules partnership. B is almost the opposite of A. Where A needs to be independent, B is more partnership-oriented. They look to others for answers, support, decisions—well someone has to do it. Where As are leaders, Bs are followers. They often prefer to be the power behind the throne. B-named people are open-minded, and offer great support with little or no recognition for their efforts. Sometimes they cling to ideas long after they have outlived their usefulness. Some B names must learn to change more with the times. Most people with B names provide insight and valuable perspective to those in leadership positions. They make great "behind the scenes" helpers. Usually they are too shy to be in the direct limelight. B names willingly accept their position as a valuable helper you couldn't do without.

We have some independent B names. For example, Barbara, with all those As in her name, will be sensitive and partnership-oriented. At times she will need to be independent and will naturally be more competitive. Three famous Barbaras, Barbara Streisand, Barbara Walters, and Barbara

Stanwyck, are sensitive to the needs of others, but at the same time feel a need to stand alone, independently. Although the B is a social letter, Barbara sums up to a 7 power number, so most likely all Barbaras need their solitude. The average B, however, is very social and dependent by nature.

A B-named person will yearn for a partner if single, and if married will be the better half. They are attentive to their partner's needs. This 2-ruled letter is similar to the astrological signs Taurus and Libra. Venus rules Taurus and Libra and the number 2. The influence of this social vibration brings good taste in the finer things of life. These individuals enjoy good food, company, art, and music. Consequently it seems as if we have two types of this 2-ruled letter. One is the down-to-earth "Taurean" type. The other is the more intellectual "Libra" type. Both have a good head for business. Along with the numbers 4 and 8, 2-ruled letters tend to make excellent businesspeople. Don't hesitate to put them in charge of the books.

B types are often musically talented and have a great sense of rhythm. Peace and harmony are essential to their happiness. They are known to quickly snap off the volume of music that is too loud or obnoxious. For instance, employers with names that begin with B, such as Betty or Bob, usually want to provide music for their workers. They are moved by music and will be impelled to provide a harmonic environment.

B-named people can get very upset if conflict arises among their employees, family, or friends. They usually get more upset than those actually having the conflict. That's how sensitive they are. B or 2 types are happiest when everyone is getting along. That's why they are dubbed "the mediator." The second letter serves best in a situation where they can bring two or more parties together in agreement. They're naturals at it.

B-named actors Brad Pitt, Bruce Willis, and Ben Affleck seem to have no difficulty displaying tearful emotions on screen. Most men don't cry readily, so this is no easy task. One actress, upon a movie debut, told her interviewer that she had to cry in a particular scene. She went on to say that her co-star, Bruce Willis, taught her how to cry upon demand. Imagine that, a man teaching a woman how to cry! Young children whose names begin with B can be quick to cry. B-named children get their feelings hurt ever so easily on the playground. They will need lots of hugs for healthy emotional development. These children love to give hugs as well. The B-named child is among the most sympathetic and kindest of all. He or she will tend to be more intuitive and may be interested in psychic studies.

Adults with names that begin with B may be natural partners, but can find parenthood a little difficult. They are better as a parent if they have a partner to help them with the children. They often later become friends with their children.

You can recognize a B personality by the frequent use of the words "we," "let's," "us," and "we're." When a breakup occurs, a B could pine away for weeks, months, or even years. As soon as the healing takes place, they are out in the sunshine, looking for another mate. The yearning for a partner calls out to them so strongly. B names need people and social contact more than most other names. Those of us who are looking for a good partner should turn to a B-named person. They'll not only be a wonderful partner, they'll be your best friend.

Bob Dole is a good example of how a B-named person makes a great partner. Just look at the way Bob supports his wife, Elizabeth Dole. Bob was willing to be the "First Man" of the White House. Senator Elizabeth Dole was a candidate for President of the United States in 1999. She is also a former President of the American Red Cross. This goes to show that behind every successful woman is a B-named man.

Bill Clinton is another B-named man who supports his partner. Just like Bob, he too is willing to take a back seat to his wife Senator Hillary Clinton's ambitions. Remember the famous sensitive remark Bill Clinton is quoted as saying, "I feel your pain." This is true of a B personality. They are that sensitive.

Some other famous B names: Benjamin Franklin, Billy Graham, Bob Newhart, Ben Stiller, Britney Spears, Beyonce Knowles, Bo Derek, Barry Manilow, Brad Pitt, Bernadette Peters, Bobby Darin, Brooke Shields, Bette Midler, Burt Lancaster, Betty Grable, Buddy Ebsen, Bob Dylan, Bob Marley, Barbara Eden, Barry White, Billy Joel, Benjamin Bratt, Bonnie Raitt, Bono, Burt Reynolds, Babe Ruth, Buddy Hackett, and Bob Hope.

Quick Reference of "B" Names

Babe, 10: Anticipates next move. Independent, critical of self and others. Sensitive and emotional. Loves adventure and excitement.

Babette, 10: Anticipates next move. Independent, critical of self and others. Emotional and sensitive. A free spirit, very adaptable. Dynamic, very busy lifestyle. Needs to slow down. Loves adventure and excitement.

Babs, 6: Creative in a practical way. Pioneer and risk taker. Emotional and sensitive. Charming and devoted.

Baby, 3: Loyal and understanding. Aims to please. Emotional and sensitive. Dislikes limitations.

Bahram, 7: Quietly supportive. Not easily influenced. Great judge of character. Gentle, kind, a hard worker. Independent, critical of self and others. Systematic, organized.

Bailey, 9: Generous and caring. Hardworking, sincere. Blessed in some ways. Strong verbal skills. A free spirit, very adaptable. Dislikes limitations.

Balazs, 7: Quietly supportive. Not easily influenced. Strong verbal skills. Independent, self-motivated. Great mediator. Charming and devoted.

Baldwin, 11: Good business partner. Intuitive, perceptive. Communicates skillfully. Reliable, responsible. Likes to meet new people. Blessed in some ways. Romantic and sensual.

Barbara, 7: Quietly supportive. Not easily influenced. Gentle, kind, a hard worker. Affectionate and social. Bold, courageous, a bit stubborn. A tendency to lose items. Independent, critical of self and others.

Barbie, 10: Anticipates next move. Independent, critical of self and others. Gentle, kind, a hard worker. Loyal and understanding. Artistic, having good taste. Loves adventure and excitement.

Barclay, 8: Enjoys luxury items. Resolute and purposeful. Diligent, helpful. Self-expressive, cheerful. Strong verbal skills. Bold, courageous, a bit stubborn. Needs a lot of freedom.

Barnabas, 4: Natural business aptitude. Natural teaching ability. Strong and healthy. Creative, opinionated. Bold, courageous, a bit stubborn. Affectionate and social. Resolute and purposeful. Charming and devoted.

Barnaby, 9: Generous and caring. Hardworking, sincere. Gentle, kind, diligent. Creative, opinionated. Bold, courageous, a bit stubborn. Affectionate and social. Needs a lot of freedom.

Barnard, 4: Natural business aptitude. Natural teaching ability. Intense inner power. Creative, opinionated. Bold, courageous, a bit stubborn. Tendency to lose items. Down-to-earth, faithful.

Barney, 11: Good business partner. Resolute, purposeful. Strives to improve humanity. Original and unconventional. Loves adventure and excitement. Needs a lot of freedom.

Baron, 5: Sparkling emotional outlook. Pioneer and risk taker. Diligent, helpful. Natural counselor and healer. Original and unconventional.

Barry, 10: Anticipates next move. Independent, critical of self and others. Gentle, kind, a hard worker. Intense inner power. Needs a lot of freedom.

Bart, 5: Sparkling emotional outlook. Bold, courageous, a bit stubborn. Intense inner power. Dynamic, very busy lifestyle.

Barth, 4: Natural business aptitude. Natural teaching ability. Gentle, kind, a hard worker. Dynamic, very busy lifestyle. Self-reliant, successful.

Bartholomew, 6: Creative in a practical way. Pioneer and risk taker. Diligent, helpful. Dynamic, busy lifestyle. Self-reliant, successful. Natural counselor and healer. Frequent traveler. Musically talented. Systematic, organized. A free spirit, very adaptable. Likes to meet new people.

Bartley, 11: Good business partner. Intuitive, perceptive. Intense inner power. Dynamic, busy lifestyle. Strong verbal skills. A free spirit, very adaptable. Needs a lot of freedom.

Barton, 7: Quietly supportive. Not easily influenced. Gentle, kind, a hard worker. Dynamic, busy lifestyle. Natural counselor and healer. Original and unconventional.

Basil, 7: Quietly supportive. Not easily influenced. Charming and devoted. Artistic, having good taste. Strong verbal skills.

Baxter, 7: Quietly supportive. Not easily influenced. Artistic, sensual and perceptive. Dynamic, busy lifestyle. A free spirit, very adaptable. Gentle, kind, a hard worker.

Bea, 8: Enjoys luxury items. Original and creative. Resolute and purposeful.

Beatrice, 9: Generous and caring. Enjoys giving gifts. Bold, courageous, a bit stubborn. Dynamic, busy lifestyle. Gentle, kind, a hard worker. Artistic, having good taste. Self-expressive, cheerful. Likes to entertain.

Beau, 11: Good business partner. Keenly perceptive. Independent, critical of self and others. Attractive and charming.

Beaufort, 7: Quietly supportive. Not easily fooled. Independent, critical of self and others. Attractive and charming. Self-sacrificing, loving. Natural counselor and healer. Gentle, kind, a hard worker. Dynamic, busy lifestyle.

Beauregard, 10: Anticipates next move. Likes change and variety. Independent, critical of self and others. Attractive and charming. Gentle, kind, a hard worker. Loves adventure and excitement. Scientific and philosophical. Bold, courageous, a bit stubborn. Tendency to lose items. Down-to-earth, faithful.

Becca, 5: Sparkling emotional outlook. Physical and passionate. Self-expressive, cheerful. Optimistic and outspoken. Bright, adventuresome.

Becky, 10: Anticipates next move. Likes change and variety. Inspiring and creative. Strong desire to succeed. Needs a lot of freedom.

Behrang, 10: Anticipates next move. Likes change and variety. Self-reliant, successful. Gentle, kind, a hard worker. Independent, critical of self and others. Original and unconventional. Scientific and philosophical.

Behrooz, 8: Enjoys luxury items. Original and creative. Great judge of character. Intense inner power. Natural counselor and healer. Respects rules. Uses common sense.

Behzad, 10: Anticipates next move. Likes change and variety. Self-reliant, successful. Uses common sense. Independent, critical of self and others. Reliable, responsible.

Beldon, 7: Quietly supportive. Not easily fooled. Strong verbal skills. Reliable, responsible. Natural counselor and healer. Original and unconventional.

Belinda, 11: Good business partner. Keenly perceptive. Strong verbal skills. Artistic, having good taste. Original and unconventional. Natural authority. Resolute and purposeful.

Bella, 5: Sparkling emotional outlook. Likes change, very adaptable. Communicates skillfully. Ups and downs financially. Pioneer and risk taker.

Belle, 9: Generous and caring. Enjoys giving gifts. Strong verbal skills. Frequent traveler. A free spirit, very adaptable.

Ben, 3: Loyal and understanding. A free spirit, very adaptable. Romantic and creative.

Benedict, 8: Enjoys luxury items. Creative, original, and unconventional. Likes change and variety. Systematic, organized. Artistic, having good taste. Outgoing and cheerful. Dynamic, busy lifestyle.

Benita, 6: Creative in a practical way. A step ahead of others. Unconventional, opinionated. Artistic, having good taste. Dynamic, busy lifestyle. Pioneer and risk taker.

Benjamin, 5: Sparkling emotional outlook. Physical and passionate. Original, opinionated. Clever and talented. Bright, adventuresome. Domestic, hardworking. Blessed in some ways. Creative, unconventional.

Benjie, 9: Generous and caring. Enjoys giving gifts. Original and unconventional. Clever and talented. Blessed in some ways. Loves adventure and excitement.

Benny, 6: Creative in a practical way. A step ahead of others. Unconventional, opinionated. Romantic and sensual. Needs a lot of freedom.

Benson, 6: Creative in a practical way. A step ahead of others. Romantic and original. Charming and devoted. Natural counselor and healer. Unconventional and opinionated.

Bentley, 11: Good business partner. Keenly perceptive. Original and unconventional. Dynamic, busy lifestyle. Communicates skillfully. Physical and passionate. Dislikes limitations.

Benton, 7: Quietly supportive. Not easily fooled. Original and unconventional. Dynamic, busy lifestyle. Natural counselor and healer. Creative and opinionated.

Berkley, 6: Creative in a practical way. A step ahead of others. Gentle, kind, a hard worker. Strong desire to succeed. Communicates skillfully. Physical and passionate. Dislikes limitations.

Bernadette, 22: Good business partner. Has big plans and ideas. Strives to improve humanity. Original and unconventional. Not easily influenced. Reliable, responsible. Physical and passionate. Dynamic, busy lifestyle. Sensitive and easily hurt. Loves adventure and excitement.

Bernadine, 9: Generous and caring. Enjoys giving gifts. Gentle, kind, a hard worker. Original and unconventional. Helpful, sincere. Reliable, responsible. Blessed in some ways. Romantic and sensual. A free spirit, very adaptable.

Bernard, 8: Enjoys luxury items. Original and creative. Uses good judgment. Romantic, sensual. Resolute and purposeful. Tendency to lose items. Has natural authority.

Bernice, 11: Good business partner. Keenly perceptive. Gentle, kind, a hard worker. Original and unconventional. Artistic, having good taste. Self-expressive, cheerful. Physical and passionate.

Bernie, 8: Enjoys luxury items. Original, creative, and unconventional. Intense inner power. Blessed in some ways. Physical and passionate.

Bert, 9: Generous and caring. Enjoys giving gifts. Diligent, helpful. Dynamic, busy lifestyle.

Bertha, 9: Generous and caring. Enjoys giving gifts. Considerate and kind. Dynamic, busy lifestyle. Great judge of character. Not easily influenced.

Bertie, 5: Sparkling emotional outlook. Physical and passionate. Intense inner power. Dynamic, busy lifestyle. Artistic, having good taste. Keenly perceptive.

Beryl, 8: Enjoys luxury items. Original and creative. Intense inner power. Needs a lot of freedom. Strong verbal skills.

Bess, 9: Generous and caring. Enjoys giving gifts. Charming and devoted. Impulsive and extreme.

Bessie, 5: Sparkling emotional outlook. Physical and passionate. Charming and devoted. Impulsive and extreme. Blessed in some ways. Keenly perceptive.

Beth, 8: Enjoys luxury items. Original and creative. Dynamic, busy lifestyle. Great judge of character.

Betsy, 8: Enjoys luxury items. Original and creative. Dynamic, busy lifestyle. Charming and devoted. Needs a lot of freedom.

Bette, 7: Quietly supportive. Not easily fooled. Dynamic, busy lifestyle. Sensitive and easily hurt. Physical and passionate.

Betty, 9: Generous and caring. Enjoys giving gifts. Dynamic, busy lifestyle. Sensitive and easily hurt. Dislikes limitations.

Beulah, 22: Good business partner. Has big plans and ideas. Attractive and charming. Strong verbal skills. Resolute and purposeful. Self-reliant, successful.

Beverly, 8: Enjoys luxury items. Original and creative. Intuitive and inspired. Likes change and variety. Gentle, kind, a hard worker. Strong verbal skills. Dislikes limitations.

Bevis, 3: Loyal and understanding. A free spirit, very adaptable. Strong imagination. Blessed in some ways. Charming and devoted.

Bian, 8: Enjoys luxury items. Original and creative. Not easily influenced. Romantic, opinionated.

Bianca, 3: Loyal and understanding. Blessed in some ways. Pioneer and risk taker. Original and unconventional. Self-expressive, cheerful. Bold, courageous, a bit stubborn.

Bibi, 22: Good business partner. Considerate, understanding. Emotional and sensitive. Artistic, having good taste.

Bill, 8: Enjoys luxury items. Blessed in some ways. Strong verbal skills. Financial ups and downs.

Billie, 4: Natural business aptitude. Considerate, understanding. Communicates skillfully. Frequent traveler. Artistic, having good taste. A free spirit, very adaptable.

Billy, 6: Creative in a practical way. Artistic, having good taste. Strong verbal skills. Frequent traveler. Dislikes limitations.

Bina, 8: Enjoys luxury items. Practical when giving. Romantic, sensual. Independent, critical of self and others.

Bing, 5: Sparkling emotional outlook. Idealistic, humanitarian. Romantic, sensual. Scientific and philosophical.

Binh, 6: Creative in a practical way. Blessed in some ways. Original, opinionated. Great judge of character.

Binti, 9: Generous and caring. Artistic, having good taste. Original and unconventional. Dynamic, busy lifestyle. Idealistic and humanitarian.

Biolulfo, 11: Good business partner. Blessed in some ways. Natural counselor and healer. Strong verbal skills. Attractive and charming. Frequent traveler. Self-sacrificing, loving. May have musical abilities.

Birdie, 11: Good business partner. Considerate, understanding. Gentle, kind, a hard worker. Reliable, responsible. Artistic, having good taste. A free spirit, very adaptable.

Bishop, 6: Creative in a practical way. Idealistic, humanitarian. Charming and devoted. Great judge of character. Natural counselor and healer. Intelligent and knowledgeable.

Bjorn, 5: Sparkling emotional outlook. Clever and talented. Natural counselor and healer. Intense inner power. Creative, opinionated.

Blade, 6: Creative in a practical way. Frequent traveler. Pioneer and risk taker. Workaholic, determined. Likes to entertain.

Blaine, 7: Quietly supportive. Strong verbal skills. Resolute and purposeful. Blessed in some ways. Original and unconventional. A free spirit, very adaptable.

Blair, 6: Creative in a practical way. Easygoing attitude. Pioneer and risk taker. Blessed in some ways. Gentle, kind, a hard worker.

Blake, 22: Good business partner. Frequent traveler. Not easily influenced. Strong desire to succeed. A free spirit, very adaptable.

Blanca, 6: Creative in a practical way. Easygoing attitude. Resolute and purposeful. Original and unconventional. Self-expressive, cheerful. Pioneer and risk taker.

Blanche, 9: Generous and caring. Strong verbal skills. Not easily influenced. Original and unconventional. Self-expressive, cheerful. Great judge of character. A free spirit, very adaptable.

Blane, 7: Quietly supportive. Intellectually sound. Independent, critical of self and others. Original and unconventional. A free spirit, very adaptable.

Blayne, 5: Sparkling emotional outlook. Communicates skillfully. Independent, critical of self and others. Highly perceptive. Original, unconventional. A free spirit, very adaptable.

Bliss, 7: Quietly supportive. Intellectually sound. Blessed in some ways. Charming and devoted. Impulsive and extreme.

Blossom, 5: Sparkling emotional outlook. Frequent traveler. Natural counselor and healer. Charming and devoted. Impulsive and extreme. Has musical talent. Domestic and hardworking.

Blythe, 9: Generous and caring. Strong verbal skills. Needs a lot of freedom. Dynamic, busy lifestyle. Great judge of character. Loves adventure and excitement.

Bo, 8: Enjoys luxury items. Natural counselor and healer. Successful.

Bob, 10- Anticipates next move. Ambitious and innovative. Good mediator.

Bobbi, 3: Loyal and understanding. Likes harmony and beauty. Emotional and sensitive. May be psychic. Artistic, having good taste.

Bobbie, 8: Enjoys luxury items. Competitive in business. Emotional and sensitive. May be psychic. Artistic, having good taste. Physical and passionate.

Bobby, 10: Anticipates next move. Natural counselor and healer. Emotional and sensitive. Friendly, but shy. Needs a lot of freedom.

Boden, 22: Good business partner. Creates group harmony. Workaholic, determined. A free spirit, very adaptable. Original and unconventional.

Bogart, 9: Generous and caring. Transforms others with love. Scientific and philosophical. Pioneer and risk taker. Gentle, kind, a hard worker. Dynamic, busy lifestyle.

Bonita, 7: Quietly supportive. Respects rules. Original and unconventional. Blessed in some ways. Dynamic, busy lifestyle. Independent, critical of self and others.

Bonne, 5: Sparkling emotional outlook. Versatile in service. Original and unconventional. Romantic, sensual. A free spirit, very adaptable.

Bonnie, 5: Sparkling emotional outlook. Natural counselor and healer. Original and opinionated. Romantic, sensual. Artistic, having good taste. A free spirit, very adaptable.

Boone, 6: Creative in a practical way. May have musical abilities. Magnetic personality. Original and unconventional. A free spirit, very adaptable.

Boris, 9: Generous and caring. Natural counselor and healer. Gentle, kind, a hard worker. Blessed in some ways. Charming and devoted.

Boswell, 7: Quietly supportive. Open to opportunities. Charming and devoted. Likes to meet new people. A free spirit, very adaptable. Strong verbal skills. Frequent traveler.

Bosworth, 3: Loyal and understanding. Natural counselor and healer. Charming and devoted. Likes to meet new people. Respects rules. Gentle, kind, a hard worker. Dynamic, busy lifestyle. Great judge of character.

Bowie, 9: Generous and caring. Transforms others with love. Likes to meet new people. Artistic, having good taste. A free spirit, very adaptable.

Boyce, 5: Sparkling emotional outlook. Natural counselor and healer. Needs a lot of freedom. Self-expressive, cheerful. Physical and passionate.

Boyd, 10: Anticipates next move. Natural counselor and healer. Dislikes limitations. Workaholic, determined.

Brad, 7: Quietly supportive. Gentle, kind, a hard worker. Not easily influenced. Domestic, responsible.

Braden, 8: Enjoys luxury items. Diligent, helpful. Resolute and purposeful. Reliable, responsible. Physical, passionate. Creative and opinionated.

Bradford, 5: Sparkling emotional outlook. Gentle and kind. Bright, adventuresome. Down-to-earth, faithful. Self-sacrificing, loving. Natural counselor and healer. Tendency to lose items. Workaholic, determined.

Bradley, 4: Natural business aptitude. Diligent, helpful. Excellent teaching skills. Systematic, organized. Communicates skillfully. Loves adventure and excitement. Highly perceptive.

Brady, 5: Sparkling emotional outlook. Gentle, kind, a hard worker. Not easily influenced. Has a natural authority. Needs a lot of freedom.

Bram, 7: Quietly supportive. Diligent, helpful. Not easily influenced. Domestic, hardworking.

Bramwell, 5: Sparkling emotional outlook. Intense inner power. Not easily influenced. Domestic, hardworking. Likes to meet new people. A free spirit, very adaptable. Strong verbal skills. Financial ups and downs.

Brandon, 5: Sparkling emotional outlook. Gentle, kind, a hard worker. Bright, adventuresome. Original and opinionated. Reliable, responsible. Natural counselor and healer. Romantic, sensual.

Brandy, 10: Anticipates next move. Diligent, helpful. Independent, critical of self and others. Original and unconventional. Reliable, responsible. Needs a lot of freedom.

Brant, 10: Anticipates next move. Diligent, helpful. Independent, critical of self and others. Original and unconventional. Dynamic, very busy lifestyle.

Brawley, 5: Sparkling emotional outlook. Intense inner power. Bright, adventuresome. Likes to meet new people. Strong verbal skills. Physical, passionate. Needs a lot of freedom.

Breanna, 10: Anticipates next move. Hardworking, diligent. A free spirit, very adaptable. Independent, critical of self and others. Romantic and sensual. Creative and opinionated. Bold, courageous, a bit stubborn.

Bree, 3: Loyal and understanding. Gentle, kind, a hard worker. A free spirit, very adaptable. Physical and passionate.

Bren, 3: Loyal and understanding. Gentle, kind, a hard worker. A free spirit, very adaptable. Romantic and sensual.

Brenda, 8: Enjoys luxury items. Intense inner power. Physical and passionate. Creative, opinionated. Reliable, responsible. Resolute and purposeful.

Brenna, 9: Generous and caring. Gentle, kind, a hard worker. A free spirit, very adaptable. Romantic and sensual. Creative and opinionated. Helpful, sincere.

Brent, 5: Sparkling emotional outlook. Gentle, kind, a hard worker. Physical and passionate. Creative, opinionated. Dynamic, busy lifestyle.

Bret, 9: Generous and caring. Gentle, kind, a hard worker. A free spirit, very adaptable. Dynamic, busy lifestyle.

Brett, 20: Emotional, sensitive. Diligent, helpful. A free spirit, very adaptable. Dynamic, busy lifestyle. Sensitive and easily hurt.

Brewster, 11: Good business partner. Idealistic, humanitarian. A free spirit, very adaptable. Likes to meet new people. Charming and devoted. Dynamic, busy lifestyle. Loves adventure and excitement. Tendency to lose items.

Brian, 8: Enjoys luxury items. Gentle, kind, a hard worker. Blessed in some ways. Resolute and purposeful. Romantic and opinionated.

Brianna, 5: Sparkling emotional outlook. Intense inner power. Artistic, having good taste. Not easily influenced. Original and unconventional. Romantic and sensual. Pioneer and risk taker.

Brice, 10: Anticipates next move. Diligent, helpful. Blessed in some ways. Self-expressive, cheerful. Likes change and variety.

Bridget, 11: Good business partner. Idealistic, humanitarian. Blessed in some ways. Reliable, responsible. Scientific and philosophical. A free spirit, very adaptable. Dynamic, busy lifestyle.

Brie, 7: Quietly supportive. Gentle, kind, a hard worker. Blessed in some ways. Not easily fooled.

Brienna, 9: Generous and caring. Gentle, kind, a hard worker. Blessed in some ways. A free spirit, very adaptable. Original and unconventional. Romantic and sensual. Helpful, sincere.

Brieta, 10: Anticipates next move. Diligent, helpful. Works for group effort. A free spirit, very adaptable. Dynamic, busy lifestyle. Independent, critical of self and others.

Brietta, 3: Loyal and understanding. Optimistic, very kind. Artistic, having good taste. A free spirit, very adaptable. Dynamic, busy lifestyle. Sensitive and easily hurt. Aims to please.

Brigette, 5: Sparkling emotional outlook. Gentle, kind, a hard worker. Blessed in some ways. Scientific and philosophical. A free spirit, very adaptable. Dynamic, busy lifestyle. Sensitive and easily hurt. Physical and passionate.

Brina, 8: Enjoys luxury items. Diligent, helpful. Practical when giving. Creative, opinionated. Resolute and purposeful.

Brita, 5: Sparkling emotional outlook. Gentle, kind, a hard worker. Artistic, having good taste. Dynamic, busy lifestyle. Bright, adventuresome.

Britney, 3: Loyal and understanding. Gentle, kind, a hard worker. Blessed in some ways. Dynamic, busy lifestyle. Romantic, sensual. A free spirit, very adaptable. Needs a lot of freedom.

Broderick, 4: Natural business aptitude. Strong and healthy. Assumes responsibility. Systematic, organized. Physical and passionate. Tendency to lose items. Artistic, having good taste. Inspiring, very creative. Strong desire to succeed.

Brodie, 8: Enjoys luxury items. Intense inner power. Natural counselor and healer. Reliable and responsible. Artistic, having good taste. Physical and passionate.

Bron, 22: Good business partner. Diligent, helpful. Natural counselor and healer. Original and unconventional.

Bronson, 7: Quietly supportive. Intense inner power. Natural counselor and healer. Original and unconventional. Charming and devoted. Magnetic personality. Romantic and sensual.

Brook, 7: Quietly supportive. Gentle, kind, a hard worker. Natural counselor and healer. Magnetic personality. Strong desire to succeed.

Brooke, 3: Loyal and understanding. Optimistic, very kind. Natural counselor and healer. Magnetic personality. Strong desire to succeed. A free spirit, very adaptable.

Brooklyn, 4: Natural business aptitude. Strong and healthy. Assumes responsibility. Natural counselor and healer. Intuitive and inspired. Great verbal skills. Needs a lot of freedom. Romantic and opinionated.

Bruce, 22: Good business partner. Diligent, helpful. Attractive and charming. Optimistic and outspoken. A free spirit, very adaptable.

Brucia, 9: Generous and caring. Sometimes naive. Youthful, appealing. Self-expressive, cheerful. Blessed in some ways. Resolute and purposeful.

Bruno, 7: Quietly supportive. Gentle, kind, a hard worker. Attractive and charming. Original and unconventional. Natural counselor and healer.

Bryan, 6: Creative in a practical way. Diligent, helpful. Needs a lot of freedom. Pioneer and risk taker. Original and unconventional.

Bryanna, 30: Loyal and understanding. Gentle, kind, a hard worker. Needs a lot of freedom. Pioneer and risk taker. Romantic and sensual. Creative, opinionated. Bold, courageous, a bit stubborn.

Bryant, 8: Enjoys luxury items. Intense inner power. Needs a lot of freedom. Resolute and purposeful. Romantic, sensual. Dynamic, busy lifestyle.

Bryce, 8: Enjoys luxury items. Diligent, helpful. Dislikes restrictions. Self-expressive, cheerful. Physical and passionate.

Bryna, 6: Creative in a practical way. Diligent, helpful. Needs a lot of freedom. Original and unconventional. Not easily influenced.

Bud, 9: Generous and caring. Attractive and charming. Reliable and responsible.

Buddy, 20- Emotional, sensitive. Socially charming. Practical, conservative. Down-to-earth, domestic. Needs a lot of freedom.

Bunny, 22- Good business partner. Creative, intuitive. Original and unconventional. Romantic, sensual. Stylish and refined.

Burke, 30: Loyal and understanding. Attractive and charming. Gentle, kind, a hard worker. Strong desire to succeed. A free spirit, very adaptable.

Burl, 8: Enjoys luxury items. Slow to make decisions. Intense inner power. Strong verbal skills.

Burt, 7: Quietly supportive. Attractive and charming. Gentle, kind, a hard worker. Dynamic, busy lifestyle.

Burton, 9: Generous and caring. Go with the flow attitude. Idealistic, humanitarian. Dynamic, busy lifestyle. Natural counselor and healer. Original and unconventional.

Busby, 6: Creative in a practical way. Very lucky. Can be moody. Affectionate and friendly. Dislikes limitations.

Buzz, 3: Loyal and understanding. Attractive and charming. Uses common sense. Excellent mediator.

Byford, 7: Quietly supportive. Needs a lot of freedom. Self-sacrificing, loving. Natural counselor and healer. Gentle, kind, a hard worker. Reliable and responsible.

Byram, 5: Sparkling emotional outlook. Stylish and refined. Intense inner power. Bright, adventuresome. Systematic, organized.

Byron, 11: Good business partner. Needs a lot of freedom. Gentle, kind, a hard worker. Natural counselor and healer. Original and unconventional.

$\mathcal{C}$

If a name begins with C, has more than one C, or ends with a C, this person is cheerful, self-expressive, creative, and likable.

C is for communication. The C individual excels in the art of communication. They want to be sure the lines of communication are clear; and that everyone understands one another. They are exceptionally gifted in the areas of writing and holding conversations. They excel professionally in the entertainment industry, theatre, sales, writing, comedy, or any other profession related to communication or transportation. They are good with words and people. C types know how to make people feel comfortable and at ease. They have good manners and look almost as well dressed as those with an E in their name.

Because this letter is ruled by the number 3, most people with a C anywhere in their first name are a little "car happy." C-named people usually love their vehicles as well as other people's vehicles. This letter likes to go places, fast. Oddly enough, as much as they like to go fast, they are a little slow about making decisions. This letter, as well as the other number 3-ruled letters (L and U), like to intellectualize their experiences, making it difficult for them to make up their minds.

The typical C is a social delight and has the keen ability to not only hold up their end of a conversation, but to listen well too. They have a great sense of humor. Carol Burnett, Charlie Chaplin, and Cloris Leachman all have a comical, animated sense of humor. Even comedian Lucille Ball has a C in her name. This letter rules the "natural comedian." We can recognize a C personality at the supermarket—they're the person that tells a joke at just the right moment, making everyone laugh. Their sense of humor eases most tense situations. C-named people have a "stage presence" about them. It's as if they are putting on a performance all the time. It's a youthful letter; remember, child starts with C. There's a little child in all C people.

Those with names that begin with C are often extravagant and melo-dramatic. This letter needs a creative outlet, or the C person can become moody and overly dramatic. Similar to the third sign of the zodiac, Gemini, the C personality usually can't resist painting a story as a little more colorful than it actually is. This letter, as well as its siblings L and U, is rich in imagination. We should say to all those 3-ruled people out there, "I've told you a million times not to exaggerate!" They can be storytell-ers. This is also true of those with a power number or intensity number 3. If carried too far, this letter is known to exaggerate to the point of outright lying.

C is the third letter of the alphabet, so it is ruled by the number 3 vibration. The number 3 in numerology reflects balance. Picture a teeter-totter going up and down. If we stood in the middle of the teeter-totter, we wouldn't move up or down. We would remain steady while the two sides of the teeter-totter moved up and down. The C- or 3-ruled indi-vidual also needs to go in the middle for balance. They should go within themselves and meditate to achieve this balance. Escapist tendencies are not uncommon to the C, but if the C-named person practices medita-tion they will be more balanced and more able to apply themselves to a steady path toward inner peace. People in their lives can pull them up or down; they need to find a middle so this doesn't happen. The Bible says, "Thy body is thy temple, worship within it." What a perfect passage for this letter to remember. C or 3 types that don't achieve this balance often scatter their energies and express little sense of purpose.

The typical C will make many short trips around town. Their housing situation may be temporary. C-named people usually experience many ups and downs financially. This letter often adopts the saying, "I'm spending my children's inheritance." If they have money, they spend it; if not, they don't. It's a cheerful, happy-go-lucky letter and hardly serious about life. Fortunately, what they lack in concern for money, they make up for in luck. Along with letters L and U, C people tend to strike it rich in the lottery, inheritance, or with just plain dumb luck. Another special bonus is that they tend to bounce back rapidly from physical and mental setbacks. C first names have an easygoing manner. Some may appear too easygoing, with a devil-may-care attitude. And there is a reason Chatty Cathy starts with the letter C. Some C names will talk your ear off!

Speaking of talking, another interesting observation about people with letters ruled by the number 3 is their mouths. People with the letters C, L, or U in their names seem to have interesting mouths. Either the mouth is too big for their faces, or they have a noticeable space between their teeth, a cute lisp, or an overbite. This is also true of those with intensity and power number 3. There's just something about their mouths.

Those born with CH in the beginning of their names always seem young and sexy. Just look at how young and sexy Cher is. Long after she's gone people will remember her youthful appearance as well as her sex appeal. The C is youthful and the Scorpio-like H makes for quite a combination. Christian Slater also looks young and sexy on- or off-screen. CH people tend to think and act young, but also have a touch of Scorpio blended in their personalities. Another CH person is Cheryl Tiegs—she's over fifty and still looks great. Christie Brinkley also drinks from the same fountain of youth. Charlie Sheen is another remarkably young-looking older actor. He just never seems to age.

Charlie Chaplin, although today not considered "young and sexy," still had the Gemini/Scorpio influence of his first two letters. The third letter of the alphabet has a natural talent for comedy. The H or eighth letter has everything to do with control, just like Scorpio does. At a very early age, during the Depression, Charlie controlled the stage and brought laughter to many when happiness was a rare commodity. And typical to the H in his name, Charlie made out quite well financially when most of the world was struggling. The H helped him master the material side of life, with the letter C, in a fun way.

If there were a letter that symbolized the "spice of life," it would have to be C. Food would be bland without spices and the world would be boring without C or 3 vibration types. Their sparkling emotional outlooks and vibrant, witty personalities can be like a cold drink on a hot day. Very refreshing indeed. The entertainment industry is full of C-named people.

Some more famous C names: Chelsea Handler, Christopher Walken, Cary Grant, Christina Aguilera, Conan O'Brien, Carol Channing, Chubby Checker, Christopher Reeve, Carrie Fisher, Charlize Theron, Christina Applegate, Celine Dion, Clark Gable, Chevy Chase, Cecil B. DeMille, Chuck Berry, Charlton Heston, Charles Bronson, Cameron Diaz, Clint Eastwood, Cindy Crawford, Carl Reiner, Catherine Zeta-Jones, Cesar Chavez, Condoleezza Rice, Carmen Electra, and Cate Blanchett.

QUICK REFERENCE OF "C" NAMES

Cadence, 8: Ups and downs financially. Resolute and purposeful. Reliable, responsible. Physical and passionate. Original and unconventional. Self:expressive, cheerful. Loves adventure and excitement.

Caesar, 11: Inspiring and highly creative. Intuitive, perceptive. A free spirit, very adaptable. Charming and devoted. Bold, courageous, a bit stubborn. Gentle, kind, a hard worker.

Cahil, 6: Mellow, yet tactful. Pioneer and risk taker. Great judge of character. Blessed in some ways. Strong verbal skills.

Cain, 9: Artistically creative. Helpful, sincere. Blessed in some ways. Original and unconventional.

Caitlin, 5: Quick sense of humor. Bright, adventuresome. Enjoys giving to others. Dynamic, busy lifestyle. Strong verbal skills. Artistic, having good taste. Romantic, opinionated.

Cal, 7: Sees the irony in situations. Not easily influenced. Strong verbal skills.

Calandra, 9: Artistically creative. Independent, critical of self and others. Frequent traveler. Bold, courageous, a bit stubborn. Original and unconventional. Reliable, responsible. Gentle, kind, hard worker. Pioneer and risk taker.

Caldwell, 9: Artistically creative. Helpful, sincere. Communicates skillfully. Reliable, responsible. Likes to meet new people. A free spirit, very adaptable. Frequent traveler. Slow to make decisions.

Caleb, 5: Quick sense of humor. Bright, adventuresome. Strong verbal skills. A free spirit, very adaptable. Affectionate, social.

Calhoun, 11: Inspiring and highly creative. Intuitive, perceptive. Strong verbal skills. Great judge of character. Natural counselor and healer. Attractive and charming. Original and unconventional.

Calista, 11: Inspiring and highly creative. Intuitive, perceptive. Strong verbal skills. Blessed in some ways. Charming and devoted. Dynamic, busy lifestyle. Bold, courageous, a bit stubborn.

Calixto, 30: Cheerful, lighthearted. Aims to please. Communicates skillfully. Blessed in some ways. Artistic, sensual, perceptive. Dynamic, busy lifestyle. Natural counselor and healer.

Calla, 11: Inspiring and highly creative. Intuitive, perceptive. Strong verbal skills. Frequent traveler. Bold, courageous, a bit stubborn.

Calum, 5: Quick sense of humor. Bright, adventuresome. Optimistic, outspoken. Attractive and charming. Domestic, hardworking.

Calvert, 9: Artistically creative. Helpful, sincere. Strong verbal skills. Intuitive and inspired. A free spirit, very adaptable. Gentle, kind, a hard worker. Dynamic, busy lifestyle.

Calvin, 7: Sees the irony in situations. Not easily influenced. Frequent traveler. A little eccentric. Blessed in some ways. Original and unconventional.

Calypso, 10: Independent, critical of self and others. Strong verbal skills. Needs a lot of freedom. Intelligent and knowledgeable. Charming and devoted. Natural counselor and healer.

Cam, 8: Ups and downs financially. Resolute and purposeful. Domestic and hardworking.

Camella, 20: Has a sociable demeanor. Reads people easily. Domestic and hardworking. A free spirit, very adaptable. Strong verbal skills. Frequent traveler. Bold, courageous, a bit stubborn.

Cameo, 10: Great verbal expressions. Independent, critical of self and others. Domestic and hardworking. A free spirit, very adaptable. Natural counselor and healer.

Cameron, 6: Mellow, yet tactful. Pioneer and risk taker. Systematic and organized. A free spirit, very adaptable. Gentle, kind, a hard worker. Natural counselor and healer. Original and unconventional.

Camilla, 6: Mellow, yet tactful. Pioneer and risk taker. Domestic and hardworking. Blessed in some ways. Strong verbal skills. Frequent traveler. Bold, courageous, a bit stubborn.

Camille, 10: Independent, critical of self and others. Domestic and hardworking. Blessed in some ways. Strong verbal skills. Frequent traveler. A free spirit, very adaptable.

Campbell, 10: Independent, critical of self and others. Domestic and hardworking. Intelligent and knowledgeable. Affectionate, loyal. A free spirit, very adaptable. Strong verbal skills. Frequent traveler.

Candace, 22: Inspiring and highly creative. Resolute and purposeful. Original and unconventional. Reliable, responsible. Bold, courageous, a bit stubborn. Optimistic and outspoken. A free spirit, very adaptable.

Candi, 22: Inspiring and highly creative. Resolute and purposeful. Original and unconventional. Reliable, responsible. Blessed in some ways.

Candice, 30: Cheerful, lighthearted. Pioneer and risk taker. Creative, opinionated. Reliable, responsible. Blessed in some ways. Optimistic and outspoken. A free spirit, very adaptable.

Candida, 9: Artistically creative. Hardworking, helpful. Original and unconventional. Reliable, responsible. Blessed in some ways. Down:to:earth, faithful. Bold, courageous, a bit stubborn.

Candido, 5: Quick sense of humor. Bright, adventuresome. Romantic, sensual. Reliable, responsible. Blessed in some ways. Workaholic, determined. Natural counselor and healer.

Candie, 9: Artistically creative. Pioneer and risk taker. Physical and passionate. Reliable, responsible. Artistic, having good taste. A free spirit, very adaptable.

Candy, 20: Has a sociable demeanor. Reads people easily. Original and unconventional. Reliable, responsible. Needs a lot of freedom.

Canute, 10: Great verbal expressions. Independent, critical of self and others. Original and unconventional. Charming and attractive. Dynamic, busy lifestyle. A free spirit, very adaptable.

Caprice, 10: Great verbal expressions. Independent, critical of self and others. Intelligent and knowledgeable. Gentle, kind, a hard worker. Blessed in some ways. Outgoing, youthful outlook. A free spirit, very adaptable.

Cara, 5: Quick sense of humor. Bright, adventuresome. Gentle, kind, a hard worker. Pioneer and risk taker.

Carey, 7: Sees the irony in situations. Not easily influenced. Gentle, kind, a hard worker. Loves adventure and excitement. Needs a lot of freedom.

Carie, 9: Artistically creative. Helpful, sincere. Gentle, kind, a hard worker. A free spirit, very adaptable.

Carin, 9: Artistically creative. Helpful, sincere. Gentle, kind, a hard worker. Considerate, understanding. Original, opinionated.

Carissa, 7: Sees the irony in situations. Not easily influenced. Gentle, kind, a hard worker. Blessed in some ways. Charming and devoted. Impulsive and extreme. Bold, courageous, a bit stubborn.

Carita, 7: Sees the irony in situations. Not easily influenced. Diligent, helpful. Blessed in many ways. Dynamic, busy lifestyle. Bold, courageous, a bit stubborn.

Carl, 7: Sees the irony in situations. Not easily influenced. Gentle, kind, a hard worker. Strong verbal skills.

Carla, 8: Ups and downs financially. Resolute and purposeful. Intense inner power. Communicates skillfully. Bold, courageous, a bit stubborn.

Carleton, 7: Sees the irony in situations. Not easily influenced. Gentle, kind, a hard worker. Strong verbal skills. A free spirit, very adaptable. Dynamic, busy lifestyle. Natural counselor and healer. Original and unconventional.

Carlie, 30: Cheerful, lighthearted. Aims to please. Gentle, kind, a hard worker. Strong verbal skills. Blessed in some ways. A free spirit, very adaptable.

Carlin, 30: Cheerful, lighthearted. Aims to please. Gentle, kind, a hard worker. Strong verbal skills. Blessed in some ways. Original and unconventional.

Carlisle, 7: Sees the irony in situations. Not easily influenced. Gentle, kind, a hard worker. Strong verbal skills. Blessed in some ways. Charming and devoted. Frequent traveler. A free spirit, very adaptable.

Carlo, 4: Happily takes care of business. Resolute and purposeful. Diligent, helpful. Strong verbal skills. Natural counselor and healer.

Carlos, 5: Quick sense of humor. Bright, adventuresome. Intense inner power. Communicates skillfully. Natural counselor and healer. Charming and devoted.

Carlotta, 9: Artistically creative. Pioneer and risk taker. Gentle, kind, a hard worker. Strong verbal skills. Natural counselor and healer. Dynamic, busy lifestyle. Sensitive and easily hurt. Bold, courageous, a bit stubborn.

Carly, 5: Quick sense of humor. Bright, adventuresome. Intense inner power. Communicates skillfully. Needs a lot of freedom.

Carma, 9: Artistically creative. Helpful, sincere. Gentle, kind, a hard worker. Systematic, organized. Pioneer and risk taker.

Carmel, 7: Sees the irony in situations. Not easily influenced. Gentle, kind, a hard worker. Systematic, organized. A free spirit, very adaptable. Strong verbal skills.

Carmela, 8: Ups and downs financially. Resolute and purposeful. Intense inner power. Systematic, organized. Physical and passionate. Strong verbal skills. Bold, courageous, a bit stubborn.

Carmelita, 10: Independent, critical of self and others. Gentle, kind, a hard worker. Systematic, organized. A free spirit, very adaptable. Strong verbal skills. Blessed in some ways. Dynamic, busy lifestyle. Bold, courageous, a bit stubborn.

Carmen, 9: Artistically creative. Helpful, sincere. Gentle, kind, a hard worker. Systematic, organized. A free spirit, very adaptable. Romantic, opinionated.

Carmenata, 4: Happily takes care of business. Natural teaching ability. Gentle, kind, a hard worker. Systematic, organized. A free spirit, very adaptable. Original and unconventional. Bold, courageous, a bit stubborn. Dynamic, busy lifestyle. Pioneer and risk taker.

Carmine, 9: Artistically creative. Pioneer and risk taker. Gentle, kind, a hard worker. Systematic, organized. Blessed in some ways. Original and unconventional. A free spirit, very adaptable.

Carney, 30: Cheerful, lighthearted. Aims to please. Diligent, helpful. Original and unconventional. Loves adventure and excitement. Needs a lot of freedom.

Carol, 22: Inspiring and highly creative. Resolute and purposeful. Gentle, kind, a hard worker. Natural counselor and healer. Communicates skillfully.

Carola, 5: Quick sense of humor. Bright, adventuresome. Intense inner power. Natural counselor and healer. Strong verbal skills. Bold, courageous, a bit stubborn.

Carole, 9: Artistically creative. Helpful, sincere. Gentle, kind, a hard worker. Natural counselor and healer. Strong verbal skills. A free spirit, very adaptable.

Carolina, 10: Independent, critical of self and others. Diligent, helpful. Natural counselor and healer. Strong verbal skills. Blessed in some ways. Original and unconventional. Bold, courageous, a bit stubborn.

Caroline, 5: Quick sense of humor. Bright, adventuresome. Gentle, kind, a hard worker. Natural counselor and healer. Strong verbal skills. Blessed in some ways. Original and unconventional. A free spirit, very adaptable.

Carolyn, 7: Sees the irony in situations. Not easily influenced. Diligent, helpful. An opportunist. Strong verbal skills. Needs a lot of freedom. Original and unconventional.

Caron, 6: Mellow, yet tactful. Pioneer and risk taker. Gentle, kind, a hard worker. Natural counselor and healer. Creative, opinionated.

Carrie, 9: Artistically creative. Helpful, sincere. Intense inner power. A bit of a bully. Blessed in some ways. A free spirit, very adaptable.

Carroll, 7: Sees the irony in situations. Not easily influenced. Diligent, helpful. Tendency to lose items. An opportunist. Strong verbal skills. Slow to make decisions.

Carson, 7: Sees the irony in situations. Independent, critical of self and others. Diligent, helpful. Charming and devoted. An opportunist. Original and unconventional.

Carter, 11: Inspiring and highly creative. Intuitive, perceptive. Diligent, helpful. Dynamic, busy lifestyle. A free spirit, very adaptable. Tendency to lose items.

Carver, 4: Happily takes care of business. Natural teaching ability. Gentle, kind, a hard worker. Intuitive and inspired. A free spirit, very adaptable. Tendency to lose items.

Cary, 11: Inspiring and highly creative. Intuitive, perceptive. Diligent, helpful. Needs a lot of freedom.

Caryl, 5: Quick sense of humor. Bright, adventuresome. Gentle, kind, a hard worker. Dislikes restrictions. Optimistic and outspoken.

Caryn, 7: Sees the irony in situations. Not easily influenced. Diligent, helpful. Needs a lot of freedom. Original and unconventional.

Casey, 8: Ups and downs financially. Resolute and purposeful. Charming and devoted. Physical and passionate. Needs a lot of freedom.

Cash, 4: Happily takes care of business. Natural teaching ability. Charming and devoted. Great judge of character.

Casie, 10: Great verbal expressions. Independent, critical of self and others. Charming and devoted. Blessed in some ways. A free spirit, very adaptable.

Casper, 8: Ups and downs financially. Resolute and purposeful. Charming and devoted. Intelligent and knowledgeable. A free spirit, very adaptable. Gentle, kind, a hard worker.

Cass, 6: Mellow, yet tactful. Pioneer and risk taker. Charming and devoted. Intense and extreme.

Cassandra, 8: Ups and downs financially. Resolute and purposeful. Charming and devoted. Intense and extreme. Bold, courageous, a bit stubborn. Original and unconventional. Reliable, responsible. Gentle, kind, a hard worker. Independent, critical of self and others.

Cassidy, 8: Ups and downs financially. Resolute and purposeful. Charming and devoted. Intense and extreme. Blessed in some ways. Reliable, responsible. Needs a lot of freedom.

Cassie, 11: Inspiring and highly creative. Intuitive, perceptive. Very charismatic. Intense and extreme. Blessed in some ways. A free spirit, very adaptable.

Cassius, 10: Great verbal expressions. Independent, critical of self and others. Loving and devoted. Intense and extreme. Blessed in some ways. Attractive and charming. Impulsive.

Castel, 6: Mellow, yet tactful. Pioneer and risk taker. Charming and devoted. Dynamic, busy lifestyle. A free spirit, very adaptable. Strong verbal skills.

Cat, 6: Mellow, yet tactful. Pioneer and risk taker. Dynamic, busy lifestyle.

Catherine, 11: Inspiring and highly creative. Intuitive, perceptive. Dynamic, busy lifestyle. Great judge of character. A free spirit, very adaptable. Gentle, kind, a hard worker. Blessed in some ways. Original and unconventional. Physical and passionate.

Cathleen, 5: Quick sense of humor. Bright, adventuresome. Dynamic, busy lifestyle. Great judge of character. Strong verbal skills. A free spirit, very adaptable. Physical and passionate. Creative, opinionated.

Cato, 3: Quick sense of humor. Aims to please. Dynamic, busy lifestyle. Natural counselor and healer.

Cavell, 10: Independent, critical of self and others. Intuitive and inspired. A free spirit, very adaptable. Strong verbal skills. Frequent traveler.

Cecil, 5: Quick sense of humor. Physical and passionate. Spontaneous, lighthearted. Blessed in some ways. Ups and downs financially.

Cecile, 10: A free spirit, very adaptable. Self-expressive, cheerful. Blessed in some ways. Strong verbal skills. Likes change and variety.

Cecilia, 6: Mellow, yet tactful. A step ahead of others. Inspiring and creative. Blessed in some ways. Strong verbal skills. Artistic, having good taste. Pioneer and risk taker.

Cecily, 30: Cheerful, lighthearted. A free spirit, very adaptable. Optimistic, outspoken. Blessed in some ways. Communicates skillfully. Needs a lot of freedom.

Cedric, 6: Mellow, yet tactful. Physical, passionate. Natural authority. Gentle, kind, a hard worker. Artistic, having good taste. Creative and inspiring.

Celeste, 6: Mellow, yet tactful. A free spirit, very adaptable. Strong verbal skills. Physical and passionate. Charming and devoted. Dynamic, busy lifestyle. Loves adventure and excitement.

Celia, 3: Cheerful, lighthearted. Likes to entertain. Slow to make decisions. Artistic, having good taste. Pioneer and risk taker.

Celina, 8: Ups and downs financially. Original, creative, and unconventional. Strong verbal skills. Blessed in some ways. Resolute and purposeful.

Celine, 30: Cheerful, lighthearted. Likes change and variety. Communicates skillfully. Blessed in some ways. Romantic, sensual. A free spirit, very adaptable.

Cerise, 5: Great sense of humor. Physical and passionate. Gentle, kind, a hard worker. Blessed in some ways. Charming and devoted. Tendency to overindulge.

Cesar, 10: Great verbal expressions. A free spirit, very adaptable. Charming and devoted. Independent, critical of self and others. Gentle, kind, a hard worker.

Chad, 7: Sees the irony in situations. Great judge of character. Independent, critical of self and others. Reliable, responsible.

Chambrea, 6: Mellow, yet tactful. Creative and original. Resolute and purposeful. Domestic, hardworking. Friendly, but shy. Diligent, helpful. A free spirit, very adaptable. Bold, courageous, a bit stubborn.

Chance, 7: Sees the irony in situations. Great judge of character. Bold, courageous, adventuresome. Original and unconventional. Outgoing, youthful outlook. A free spirit, very adaptable.

Chancelor, 7: Sees the irony in situations. Great judge of character. Bold, courageous, adventuresome. Original and unconventional. Outgoing, youthful outlook. A free spirit, very adaptable. Strong verbal skills. Natural counselor and healer. Gentle, kind, a hard worker.

Chandler, 11: Inspiring and highly creative. Self-reliant, successful. Intuitive, perceptive. Original and unconventional. Reliable, responsible. Strong verbal skills. A free spirit, very adaptable. Intense inner power.

Chandra, 4: Happily takes care of business. Relies on own judgment. Natural teaching ability. Original and unconventional. Systematic, organized. Gentle, kind, a hard worker. Bold, courageous, a bit stubborn.

Chan-ho, 4: Happily takes care of business. Great judge of character. Natural teaching ability. Original and unconventional. Self-reliant, successful. Natural counselor and healer.

Channing, 7: Sees the irony in situations. Self-reliant, successful. Not easily influenced. Original and unconventional. Romantic, sensual. Blessed in some ways. Creative, opinionated. Scientific and philosophical.

Chaplin, 9: Artistically creative. Self-reliant, successful. Hardworking, helpful. Intelligent and knowledgeable. Strong verbal skills. Blessed in some ways. Original and unconventional.

Charity, 3: Cheerful, lighthearted. Relies on own judgment. Pioneer and risk taker. Gentle, kind, a hard worker. Blessed in some ways. Dynamic, busy lifestyle. Needs a lot of freedom.

Charlene, 3: Cheerful, lighthearted. Relies on own judgment. Pioneer and risk taker. Gentle, kind, a hard worker. Strong verbal skills. A free spirit, very adaptable. Original and unconventional. Tendency to overindulge.

Charles, 30: Cheerful, lighthearted. Self-reliant, successful. Pioneer and risk taker. Gentle, kind, a hard worker. Strong verbal skills. A free spirit, very adaptable. Charming and devoted.

Charley, 9: Artistically creative. Influential, successful. Hardworking, helpful. Intense inner power. Frequent traveler. Loves adventure and excitement. Needs a lot of freedom.

Charlie, 11: Inspiring and highly creative. Self-reliant, successful. Intuitive, perceptive. Gentle, kind, a hard worker. Strong verbal skills. Blessed in some ways. A free spirit, very adaptable.

Charlize, 10: Relies on own judgment. Independent, critical of self and others. Gentle, kind, a hard worker. Strong verbal skills. Blessed in some ways. Uses common sense. A free spirit, very adaptable.

Charlotte, 3: Cheerful, lighthearted. Financial ups and downs. Pioneer and risk taker. Gentle, kind, a hard worker. Strong verbal skills. Natural counselor and healer. Dynamic, busy lifestyle. Sensitive and easily hurt. A free spirit, very adaptable.

Charlton, 10: Great verbal expressions. Sometimes a loner. Independent, critical of self and others. Gentle, kind, a hard worker. Communicates skillfully. Dynamic, busy lifestyle. Natural counselor and healer. Romantic, opinionated.

Charmaine, 9: Artistically creative. Great judge of character. Not easily influenced. Gentle, kind, a hard worker. Systematic, organized. Bold, courageous, a bit stubborn. Blessed in some ways. Original and unconventional. A free spirit, very adaptable.

Chas, 4: Happily takes care of business. Great judge of character. Independent, critical of self and others. Charming and devoted.

Chase, 9: Artistically creative. Self-reliant, successful. Hardworking and helpful. Charming and devoted. A free spirit, very adaptable.

Chauncey, 8: Ups and downs financially. Appreciates quality. Resolute and purposeful. Attractive and charming. Original and unconventional. Physical and passionate. Needs a lot of freedom.

Che, 7: Sees the irony in situations. Great judge of character. A free spirit, very adaptable.

Chelsea, 8: Ups and downs financially. Appreciates quality. Physical and passionate. Communicates skillfully. Charming and devoted. Original and creative. Resolute and purposeful.

Chen, 3: Cheerful, lighthearted. Financial ups and downs. Physical and passionate. Original and opinionated.

Cheol-soo, 11: Inspiring and highly creative. Great judge of character. A free spirit, very adaptable. Natural counselor and healer. Strong verbal skills. Charming and devoted. Good parental skills. Has musical talent.

Cher, 7: Sees the irony in situations. Great judge of character. A free spirit, very adaptable. Gentle, kind, a hard worker.

Cherie, 3: Cheerful, lighthearted. Financial ups and downs. A free spirit, very adaptable. Gentle, kind, a hard worker. Blessed in some ways. Physical and passionate.

Cherilyn, 4: Happily takes care of business. Great judge of character. Loves adventure and excitement. Gentle, kind, a hard worker. Blessed in some ways. Strong verbal skills. Needs a lot of freedom. Original and unconventional.

Cherry, 5: Quick sense of humor. Creative and original. Physical and passionate. Gentle, kind, a hard worker. Could be forgetful. Needs a lot of freedom.

Cheryle, 4: Happily takes care of business. Great judge of character. Loves adventure and excitement. Gentle, kind, a hard worker. Needs a lot of freedom. Strong verbal skills. Physical and passionate.

Chester, 6: Mellow, yet tactful. Creative and original. A free spirit, very adaptable. Charming and devoted. Dynamic, busy lifestyle. Loves adventure and excitement. Gentle, kind, a hard worker.

Chet, 9: Artistically creative. Self-reliant, successful. A free spirit, very adaptable. Dynamic, busy lifestyle.

Chevy, 9: Artistically creative. Original, perceptive. A free spirit, very adaptable. Intuitive and inspired. Needs a lot of freedom.

Cheyenne, 7: Sees the irony in situations. Great judge of character. A free spirit, very adaptable. Needs a lot of freedom. Tendency to overindulge. Romantic and sensual. Original and unconventional. Loves adventure and excitement.

Chile, 10: Great verbal expressions. Makes and loses money easily. Artistic, having good taste. Communicates skillfully. Loves adventure and excitement.

China, 8: Ups and downs financially. Self-reliant, successful. Blessed in some ways. Original and unconventional. Resolute and purposeful.

Chiquita, 7: Sees the irony in situations. Great judge of character. Blessed in some ways. Attracts wealth. Youthful, appealing. Artistic, having good taste. Dynamic, busy lifestyle. Independent, critical of self and others.

Chloe, 7: Sees the irony in situations. Great judge of character. Strong verbal skills. Natural counselor and healer. A free spirit, very adaptable.

Chloris, 3: Cheerful, lighthearted. Financial ups and downs. Frequent traveler. Parental nature. Gentle, kind, a hard worker. Blessed in some ways. Charming and devoted.

Choong-Wan, 10: Great verbal expressions. Self-reliant, success-ful. Natural counselor and healer. Has musical abilities. Original and unconventional. Scientific and philosophical. Likes to meet new people. Independent, critical of self and others. Romantic, sensual.

Chris, 30: Cheerful, lighthearted. Financial ups and downs. Gentle, kind, a hard worker. Blessed in some ways. Charming and devoted.

Chrissy, 11: Inspiring and highly creative. Self-reliant, successful. Gentle, kind, a hard worker. Blessed in some ways. Charming and devoted. Impulsive and extreme. Needs a lot of freedom.

Christa, 6: Mellow, yet tactful. Creative and original. Hardworking and kind. Blessed in some ways. Charming and devoted. Dynamic, busy lifestyle. Pioneer and risk taker.

Christal, 9: Artistically creative. Great judge of character. Intense inner power. Forgive and be happy. Charming and devoted. Dynamic, busy lifestyle. Not easily influenced. Strong verbal skills.

Christian, 11: Inspiring and highly creative. Self-reliant, successful. Gentle, kind, a hard worker. Blessed in some ways. Charming and devoted. Dynamic, busy lifestyle. Artistic, having good taste. Inde-pendent, critical of self and others. Original and unconventional.

Christie, 10: Great verbal expressions. Self-reliant, successful. Gentle, kind, a hard worker. Blessed in some ways. Charming and devoted. Dynamic, busy lifestyle. Artistic, having good taste. A free spirit, very adaptable.

Christina, 11: Inspiring and highly creative. Self-reliant, successful. Gentle, kind, a hard worker. Blessed in some ways. Charming and devoted. Dynamic, busy lifestyle. Artistic, having good taste. Original and unconventional. Resolute and purposeful.

Christine, 6: Mellow, yet tactful. Creative and original. Gentle, kind, a hard worker. Blessed in some ways. Charming and devoted. Dynamic, busy lifestyle. Artistic, having good taste. Romantic, sensual. A step ahead of others.

Christopher, 4: Happily takes care of business. Great judge of character. Gentle, kind, a hard worker. Blessed in some ways. Charming and devoted. Dynamic, busy lifestyle. Natural counselor and healer. Intelligent and knowledgeable. Self-reliant, successful. A free spirit, very adaptable. Intense inner power.

Chuck, 10: Great verbal expressions. Self-reliant, successful. Attractive and charming. Self-expressive, cheerful. Strong desire to succeed.

Chuy, 3: Cheerful, lighthearted. Creative and original. Attractive and charming. Needs a lot of freedom.

Cicero, 8: Ups and downs financially. Blessed in some ways. Optimistic, outspoken. Physical and passionate. Intense inner power. Natural counselor and healer.

Cicily, 7: Sees the irony in situations. Blessed in some ways. Spontaneous, cheerful. Artistic, having good taste. Slow to make decisions. Needs a lot of freedom.

Cindy, 10: Great verbal expressions. Blessed in some ways. Original and unconventional. Reliable, responsible. Needs a lot of freedom.

Claire, 30: Cheerful, lighthearted. Communicates skillfully. Independent, critical of self and others. Blessed in some ways. Gentle, kind, a hard worker. A free spirit, very adaptable.

Clara, 8: Ups and downs financially. Recuperates quickly. Not easily influenced. Intense inner power. Bold, courageous, a bit stubborn.

Clare, 3: Cheerful, lighthearted. Communicates skillfully. Independent, critical of self and others. Gentle, kind, a hard worker. A free spirit, very adaptable.

Clarence, 7: Sees the irony in situations. Strong verbal skills. Independent, critical of self and others. Gentle, kind, a hard worker. A free spirit, very adaptable. Original and unconventional. Optimistic and outspoken. Tendency to overindulge.

Clareta, 6: Mellow, yet tactful. Frequent traveler. Pioneer and risk taker. Diligent, helpful. A free spirit, very adaptable. Dynamic, very busy lifestyle. Bold, courageous, a bit stubborn.

Clarice, 6: Mellow, yet tactful. Frequent traveler. Pioneer and risk taker. Diligent, helpful. Blessed in some ways. Inspiring and creative. A step ahead of others.

Clarissa, 10: Strong verbal skills. Independent, critical of self and others. Gentle, kind, a hard worker. Blessed in some ways. Charming and devoted. Impulsive and extreme. Bold, courageous, a bit stubborn.

Clark, 9: Artistically creative. Frequent traveler. Pioneer and risk taker. Gentle, kind, a hard worker. Strong desire to succeed.

Claud, 5: Quick sense of humor. Moves and travels often. Bold, courageous, a bit stubborn. Attractive and charming. Reliable and responsible.

Claude, 10: Strong verbal skills. Independent, critical of self and others. Attractive and charming. Reliable, responsible. A free spirit, very adaptable.

Claudell, 7: Sees the irony in situations. Strong verbal skills. Not easily influenced. Attractive and charming. Reliable, responsible.

Claudia, 6: Mellow, yet tactful. Frequent traveler. Independent, critical of self and others. Attractive and charming. Reliable, responsible. Blessed in some ways. Bold, courageous, a bit stubborn.

Clay, 5: Quick sense of humor. Moves and travels often. Independent, critical of self and others. Needs a lot of freedom.

Clayton, 9: Artistically creative. Strong verbal skills. Pioneer and risk taker. Needs a lot of freedom. Dynamic, busy lifestyle. Natural counselor and healer. Original and unconventional.

Clem, 6: Mellow, yet tactful. Frequent traveler. A free spirit, very adaptable. Domestic, hardworking.

Clement, 9: Artistically creative. Strong verbal skills. A free spirit, very adaptable. Domestic, hardworking. Loves adventure and excitement. Original and unconventional. Dynamic, a busy lifestyle.

Clementine, 10: Great verbal expressions. Frequent traveler. A free spirit, very adaptable. Domestic, hardworking. Loves adventure and excitement. Original and unconventional. Dynamic, a busy lifestyle. Blessed in some ways. Romantic, sensual. Tendency to overindulge.

Cleo, 8: Ups and downs financially. Appreciates quality. Physical and passionate. Natural counselor and healer.

Cleopatra, 10: Great verbal expressions. Optimistic, outspoken. A free spirit, very adaptable. Natural counselor and healer. Intelligent and knowledgeable. Independent, critical of self and others. Dynamic, busy lifestyle. Gentle, kind, a hard worker. Bold, courageous, a bit stubborn.

Cliff, 9: Artistically creative. Strong verbal skills. Blessed in some ways. Self-sacrificing, loving. Easygoing nature.

Clifford, 10: Great verbal expressions. Optimistic, outspoken. Blessed in some ways. Self-sacrificing, loving. Very considerate. Natural counselor and healer. Gentle, kind, a hard worker. Reliable, responsible.

Clifton, 7: Sees the irony in situations. Strong verbal skills. Blessed in some ways. Self-sacrificing, loving. Dynamic, busy lifestyle. Natural counselor and healer. Original and unconventional.

Clint, 22: Inspiring and highly creative. Travels frequently. Blessed in some ways. Romantic and opinionated. Dynamic, busy lifestyle.

Clinton, 6: Mellow, yet tactful. Optimistic and outspoken. Artistic, having good taste. Original and unconventional. Dynamic, busy lifestyle. Natural counselor and healer. Romantic and sensual.

Clive, 6: Mellow, yet tactful. Optimistic and outspoken. Artistic, having good taste. Intuitive and inspired. A free spirit, very adaptable.

Clovis, 8: Ups and downs financially. Recuperates quickly. Natural counselor and healer. Intuitive and inspired. Blessed in some ways. Charming and devoted.

Clyde, 22: Inspiring and highly creative. Strong verbal skills. Needs a lot of freedom. Reliable, responsible. Loves adventure and excitement.

Coby, 9: Artistically creative. Creates group harmony. Affectionate, social. Needs a lot of freedom.

Cody, 20: Has a sociable demeanor. Respects rules. Reliable and responsible. Needs a lot of freedom.

Colan, 9: Artistically creative. Creates group harmony. Strong verbal skills. Independent, critical of self and others. Original and unconventional.

Colbert, 30: Cheerful, lighthearted. Natural counselor and healer. Communicates skillfully. Friendly, but shy. A free spirit, very adaptable. Gentle, kind, a hard worker. Dynamic, busy lifestyle.

Colby, 3: Cheerful, lighthearted. Natural counselor and healer. Communicates skillfully. Affectionate, social. Needs a lot of freedom.

Cole, 7: Sees the irony in situations. Open to opportunities. Strong verbal skills. A free spirit, very adaptable.

Colette, 7: Sees the irony in situations. Open to opportunities. Strong verbal skills. A free spirit, very adaptable. Dynamic, busy lifestyle. A force of nature. Tendency to overindulge.

Colin, 8: Ups and downs financially. Competitive in business. Communicates skillfully. Blessed in some ways. Original and unconventional.

Colleen, 30: Cheerful, lighthearted. Natural counselor and healer. Optimistic, outspoken. Frequent traveler. A free spirit, very adaptable. Tendency to overindulge. Romantic and sensual.

Collier, 11: Inspiring and highly creative. Open to opportunities. Strong verbal skills. Frequent traveler. Considerate, understanding. Likes to entertain. Gentle, kind, a hard worker.

Conan, 20: Has a sociable demeanor. Natural counselor and healer. Creative and opinionated. Perceptive, reads people easily. Romantic and sensual.

Concepcion, 7: Sees the irony in situations. Open to opportunities. Original and unconventional. Optimistic, outspoken. A free spirit, very adaptable. Intelligent and knowledgeable. Outgoing, youthful outlook. Blessed in some ways. Natural counselor and healer. Romantic and sensual.

Conception, 6: Mellow, yet tactful. Natural counselor and healer. Original and unconventional. Inspiring and creative. A free spirit, very adaptable. Intelligent and knowledgeable. Dynamic, busy lifestyle. Blessed in some ways. May have musical abilities. Romantic and sensual.

Condoleezza, 9: Artistically creative. Creates group harmony. Original and romantic. Reliable, responsible. Nurturing, loving. Strong verbal skills. A free spirit, very adaptable. Loves adventure and excitement. Uses common sense. Is a great mediator. Resolute and purposeful.

Condolisa, 11: Inspiring and highly creative. Open to opportunities. Original and unconventional. Reliable, responsible. Nurturing, loving. Strong verbal skills. Blessed in some ways. Charming and devoted. Resolute and purposeful.

Conner, 6: Mellow, yet tactful. Natural counselor and healer. Original and unconventional. Creative, opinionated. A free spirit, very adaptable. Gentle, kind, a hard worker.

Connie, 6: Mellow, yet tactful. Natural counselor and healer. Original and unconventional. Creative, opinionated. Blessed in some ways. A free spirit, very adaptable.

Connor, 7: Sees the irony in situations. Open to opportunities. Original and unconventional. Romantic and sensual. May have musical abilities. Gentle, kind, a hard worker.

Conrad, 10: Great verbal expressions. Self-sacrificing, devoted. Romantic, opinionated. Intense inner power. Independent, critical of self and others. Reliable and responsible.

Conroy, 9: Artistically creative. Creates group harmony. Original and unconventional. Gentle, kind, a hard worker. Respects rules. Needs a lot of freedom.

Constance, 4: Happily takes care of business. Respects rules. Original and unconventional. Charming and devoted. Dynamic, busy lifestyle. Independent, critical of self and others. Romantic and sensual. Inspiring and very creative. A free spirit, very adaptable.

Consuelo, 5: Quick sense of humor. Natural counselor and healer. Romantic, opinionated. Charming and devoted. Creative, intuitive. A free spirit, very adaptable. Strong verbal skills. May have musical abilities.

Conway, 9: Artistically creative. Creates group harmony. Original and unconventional. Likes to meet new people. Pioneer and risk taker. Needs a lot of freedom.

Cooper, 9: Artistically creative. Creates group harmony. Nurturing, loving. Intelligent, knowledgeable. A free spirit, very adaptable. Gentle, kind, a hard worker.

Cora, 10: Great verbal expressions. Self-sacrificing, devoted. Gentle, kind, a hard worker. Independent, critical of self and others.

Coral, 22: Inspiring and highly creative. Natural counselor and healer. Gentle, kind, a hard worker. Resolute and purposeful. Strong verbal skills.

Corbin, 7: Sees the irony in situations. Open to opportunities. Gentle, kind, a hard worker. Friendly, loyal. Artistic, having good taste. Original and unconventional.

Coretta, 10: Great verbal expressions. Self-sacrificing, devoted. Intense inner power. Loves adventure and excitement. Dynamic, busy lifestyle. Needs to slow down. Bold, courageous, a bit stubborn.

Corey, 30: Cheerful, lighthearted. Natural counselor and healer. Intense inner power. A free spirit, very adaptable. Dislikes limitations.

Corinne, 6: Mellow, yet tactful. Natural counselor and healer. Diligent, helpful. Considerate, understanding. Original and unconventional. Romantic, sensual. Likes to entertain.

Corliss, 5: Quick sense of humor. Enjoys working. Intense inner power. Strong verbal skills. Artistic, having good taste. Charming and devoted. Extreme.

Cornel, 4: Happily takes care of business. Respects rules. Gentle, kind, a hard worker. Original and unconventional. A free spirit, very adaptable. Strong verbal skills.

Cornelia, 5: Quick sense of humor. Natural counselor and healer. Gentle, kind, a hard worker. Original and unconventional. Physical and passionate. Strong verbal skills. Blessed in some ways. Independent, critical of self and others.

Cornelius, 8: Ups and downs financially. Competitive in business. Intense inner power. Creative, opinionated. Physical, passionate. Optimistic, outspoken. Artistic, having good taste. Attractive and charming. Many mood swings.

Cory, 7: Sees the irony in situations. Open to opportunities. Gentle, kind, a hard worker. Needs a lot of freedom.

Courtney, 4: Happily takes care of business. Respects rules. Attractive and charming. Gentle, kind, a hard worker. Dynamic, busy lifestyle. Original, unconventional. Loves adventure and excitement. Needs a lot of freedom.

Craig, 11: Inspiring and highly creative. Intense inner power. Not easily influenced. Blessed in some ways. Scientific and philosophical.

Cris, 22: Inspiring and highly creative. Gentle, kind, a hard worker. Blessed in some ways. Charming and devoted.

Cristo, 30: Cheerful, lighthearted. Gentle, kind, a hard worker. Blessed in some ways. Charming and devoted. Dynamic, busy lifestyle. Natural counselor and healer.

Cruz, 5: Quick sense of humor. Intense inner power. Attractive and charming. A tendency to look on the bright side.

Crystal, 8: Ups and downs financially. Intense inner power. Needs a lot of freedom. Charming and devoted. Dynamic, busy lifestyle. Resolute and purposeful. Strong verbal skills.

Cullen, 22: Inspiring and highly creative. Attractive and charming. Strong verbal skills. Frequent traveler. Likes to entertain. Romantic, sensual.

Culver, 9: Artistically creative. Attractive and charming. Strong verbal skills. Intuitive and inspired. A free spirit, very adaptable. Gentle, kind, hard worker.

Curt, 8: Ups and downs financially. Attractive and charming. Intense inner power. Dynamic, busy lifestyle.

Curtis, 9: Artistically creative. Attractive and charming. Gentle, kind, a hard worker. Dynamic, busy lifestyle. Blessed in some ways. Many mood swings.

Cyndi, 10: (Same as Cindy.)

Cynthia, 8: Ups and downs financially. Dislikes limitations. Romantic, sensual. Dynamic, busy lifestyle. Self-reliant, successful. Artistic, having good taste. Resolute and purposeful.

Cyrena, 30: Cheerful, lighthearted. Needs a lot of freedom. Gentle, kind, a hard worker. Tendency to overindulge. Romantic, sensual. Pioneer and risk taker.

Cyril, 4: Happily takes care of business. Needs a lot of freedom. Gentle, kind, a hard worker. Blessed in some ways. Strong verbal skills.

Cyrilla, 8: Ups and downs financially. Dislikes limitations. Intense inner power. Blessed in some ways. Strong verbal skills. Frequent traveler. Independent, critical of self and others.

Cyrinda, 11: Inspiring and highly creative. Stylish and refined. Gentle, kind, a hard worker. Artistic, having good taste. Original and unconventional. Reliable, responsible. Resolute and purposeful.

Cyrus, 5: Quick sense of humor. Needs a lot of freedom. Gentle, kind, a hard worker. Attractive and charming. Impulsive and extreme.

D

If a name begins with D, has more than one D, or ends with a D, this person is down-to-earth, systematic, practical, and organized.

If you want to get something done, give it to a D person. They're very responsible and efficient about everything they do. Even when they are planning a fun trip, they seem so businesslike that it's difficult to imagine them actually having fun. The fun part of a trip for a D person might very well be in the planning and taking care of all the last minute details and obligations. It's not that they are "stick-in-the-muds," it's just that they enjoy being efficient. It's their nature, that's all. Children with D names will give you their game plan well in advance to ensure success.

D-named people are almost as hard-driven as A types. They're more domesticated, though, as D is the fourth letter in the alphabet, ruled by the number 4. The number 4 vibration rules work and family. Consequently, the D person is all about work and family. Hard work is complementary to this person's nature. The typical D-named person is fine with the chores the rest of us find difficult. They don't mind weeding the garden, cleaning out storage areas, paying the bills, and cooking dinner. Most consider themselves lucky to be married to a D-named person for this reason. The letters D, M, and V are all ruled by the number 4. Anyone with the letters D, M, or V anywhere in their name will be task-oriented, down-to-earth, systematic, and practical.

Anyone that likes having a roof over his or her head and the bills paid on time can sleep well if married to a D. The D person is one of the most shrewd and determined letters in the alphabet. Those married to a D are in for a special bonus. Cheating goes against their grain, if they are a typical D person. It's not that they aren't capable of cheating on their partners; it's that when they have invested time and money into a relationship, why chance it? Gamblers they're not. We won't find many D types throwing money away in the casinos either. It just isn't practical; it's non-productive and wasteful.

In astrology we like to see a little earth in a chart to help ground a person so the person actually gets something done during their short time on earth. This is also true of a name. One 4-ruled letter could give a name just enough ability to get something accomplished during their lifetime. D types are down-to-earth, goal-oriented, shrewd, and similar to Capricorns, yet they are as domestic and security-oriented as Cancer the crab.

A person with the name of David would have three 4-ruled letters in his name. Not only would he have a 4 intensity number, but also a 4 power number. It is possible to have too much of a good thing with this much 4 in a name. The numbers 4 and 8 are karmic. These numbers attract hard lessons in life to the ones who have them in their names. A little seven-year-old girl, Danielle van Dam, disappeared on February 2, 2002 (2/2/2002). If we add up the date she disappeared it adds up to 8, a karmic number. Her name has four 4-ruled letters. Her mother, Brenda van Dam, also has four 4-ruled letters. Danielle's father, Damon van Dam, has five 4-ruled letters. And last but not least, David Westerfield, the man who was convicted of the crime with DNA evidence, also has four 4-ruled letters in his first name. Danielle's two brothers' names also started with D. They thought they would find Danielle's body in the desert, but found her on Dehesa Road. And let's not forget the bar that got so much publicity during the trial, "Dad's." Too many D names added up to disaster and death. Although Danielle's parents won a civil suit against Westerfield, no one mentioned above really won. They all lost, didn't they? The lessons brought about by karmic numbers can be harsh and brutal.

Look at the name Saddam Hussein. This terrorist leader had all 1s and 4s in his first name. How harsh is that? Extremely harsh. Almost as harsh as Adolf Hitler; the A and D in the front of his name were enough to predict this man's reputation for harsh and cruel behavior.

Before deciding to change little David's name to Barney, consider the fact that no matter how many harsh letters in a name, heredity and upbringing can have an overwhelming effect on a person's potential. The 4-ruled, similar to the 1-ruled, have bullies in their heads driving them to do their best. They make wonderful teachers, accountants, lawyers, government officials, and managers. Most D-named people are workaholics, driven by contempt for anyone who is lazy, phony, or unpredictable. They aren't as easily put off as some of the other letters. This 4-ruled letter has follow-through ability. Next time you attend an award ceremony, observe how many of the people who win awards have the letters D or M or V in their names. Almost every award winner does, or they have a 4 power number.

The D in Arnold Schwarzenegger's name was enough to make him play the role of terminator well. If a D appears anywhere in a name it gives the person the ability to systematically size up any situation. It's sort of a human computer effect. D names can enter a room, look around, assess and know what's right or wrong about it. I know a school teacher named Diane who can tell who the trouble makers are in the first five minutes. If Arnold does well as governor of California, it's because of the D in his name. D is for determination.

Another interesting observation about D and other 4-ruled letters is the skin color of the person with this influence. It seems even a hidden 4 can denote a darker skin coloring. Some D names are blonde with light skin, but they look as if they should be brunette. They look more serious than the average blonde. The more 4-ruled letters or number 4 influence in a name, the darker the skin, in most cases.

A softer D type would be the late Princess Di. She suffered some of the problems of the number 4 vibration such as depression and hardships in her marriage. The I in her name made her a humanitarian. People looked up to her, right or wrong. She was blessed, but the I made her not happy unless able to forgive others for wrongdoing toward her. Her power number added up to the unlucky 13 which condensed down to a 4. She was a natural teacher and taught the world a thing or two about compassion. She was down-to-earth yet elegant, a combination only Princess Di could pull off.

Some other famous D names are: Daryl Hannah, David Letterman, Dean Martin, David Carradine, Dan Aykroyd, Donald Trump, Davy Crockett, Debbie Reynolds, Dan Rather, Duke Cunningham,

Dionne Warwick, Diana Ross, Dennis Quaid, Dave Mathews, Demi Moore, Dennis Hopper, Dustin Hoffman, Donny Osmond, Dana Carvey, Della Reese, Dom DeLuise, Donald Sutherland, Don Henley, and Dolly Parton.

QUICK REFERENCE OF "D" NAMES

Dacha, 8: Reliable, responsible. Not easily influenced. Optimistic, outspoken. Great judge of character. Bold, courageous, a bit stubborn.

Daffi, 8: Reliable, responsible. Resolute and purposeful. Self-sacrificing, loving. High moral standards. Artistic, having good taste.

Daffodil, 3: Serious, yet fun-loving. Aims to please. Self-sacrificing, loving. High moral standards. Natural counselor and healer. Down-to-earth, faithful. Blessed in some ways. Strong verbal skills.

Daffy, 6: Creative problem solver. Pioneer and risk taker. Self-sacrificing, loving. Service-oriented. Needs a lot of freedom.

Daghlawi, 11: Workaholic, determined. Intuitive, perceptive. Scientific and philosophical. Self-reliant, successful. Strong verbal skills. Bold, courageous, a bit stubborn. Likes to meet new people. Blessed in some ways.

Dagmar, 8: Reliable, responsible. Resolute and purposeful. Scientific and philosophical. Domestic, hardworking. Resolute and purposeful. Intense inner power.

Dahlia, 8: Reliable, responsible. Resolute and purposeful. Self-reliant, successful. Strong verbal skills. Artistic, having good taste. Bold, courageous, a bit stubborn.

Daisie, 11: Workaholic, determined. Intuitive, perceptive. Artistic, having good taste. Charming and devoted. Blessed in some ways. Likes to entertain. .

Daisy, 22: Workaholic, determined. Ambitious leader, great vision. Artistic, having good taste. Charming and devoted. Dislikes limitations.

Dakota, 7: Systematic, organized. Not easily influenced. Strong desire to succeed. Natural counselor and healer. Dynamic, busy lifestyle. Bold, courageous, a bit stubborn.

Dale, 4: Down-to-earth, faithful. Natural teaching ability. Strong verbal skills. A free spirit, very adaptable.

Daleen, 5: Enjoys working. Bright, adventuresome. Communicates skillfully. A free spirit, very adaptable. Tendency to overindulge. Romantic, sensual.

Dalin, 22: Workaholic, determined. Ambitious leader, great vision. Frequent traveler. Blessed in some ways. Creative, opinionated.

Dallan, 8: Reliable, responsible. Resolute and purposeful. Strong verbal skills. Ups and downs financially. Self-motivated, determined. Romantic, sensual.

Dallas, 4: Down-to-earth, faithful. Natural teaching ability. Strong verbal skills. Frequent traveler. Bold, courageous, a bit stubborn. Charming and devoted.

Dalton, 3: Serious, yet fun:loving. Aims to please. Communicates skillfully. Dynamic, busy lifestyle. Natural counselor and healer. Romantic, sensual.

Damian, 6: Creative problem solver. Pioneer and risk taker. Systematic, organized. Artistic, having good taste. Original and unconventional.

Damien, 10: Natural authority. Independent, critical of self and others. Domestic, hardworking. Blessed in some ways. A free spirit, very adaptable. Creative, opinionated.

Damon, 20: Practical, conservative. Reads people easily. Desires financial security. Natural counselor and healer. Romantic, sensual.

Dan, 10: Natural authority. Independent, critical of self and others. Creative, opinionated.

Dana, 11: Workaholic, determined. Intuitive, perceptive. Romantic, sensual. Bold, courageous, a bit stubborn.

Dane, 6: Creative problem solver. Pioneer and risk taker. Original and opinionated. Physical and passionate.

Daniel, 9: Trustworthy, dependable. Helpful, sincere. Original and unconventional. Blessed in some ways. A free spirit, very adaptable. Communicates skillfully.

Daniela, 10: Natural authority. Independent, critical of self and others. Original and unconventional. Blessed in some ways. Loves adventure and excitement. Frequent traveler. Bold, courageous, a bit stubborn.

Danielle, 8: Reliable, responsible. Resolute and purposeful. Creative, opinionated. Artistic, having good taste. A free spirit, very adaptable. Strong verbal skills. Frequent traveler. Physical and passionate.

Danilo, 10: Natural authority. Independent, critical of self and others. Original and unconventional. Blessed in some ways. Strong verbal skills. Natural counselor and healer.

Danita, 22: Workaholic, determined. Ambitious leader, great vision. Romantic, opinionated. Blessed in some ways. Dynamic, busy lifestyle. Resolute and purposeful.

D'Anna, 7: Systematic, organized. Not easily influenced. Original and unconventional. Romantic, sensual. Bold, courageous, a bit stubborn.

Dannen, 7: Systematic, organized. Not easily influenced. Original and unconventional. Romantic, sensual. Tendency to overindulge. Creative, opinionated.

Danny, 22: Workaholic, determined. Ambitious leader, great vision. Original and unconventional. Creative, opinionated. Needs a lot of freedom.

Dante, 8: Reliable, responsible. Resolute and purposeful. Original and unconventional. Dynamic, very busy lifestyle. Physical and passionate.

Daphne, 30: Serious, yet fun:loving. Aims to please. Intelligent and knowledgeable. Great judge of character. Romantic and sensual. A free spirit, very adaptable.

Dar, 5: Enjoys working. Bright, adventuresome. Gentle, kind, a hard worker.

Dara, 6: Creative problem solver. Pioneer and risk taker. Compassionate, understanding. Natural authority.

Darby, 5: Enjoys working. Bright, adventuresome. Intense inner power. Affectionate, social. Needs a lot of freedom.

Darcie, 4: Down-to-earth, faithful. Natural teaching ability. Gentle, kind, a hard worker. Self-expressive, cheerful. Blessed in some ways. A free spirit, very adaptable.

Darcy, 6: Creative problem solver. Pioneer and risk taker. Compassionate, understanding. Optimistic, cheerful. Needs a lot of freedom.

Darei, 10: Natural authority. Independent, critical of self and others. Gentle, kind, a hard worker. A free spirit, very adaptable. Blessed in some ways.

Daria, 6: Creative problem solver. Pioneer and risk taker. Compassionate, understanding. Artistic, having good taste. Self-motivated, determined.

Dariel, 4: Down-to-earth, faithful. Natural teaching ability. Compassionate, understanding. Blessed in some ways. A free spirit, very adaptable. Communicates skillfully.

Darius, 9: Trustworthy, dependable. Helpful, sincere. Intense inner power. Blessed in some ways. Attractive and charming. Loving and devoted.

Darleen, 5: Enjoys working. Bright, adventuresome. Gentle, kind, a hard worker. Great verbal skills. A free spirit, very adaptable. Tendency to overindulge. Romantic, sensual.

Darlene, 5: (Same as Darleen.)

Darlin, 4: Down-to-earth, faithful. Natural teaching ability. Gentle, kind, a hard worker. Strong verbal skills. Blessed in some ways. Romantic, sensual.

Darrah, 5: Enjoys working. Bright, adventuresome. Gentle, kind, a hard worker. Tendency to lose items. Pioneer and risk taker. Self-reliant, successful.

Darrel, 4: Down-to-earth, faithful. Natural teaching ability. Gentle, kind, a hard worker. Tendency to lose items. A free spirit, very adaptable. Strong verbal skills.

Darrell, 7: Systematic, organized. Not easily influenced. Intense inner power. Tendency to lose items. A free spirit, very adaptable. Strong verbal skills. Frequent traveler.

Darren, 6: Creative problem solver. Pioneer and risk taker. Gentle, kind, a hard worker. Could be forgetful. A free spirit, very adaptable. Original, unconventional.

Daryl, 6: Creative problem solver. Pioneer and risk taker. Gentle, kind, a hard worker. Needs a lot of freedom. Strong verbal skills.

DaShaun, 5: Enjoys working. Bright, adventuresome. Charming and devoted. Self-reliant, successful. Bold, courageous, a bit stubborn. Very lucky. Physical and passionate.

Dave, 5: Enjoys working. Bright, adventuresome. Intuitive and inspired. Physical and passionate.

David, 22: Workaholic, determined. Ambitious leader, great vision. Intuitive and inspired. Artistic, having good taste. Down-to-earth, faithful.

Davie, 5: Enjoys working. Bright, adventuresome. Intuitive and inspired. Artistic, having good taste. Physical and passionate.

Davy, 7: Systematic, organized. Not easily influenced. Intuitive and inspired. Needs a lot of freedom.

Dawn, 6: Creative problem solver. Pioneer and risk taker. Likes to meet new people. Original and unconventional.

Dean, 6: Creative problem solver. A step ahead of others. Pioneer and risk taker. Romantic, opinionated.

Deandra, 11: Workaholic, determined. Physical and passionate. Intuitive, perceptive. Creative, opinionated. Down-to-earth, faithful. Gentle, kind, a hard worker. Bold, courageous, a bit stubborn.

Deane, 20: Practical, conservative. Social and entertaining. Resolute and purposeful. Romantic, sensual. A free spirit, very adaptable.

Deanna, 3: Serious, yet fun:loving. A free spirit, very adaptable. Self-motivated, independent. Original and unconventional. Romantic, sensual. Pioneer and risk taker.

Deb, 11: Workaholic, determined. Intuitive, perceptive. Affectionate, social.

Debbie, 9: Trustworthy, dependable. Enjoys giving gifts. Loyal, understanding. Emotional, sensitive. Blessed in some ways. Physical and passionate.

Debby, 20: Practical, conservative. Likes to entertain. Affectionate, social. Emotional, sensitive. Needs a lot of freedom.

Debora, 9: Trustworthy, dependable. Enjoys giving gifts. Loyal, understanding. Natural counselor and healer. Gentle, kind, a hard worker. Helpful, sincere.

Deborah, 8: Reliable, responsible. Original and creative. Friendly, but shy. Natural counselor and healer. Intense inner power. Bold, courageous, a bit stubborn. Great judge of character.

Debra, 3: Serious, yet fun:loving. A free spirit, very adaptable. Social, affectionate. Gentle, kind, a hard worker. Creative, aims to please.

Dede, 9: Trustworthy, dependable. Enjoys giving gifts. Domestic, responsible. Physical, passionate.

Dee, 5: Enjoys working. Physical and passionate. Perceptive, socially adept.

Deedee, 10: Natural authority. Likes change and variety. Perceptive, socially adept. Down-to-earth, practical. Likes to entertain. Physical and passionate.

Deidre, 9: Trustworthy, dependable. Enjoys giving gifts. Artistic, having good taste. Workaholic, shrewd, determined. Tendency to lose things. Physical, passionate.

Dejuan, 10: Natural authority. Likes change and variety. Clever and talented. Attractive and charming. Self-motivated, purposeful. Romantic, sensual.

Delano, 6: Creative problem solver. A step ahead of others. Strong verbal skills. Pioneer and risk taker. Original and unconventional. Natural counselor and healer.

Delia, 22: Workaholic, determined. Has big plans and ideas. Frequent traveler. Blessed in some ways. Independent, self-motivated.

Delight, 11: Workaholic, determined. Keenly perceptive. Strong verbal skills. Artistic, having good taste. Willpower and determination. Great judge of character. Dynamic, busy lifestyle.

Delilah, 6: Creative problem solver. A step ahead of others. Financial ups and downs. Blessed in some ways. Frequent traveler. Pioneer and risk taker. Great judge of character.

Della, 7: Systematic, organized. Not easily fooled. Strong verbal skills. Frequent traveler. Resolute and purposeful.

Deloris, 10: Natural authority. Likes change and variety. Strong verbal skills. Natural counselor and healer. Gentle, kind, a hard worker. Blessed in some ways. Charming and devoted.

Delphine, 10: Natural authority. Likes change and variety. Frequent traveler. Intelligent and knowledgeable. Self-reliant, successful. Blessed in some ways. Romantic, sensual. Loves adventure and excitement.

Delta, 6: Creative problem solver. A step ahead of others. Strong verbal skills. Dynamic, busy lifestyle. Pioneer and risk taker.

Demetra, 30: Serious, yet fun:loving. A free spirit, very adaptable. Domestic, hardworking. Likes to entertain. Dynamic, busy lifestyle. Tendency to lose things. Independent, self-motivated.

Demetria, 3: Serious, yet fun:loving. A free spirit, very adaptable. Domestic, hardworking. Likes to entertain. Dynamic, busy lifestyle. Tendency to lose things. Blessed in some ways. Independent, self-motivated.

Demetrius, 6: Creative problem solver. A step ahead of others. Tolerant, endures hardships. Adaptable to change. Dynamic, busy lifestyle. Diligent, helpful. Considerate, understanding. Youthful, appealing. Charming and devoted.

Demi, 22: Workaholic, determined. A free spirit, very adaptable. Energetic, hardworking. Blessed in some ways.

Demitra, 7: Systematic, organized. Not fooled easily. Domestic, hardworking. Artistic, having good taste. Dynamic, busy lifestyle. Self-sacrificing, helpful. Independent, critical of self and others.

Demmie, 4: Down-to-earth, faithful. A free spirit, very adaptable. Energetic, hardworking. Tolerant, endures hardships. Blessed in some ways. Physical and passionate.

Dena, 6: Creative problem solver. A step ahead of others. Romantic, sensual, perceptive. Independent, ambitious.

Denise, 11: Workaholic, determined. Physical and passionate. Opinionated, original. Blessed in some ways. Charming and devoted. Learns through experiences.

Deniz, 4: Down-to-earth, faithful. Accesses quickly. Romantic, sensual. Blessed in some ways. Uses common sense.

Dennis, 11: Workaholic, determined. Intuitive, perceptive. Original and unconventional. Romantic and sensual. Blessed in some ways. Charming and devoted.

Denny, 8: Reliable, responsible. Original and creative. Romantic, sensual. Unconventional, opinionated. Needs a lot of freedom.

Denton, 9: Trustworthy, dependable. Enjoys giving gifts. Creative, opinionated. Dynamic, very busy lifestyle. Natural counselor and healer. Romantic and sensual.

Denver, 5: Enjoys working. Physical and passionate. Original and opinionated. Intuitive and inspired. A free spirit, very adaptable. Gentle, kind, a hard worker.

Denys, 22: Workaholic, determined. Has big plans and ideas. Opinionated and unconventional. Needs a lot of freedom. Charming and devoted.

Denzel, 30: Serious, yet fun:loving. A free spirit, very adaptable. Romantic, sensual. Uses common sense. Likes change and variety. Communicates skillfully.

Derek, 7: Systematic, organized. Not easily fooled. Gentle, kind, a hard worker. Likes change and variety. Strong desire to succeed.

Dermot, 30: Serious, yet fun:loving. A free spirit, very adaptable. Intense inner power. Domestic, hardworking. Natural counselor and healer. Dynamic, busy lifestyle.

Derrick, 5: Enjoys working. Physical and passionate. Gentle, kind, a hard worker. Intense inner power. Artistic, having good taste. Self-expressive, cheerful. Strong desire to succeed.

Derwin, 10: Natural authority. Likes change and variety. Diligent, helpful. Likes to meet new people. Humanitarian, emotional. Original and unconventional.

Desi, 10: Natural authority. Likes change and variety. Charming and devoted. Blessed in some ways.

Desiree, 11: Workaholic, determined. Intuitive, perceptive. Charming and devoted. Artistic, having good taste. Intense inner power. Physical and passionate. Loves adventure and excitement.

Desma, 6: Creative problem solver. A step ahead of others. Devoted, loving. Domestic, hardworking. Independent, ambitious.

Desmond, 11: Workaholic, determined. Intuitive, perceptive. Charming and devoted. Domestic, hardworking. Natural counselor and healer. Creative, opinionated. Down-to-earth, faithful.

Destiny, 6: Creative problem solver. A step ahead of others. Passionate, loving. Dynamic, busy lifestyle. Artistic, having good taste. Original, opinionated. Needs a lot of freedom.

Deva, 5: Enjoys working. Physical and passionate. Intuitive and inspired. Independent, pioneer and risk taker.

Devin, 9: Trustworthy, dependable. Enjoys giving gifts. Strong imagination. Blessed in some ways. Original and unconventional.

Devon, 6: Creative problem solver. A step ahead of others. Intuitive and inspired. Natural counselor and healer. Unconventional, opinionated.

Devona, 7: Systematic, organized. Not easily fooled. Strong imagination. Creates group harmony. Original and unconventional.

Dewey, 8: Reliable, responsible. Original and creative. Likes to meet new people. Physical and passionate. Needs a lot of freedom.

Dexter, 4: Down-to-earth, faithful. A free spirit, very adaptable. Artistic, sensual, perceptive. Dynamic, busy lifestyle. Loves adventure and excitement. Gentle, kind, a hard worker.

Dextra, 9: Trustworthy, dependable. Adaptable to change. Artistic, sensual, perceptive. Dynamic, busy lifestyle. Intense inner power. Pioneer and risk taker.

Di, 4: Down-to-earth, faithful. Teaches kindness. Desires financial security.

Diana, 20: Practical, conservative. Emotional, considerate. Reads people easily. Original and creative. Bold, courageous, a bit stubborn.

Diane, 6: Creative problem solver. Artistic, having good taste. Resolute and purposeful. Original and opinionated. A free spirit, very adaptable.

Dick, 9: Trustworthy, dependable. Idealistic and humanitarian. Self-expressive, cheerful. Strong desire to succeed.

Didi, 8: Reliable, responsible. Blessed in some ways. Down-to-earth, faithful. Artistic, having good taste.

Diego, 4: Down-to-earth, faithful. Idealistic and humanitarian. Loves adventure and excitement. Has willpower and determination. Natural counselor and healer.

Dierdre, 9: Trustworthy, dependable. Artistic, having good taste. Likes to entertain. Gentle, kind, a hard worker. Domestic, responsible. Tendency to lose items. A free spirit, very adaptable.

Digna, 8: Reliable, responsible. Blessed in some ways. Stylish and refined. Romantic, sensual. Resolute and purposeful.

Dillon, 30: Serious, yet fun:loving. Blessed in some ways. Strong verbal skills. Financial ups and downs. Natural counselor and healer. Original and unconventional.

Dimitra, 11: Workaholic, determined. Considerate, understanding. Domestic, hardworking. Artistic, having good taste. Dynamic, busy lifestyle. Could be forgetful. Ambitious, self-motivated.

Dinah, 9: Trustworthy, dependable. Idealistic and humanitarian. Original and unconventional. Bold, courageous, a bit stubborn. Great judge of character.

Dion, 6: Creative problem solver. Artistic, having good taste. Natural counselor and healer. Original and unconventional.

Dione, 11: Workaholic, determined. Considerate, understanding. Loving and nurturing. Original and unconventional. Loves adventure and excitement.

Dionisio, 4: Down-to-earth, faithful. Blessed in some ways. Natural counselor and healer. Romantic, sensual. Idealistic and humanitarian. Charming and devoted. Artistic, having good taste. May have musical abilities.

Dirk, 6: Creative problem solver. Considerate, understanding. Diligent and helpful. Strong desire to succeed.

Dixie, 6: Creative problem solver. Blessed in some ways. Artistic, sensual, perceptive. Idealistic and humanitarian. Adaptable to change.

Dixon, 30: Serious, yet fun:loving. Blessed in some ways. Artistic, sensual, perceptive. Natural counselor and healer. Original and unconventional.

D.J., 5: Enjoys working. Very clever and talented. Freedom loving.

Dodi, 5: Enjoys working. Natural counselor and healer. Down-to-earth, faithful. Artistic, having good taste.

Dodong, 5: Enjoys working. Natural counselor and healer. Hardworking, faithful. May have musical abilities. Romantic, sensual. Willpower and determination.

Dolan, 10: Natural authority. Natural counselor and healer. Strong verbal skills. Independent, critical of self and others. Original and unconventional.

Dolley, 10: Natural authority. Natural counselor and healer. Strong verbal skills. Frequent traveler. Loves adventure and excitement. Needs a lot of freedom.

Dollie, 30: Serious, yet fun:loving. Good parenting abilities. Communicates skillfully. Financial ups and downs. Blessed in some ways. A free spirit, very adaptable.

Dolly, 5: Enjoys working. Creates group harmony. Strong verbal skills. Ups and downs financially. Dislikes limitations.

Dolores, 7: Systematic, organized. Natural counselor and healer. Frequent traveler. May have musical abilities. Intense inner power. Likes change, very adaptable. Charming and devoted.

Dom, 5: Enjoys working. Natural counselor and healer. Domestic, faithful, hardworking.

Dominic, 4: Down-to-earth, faithful. Respects rules. Domestic, hardworking. Blessed in some ways. Romantic, sensual. Artistic, having good taste. Optimistic, cheerful.

Dominica, 5: Enjoys working. Natural counselor and healer. Domestic, hardworking. Blessed in some ways. Romantic, sensual. Artistic, having good taste. Loyal, understanding. Pioneer and risk taker.

Dominick, 6: Creative problem solver. Loving and nurturing. Domestic, hardworking. Blessed in some ways. Creative, opinionated. Artistic, having good taste. Self-expressive, cheerful. Strong desire to succeed.

Dominique, 8: Reliable, responsible. Natural counselor and healer. Domestic, hardworking. Blessed in some ways. Creative, opinionated. Artistic, having good taste. Attracts wealth. Attractive and charming. Likes change, very adaptable.

Don, 6: Creative problem solver. Nurturing, loving, responsible. Original and unconventional.

Donald, 5: Enjoys working. Natural counselor and healer. Original and unconventional. Pioneer and risk taker. Strong verbal skills. Down-to-earth, faithful.

Donalt, 3: Serious, yet fun:loving. Creates group harmony. Romantic, sensual. Pioneer and risk taker. Strong verbal skills. Dynamic, busy lifestyle.

Donn, 20: Practical, conservative. Natural counselor and healer. Romantic, sensual. Creative and opinionated.

Donna, 3: Serious, yet fun:loving. Good parenting skills. Creative, opinionated. Romantic, sensual. Bold, courageous, a bit stubborn.

Donnell, 4: Down-to-earth, faithful. Natural counselor and healer. Original and unconventional. Creative, opinionated. Physical and passionate. Strong verbal skills. Frequent traveler.

Donny, 9: Trustworthy and dependable. Creates group harmony. Creative, opinionated. Romantic, sensual. Needs a lot of freedom.

Donovan, 4: Down-to-earth, faithful. Natural counselor and healer. Original and unconventional. Strong parenting skills. Intuitive and inspired. Independent, critical of self and others. Romantic and sensual.

Dooley, 4: Down-to-earth, faithful. Strong parenting skills. May have musical abilities. Frequent traveler. Adaptable to change. Needs a lot of freedom.

Dora, 20: Practical, conservative. Creates group harmony. Gentle, kind, a hard worker. Not easily influenced.

Doreen, 7: Systematic, organized. Respects rules. Diligent, helpful. Physical, passionate. A free spirit, very adaptable. Creative, opinionated.

Dori, 10: Natural authority. Self-sacrificing, devoted. Intense inner power. Artistic, having good taste.

Doria, 11: Workaholic, determined. Natural counselor and healer. Gentle, kind, a hard worker. Blessed in some ways. Independent, critical of self and others.

Dorian, 7: Systematic, organized. Respects rules. Intense inner power. Blessed in some ways. Independent, critical of self and others. Creative, opinionated.

Dorie, 6: Creative problem solver. Strong parenting skills. Gentle, kind, a hard worker. Blessed in some ways. A free spirit, very adaptable.

Dorien, 11: Workaholic, determined. Creates group harmony. Intense inner power. Artistic, having good taste. Physical, passionate. Creative, opinionated.

Doris, 11: Workaholic, determined. Creates group harmony. Intense inner power. Blessed in some ways. Charming and devoted.

Dorothea, 5: Enjoys working. Respects rules. Intense inner power. May have musical abilities. Dynamic, busy lifestyle. Likes to delegate. Enjoys entertaining. Not easily influenced.

Dorothy, 6: Creative problem solver. Natural counselor and healer. Highly emotional. May have musical abilities. Dynamic, busy lifestyle. Great judge of character. Needs a lot of freedom.

Dorrie, 6: Creative problem solver. Nurturing and loving. Gentle, kind, a hard worker. Tendency to lose items. Blessed in some ways. A free spirit, very adaptable.

Dorry, 8: Reliable, responsible. Natural counselor and healer. Intense inner power. Highly emotional. Needs a lot of freedom.

Dory, 8: Reliable, responsible. Natural counselor and healer. Gentle, kind, a hard worker. Needs a lot of freedom.

Dot, 3: Serious, yet fun:loving. Creates group harmony. Dynamic, busy lifestyle.

Dottie, 10: Natural authority. Natural counselor and healer. Dynamic, busy lifestyle. Sensitive and easily hurt. Artistic, having good taste. Likes to entertain.

Dotty, 3: Serious, yet fun:loving. Creates group harmony. Dynamic, busy lifestyle. Sensitive and easily hurt. Needs a lot of freedom.

Doug, 20: Practical, conservative. Natural counselor and healer. Attractive and charming. Scientific and philosophical.

Douglas, 7: Systematic, organized. Respects rules. Attractive and charming. Scientific and philosophical. Strong verbal skills. Not easily influenced. Many mood swings.

Doyle, 7: Systematic, organized. Respects rules. Needs a lot of freedom. Frequent traveler. Loves adventure and excitement.

Do:young, 11: Workaholic, determined. Creates group harmony. Needs a lot of freedom. May have musical abilities. Attractive and charming. Original and unconventional. Scientific and philosophical.

Drake, 30: Serious, yet fun:loving. Gentle, kind, a hard worker. Independent, critical of self and others. Strong desire to succeed. Loves adventure and excitement.

Drew, 5: Enjoys working. Diligent, helpful. Physical, passionate. Friendly, adaptable to change.

Duane, 9: Trustworthy, dependable. Attractive and charming. Independent, critical of self and others. Original and unconventional. A free spirit, very adaptable.

Dude, 7: Systematic, organized. Attractive and charming. Down-to-earth, faithful. A free spirit, very adaptable.

Dudley, 8: Reliable, responsible. Attractive and charming. Down-to-earth, faithful. Strong verbal skills. Physical, passionate. Dislikes limitations.

Dugan, 20: Practical, conservative. Attractive and charming. Scientific and philosophical. Independent, critical of self and others. Original and unconventional.

Duke, 5: Enjoys working. Attractive and charming. Strong desire to succeed. A free spirit, very adaptable.

Duncan, 3: Serious, yet fun:loving. Slow to make decisions. Original and unconventional. Self-expressive, cheerful. Independent, critical of self and others. Romantic and sensual.

Dunstan, 3: Serious, yet fun:loving. Slow to make decisions. Original and unconventional. Charming and devoted. Dynamic, busy lifestyle. Pioneer and risk taker. Romantic and sensual.

Durand, 8: Reliable, responsible. Attractive and charming. Intense inner power. Resolute and purposeful. Romantic, sensual. Down-to-earth, faithful.

Durant, 6: Creative problem solver. Youthful, appealing. Gentle, kind, a hard worker. Independent, critical of self and others. Original and unconventional. Dynamic, very busy lifestyle.

Dustin, 6: Creative problem solver. Youthful, appealing. Charming and devoted. Dynamic, busy lifestyle. Blessed in some ways. Original and opinionated.

Dusty, 8: Reliable, responsible. Attractive and charming. Many mood swings. Dynamic, busy lifestyle. Needs a lot of freedom.

Dutch, 20: Practical, conservative. Attractive and charming. Dynamic, busy lifestyle. Loyal and understanding. Excellent judge of character.

Dwane, 20: Practical, conservative. Likes to meet new people. Independent, critical of self and others. Romantic, sensual. A free spirit, very adaptable.

Dwayne, 9: Trustworthy and dependable. Likes to meet new people. Pioneer and risk taker. Needs a lot of freedom. Romantic, sensual. Enjoys giving gifts.

Dwight, 8: Reliable, responsible. Likes to meet new people. Blessed in some ways. Scientific and philosophical. Excellent judge of character. Dynamic, busy lifestyle.

Dylan, 20: Practical, conservative. Dislikes limitations. Frequent traveler. Independent, critical of self and others. Romantic, sensual.

E

If a name begins with E, has E as the first vowel, has more than one E, or ends with an E, this person is a free spirit, adaptable to change, physical, passionate, and loves adventure.

E is for entertainment. The E person could be bored to tears in a humdrum routine. They're versatile, adventurous, and freedom-oriented. An E anywhere in a person's name will give them the edge in interior decorating. E names have a natural flair, or at the very least an interesting concept, and are one of the best dressed of all the letters. Also, E types can wrap a gift better than any other letter in the alphabet.

Those with names that begin with E enjoy giving more than receiving. It's important to remember that an E person delights in the reaction of others receiving a gift from them. Elvis Presley would take off jewelry and throw it to the audience. That's the E in his name; he loved surprising others. Even his famous "Graceland," where he lived, reflected a sort of freedom in its décor. Since Elvis begins with a vowel, he wore his heart's desire letter up front for the world to see. Speaking of world, his name adds up to a 22 power number. This means he was a master on the global playing field. The number 22 is a master number and gives the bearer an ability to be big on an international level. The world knows and loves Elvis. Almost everyone around the world has heard of him.

E represents the change aspect of a personality. E is the fifth letter and 5 rules change. This 5-ruled letter often changes circumstances beyond our control. An E anywhere in a name gives the bearer the feeling that, "The only thing constant in life is change." Often change is a blessing for anyone with the 5-ruled letters E, N, or W in their name. Similar to cats, they generally land on their feet.

E-named people are also excellent dressers, if not a bit flashy. They seem to always remember the hair, earrings, and makeup. Both male and female under the E influence won't mind getting ready for a date. They'll look good, smell good, and feel good. E types are into the five senses: feel, sound, touch, smell, and sight. This makes the E very sensual. They'll want to have all the effects just right: lighting, candle scents, music, and atmosphere. This letter, next to N, W, and X, is one of the sexiest of letters. Elvis was one of the biggest heartthrobs of all time. The Beatles had an E first vowel. The Beatles weren't all that sexy by themselves, but as a group under a name with an E first vowel, well, the girls went crazy over them.

E names as well as N names tend to fall in and out of love often, especially early in life. Yet, if they are lucky enough to find the right mate, their marriages are models of happiness. The paradox of this letter is that they love their freedom. So in order to stay happy in a relationship with this 5-ruled letter, one must allow the person with the E in their name freedom, without suspicion or jealousy. This is a tall order because E-named people are so desirable. The typical E will run the other way when jealousy is displayed. Not holding on too tightly is the key to staying with an E. Patience is also a virtue; ask Shannon Tweed, long time girlfriend of rock star Gene Simmons from Kiss. Fortunately, she has plenty of 5-ruled letters in her own name, which aids in compatibility and understanding.

This letter is similar to the astrological sign Leo in the way of romance and creativity; yet it also has qualities of Aquarius in that they enjoy their friends and freedom. This is truly one of the most fun and exciting letters to have in a name. E people light up the room with their smiles. The person with this letter anywhere in their name will adapt easily to change. Some fit in well with the military because change in residence is highly possible. This letter, as well as N and W, are capable of role reversal. It's not uncommon for the wife to go to work and leave the husband home to take care of the kids. This letter is not afraid to defy the natural order of things. Different and unusual is their wavelength. E-named people also manage to look as if they are listening, when they are really a million miles away. Don't underestimate their power of concentration. Often while they are nodding their head as if listening to you, they are solving a problem that has been perplexing their co-workers for weeks.

108

Emeril Lagasse, chef, restaurateur, television personality, and author of twelve cook books (so far), exemplifies his E name by popularizing the word, "Bam!" Such an exciting word for this chef with two Es in his name. He's very domestic and hardworking with his first consonant M. Still, two Es give him an intensity 5, so he loves excitement, change, and variety. No doubt all his recipes are a delight to the senses. He's unorthodox and different from any other chef to say the least. Also, the R and I give him an intensity 9, so he's very much a humanitarian with friends of all race and color. His name sums up to a power number 8, so he's a survivor and will no doubt receive financial rewards in this lifetime.

Elvira, "Mistress of the Dark" or "The Queen of Halloween," also seems to fit her name well. Although her real name is Cassandra Peterson, both the letters C and L give way to a natural comedian. Her character is funny, sexy, and delivers one-liners in a low-cut black skintight evening gown. With an E first name she can get away with being "shocking" better than most. Also the 5-ruled E next to her 3-ruled L adds up to a hidden 8, which is also comfortable with Halloween. The number 8 rules the eighth astrological sign of Scorpio and it is the sexiest of influences. Also this hidden 8 is a little frightening or scary, but with the E and L it's delivered in a crazy-fun sort of way. She also never seems to age! This can be attributed to the C in her birth name, or the L in Elvira. C and L types are ruled by the number 3 and have a youthful appearance for much longer than the other letters, except for the letter U which is also ruled by the number 3.

Too much of this letter in a name could give one a tendency to overindulge. Many E names are candidates for Jenny Craig. Who better to understand a tendency to overindulge than an intensity 5 name like Jenny? Weight Watchers also has two 5-ruled letters in the beginning of its name. An abundance of this letter, or the letter N or W, in a name can also promote a desire for escapism. The escapist tendencies could fall into many categories including television, books, and overeating; however, sadly, some fall into dangerous forms of escapism such as drugs and alcohol. This letter, as well as other 5-ruled letters, can get burned out easily by overdoing and overindulging. This usually has to do with certain foods, driving, people, hobbies, a particular job, or any activity on which they get hooked. This letter along with the 5-ruled letters N and W need to adopt the attitude, "Everything in moderation!"

The 5-ruled person knows how to motivate others and seems to have some teaching ability. Some can master the art of communication better than a C or L person! Their sense of humor can be spontaneous and highly acute. The typical E is very intelligent and good with their hands. They seem to have some mechanical ability. Some can hit the TV just right so it stops making that noise. E-named people make excellent salespersons, politicians, public relations persons, lawyers, and teachers. Some Es succeed in more shocking careers such as rock band members. Gene Simmons has two Es in his name. Anyone with an E in their name is bound to be more colorful. Often E types are gamblers, playing for high stakes with a great enthusiasm which others find attractive. Their desire to gamble or take chances can backfire, causing them to take another course of action. That's okay, because who's better equipped to adapt to change than an E person? It complements their nature. For them, life's an adventure waiting to happen.

Other famous people whose names begin with E are: Elizabeth Taylor, Elton John, Ernest Hemingway, Elijah Wood, Elizabeth Hurley, Edgar Allan Poe, Ellen Bernstein, Eddie Murphy, Evita Peron, Eleanor Roosevelt, Eve Arden, Esther Williams, Eminem, Enya, Edgar Cayce, Ethel Merman, Eartha Kitt, Eric Clapton, Eva Gabor, Ed McMahon, Ed Sullivan, Efrem Zimbalist, Jr., Elizabeth Montgomery, Elle Macpherson, Elizabeth, The Queen Mother, Ellen DeGeneres, Elliott Gould, Elvis Costello, Evel Knievel, and Errol Flynn.

QUICK REFERENCE OF "E" NAMES

Earl, 9: True humanitarian. Resolute and purposeful. Gentle, kind, a hard worker. Strong verbal skills.

Earle, 5: Physical and passionate. Bold, adventuresome. Intense inner power. Frequent traveler. Loves excitement and change.

Earlene, 6: A step ahead of others. Pioneer and risk taker. Gentle, kind, a hard worker. Strong verbal skills. Physical and passionate. Original and unconventional. Loves adventure and excitement.

Earline, 10: Likes change and variety. Self-motivated, courageous. Diligent, helpful. Strong verbal skills. Blessed in some ways. Original and opinionated. Loves adventure and excitement.

Eartha, 8: Original and creative. Bold, courageous, a bit stubborn. Intense inner power. An excellent mediator. Self-reliant, successful. Pioneer and risk taker.

Easter, 5: Physical and passionate. Pioneer and risk taker. Charming and devoted. Dynamic, busy lifestyle. Loves freedom and adventure. Considerate and kind.

Eaton, 10: Likes change and variety. Independent, critical of self and others. Dynamic, busy lifestyle. Natural counselor and healer. Original and opinionated.

Ebba, 10: Likes change and variety. Emotional and sensitive. Affectionate and loyal. Not easily influenced.

Eben, 8: Original and creative. Loyal and understanding. Physical and passionate. Unconventional, opinionated.

Ebenezer, 8: Original and creative. Great mediator. Physical and passionate. Unconventional, opinionated. Loves adventure and excitement. Uses common sense. Needs change and variety. Intense inner power.

Ebrahim, 11: Keenly perceptive. Friendly, but shy. Gentle, kind, a hard worker. Reads people easily. Great judge of character. Blessed in some ways. Systematic and organized.

Echo, 22: Has big plans. Optimistic, outspoken. Excellent judge of character. Has musical abilities.

Ed, 9: True humanitarian. Down-to-earth, faithful. A natural teacher.

Eda, 10: Likes change and variety. Natural authority and leader. Independent, critical of self and others.

Edan, 6: A step ahead of others. Reliable, responsible. Pioneer and risk taker. Romantic and sensual.

Edana, 7: Not easily fooled. Down-to-earth, faithful. Independent, critical of self and others. Original and unconventional. Bold, courageous, a bit stubborn.

Eddie, 9: True humanitarian. Reliable, responsible. Down-to-earth, faithful. Artistic, having good taste. A free spirit, very adaptable.

Ede, 5: Physical and passionate. Quick problem solver. Loves adventure and excitement.

Eden, 10: Likes change and variety. Natural authority. A free spirit, very adaptable. Romantic, sensual.

Edgar, 8: Original and creative. Systematic, organized. Willpower and determination. Not easily influenced. Intense inner power.

Edgardo, 9: True humanitarian. Reliable, responsible. Scientific and philosophical. Natural authority. Gentle, kind, a hard worker. Down-to-earth, faithful. Natural counselor and healer.

Edie, 5: Physical and passionate. Systematic, organized. Blessed in some ways. A free spirit, very adaptable.

Edina, 6: A step ahead of others. Reliable, responsible. Artistic, having good taste. Creative, opinionated. Pioneer and risk taker.

Edison, 30: A free spirit, very ,adaptable. Creative problem solver. Blessed in some ways. Charming and devoted. Natural counselor and healer. Romantic, opinionated.

Edith, 10: Likes change and variety. A natural authority. Artistic, having good taste. Dynamic, busy lifestyle. Excellent judge of character.

Edmond, 10: Likes change and variety. Practical and determined. Domestic, hardworking. Natural counselor and healer. Creative, opinionated. Down-to-earth, faithful.

Edmund, 7: Not easily fooled. Systematic, organized. Domestic, hardworking. Attractive and charming. Original and unconventional. Down-to-earth, faithful.

Edna, 6: A step ahead of others. Reliable, responsible. Creative, opinionated. Pioneer and risk taker.

Edsel, 9: True humanitarian. Natural authority. Charming and devoted. Physical and passionate. Strong verbal skills.

Eduardo, 5: Physical and passionate. Systematic, organized. Attractive and charming. Not easily influenced. Intense inner power. Down-to-earth, practical. Natural counselor and healer.

Edward, 10: Likes change and variety. Creative problem solver. Enjoys meeting new people. Independent, critical of self and others. Gentle, kind, a hard worker. Down-to-earth, practical.

Edwin, 10: Likes change and variety. Creative problem solver. Enjoys meeting new people. Blessed in some ways. Romantic, sensual.

Edwina, 11: Keenly perceptive. Natural authority. Creative and determined. Blessed in some ways. Original and unconventional. Reads people easily.

Effie, 4: Accesses quickly. Self-sacrificing, loving. High moral standards. Artistic, having good taste. Likes change and variety.

Efrem, 11: Keenly perceptive. Self-sacrificing, loving. Intense inner power. Loves adventure and excitement. Domestic, hardworking.

Efren, 30: A free spirit, very adaptable. Self-sacrificing, loving. Gentle, kind, a hard worker. Physical and passionate. Original and opinionated.

Egan, 9: True humanitarian. Scientific and philosophical. Pioneer and risk taker. Original and unconventional.

Egbert, 30: A free spirit, very adaptable. Philosophical and scientific. Friendly and affectionate. Likes to entertain. Gentle, kind, a hard worker. Dynamic, busy lifestyle.

Egill, 9: True humanitarian. Scientific, philosophical. Idealistic. Strong verbal skills. Frequent traveler.

Egon, 5: Physical and passionate. Extremely intelligent. Nurturing, loving. Creative and opinionated.

Eileen, 5: Physical and passionate. Blessed in some ways. Communicates skillfully. Tendency to overindulge. A free spirit, very adaptable. Creative and opinionated.

Eirene, 11: Keenly perceptive. Artistic, having good taste. Gentle, kind, a hard worker. Good entertainer. Original and unconventional. Physical, passionate.

Elaina, 6: A step ahead of others. Strong verbal skills. Independent, critical of self and others. Blessed in some ways. Creative and original. Bold, courageous, a bit stubborn.

Elaine, 10: Likes change and variety. Strong verbal skills. Independent, critical of self and others. Artistic, having good taste. Romantic, sensual. Social, friendly.

Elan, 5: Physical and passionate. Communicates skillfully. Self-motivated, stubborn. Original and unconventional.

Elayne, 8: Original and creative. Frequent traveler. Resolute and purposeful. Needs a lot of freedom. Unconventional, opinionated. Physical and passionate.

Elberta, 9: True humanitarian. Strong verbal skills. Friendly, but shy. A free spirit, very adaptable. Gentle, kind, a hard worker. Dynamic, busy lifestyle. Independent, critical of self and others.

Elden, 22: Has big plans. Frequent traveler. Systematic, organized. Physical and passionate. Original and unconventional.

Eldon, 5: Physical and passionate. Strong verbal skills. Reliable, responsible. Natural counselor and healer. Creative, opinionated.

Eldora, 10: Likes change and variety. Frequent traveler. Systematic, organized. Loving and nurturing. Gentle, kind, a hard worker. Independent, critical of self and others.

Eldrick, 8: Original and creative. Communicates skillfully. Reliable, responsible. Intense inner power. Blessed in some ways. Self-expressive, cheerful. Strong desire to succeed.

Eldridge, 10: Likes change and variety. Strong verbal skills. Systematic, organized. Gentle, kind, a hard worker. Blessed in some ways. Down-to-earth, faithful. Stylish and refined. Physical and passionate.

Eleanor, 7: Not easily fooled. Strong verbal skills. Physical and passionate. Resolute and purposeful. Original and opinionated. Natural counselor and healer. Gentle, kind, a hard worker.

Eleazar, 5: Physical and passionate. Ups and downs financially. Loves adventure and excitement. Pioneer and risk taker. A good mediator. Not easily influenced. Intense inner power.

Elecio, 4: Accesses quickly. Communicates skillfully. Physical and passionate. Self-expressive, cheerful. Blessed in some ways. Natural counselor and healer.

Electra, 10: Likes change and variety. Frequent traveler. Physical and passionate. Optimistic, outspoken. Dynamic, busy lifestyle. Gentle, kind, a hard worker. Independent, critical of self and others.

Elena, 10: Likes change and variety. Strong verbal skills. Physical and passionate. Original and unconventional. Independent, critical of self and others.

Eleni, 9: True humanitarian. Frequent traveler. Loves adventure and excitement. Creative and opinionated. Blessed in some ways.

Elese, 10: Likes change and variety. Strong verbal skills. Physical and passionate. Charming and devoted. Loves adventure and excitement.

Elexa, 20: Social and entertaining. Communicates well. Physical and passionate. Artistic, sensual, perceptive. Reads people easily.

Elfreda, 6: A step ahead of others. Strong verbal skills. Self-sacrificing, loving. Gentle, kind, a hard worker. Physical, passionate. Reliable, responsible. Pioneer and risk taker.

Elga, 7: Not easily fooled. Frequent traveler. Scientific and philosophical. Independent, courageous, bold.

Eli, 8: Original and creative. Recuperates quickly. Blessed in some ways.

Elia, 9: True humanitarian. Communicates skillfully. Forgive and be happy. Pioneer and risk taker.

Elias, 10: Likes change and variety. Strong verbal skills. Blessed in some ways. Independent, critical of self and others. Charming and devoted.

Elijah, 9: True humanitarian. Frequent traveler. Forgive and be happy. Clever and talented. Hardworking, helpful, sincere. Excellent judge of character.

Elinore, 6: A step ahead of others. Strong verbal skills. Artistic, having good taste. Creative, opinionated. Natural counselor and healer. Gentle, kind, a hard worker. Physical and passionate.

Eliot, 7: Not easily fooled. Strong verbal skills. Blessed in some ways. Natural counselor and healer. Dynamic, busy lifestyle.

Elisa, 10: Likes change and variety. Frequent traveler. Considerate, understanding. Charming and devoted. Not easily influenced.

Elise, 5: Physical and passionate. Communicates skillfully. Blessed in some ways. Charming and devoted. A free spirit, adaptable to change.

Elisha, 9: True humanitarian. Strong verbal skills. Artistic, having good taste. Devoted, loving. Great judge of character. Pioneer and risk taker.

Elissa, 20: Social and entertaining. Communicates skillfully. Blessed in some ways. Charming and devoted. Impulsive and extreme. Independent, critical of self and others.

Elite, 6: A step ahead of others. Strong verbal skills. Artistic, having good taste. Dynamic, busy lifestyle. A free spirit, very adaptable.

Eliza, 8: Original and creative. Strong powers of recuperation. Blessed in some ways. Has common sense. Independent, critical of self and others.

Elizabeth, 7: Not easily fooled. Strong verbal skills. Blessed in some ways. Has common sense. Independent, critical of self and others. Friendly, but shy. Loves adventure and excitement. Dynamic, busy lifestyle. Excellent judge of character.

Ella, 3: A free spirit, very adaptable. Slow to make decisions. Communicates skillfully. Pioneer and risk taker.

Ellamay, 6: A step ahead of others. Skilled communicator. Frequent traveler. Independent, critical of self and others. Domestic, hardworking. Pioneer and risk taker. Needs a lot of freedom.

Elle, 7: Not easily fooled. Has gift of gab. Listens well too. Loves freedom and adventure.

Ellen, 3: A free spirit, very adaptable. Has gift of gab. Listens well too. Tendency to overindulge. Romantic and sensual.

Ellery, 5: Physical and passionate. Communicates skillfully. Financial ups and downs. A free spirit, very adaptable. Gentle, kind, a hard worker. Needs a lot of freedom.

Ellie, 7: Not easily fooled. Strong verbal skills. Frequent traveler. Blessed in some ways. Physical and passionate.

Ellin, 7: Not easily fooled. Strong verbal skills. Frequent traveler. Blessed in some ways. Romantic and sensual.

Elliott, 30: A free spirit, very adaptable. Gift of gab. Listens well too. Blessed in some ways. Natural counselor and healer. Dynamic, busy lifestyle. Sensitive and easily hurt.

Ellis, 3: A free spirit, very adaptable. Gift of gab. Listens well too. Blessed in some ways. Charming and devoted.

Elma, 4: Accesses quickly. Strong powers of recuperation. Domestic, hardworking. Resolute and purposeful.

Elmer, 8: Original and creative. Communicates skillfully. Desires financial security. Likes change and variety. Gentle, kind, a hard worker.

Elmira, 4: Accesses quickly. Strong powers of recuperation. Domestic, hardworking. Artistic, having good taste. Diligent, thoughtful. Resolute and purposeful.

Elmo, 9: True humanitarian. Communicates skillfully. Systematic, organized. Natural counselor and healer.

Eloise, 11: Keenly perceptive. Strong verbal skills. Natural counselor and healer. Artistic, having good taste. Charming and devoted. Physical and passionate.

Elroy, 30: A free spirit, very adaptable. Slow to make decisions. Gentle, kind, a hard worker. Natural counselor and healer. Needs a lot of freedom.

Elsa, 10: Likes change and variety. Strong verbal skills. Charming and devoted. Independent, critical of self and others.

Elsbeth, 8: Original and creative. Recuperates quickly. Devoted and loving. Great mediator. Physical and passionate. Dynamic, busy lifestyle. Self-reliant, successful.

Elsie, 5: Physical and passionate. Frequent traveler. Charming and devoted. Artistic, having good taste. Likes change and variety.

Elton, 3: A free spirit, very adaptable. Slow to make decisions. Dynamic, busy lifestyle. Natural counselor and healer. Creative and opinionated.

Elvina, 9: True humanitarian. Frequent traveler. Intuitive and inspired. Artistic, having good taste. Creative and opinionated. Pioneer and risk taker.

Elvira, 4: Accesses quickly. Strong powers of recuperation. Intuitive and inspired. Blessed in some ways. Gentle, kind, a hard worker. Resolute and purposeful.

Elvis, 22: Has big plans. Communicates skillfully. Intuitive and inspired. Blessed in some ways. Charming and devoted.

Elwin, 9: True humanitarian. Communicates skillfully. Likes to meet new people. Considerate, understanding. Romantic and sensual.

Ely, 6: A step ahead of others. Communicates skillfully. Needs a lot of freedom.

Elyce, 5: Physical and passionate. Frequent traveler. Dislikes limitations. Sense of humor. A free spirit, adaptable to change.

Elyse, 3: A free spirit, very adaptable. Slow to make decisions. Needs a lot of freedom. Charming and devoted. Physical and passionate.

Elysia, 8: Original and creative. Recuperates quickly. Dislikes limitations. Charming and devoted. Blessed in some ways. Independent, critical of self and others.

Em, 9: A true humanitarian. Systematic, organized. Generous, enjoys giving gifts.

Emanuel, 8: Original and creative. Domestic, hardworking. Resolute and purposeful. Unconventional, opinionated. Attractive and charming. Physical and passionate. Communicates skillfully.

Emeril, 8: Original and creative. Domestic, hardworking. Physical and passionate. Intense inner power. Blessed in some ways. Communicates skillfully.

Emerson, 8: Original and creative. Domestic, hardworking. Likes variety and change. Intense inner power. Charming and devoted. Natural counselor and healer. Romantic, sensual.

Emery, 30: A free spirit, very adaptable. Systematic, organized. Loves adventure and excitement. Gentle, kind, a hard worker. Dislikes limitations.

Emil, 3: A free spirit, very adaptable. Systematic, hardworking. Blessed in some ways. Communicates skillfully.

Emile, 8: Original and creative. Systematic, organized. Artistic, having good taste. Strong verbal skills. Likes change and variety.

Emilia, 4: Accesses quickly. Domestic, hardworking. Blessed in some ways. Communicates skillfully. Artistic, having good taste. Not easily influenced.

Emily, 10: Likes change and variety. Systematic, organized. Blessed in some ways. Strong verbal skills. Dislikes limitations.

Eminem, 5: Physical and passionate. Domestic, hardworking. Artistic, having good taste. Original and opinionated. A free spirit, very adaptable. Desires financial security.

Emlyn, 6: A step ahead of others. Systematic, organized. Communicates skillfully. Dislikes limitations. Romantic, opinionated.

Emma, 5: Physical and passionate. Domestic, hardworking. Desires financial security. Self-motivated, determined.

Emmanuel, 30: A free spirit, very adaptable. Domestic, hardworking. Desires financial security. Independent, critical of self and others. Original and unconventional. Attractive and charming. Escapist tendencies. Strong verbal skills.

Emme, 9: True humanitarian. Systematic, organized. Domestic, hardworking. Enjoys freedom for adventure.

Emmet, 20: Social and entertaining. Domestic, hardworking. Desires financial security. Physical, passionate. Dynamic, busy lifestyle.

Emory, 4: Accesses quickly. Domestic, hardworking. Natural counselor and healer. Diligent, helpful. Dislikes limitations.

Engelbert, 7: Not easily fooled. Creative, opinionated. Extremely intelligent. A free spirit, very adaptable. Strong verbal skills. Friendly, but shy. Physical and passionate. Gentle, kind, a hard worker. Dynamic, busy lifestyle.

Enid, 5: Physical and passionate. Original and unconventional. Considerate and understanding. Reliable, responsible.

Enrico, 10: Likes change and variety. Creative, opinionated. Gentle, kind, a hard worker. Artistic, having good taste. Cheerful, light-hearted. Natural counselor and healer.

Enya, 9: True humanitarian. Romantic, opinionated. Needs a lot of freedom. Pioneer and risk taker.

Ephraim, 7: Not easily fooled. Intelligent and knowledgeable. Excellent judge of character. Gentle, kind, a hard worker. A natural authority. Blessed in some ways. Desires financial security.

Ephrem, 11: Keenly perceptive. Intelligent and knowledgeable. Excellent judge of character. Gentle, kind, a hard worker. Physical and passionate. Desires financial security.

Epifanio, 3: A free spirit, very adaptable. Levelheaded. Blessed in some ways. Self-sacrificing, loving. Pioneer and risk taker. Original and unconventional. Artistic, having good taste. Natural counselor and healer.

Epsilon, 9: True humanitarian. Intelligent and knowledgeable. Charming and devoted. Blessed in some ways. Strong verbal skills. Natural counselor and healer. Original and unconventional.

Erasmus, 6: A step ahead of others. Intense inner power. Pioneer and risk taker. Charming and devoted. Domestic, hardworking. Attractive, youthful. Impulsive and extreme.

Eric, 8: Original and creative. Gentle, kind, a hard worker. Considerate, understanding. Self-expressive, cheerful.

Erica, 9: True humanitarian. Understanding, helpful. Artistic, having good taste. Self-expressive, cheerful. Pioneer and risk taker.

Erik, 7: Not easily fooled. Diligent, helpful. Blessed in some ways. Strong desire to succeed.

Erika, 8: Original and creative. Gentle, kind, a hard worker. Idealistic, humanitarian. Strong desire to succeed. Independent, critical of self and others.

Erin, 10: Likes change and variety. Compassionate, understanding. Blessed in some ways. Romantic, opinionated.

Erle, 22: Has big plans. Gentle, kind, a hard worker. Frequent traveler. Physical and passionate.

Erma, 10: Likes change and variety. Diligent, helpful. Domestic, hardworking. Independent, critical of self and others.

Erna, 20: Social and entertaining. Compassionate, understanding. Romantic, opinionated. Resolute and purposeful.

Ernest, 9: True humanitarian. Considerate, helpful. Original and unconventional. Physical and passionate. Charming and devoted. Dynamic, busy lifestyle.

Ernestine, 10: Likes change and variety. Gentle, kind, a hard worker. Original and unconventional. Physical and passionate. Charming and devoted. Dynamic, busy lifestyle. Blessed in some ways. Creative and opinionated. Loves adventure and excitement.

Ernesto, 6: A step ahead of others. Gentle, kind, a hard worker. Original and unconventional. Physical and passionate. Charming and devoted. Dynamic, busy lifestyle. Natural counselor and healer.

Errol, 5: Physical and passionate. Intense inner power. Could be forgetful. Natural counselor and healer. Strong verbal skills.

Erwin, 6: A step ahead of others. Gentle, kind, a hard worker. Likes to meet new people. Artistic, having good taste. Romantic, opinionated.

Erwina, 7: Not easily fooled. Hardworking and kind. Likes to meet new people. Blessed in some ways. Creative, opinionated. Self-motivated, determined.

Esau, 10: Likes change and variety. Charming and devoted. Independent, critical of self and others. Attractive, youthful.

Eskel, 7: Not easily fooled. Charming and devoted. Strong desire to succeed. Physical and passionate. Communicates skillfully.

Esmeralda, 6: A step ahead of others. Charming and devoted. Systematic, organized. Physical and passionate. Gentle, kind, hard worker. Independent, critical of self and others. Strong verbal skills. Reliable, responsible. Bold, courageous, a bit stubborn.

Estella, 20: Social and entertaining. Charming and devoted. Dynamic, busy lifestyle. Physical and passionate. Strong verbal skills. Financial ups and downs. Perceptive, reads people easily.

Estelle, 6: A step ahead of others. Devoted and loving. Dynamic, busy lifestyle. Physical and passionate. Strong verbal skills. Financial ups and downs. Loves adventure and excitement.

Estes, 5: Physical and passionate. Charming and devoted. Dynamic, busy lifestyle. Needs freedom and adventure. Intense and extreme.

Esther, 30: A free spirit, very adaptable. Charming and devoted. Dynamic, busy lifestyle. Excellent judge of character. Physical and passionate. Gentle, kind, a hard worker.

Ethan, 3: A free spirit, very adaptable. Dynamic, busy lifestyle. Financial ups and downs. Independent, critical of self and others. Romantic and sensual.

Ethel, 5: Physical and passionate. Dynamic, busy lifestyle. Original and creative. A free spirit, very adaptable. Strong verbal skills.

Etta, 10: Loves change and variety. Dynamic, busy lifestyle. Needs to slow down. Independent, critical of self and others.

Eugene, 30: A free spirit, very adaptable. Attractive and charming. Scientific and philosophical. Tendency to overindulge. Romantic and sensual. Loves adventure and excitement.

Eugenia, 8: Original and creative. Attractive and charming. Scientific and philosophical. Likes freedom and variety. Physical and passionate. Blessed in some ways. Self-motivated, successful.

Eulalee, 7: Not easily fooled. Attractive and charming. Excellent verbal skills. Pioneer and risk taker. Financial ups and downs. Physical and passionate. Needs change and variety.

Eun, 4: Accesses quickly. Attractive and charming. Romantic and opinionated.

Eun-hee, 4: Accesses quickly. Attractive and charming. Original and unconventional. Great judge of character. Physical and passionate. Loves adventure and excitement.

Eunice, 30: A free spirit, very adaptable. Youthful, appealing. Creative, opinionated. Artistic, having good taste. Great sense of humor. Loves freedom and adventure.

Eun-ju, 8: Original, creative, and unconventional. Attractive and charming. Clever and talented. Difficulty making decisions.

Eustace, 20: Social and entertaining. Attractive and charming. Devoted, loving. Dynamic, busy lifestyle. Perceptive, reads people easily. Self-expressive, cheerful. Physical and passionate.

Eva, 10: Likes change and variety. Intuitive and inspired. Independent, critical of self and others.

Evan, 6: A step ahead of others. Responsible, trustworthy. Self-motivated, independent. Romantic, opinionated.

Evangeline, 4: Accesses quickly. Strong imagination. Resolute and purposeful. Original and unconventional. Has willpower and determination. Physical and passionate. Strong verbal skills. Blessed in some ways. Creative, opinionated. A free spirit, very adaptable.

Eve, 5: Physical and passionate. Intuitive and inspired. Loves adventure and excitement.

Eveline, 9: True humanitarian. Has big plans and ideas. Needs change and variety. Communicates well. Artistic, having good taste. Creative, opinionated. Loves adventure and excitement.

Evelyn, 11: Keenly perceptive. Intuitive and inspired. Physical and passionate. Strong verbal skills. Needs a lot of freedom. Original and opinionated.

Everett, 5: Physical and passionate. Strong imagination. A free spirit, very adaptable. Gentle, kind, a hard worker. Likes to entertain. Dynamic, busy lifestyle. Social, affectionate.

Evita, 3: A free spirit, very adaptable. Intuitive and inspired. Blessed in some ways. Dynamic, busy lifestyle. Pioneer and risk taker.

Evona, 3: A free spirit, very adaptable. Responsible and trustworthy. Natural counselor and healer. Original and unconventional. Pioneer and risk taker.

Evonne, 30: A free spirit, very adaptable. Intuitive and inspired. Natural counselor and healer. Original and unconventional. Romantic, sensual. Needs change and variety.

Ewald, 9: True humanitarian. Likes to meet new people. Pioneer and risk taker. Communicates skillfully. Natural authority.

Ewan, 7: Not easily fooled. Creative and determined. Independent, self-motivated. Romantic and sensual.

Exene, 8: Original and creative. Artistic, sensual, perceptive. Tendency to overindulge. Unconventional and opinionated. Physical and passionate.

Ezekial, 6: A step ahead of others. Uses common sense. Physical and passionate. Sensitive, diplomatic. Blessed in some ways. Pioneer and risk taker. Strong verbal skills.

Ezekiel, 10: Likes change and variety. Uses common sense. Physical and passionate. Strong desire to succeed. Blessed in some ways. Loves adventure and excitement. Strong verbal skills.

Ezra, 5: Physical and passionate. An excellent mediator. Gentle, kind, a hard worker. Self-motivated, determined.

F

If a name begins with F, has more than one F, or ends with an F, this person is loving, nurturing, able to counsel, can carry a tune, has a strong parental nature, and is self-sacrificing.

The sixth letter rules love. F is capable of jealousy, although not all F people are the jealous type. The devoted F person is a little more territorial than the other letters. Fidel Castro of Cuba was insistent on protecting and keeping his people in Cuba. The cartoon character Fred Flintstone often showed a jealous streak when his wife, Wilma, was wooed by a good-looking movie star.

F people need someone to love. If they think the object of their affection is planning on leaving them, they will take steps to protect what they feel is rightfully theirs. Or, as in the case of Farrah Fawcett, when her husband, Lee Majors, wasn't around for her to give her love to, she left him. It's important to let the F person have someone to love and take care of. Those whose names begin with F will need to have kids, pets, or at least a garden to love and nurture. It's not surprising the words flower and florist begin with the nurturing, loving letter F. After all, gardens need lots of love, care, and attention too.

We can often recognize an F person by their conversations. Everything they do is for their loved ones. They are one of the most responsible and duty-bound of all the letters. Chances are you won't find Fiona or Frank out partying all night. You'll find them taking care of their loved ones, working to support them, thinking about them, talking about them, or doing something for them. If they have children, the children become their whole world. If they don't have children, they will treat their pets like children. They often like to dress up their pets and take them everywhere. Some spend time tending their gardens daily. Similar to letters O and X, this letter can manage large groups of people. I know one woman whose name starts with an F who thought of her business as a "child."

She started it, or gave birth to it, nurtured it, and helped it to grow; so for some, a business can be like a child for them to love. Either way, this letter needs to give out love!

F types are magnetic. Fabio is quite attractive to most females; he's famous for it. Sure he's good-looking, but it's more than that. This 6-ruled letter makes people stop dead in their tracks and take notice. Franklin D. Roosevelt, the only president to serve three terms, had that magnetic quality. Everyone felt "taken care of" under the democratic President. We already know Fidel Castro had an alluring hold on his people for many decades. It's that loving, nurturing energy that Fidel gave out. People were drawn to him. The famous were also drawn to Fidel's magnetic personality. Jack Nicholson, Steven Spielberg, and Robert Redford all visited the long-time leader of Cuba. This love-ruled letter holds the power of attraction. Even the profane F word has something to do with love. Those who use the F word frequently may be drawn to the subject of love for some reason.

The F-named person is a mother and father all wrapped up in one. They are so nurturing and duty-bound they usually end up in managerial positions. That's why F people tend to navigate toward leadership positions early in life. When trying to decide which employee to put in charge, consider a person with an F in their name. They are all about service and duty. They don't need someone to hold their hand. They will take on all the duties and responsibilities one person can handle. The rest of the employees seem like mere children compared to the responsible, duty-bound F-named employee. Consequently, because they are so capable of handling the responsibility of managing large tasks, they resent having anyone look over their shoulder while doing so. Just leave them alone so they can work some miracles for you.

A famous person whose name began with F is Florence Nightingale. She truly lived out this loving and nurturing vibration as the founder of the nursing profession. Not only did she have two letters in her name ruled by the number 6, but her name summed up to a 6 power number as well. She was born into a wealthy family in Italy and didn't have to work. Her parents couldn't understand why she chose a life of duty and service. With all that 6 energy in her name, how could she escape it? She was destined to sacrifice herself to the service and care of others. And as with most F names, she excelled in providing a much-needed service at that time.

Another fascinating F name is Frank Lloyd Wright. He has been described as a creative genius in the field of American architecture. F people create children of their minds and bodies. This 6-ruled letter desires to create. During Frank's lifetime he designed over eight hundred buildings! He was ninety-two years old when he died. He had never stopped working. F-named people are very devoted, but the R in his name made him a very hard worker. His first vowel, A, is responsible for his critical eye. The K at the end of his name gave him a strong desire to succeed. The N and power number 5 gave him a desire to change the existing order of things. His contribution was to build houses that looked as if they were a natural part of the place they were in. The 5 is adaptable to change—and so were his buildings. Although they were foreign, he designed them to adapt or fit into their environment in an aesthetically pleasing way. Today it's an honor to graduate from one of his schools.

Before we get too carried away with all the wonderfulness of this 6-ruled letter of love, consider that F is one of the most meddlesome of all the letters. Sometimes they become jealous or try to interfere with other people's lives. Similar to the letter O, they could take what does not belong to them, if they are not taught good moral values early in life. Often the F-named will find themselves in a power struggle between opposing parties. They often bring peace to a volatile situation, similar to the role of a parent. The F-named person needs to learn to have an open mind in disputes, without taking sides or interfering. This includes disputes with family, co-workers, and friends. Similar to the letter O, men with an F in their name can be drawn to the damsel in distress; and the woman with this letter can be drawn to a mama's boy who needs lots of nurturing and care. Duty-bound F tends to attract the meek and needy.

This letter is similar to the astrological sign Virgo. Like Virgo, the F name tends to have a stocked medicine cabinet at home. They are natural counselors and healers, similar to the O names. Many are vegetarians and have their own herb garden. Don't hesitate to ask your F-named friend for health advice; they are usually right on the money in diagnosing illness. This letter tends to have allergies and to be sensitive to odors and perfumes. They will be the first to complain if something smells bad. Some F names cannot tolerate perfume at all.

F people make excellent counselors, healers, teachers, social workers, singers, psychologists, gardeners, farmers, florists, artists, and designers. This letter has something musical about it. Similar to the letter O, F can go far in the music industry. Unfortunately, the F-named person is usually too busy trying to make a living to pursue a career in music. So at the very least, we should consider our F-named friends when we need good singers at our next karaoke party.

Other famous people with names that begin with F are: Flip Wilson, Fiona Apple, Fred Astaire, Fantasia Barrino, Franz Liszt, F. Scott Fitzgerald, Faith Hill, Fred McMurray, Frank Sinatra, Finola Hughes, Florence Henderson, Frances Fisher, Franklin Pierce, Frankie J, Federico Fellini, Frédéric Chopin, Faith Evans, Francis Scott Key, Fernando Lamas, Frankie Avalon, Franz Ferdinand, and Fats Domino.

QUICK REFERENCE OF "F" NAMES

Fabia, 10: Wonderful leadership abilities. Independent, critical of self and others. Affectionate, social. Blessed in some ways. Not easily inflenced.

Fabian, 6: Very devoted, loving. Pioneer and risk taker. Friendly, but shy. Artistic, having good taste. Independent, self-motivated. Romantic, sensual.

Fabio, 6: Very devoted, loving. Pioneer and risk taker. Friendly, but shy. Artistic, having good taste. Magnetic personality.

Fabiola, 10: Wonderful leadership abilities. Independent, critical of self and others. Loyal, understanding. Blessed in some ways. Natural counselor and healer. Strong verbal skills. Bold, courageous, a bit stubborn.

Fairleigh, 3: Lucky in timing. Pioneer and risk taker. Blessed in some ways. Gentle, kind, a hard worker. Communicates well. A free spirit, very adaptable. Artistic, having good taste. Scientific, philosophical. Self-reliant, successful.

Faith, 8: Likes competition. Resolute and purposeful. Blessed in some ways. Dynamic, busy lifestyle. Self-reliant, successful.

Fannie, 4: Responsible, duty-bound. Independent, critical of self and others. Opinionated, original. Romantic, sensual. Blessed in some ways. A free spirit, very adaptable.

Fanny, 6: Very devoted, loving. Independent, self-motivated. Original and unconventional. Romantic, creative. Needs a lot of freedom.

Fantasia, 8: Likes competition. Not easily influenced. Creative, opinionated. Dynamic, busy lifestyle. Pioneer and risk taker. Charming and devoted. Blessed in some ways. Bold, courageous, a bit stubborn.

Fara, 8: Likes competition. Independent, critical of self and others. Gentle, kind, a hard worker. Bold, courageous, a bit stubborn.

Faris, 8: Likes competition. Not easily influenced. Intense inner power. Artistic, having good taste. Can be moody.

Farley, 4: Responsible, duty-bound. Resolute and purposeful. Gentle, kind, a hard worker. Strong verbal skills. A free spirit, very adaptable. Dislikes limitations.

Farr, 7: Enjoys working alone. Not easily influenced. Intense inner power. Diligent, helpful, kind.

Farrah, 7: Enjoys working alone. Independent, critical of self and others. Gentle, kind, a hard worker. Tendency to lose items. Bold, courageous, a bit stubborn. Excellent judge of character.

Farrel, 6: Very devoted, loving. Pioneer and risk taker. Highly emotional. Diligent, hardworking. A free spirit, very adaptable. Strong verbal skills.

Fatemeh, 4: Responsible, duty-bound. Natural teaching ability. Dynamic, busy lifestyle. A free spirit, very adaptable. Domestic, hardworking. Loves adventure and excitement. Self-reliant, successful.

Fatima, 5: Original, innovative. Bright, adventuresome. Dynamic, busy lifestyle. Blessed in some ways. Domestic, hardworking. Pioneer and risk taker.

Faust, 4: Responsible, duty-bound. Natural teaching ability. Attractive and charming. Prone to mood swings. Dynamic, busy lifestyle.

Fave, 7: Enjoys working alone. Not easily influenced. A brilliant mind. Likes change and variety.

Favian, 8: Likes competition. Resolute and purposeful. Intuitive and inspired. Blessed in some ways. Bold, courageous, a bit stubborn. Romantic, sensual.

Favor, 8: Likes competition. Resolute and purposeful. Strong imagination. Magnetic personality. Intense inner power.

Fawn, 8: Likes competition. Resolute and purposeful. Likes to meet new people. Romantic, sensual.

Fawna, 9: Easygoing nature. Helpful, sincere. Likes to meet new people. Creative, opinionated. Not easily influenced.

Fay, 5: Original, innovative. Bright, adventuresome. Needs a lot of freedom.

Faye, 10: Wonderful leadership abilities. Independent, critical of self and others. Needs a lot of freedom. Loves adventure and excitement.

Federico, 11: Task- or service-oriented. A free spirit, very adaptable. Reliable, responsible. Likes to entertain. Gentle, kind, a hard worker. Blessed in some ways. Self-expressive, cheerful. Natural counselor and healer.

Fedora, 4: Responsible, duty-bound. Likes change and variety. Down-to-earth, faithful. Natural counselor and healer. Gentle, kind, a hard worker. Resolute and purposeful.

Felice, 4: Responsible, duty-bound. Physical and passionate. Strong verbal skills. Blessed in some ways. Self-expressive, cheerful. Loves adventure and excitement.

Felicia, 9: Easygoing nature. A free spirit, very adaptable. Communicates well. Blessed in some ways. Self-expressive, cheerful. Artistic, having good taste. Pioneer and risk taker.

Feliciano, 11: Task- or service-oriented. Intuitive, perceptive. Frequent traveler. Blessed in some ways. Outgoing, youthful outlook. Artistic, having good taste. Bold, courageous, a bit stubborn. Romantic, sensual. Musically talented.

Felicity, 8: Likes competition. Original and creative. Financial ups and downs. Emotional, considerate. Self-expressive, cheerful. Artistic, having good taste. Dynamic, busy lifestyle. Needs a lot of freedom.

Felimon, 11: Task- or service-oriented. Intuitive, perceptive. Strong verbal skills. Blessed in some ways. Domestic, hardworking. Natural counselor and healer. Creative, opinionated.

Felipe, 8: Likes competition. Original and creative. Strong verbal skills. Blessed in some ways. Intelligent and knowledgeable. Loves adventure and excitement.

Felix, 11: Task- or service-oriented. Intuitive, perceptive. Frequent traveler. Emotional, considerate. Artistic, sensual.

Feliza, 5: Original, innovative. Physical and passionate. Ups and downs financially. Blessed in some ways. A great mediator. Bold, courageous, a bit stubborn.

Felton, 9: Easygoing nature. Enjoys giving gifts. Strong verbal skills. Dynamic, busy lifestyle. Natural counselor and healer. Romantic, opinionated.

Femi, 6: Very devoted, loving. A step ahead of others. Domestic, hardworking. Artistic, having good taste.

Fenton, 11: Task- or service-oriented. Intuitive, perceptive. Creative, opinionated. Dynamic, busy lifestyle. Natural counselor and healer. Romantic and sensual.

Ferdinand, 3: Lucky in timing. A free spirit, very adaptable. Gentle, kind, a hard worker. Reliable, responsible. Blessed in some ways. Original and unconventional. Pioneer and risk taker. Romantic, sensual. Down-to-earth, faithful.

Fergie, 5: Original, innovative. Physical and passionate. Gentle, kind, a hard worker. Stylish and refined. Blessed in some ways. A free spirit, very adaptable.

Fergus, 4: Responsible, duty-bound. Accesses quickly. Diligent, helpful. Scientific and philosophical. Attractive and charming. Loving and devoted.

Fermain, 3: Lucky in timing. A free spirit, very adaptable. Gentle, kind, a hard worker. Domestic, organized. Pioneer and risk taker. Blessed in some ways. Original and unconventional.

Fermin, 11: Task- or service-oriented. Intuitive, perceptive. Compassionate, understanding. Domestic, organized. Blessed in some ways. Original and unconventional.

Fern, 7: Enjoys working alone. Not easily fooled. Gentle, kind, a hard worker. Original, opinionated.

Fernando, 5: Original, innovative, and opinionated. Physical and passionate. Intense inner power. Creative and unconventional. Bold, courageous, a bit stubborn. Problem solver. Natural counselor and healer.

Ferris, 3: Lucky in timing. A free spirit, very adaptable. Gentle, kind, a hard worker. Could be forgetful. Blessed in some ways. Charming and devoted.

Fidel, 9: Easygoing nature. Artistic, having good taste. Natural authority, practical. Very entertaining, likes variety. Slow to make decisions.

Fielding, 3: Lucky in timing. Blessed in some ways. Likes to entertain. Slow to make decisions. Practical, reliable. Considerate, understanding. Creative, romantic. Scientific and philosophical.

Fifi, 30: Lucky in timing. Blessed in some ways. Great with plants, kids, and animals. Creative with easygoing attitude.

Filbert, 9: Easygoing nature. Artistic, having good taste. Strong verbal skills. Friendly, but shy. A free spirit, very adaptable. Gentle, kind, a hard worker. Dynamic, busy lifestyle.

Filmore, 6: Very devoted, loving. Artistic, having good taste. Frequent traveler. Domestic, hardworking. Natural counselor and healer. Highly emotional. A free spirit, very adaptable.

Findlay, 8: Likes competition. Idealistic, humanitarian. Romantic, sensual. Workaholic, shrewd, determined. Strong verbal skills. Resolute and purposeful. Truth seeker.

Findley, 3: Lucky in timing. Artistic, having good taste. Creative, romantic. Reliable, responsible. Slow to make decisions. Loves adventure and excitement. Needs a lot of freedom.

Finley, 8: Likes competition. Blessed in some ways. Creative, opinionated. Frequent traveler. Physical and passionate. Dislikes limitations.

Finn, 7: Enjoys working alone. Humanitarian, idealistic. Original and unconventional. Romantic, opinionated.

Fiona, 9: Easygoing nature. Artistic, having good taste. Natural counselor and healer. Original and unconventional. Pioneer and risk taker.

Fionna, 5: Original, innovative. Blessed in some ways. Magnetic personality. Creative, opinionated. Romantic, sensual. Bold, courageous, a bit stubborn.

Fiorenza, 4: Responsible, duty-bound. Blessed in some ways. Natural counselor and healer. Gentle, kind, a hard worker. Physical and passionate. Original and unconventional. Great judge of character. Pioneer and risk taker.

Fitch, 10: Wonderful leadership abilities. Artistic, having good taste. Dynamic, busy lifestyle. Self-expressive, cheerful. Excellent judge of character.

Fitzgerald, 9: Easygoing nature. Idealistic, humanitarian. Needs to slow down. Uses common sense. Extremely intelligent. A free spirit, very adaptable. Gentle, kind, a hard worker. Independent, critical of self and others. Strong verbal skills. Reliable, responsible.

Fitzpatrick, 4: Responsible, duty-bound. Artistic, having good taste. Dynamic, busy lifestyle. Uses common sense. Intelligent and knowledgeable. Independent, critical of self and others. Sensitive and easily hurt. Gentle, kind, a hard worker. Blessed in some ways. Self-expressive, cheerful. Strong desire to succeed.

Flavia, 6: Very devoted, loving. Strong verbal skills. Pioneer and risk taker. Intuitive and inspired. Blessed in some ways. Not easily influenced.

Flavian, 11: Task- or service-oriented. Communicates skillfully. Independent, critical of self and others. Intuitive and inspired. Artistic, having good taste. Bold, courageous, a bit stubborn. Original and unconventional.

Flavius, 9: Easygoing nature. Strong verbal skills. Pioneer and risk taker. Intuitive and inspired. Blessed in some ways. Attractive, flirtatious. Charming and devoted.

Fleming, 3: Lucky in timing. Frequent traveler. A free spirit, very adaptable. Domestic, hardworking. Blessed in some ways. Original and unconventional. Scientific and philosophical.

Fletch, 9: Easygoing nature. Slow to make decisions. Adaptable, likes change. Dynamic, busy lifestyle. Self-expressive, cheerful. Excellent judge of character.

Fletcher, 5: Original, innovative. Strong verbal skills. A free spirit, very adaptable. Dynamic, busy lifestyle. Self-expressive, cheerful. Excellent judge of character. Tendency to overindulge. Gentle, kind, a hard worker.

Flint, 7: Enjoys working alone. Frequent traveler. Blessed in some ways. Original and unconventional. Dynamic, busy lifestyle.

Flo, 6: Very devoted, loving. Communicates skillfully. Magnetic personality.

Flora, 7: Enjoys working alone. Strong verbal skills. Natural counselor and healer. Intense inner power. Independent, critical of self and others.

Florence, 6: Very devoted, loving. Communicates skillfully. Natural counselor and healer. Gentle, kind, a hard worker. A free spirit, very adaptable. Romantic and creative. Self-expressive, cheerful. Likes change and variety.

Floyd, 8: Likes competition. Strong verbal skills. Natural counselor and healer. Needs a lot of freedom. Natural authority.

Flynn, 8: Likes competition. Frequent traveler. Dislikes limitations. Original and unconventional. Romantic, sensual.

Forbes, 11: Task- or service-oriented. Natural counselor and healer. Gentle, kind, a hard worker. Friendly, but shy. A free spirit, very adaptable. Charming and devoted.

Ford, 7: Enjoys working alone. Respects rules. Diligent, helpful. Practical and conservative.

Forrest, 11: Task- or service-oriented. Natural counselor and healer. Intense inner power. Tendency to lose items. A free spirit, very adaptable. Charming and devoted. Dynamic, busy lifestyle.

Forrester, 7: Enjoys working alone. Natural counselor and healer. Gentle, kind, a hard worker. Tendency to lose items. A free spirit, very adaptable. Charming and devoted. Dynamic, busy lifestyle. Loves adventure and excitement. Intense inner power.

Fortune, 9: Easygoing nature. Natural counselor and healer. Gentle, kind, a hard worker. Dynamic, busy lifestyle. Attractive and charming. Original and unconventional. A free spirit, very adaptable.

Foster, 11: Task- or service-oriented. Has musical abilities. Charming and devoted. Dynamic, busy lifestyle. A free spirit, very adaptable. Gentle, kind, a hard worker.

Fostina, 30: Lucky in timing. Good parenting skills. Charming and devoted. Dynamic, busy lifestyle. Blessed in some ways. Resolute and purposeful.

Fran, 3: Lucky in timing. Diligent, helpful. Independent, critical of self and others. Romantic, opinionated.

Franc, 6: Very devoted, loving. Gentle, kind, a hard worker. Self-motivated, independent. Original and unconventional. Optimistic, cheerful.

Frances, 30: Lucky in timing. Intense inner power. Independent, critical of self and others. Romantic, opinionated. Self-expressive, cheerful. A free spirit, very adaptable. Charming and devoted.

Francine, 7: Enjoys working alone. Gentle, kind, a hard worker. Independent, critical of self and others. Original and unconventional. Self-expressive, cheerful. Blessed in some ways. Romantic, sensual. A free spirit, very adaptable.

Francis, 7: Enjoys working alone. Highly emotional. Independent, critical of self and others. Original and unconventional. Self-expressive, cheerful. Blessed in some ways. Charming and devoted.

Francisca, 11: Task- or service-oriented. Intense inner power. Independent, critical of self and others. Romantic, sensual. Outgoing, cheerful. Blessed in some ways. Charming and devoted. Inspiring and creative. Bold, courageous, a bit stubborn.

Franco, 30: Lucky in timing. Diligent, helpful. Independent, critical of self and others. Original and unconventional. Outspoken, cheerful. Natural counselor and healer.

Francois, 4: Responsible, duty-bound. Gentle, kind, a hard worker. Independent, critical of self and others. Original and unconventional. Self-expressive, cheerful. Natural counselor and healer. Blessed in some ways. Charming and devoted.

Frank, 5: Original, innovative. Diligent, hardworking. Independent, critical of self and others. Creative and unconventional. Strong desire to succeed.

Frankie, 10: Wonderful leadership abilities. Highly emotional. Independent, critical of self and others. Romantic, original. Strong desire to succeed. Blessed in some ways. A free spirit, very adaptable.

Franklin, 4: Responsible, duty-bound. Gentle, kind, a hard worker. Natural teaching ability. Original and unconventional. Strong desire to succeed. Frequent traveler. Blessed in some ways. Romantic, sensual.

Franz, 11: Task- or service-oriented. Highly emotional. Intuitive, perceptive. Original and unconventional. Uses common sense.

Fraser, 4: Responsible, duty-bound. Gentle, kind, a hard worker. Natural teaching ability. Charming and devoted. A free spirit, very adaptable. Tendency to lose items.

Frasier, 4: Responsible, duty-bound. Intense inner power. Natural teaching ability. Charming and devoted. Blessed in some ways. A free spirit, very adaptable. Tendency to lose items.

Frazer, 11: Task- or service-oriented. Emotional, considerate. Intuitive, perceptive. Good mediator. A free spirit, very adaptable. Tendency to lose things.

Frazier, 11: Task- or service-oriented. Emotional, considerate. Intuitive, perceptive. Good mediator. Blessed in some ways. Likes change and variety. Tendency to lose items.

Fred, 6: Very devoted, loving. Gentle, kind, a hard worker. A step ahead of others. Reliable, responsible.

Freda, 7: Enjoys working alone. Intense inner power. Not easily fooled. Reliable, responsible. Bold, courageous, a bit stubborn.

Freddie, 6: Very devoted, loving. Diligent, helpful. A step ahead of others. Natural authority. Down-to-earth, faithful. Blessed in some ways. Physical, passionate.

Frederic, 5: Original, innovative. Intense inner power. Physical and passionate. Creative problem solver. Loves adventure and excitement. Tendency to lose items. Blessed in some ways. Optimistic, sense of humor.

Frederica, 6: Very devoted, loving. Diligent, helpful. A step ahead of others. Faithful, down-to-earth. Likes to entertain. Tendency to lose items. Blessed in some ways. Self-expressive, cheerful. Bold, courageous, a bit stubborn.

Frederick, 7: Enjoys working alone. Gentle, kind, a hard worker. Not easily fooled. Reliable, responsible. Loves adventure and excitement. Tendency to lose items. Blessed in some ways. Self-expressive, cheerful. Strong desire to succeed.

Fredric, 9: Easygoing nature. Emotional, considerate. Enjoys giving gifts. Down-to-earth, faithful. Intense inner power. Blessed in some ways. Inspiring, very creative.

Freeman, 8: Likes competition. Diligent, helpful. Creative, original. Physical, passionate. Desires financial security. Resolute and purposeful. Stubborn, opinionated.

Freemon, 4: Responsible, duty-bound. Gentle, kind, a hard worker. Accesses quickly. Physical, passionate. Systematic, organized. Natural counselor and healer. Original and unconventional.

Freida, 7: Enjoys working alone. Intense inner power. Not easily fooled. Blessed in some ways. Reliable, responsible. Bold, courageous, a bit stubborn.

Fremont, 10: Wonderful leadership abilities. Gentle, kind, a hard worker. Likes change and variety. Systematic, organized. Respects rules. Original and unconventional. Dynamic, busy lifestyle.

Frida, 11: Task- or service-oriented. Sensitive, emotional. Considerate, understanding. Reliable, responsible. Independent, critical of self and others.

Friday, 9: Easygoing nature. Intense inner power. Artistic, having good taste. Reliable, responsible. Pioneer and risk taker. Needs a lot of freedom.

Fritz, 7: Enjoys working alone. Gentle, kind, a hard worker. Blessed in some ways. Dynamic, busy lifestyle. Uses common sense.

Fuller, 11: Task- or service-oriented. Attractive and charming. Communicates skillfully. Ups and downs financially. A free spirit, very adaptable. Gentle, kind, a hard worker.

If a name begins with G, has more than one G, or ends with a G, this person is a truth seeker, spiritual, psychic, scientific, philosophical, and needs periodic solitude.

G is ruled by the number 7 vibration. The 7-ruled letters are spiritual. There's a Neptunian feel to the seventh letter of the alphabet. G names often prefer to live by water. This letter is similar to the astrological sign Pisces, the fish. Some G names appear to "swim" across a room. It's entertaining to watch how smoothly they glide from one place to another. Also, some are known to "drink like a fish." Our nautical friends tend to either need more sleep than most, or have sleeping disorders from too much mental activity. Gs are truthseekers. Be honest, don't lie or they'll never, and I do mean never, trust you again.

G-named people are a little more psychic than most. They are also photogenic and seem to perform well in front of a camera or on the silver screen. They tend to have style and are more refined than the rest of us. Even though Lady Godiva was forced to ride naked on a horse through the middle of town, she managed to do it with style.

Unfortunately this is one of those letters that is prone to negative forms of escapism. Not all people with a G in their name are susceptible to alcohol or drug addictions. Heredity is a factor, as with all the letters. If the G-named person comes from a family of alcohol or drug addictions, they may also be prone to the same. Alcohol is often referred to as "spirits." Spiritualism and spirits are ruled by the same vibration. It won't be hard to tell which side of the line your G friends are on. I once knew a Gregg that suffered from drug and alcohol addiction. If his parents only knew that a name with three Gs in it might lead to escapist tendencies, they may have named him differently. If Gregg came from a family with strong religious beliefs, he may have turned to the spirit of God instead. Or if from a family of rocket scientists, he would take on a similar role, as this letter is so scientific. G is one of the most willful and determined of all the letters.

G is also for genius. The typical G will approach a problem in a detached, analytical sort of way. They are among the most visionary of letters. G types make great inventors, researchers, investigators, technicians, watchmakers, philosophers, and theologians. They also perform well in the entertainment industry. This spiritual letter needs to recharge its batteries from time to time. The typical G will get cranky if not allowed their own space for sleep and meditation.

G-named people need to have faith in order to be happy. If the G-named person doesn't have a solid relationship with God, then they can become wrapped up in their own egos. This letter, along with the letters P and Y, tends to have an overly inflated opinion of themselves unless grounded with a solid belief in a higher source. As the saying goes, we have those who believe in God, and those that think they are God. To have faith in God—this is their lesson. G-named people won't truly be happy unless they have faith.

A typical G person has a strong desire for knowledge and truth; however, their fine minds need to recognize the difference between reality and illusion. They could be drawn to the scientific, technological fields, or they could be dreamers, never accomplishing any of their dreams. This letter is so spiritual, some are dreamers and some are doers, but they're either one or the other; there's no in-between. Young people with this letter need to be guided early in life so that they don't waste their potential. Again, heredity is a factor. Either one will insist upon the truth and will have a strong dislike for anything other than the truth. Similar to the letters P and Y, if a G-named person doesn't like someone, they can't pretend to like that person. That would fall into the category of "not being truthful," which is against their code of ethics. They'll be downright stubborn about this too.

The famous Gwyneth Paltrow has two 7-ruled letters in her name. She has three 5-ruled letters as well, giving her more social qualities than most G names. Plus her name adds up to a 3 power number. Those with 3 power numbers are youthful, lucky, and easygoing. This actress is extremely intelligent with all those 7s and 5s in her name. The two 7s influence her ability to look good on camera. The intensity 5 helps her adapt to change more easily. I bet she can escape the paparazzi better than most. It's well known she likes to spend her free time in Europe. She was quoted in a popular magazine article in 2003 as preferring the company of Europeans to Americans. She said Europeans like to talk about philosophy, art, and other cultural matters, and gave an example of how "stupid" American conversations can be. She seeks knowledge and truth above all else. She's stylish, refined, elegant, and polished. Gwyneth gives a wonderful example of this seventh letter influence.

Another famous G name is the late actor Gregory Peck. The two Gs in his name were responsible for giving him style and grace. They also helped him look good on camera. The two Rs gave him the upper hand in a game of intimidation. R-named people can be bullies, but the Gs helped him do it with style. Plus the E as his first vowel gave him sex appeal and a love of adventure. The intensity 7 kept his private life private.

Mahatma Gandhi, better known as Gandhi, one of the great master teachers on earth, demonstrated style and grace during his peaceful resistance to British rule. This spiritual soul showed nonviolence is more powerful than violence. Furthermore, he did it with style.

Geraldo Rivera, an American television journalist, attorney, and former talk show host, is known to have an affinity for dramatic, high-profile stories. He joined Fox News in 2001 as a war correspondent, and now frequently appears as their guest. To no surprise, as dangerous as his job was, it fit in perfectly with his name. His name adds up to an 8 power number, which rules death among other things. Often 8 power numbers have a brush with death or have dealings with death during their lifetimes. He always seems to cover the most dangerous assignments. His assignments are often "life or death" in nature. G names are truth seekers, and G added to E equals a hidden 3 which rules communication. The L also rules communication as it too is ruled by 3, so this man has a double dose of the number that makes for a great news correspondent.

Our philosophical and very knowledgeable friends have much to offer the world—even if they sometimes feel as if they don't fit in. The world can learn much from these highly spiritual souls.

Some more famous G names: Gregory Smith, Gloria Estefan, Goldie Hawn, Gladys Knight, Greta Garbo, Garth Brooks, Geena Davis, Garfield, Glenn Close, Gwen Stefani, Gregory Hines, George Peppard, Golda Meir, Grace Kelly, Gabe Kaplan, Graham Nash, Gordon Lightfoot, Glenn Frey, Groucho Marx, Gene Hackman, Gilda Radner, Gina Lollobrigida, Gypsy Rose Lee, Guy Lombardo, and George Clooney.

QUICK REFERENCE OF "G" NAMES

Gabe, 6: Appreciates nature's beauty. Pioneer and risk taker. Good mediator. A free spirit, very adaptable.

Gabey, 22: Vision brings wealth. Ambitious leader. Affectionate, social. Loves adventure and excitement. Needs a lot of freedom.

Gabi, 10: A thinker, determined. Independent, critical of self and others. Friendly, but shy. Blessed in some ways.

Gabie, 6: Appreciates nature's beauty. Pioneer and risk taker. Friendly, but shy. Artistic, having good taste. Loves adventure and excitement.

Gable, 9: Quiet and reflective. Helpful, sincere. Loyal and understanding. Strong verbal skills. A free spirit, very adaptable.

Gabriel, 9: Quiet and reflective. Helpful, sincere. Friendly, but shy. Gentle, kind, a hard worker. Blessed in some ways. A free spirit, very adaptable. Communicates skillfully.

Gabriela, 10: A thinker, determined. Independent, critical of self and others. Social, loyal. Gentle, kind, a hard worker. Blessed in some ways. A free spirit, very adaptable. Strong verbal skills. Bold, courageous, a bit stubborn.

Gabriella, 4: Into family life. Natural teaching ability. Friendly, but shy. Gentle, kind, a hard worker. Blessed in some ways. A free spirit, very adaptable. Strong verbal skills. Frequent traveler. Bold, courageous, a bit stubborn.

Gabrielle, 8: Willpower, determination. Resolute and purposeful. Friendly, but shy. Gentle, kind, a hard worker. Blessed in some ways. A free spirit, very adaptable. Strong verbal skills. Frequent traveler. Physical and passionate.

Gaby, 8: Willpower, determination. Resolute and purposeful. Friendly, but shy. Needs a lot of freedom.

Gael, 7: Enjoys alone time. Not easily influenced. A free spirit, very adaptable. Great communication skills.

Gaelle, 6: Appreciates nature's beauty. Pioneer and risk taker. A free spirit, very adaptable. Strong verbal skills. Ups and downs financially. Physical and passionate.

Gail, 20: Sensitive and psychic. Reads people easily. Blessed in some ways. Communicates skillfully.

Gale, 7: Enjoys alone time. Not easily influenced. Great communication skills. A free spirit, very adaptable.

Galen, 3: Intelligent conversationalist. Aims to please. Strong verbal skills. A free spirit, very adaptable. Romantic, opinionated.

Gallagher, 8: Willpower, determination. Resolute and purposeful. Strong verbal skills. Financial ups and downs. Bold, courageous, a bit stubborn. Extremely intelligent. Excellent judge of character. A free spirit, very adaptable. Gentle, kind, a hard worker.

Gannon, 11: Vision brings wealth. Intuitive, perceptive. Original and unconventional. Romantic, sensual. Natural counselor and healer. Creative, opinionated.

Gardenia, 5: Extremely bright. Bold, adventuresome. Gentle, kind, a hard worker. Reliable, responsible. A free spirit, very adaptable. Original and unconventional. Blessed in some ways. Bold, courageous, a bit stubborn.

Garett, 8: Willpower, determination. Resolute and purposeful. Gentle, kind, a hard worker. Physical and passionate. Dynamic, very busy lifestyle. Sensitive and easily hurt.

Garfield, 8: Willpower, determination. Resolute and purposeful. Intense inner power. Self-sacrificing, loving. Blessed in some ways. A free spirit, very adaptable. Strong verbal skills. Natural authority.

Garland, 30: Intelligent conversationalist. Aims to please. Considerate, kind. Strong verbal skills. Bold, courageous, a bit stubborn. Original and unconventional. Reliable, responsible.

Garner, 9: Quiet and reflective. Helpful, sincere. Diligent, hardworking. Creative and opinionated. A free spirit, very adaptable. Tendency to lose items.

Garnet, 11: Vision brings wealth. Intuitive, perceptive. Gentle, kind, a hard worker. Original and unconventional. A free spirit, very adaptable. Dynamic, busy lifestyle.

Garrett, 8: Willpower, determination. Resolute and purposeful. Intense inner power. Tendency to lose items. A free spirit, very adaptable. Dynamic, very busy lifestyle. Sensitive and easily hurt.

Garrick, 4: Into family life. Natural teaching ability. Gentle, kind, a hard worker. Intense inner power. Blessed in some ways. Self-expressive, cheerful. Strong desire to succeed.

Garry, 6: Appreciates nature's beauty. Pioneer and risk taker. Intense inner power. Tendency to lose items. Needs a lot of freedom.

Garth, 9: Quiet and reflective. Helpful, sincere. Gentle, kind, a hard worker. Dynamic, busy lifestyle. Excellent judge of character.

Garton, 30: Intelligent conversationalist. Aims to please. Considerate, kind. Dynamic, busy lifestyle. Natural counselor and healer. Original and unconventional.

Garvey, 6: Appreciates nature's beauty. Pioneer and risk taker. Gentle, kind, a hard worker. Intuitive and inspired. Loves adventure and excitement. Needs a lot of freedom.

Gary, 6: Appreciates nature's beauty. Pioneer and risk taker. Gentle, kind, a hard worker. Needs a lot of freedom.

Gaston, 22: Vision brings wealth. Ambitious leader. Charming and devoted. Dynamic, busy lifestyle. Natural counselor and healer. Original and romantic.

Gavan, 9: Quiet and reflective. Helpful, sincere. Intuitive and inspired. Bold, courageous, a bit stubborn. Original and unconventional.

Gavin, 8: Willpower, determination. Resolute and purposeful. Intuitive and inspired. Blessed in some ways. Original and unconventional.

Gay, 6: Appreciates nature's beauty. Pioneer and risk taker. Needs a lot of freedom.

Gaye, 20:Sensitive and psychic. Reads people easily. Needs a lot of freedom. Loves adventure and excitement.

Gayle, 5: Extremely bright. Bold, adventuresome. Needs a lot of freedom. Strong verbal skills. Loves adventure and excitement.

Gaylord, 10: A thinker, determined. Independent, critical of self and others. Needs a lot of freedom. Communicates skillfully. Natural counselor and healer. Gentle, kind, a hard worker. Reliable, responsible.

Gaynor, 8: Willpower, determination. Resolute and purposeful. Needs a lot of freedom. Original and unconventional. Natural counselor and healer. Gentle, kind, a hard worker.

Gazella, 10: A thinker, determined. Independent, critical of self and others. Uses common sense. A free spirit, very adaptable. Strong verbal skills. Frequent traveler. Bold, courageous, a bit stubborn.

Geena, 5: Extremely bright. Physical and passionate. Perceptive, socially adept. Original and opinionated. Self-motivated, a pioneer.

Gem, 7: Enjoys alone time. Not easily influenced. Domestic, hardworking.

Gemma, 3: Intelligent conversationalist. A free spirit, very adaptable. Domestic, hardworking. Systematic, organized. Natural teaching ability.

Gena, 9: Quiet and reflective. Enjoys giving gifts. Original and opinionated. Helpful, sincere.

Genaro, 6: Appreciates nature's beauty. A step ahead of others. Romantic and opinionated. Pioneer and risk taker. Gentle, kind, a hard worker. Natural counselor and healer.

Gene, 22: Vision brings wealth. Has big plans and ideas. Original and opinionated. Loves adventure and excitement.

Genesis, 6: Appreciates nature's beauty. A step ahead of others. Original and opinionated. Physical and passionate. Charming and devoted. Blessed in some ways. Impulsive and extreme.

Geneva, 9: Quiet and reflective. Enjoys giving gifts. Creative and opinionated. Loves adventure and excitement. Intuitive and inspired. Independent, critical of self and others.

Genevieve, 4: Into family life. Accesses quickly. Original and unconventional. Loves adventure and excitement. Intuitive and inspired. Blessed in some ways. Physical and passionate. Strong imagination. Skilled interior decorator.

Genie, 4: Into family life. Accesses quickly. Original and unconventional. Blessed in some ways. Loves adventure and excitement.

Geof, 6: Appreciates nature's beauty. A step ahead of others. Nurturing, loving, and self-sacrificing.

Geoff, 30: Intelligent conversationalist. A free spirit, very adaptable. Natural counselor and healer. Self-sacrificing, loving. High moral standards.

Geoffrey, 6: Appreciates nature's beauty. A step ahead of others. Nurturing and care-giving. Self-sacrificing, loving. High moral standards. Gentle, kind, a hard worker. Loves adventure and excitement. Needs a lot of freedom.

Georg, 7: Enjoys alone time. Not easily fooled. Natural counselor and healer. Gentle, kind, a hard worker. Extremely intelligent, needs solitude.

George, 3: Brilliant conversationalist. A free spirit, very adaptable. Natural counselor and healer. Gentle, kind, a hard worker. Extremely intelligent. Loves adventure and excitement.

Georgette, 3: Brilliant conversationalist. A free spirit, very adaptable. Natural counselor and healer. Gentle, kind a hard worker. Extremely intelligent. Loves adventure and excitement. Dynamic, busy lifestyle. Sensitive and easily hurt. Physical and passionate.

Georgia, 8: Willpower, determination. Original, creative. Enjoys competition. Gentle, kind, a hard worker. Extremely intelligent. Blessed in some ways. Independent, critical of self and others.

Georgie, 3: Brilliant conversationalist. A free spirit, very adaptable. Natural counselor and healer. Gentle, kind, a hard worker. Extremely intelligent. Blessed in some ways. Loves adventure and excitement.

Georgiana, 5: Extremely bright. Physical and passionate. Natural counselor and healer. Intense inner power. An opportunist. Blessed in some ways. Independent, critical of self and others. Original, unconventional. Bold, courageous, a bit stubborn.

Georgina, 4: Into family life. Accesses quickly. Respects rules. Gentle, kind, a hard worker. Willpower and determination. Artistic, having good taste. Romantic, sensual. Independent, self-motivated.

Gerald, 11: Vision brings wealth. Keenly perceptive. Gentle, kind, a hard worker. Independent, critical of self and others. Strong verbal skills. Reliable, responsible.

Geraldine, 3: Intelligent conversationalist. A free spirit, very adaptable. Gentle, kind, a hard worker. Independent, critical of self and others. Strong verbal skills. Reliable, responsible. Blessed in some ways. Original and unconventional. Loves adventure and excitement.

Geraldo, 8: Willpower, determination. Original, creative. Gentle, kind, a hard worker. Self-motivated, a risk taker. Strong verbal skills. Practical, a problem solver. Enjoys competition.

Gerard, 8: Willpower, determination. Original, creative. Intense inner power. Bold, courageous, a bit stubborn. Tendency to lose items. Natural authority.

Gerda, 8: Willpower, determination. Original, creative. Intense inner power. Reliable, responsible. Resolute and purposeful.

Germain, 4: Into family life. Accesses quickly. Gentle, kind, a hard worker. Desires financial security. Independent, critical of self and others. Blessed in some ways. Original and unconventional.

German, 4: Into family life. Accesses quickly. Gentle, kind, a hard worker. Systematic, organized. Resolute and purposeful. Romantic, sensual.

Geronimo, 6: Appreciates nature's beauty. Pioneer and risk taker. Intense inner power. Natural counselor and healer. Original and unconventional. Blessed in some ways. Domestic, hardworking. Magnetic personality.

Gerry, 10: A thinker, determined. Likes change and variety. Gentle, kind, a hard worker. Emotional, intense. Dislikes limitations.

Gertrude, 8: Willpower, determination. Original, creative. Gentle, kind, a hard worker. Dynamic, busy lifestyle. Emotional, intense. Attractive and charming. Reliable, responsible. Loves adventure and excitement.

Gervase, 11: Vision brings wealth. Keenly perceptive. Diligent, hard-working. Intuitive and inspired. Independent, critical of self and others. Charming and devoted. Loves adventure and excitement.

Gibson, 30: Intelligent conversationalist. Understanding, thoughtful. Friendly, but shy. Charming and devoted. Natural counselor and healer. Original and unconventional.

Gideon, 9: Quiet and reflective. Blessed in some ways. Reliable, responsible. A free spirit, very adaptable. Natural counselor and healer. Original and unconventional.

Gifford, 11: Vision brings wealth. Idealistic, humanitarian. Self-sacrificing, loving. High moral standards. Natural counselor and healer. Gentle, kind, a hard worker. Reliable, responsible.

Gil, 10: A thinker, determined. Respectful, kind. Frequent traveler.

Gilbert, 10: A thinker, determined. Respectful, kind. Frequent traveler. Friendly, but shy. A free spirit, very adaptable. Diligent, hardworking. Dynamic, busy lifestyle.

Gilberta, 11: Vision brings wealth. Idealistic, humanitarian. Communicates skillfully. Friendly, but shy. A free spirit, very adaptable. Gentle, kind, a hard worker. Dynamic, busy lifestyle. Independent, critical of self and others.

Gilda, 6: Appreciates nature's beauty. Artistic, having good taste. Strong verbal skills. Reliable, responsible. Independent, critical of self and others.

Giles, 7: Enjoys alone time. Blessed in some ways. Strong verbal skills. A free spirit, very adaptable. Charming and devoted.

Gillian, 10: A thinker, determined. Blessed in some ways. Strong verbal skills. Financial ups and downs. Artistic, having good taste. Independent, critical of self and others. Original and unconventional.

Gillianne, 11: Vision brings wealth. Idealistic, humanitarian. Communicates skillfully. Financial ups and downs. Artistic, having good taste. Independent, critical of self and others. Original and unconventional. Romantic, sensual. A free spirit, very adaptable.

Gilmore, 7: Enjoys alone time. Blessed in some ways. Strong verbal skills. Domestic, hardworking. Natural counselor and healer. Gentle and kind. A free spirit, very adaptable.

Gilroy, 5: Extremely bright. Blessed in some ways. Strong verbal skills. Gentle, kind, a hard worker. Natural counselor and healer. Needs a lot of freedom.

Gina, 22: Vision brings wealth. Blessed in some ways. Original and unconventional. Resolute and purposeful.

Ginger, 6: Appreciates nature's beauty. Artistic, having good taste. Romantic, sensual. Extremely intelligent. A free spirit, very adaptable. Gentle, kind, a hard worker.

Ginny, 6: Appreciates nature's beauty. Artistic, having good taste. Creative, opinionated. Romantic, sensual. Needs a lot of freedom.

Giovanni, 10: A thinker, determined. Blessed in some ways. Natural counselor and healer. Intuitive and inspired. Independent, critical of self and others. Original and opinionated. Romantic, sensual. Artistic, having good taste.

Giovanny, 8: Willpower, determination. Blessed in some ways. Natural counselor and healer. Intuitive and inspired. Resolute and purposeful. Original and opinionated. Romantic, sensual. Needs a lot of freedom.

Giselle, 6: Appreciates nature's beauty. Creates group harmony. Charming and devoted. A free spirit, very adaptable. Strong verbal skills. Frequent traveler. A step ahead of others.

Gitta, 3: Intelligent conversationalist. Understanding, compassionate. Dynamic, busy lifestyle. Sensitive and easily hurt. Pioneer and risk taker.

Gladi, 6: Appreciates nature's beauty. Strong verbal skills. Independent, critical of self and others. Reliable, responsible. Blessed in some ways.

Gladys, 5: Extremely bright. Communicates skillfully. Bold, adventuresome. Reliable, responsible. Needs a lot of freedom. Charming and devoted.

Glen, 20: Sensitive and psychic. Communicates skillfully. A free spirit, very adaptable. Romantic, sensual.

Glenda, 7: Enjoys alone time. Travels frequently. Not easily fooled. Original and creative. Reliable, responsible.

Glenn, 7: Enjoys alone time. Travels frequently. Not easily fooled. Original and opinionated. Romantic, sensual.

Glenna, 8: Willpower, determination. Speaks their mind. A free spirit, very adaptable. Original and unconventional. Romantic, sensual. Resolute and purposeful.

Gloria, 8: Willpower, determination. Speaks their mind. Natural counselor and healer. Gentle, kind, a hard worker. Blessed in some ways. Resolute and purposeful.

Gloriana, 5: Extremely bright. Communicates skillfully. Natural counselor and healer. Gentle, kind, a hard worker. Blessed in some ways. Independent, critical of self and others. Original and unconventional. Bold, courageous, a bit stubborn.

Glorie, 3: Intelligent conversationalist. Strong verbal skills. Natural counselor and healer. Gentle, kind, a hard worker. Blessed in some ways. A free spirit, very adaptable.

Glory, 5: Extremely bright. Communicates skillfully. Natural counselor and healer. Gentle, kind, a hard worker. Needs a lot of freedom.

Glynis, 5: Extremely bright. Communicates skillfully. Needs a lot of freedom. Romantic, opinionated. Blessed in some ways. Charming and devoted.

Glynn, 9: Quiet and reflective. Strong verbal skills. Dislikes restrictions. Original and unconventional. Romantic, sensual.

Godfrey, 8: Willpower, determination. Enjoys competition. Reliable, responsible. Self-sacrificing, loving. Gentle, kind, a hard worker. A free spirit, very adaptable. Dislikes limitations.

Golda, 3: Intelligent conversationalist. Natural counselor and healer. Communicates skillfully. Creative problem solver. Pioneer and risk taker.

Goldie, 7: Enjoys alone time. Open to opportunities. Strong verbal skills. Workaholic, determined. Blessed in some ways. A free spirit, very adaptable.

Goran, 10: A thinker, determined. Natural counselor and healer. Gentle, kind, a hard worker. Independent, critical of self and others. Original and unconventional.

Gordon, 10: A thinker, determined. Natural counselor and healer. Gentle, kind, a hard worker. Reliable, responsible. May have musical abilities. Original and opinionated.

Gordy, 6: Appreciates nature's beauty. Nurturing, loving. Gentle, kind, a hard worker. Reliable, responsible. Needs a lot of freedom.

Gottfried, 5: Extremely bright. Natural counselor and healer. Dynamic, busy lifestyle. Sensitive and easily hurt. Warmhearted, compassionate. Intense inner power. Blessed in some ways. A free spirit, very adaptable. Reliable, responsible.

Grace, 7: Enjoys alone time. Gentle, kind, a hard worker. Not easily fooled. Self-expressive, cheerful. A free spirit, very adaptable.

Gracie, 7: Enjoys alone time. Gentle, kind a hard worker. Not easily fooled. Self-expressive, cheerful. Blessed in some ways. A free spirit, very adaptable.

Grady, 10: A thinker, determined. Hardworking, diligent. Independent, critical of self and others. Reliable, responsible. Needs a lot of freedom.

Graham, 30: Intelligent conversationalist. Gentle, kind, a hard worker. Aims to please. Excellent judge of character. Bold, courageous, a bit stubborn. Desires financial security.

Graig, 6: Appreciates nature's beauty. Intense inner power. Pioneer and risk taker. Blessed in some ways. Extremely intelligent.

Granger, 7: Enjoys alone time. Gentle, kind, a hard worker. Not easily fooled. Original and unconventional. Extremely intelligent. A free spirit, very adaptable. Intense inner power.

Grant, 6: Appreciates nature's beauty. Diligent, hardworking. Pioneer and risk taker. Original and unconventional. Dynamic, busy lifestyle.

Grayson, 9: Quiet and reflective. Gentle, kind, a hard worker. Helpful, sincere. Needs a lot of freedom. Charming and devoted. Natural counselor and healer. Original and unconventional.

Gredel, 6: Appreciates nature's beauty. Diligent, hardworking. A step ahead of others. Reliable, responsible. Loves adventure and excitement. Strong verbal skills.

Greer, 8: Willpower, determination. Gentle, kind, a hard worker. Original and creative. Loves adventure and excitement. Tendency to lose items.

Greg, 10: A thinker, determined. Gentle, kind, a hard worker. Likes change and variety. Periodically needs solitude.

Gregg, 8: Willpower, determination. Intense inner power. Original and creative. Extremely intelligent. Periodically needs solitude.

Gregorio, 4: Into family life. Gentle, kind, a hard worker. Accesses quickly. Willpower and determination. Natural counselor and healer. Tendency to lose items. Blessed in some ways. Has musical talent.

Gregory, 5: Extremely bright. Intense inner power. Not easily fooled. Scientific, philosophical. Natural counselor and healer. Tendency to lose items. Needs a lot of freedom.

Greta, 6: Appreciates nature's beauty. Emotional, understanding. A step ahead of others. Dynamic, busy lifestyle. Pioneer and risk taker.

Gretchen, 8: Willpower, determination. Gentle, kind, a hard worker. Original and creative. Dynamic, busy lifestyle. Self-expressive, cheerful. Excellent judge of character. Loves adventure and excitement. Romantic, sensual.

Gretel, 4: Into family life. Natural teaching abilities. Accesses quickly. Dynamic, busy lifestyle. A free spirit, very adaptable. Strong verbal skills.

Grier, 3: Intelligent conversationalist. Gentle, kind, a hard worker. Blessed in some ways. A free spirit, adaptable. Intense inner power.

Griselda, 3: Intelligent conversationalist. Gentle, kind, a hard worker. Blessed in some ways. Charming and devoted. A free spirit, very adaptable. Strong verbal skills. Reliable, responsible. Pioneer and risk taker.

Grover, 4: Into family life. Has teaching ability. Natural counselor and healer. Intuitive and inspired. A free spirit, very adaptable. Tendency to lose items.

Guadalupe, 7: Enjoys alone time. Attractive and charming. Not easily influenced. Reliable, responsible. Bold, courageous, a bit stubborn. Strong verbal skills. Slow to make decisions. Intelligent and knowledgeable. A free spirit, very adaptable.

Guilana, 11: Vision brings wealth. Gracious, well-mannered. Blessed in some ways. Slow to make decisions. Intuitive, perceptive. Original and unconventional. Bold, courageous, a bit stubborn.

Guiliana, 11: Vision brings wealth. Gracious, well-mannered. Artistic, having good taste. Strong verbal skills. Blessed in some ways. Intuitive, perceptive. Original and unconventional. Bold, courageous, a bit stubborn.

Guillermo, 4: Into family life. Attractive and charming. Blessed in some ways. Strong verbal skills. Slow to make decisions. A free spirit, very adaptable. Gentle, kind, a hard worker. Systematic, organized. A natural counselor and healer.

Guinevere, 7: Enjoys alone time. Stylish and refined. Blessed in some ways. Original and unconventional. A free spirit, very adaptable. Intuitive and inspired. Tendency to overindulge. Gentle, kind, a hard worker. Loves adventure and excitement.

Gunny, 9: Quiet and reflective. Attractive and charming. Original and unconventional. Romantic, sensual. Needs a lot of freedom.

Gunther, 3: Intelligent conversationalist. Attractive and charming. Original and unconventional. Always coming and going. Excellent judge of character. A free spirit, very adaptable. Gentle, kind, a hard worker.

Gus, 11: Vision brings wealth. Gracious, well-mannered. Charming and devoted.

Gustaf, 20: Sensitive and psychic. Youthful, attractive. Charming and devoted. Dynamic, busy lifestyle. Independent, critical of self and others. Self-sacrificing, loving.

Gustave, 5: Extremely bright. Fun, flirtatious. Charming and devoted. Takes the initiative. Bold, adventuresome. Intuitive and inspired. A free spirit, very adaptable.

Gustavo, 6: Appreciates nature's beauty. Attractive and charming. Loving, duty-bound. Socially busy. Independent, critical of self and others. Intuitive and inspired. Natural counselor and healer.

Guthrie, 7: Enjoys alone time. Attractive and charming. Dynamic, busy lifestyle. Excellent judge of character. Gentle, kind, a hard worker. Blessed in some ways. A free spirit, very adaptable.

Guy, 8: Willpower, determination. Attractive and charming. Needs a lot of freedom.

Gwen, 22: Vision brings wealth. Likes to meet new people. A free spirit, very adaptable. Original and unconventional.

Gwendolen, 9: Quiet and reflective. Likes to meet new people. Enjoys giving gifts. Creative and original. Reliable, responsible. Natural counselor and healer. Strong verbal skills. Likes change and variety. Romantic, sensual.

Gwendolyn, 11: Vision brings wealth. Likes to meet new people. Keenly perceptive. Original and unconventional. Reliable, responsible. Natural counselor and healer. Strong verbal skills. Needs a lot of freedom. Romantic, sensual.

Gweneth, 10: A thinker, determined. Implements original ideas. Likes change and variety. Opinionated and creative. Loves adventure and excitement. Dynamic, busy lifestyle. Excellent judge of character.

Gwyn, 6: Appreciates nature's beauty. Likes to meet new people. Needs a lot of freedom. Creative and romantic

Gwyneth, 3: Intelligent conversationalist. Expressive, outgoing. Dislikes restrictions. Romantic and opinionated. A free spirit, very adaptable. Dynamic, busy lifestyle. Excellent judge of character.

Gypsy, 11: Vision brings wealth. Needs a lot of freedom. Intelligent and knowledgeable. Charming and devoted. Highly perceptive.

H

If a name begins with H, has more than one H, or ends with an H, this person enjoys rivalry, is an excellent judge of character, is original and creative, and likes delegating authority.

H is the eighth letter of the alphabet, ruled by the number 8. This number most resembles the eighth sign of the Zodiac, Scorpio. The number 8, in numerology, rules rewards and punishment. This eighth letter is considered karmic. It can sometimes be unlucky, but other times it will bring good fortune. This depends on the person who bears this letter in their name; it depends on the karma they brought to themselves. The number 8 rules letters H, Q, and Z. Coincidently, the game Scrabble gives a lot of points for those letters. H-named people need to remember "what goes around comes around." What they give out, they will get back. They must always remember to balance the material and spiritual sides of their nature. H names need to observe their own ability to give and take, punish and reward, serve and be served. This is their lesson.

The letter H is the Hercules of letters. Its very shape is structurally sound. Oddly enough, we have few female H names compared to male H names. This gives letter H a more masculine appeal. Many "Hillary Haters" bash Hillary Clinton because of her strength of character. Most people can't understand a woman so well-equipped to handle life's ups and downs. A person whose name has an H anywhere in it has survivor capabilities, especially if the H is in the beginning of their name.

As with Dr. Jekyll and Mr. Hyde, Hyde is the strong one. Not all H people are scary; however, they seem to have tremendous strength and determination. H people aren't quitters. Most of us know Howard Hughes came from humble beginnings. H people seem to have a natural understanding of money, power, and authority. Many corporate types have the letter H in their name somewhere. Even Martha Stewart has a little Hercules in her name. So she is well-equipped to handle rough times.

The most frightful day of the year, recognized as "Halloween," is appropriately named starting with an H. This Scorpio-ruled letter is the queen of the occult. The word "occult" is defined as "beyond ordinary knowledge." It's no surprise that our H-named friends just seem to know things. As we dare to look into their eyes, it seems as if they know our very thoughts. Most of them sense this and intentionally wear sunglasses. They don't want us to feel uncomfortable while they look through us and examine our very souls.

The H influence is similar to a pot of boiling water. They appear as if about to boil over at any minute, with so much energy bottled up inside. In the event we are unable to escape the H's explosion, we may take consolation in the fact that it will only hurt for a minute. Once these volatile letters vent, they usually forget about the whole matter within minutes. They won't brood for hours and days like the F and O letters. A little bit of heaven, a little bit of hell—our H-named friends are truly a little of each.

The H person often suffers financial challenges. One of their lessons is to learn to manage their money and not let their money manage them. If they can master this lesson, the H letter is comfortable in the banking or money market field. They make good administrators, top executives, brokers, collectors, art dealers, negotiators, builders, and entrepreneurs—anything "Scorpio-like." They are attracted to matters related to joint finances, taxes, insurance, goods of the dead, restoration, and death.

In the 2002 film, *Die Another Day,* Halle Berry was declared "the strongest Bond woman ever." With an H in the front of her name, she is the Hercules of women. She also comes off strong in *X2: X-Men United,* while demonstrating her special powers. It's not surprising to find this actress in a movie that has the word "Die" in it, as this Scorpio-like letter has everything to do with death.

Another famous H person who exhibited Scorpio-like behavior was Harry Houdini. He was the greatest magician of his time. Harry was known for his "death defying" tricks. When his mother died, he tried to contact her through séances, which is another Scorpio trait.

Hugh Grant, yet another famous H person, is as financially successful as most with not only one, but two Hs in his name. In fact, Hugh's power number equals 8 as well, so his whole personality is rather Scorpio-like. His first vowel, U, makes him attractive and charming. The G in his first name makes him quite intelligent and philosophical. It also gives him style and good looks on camera. With half his first name ruled by the number 8, he's probably quite good at negotiating his own contracts. H types like to be in control. They can also evade issues better than any other letter, except Q and Z, which are also ruled by 8.

As Harry Houdini was able to escape death traps, our H-named friends have a natural talent for escaping questions they don't want to answer. If they want you to know something, they'll let you know. They are in total control at all times. This is one of those "control freak" letters. Seldom does anyone with an H in their name ever let anything get beyond their control.

Even though he's a fictional character, Harry Potter's name seems to fit him well. The whole witchcraft scene and the near-death escapes give way to his H name. Plus, the H and A add up to a hidden 9, then two Rs ruled by the number 9 make it difficult for him to forgive. Those ruled by 9 won't be happy unless they forgive others for what they've done. Harry always seems unhappy because of the past. The Y in his name makes him need a lot of freedom. So he's always running away from his guardians. Although this is only a character in a book or movie, his name still fits him perfectly!

Some other famous people whose names start with H are: Hank Aaron, Hilary Duff, Howie Mandel, Hulk Hogan, Heather Locklear, Howard Stern, Hayley Mills, Harrison Ford, Harpo Marx, Henry Winkler, Huey Louis, Humphrey Bogart, Heidi Klum, Hilary Swank, Hugh Jackman, Hedda Hopper, Helen Keller, Henry Fonda, Harvey Korman, Howard Cosell, Hedy Lamarr, Ho Chi Minh, Helen Reddy, Herschel Walker, H. G. Wells, Holly Hunter, and Hank Williams, Jr.

QUICK REFERENCE OF "H" NAMES

Habib, 22: Self-reliant, successful. Ambitious leader, great vision. Friendly, but shy. Blessed in some ways. Emotional, sensitive.

Hadden, 9: Likes helping others. Hardworking, sincere. Reliable, responsible. Down-to-earth, faithful. A free spirit, very adaptable. Original and unconventional.

Haden, 5: A passionate soul. Bright, adventuresome. Enjoys hard work. Physical, passionate. Original and unconventional.

Hadlee, 8: Enjoys competition. Resolute and purposeful. Reliable, responsible. Strong verbal skills. A free spirit, very adaptable. Physical and passionate.

Hadley, 10: Sometimes a loner. Independent, critical of self and others. Reliable, responsible. Strong verbal skills. Loves adventure and excitement. Needs a lot of freedom.

Haidar, 5: A passionate soul. Bright, adventuresome. Blessed in some ways. Reliable, responsible. Bold, courageous, a bit stubborn. Gentle, kind, a hard worker.

Hailey, 6: Creative in business. Pioneer and risk taker. Blessed in some ways. Strong verbal skills. A free spirit, very adaptable. Dislikes limitations.

Hakeem, 7: Perceptive, psychic. Not easily influenced. Strong desire to succeed. A free spirit, very adaptable. Loves adventure and excitement. Domestic, hardworking.

Hal, 3: Makes and loses money easily. Aims to please. Travels frequently.

Halbert, 30: Makes and loses money easily. Aims to please. Strong verbal skills. Friendly, but shy. A free spirit, very adaptable. Gentle, kind, a hard worker. Dynamic, busy lifestyle.

Hale, 8: Enjoys competition. Resolute and purposeful. Communicates skillfully. Physical, passionate.

Haley, 6: Creative in business. Pioneer and risk taker. Easygoing attitude. A free spirit, very adaptable. Dislikes limitations.

Hall, 6: Creative in business. Pioneer and risk taker. Strong verbal skills. A frequent traveler.

Halle, 20: Excellent mediator. Reads people easily. Honest and sincere. Frequent traveler. A free spirit, very adaptable.

Halley, 9: Likes helping others. Hardworking, sincere. Strong verbal skills. Frequent traveler. A free spirit, very adaptable. Dislikes limitations.

Hamidi, 8: Enjoys competition. Resolute and purposeful. Domestic, hardworking. Blessed in some ways. Reliable, responsible. Idealistic, humanitarian.

Hamilton, 11: Self-reliant, successful. Intuitive, perceptive. Desires financial security. Blessed in some ways. Strong verbal skills. Dynamic, busy lifestyle. Natural counselor and healer. Original and opinionated.

Hamish, 4: Relies on own judgment. Natural teaching ability. Down-to-earth, practical. Blessed in some ways. Charming and devoted. Self-reliant, successful.

Hamlet, 5: A passionate soul. Bright, adventuresome. Domestic, hardworking. Strong verbal skills. Physical and passionate. Dynamic, busy lifestyle.

Hamlin, 30: Makes and loses money easily. Aims to please. Domestic, hardworking. Communicates skillfully. Blessed in some ways. Romantic, opinionated.

Hana, 6: Creative in business. Pioneer and risk taker. Romantic, sensual. Bold, courageous, a bit stubborn.

Hanako, 5: A passionate soul. Bright, adventuresome. Original and unconventional. Bold, courageous, a bit stubborn. Strong desire to succeed. Natural counselor and healer.

Hank, 7: Perceptive, psychic. Not easily influenced. Original and unconventional. Strong desire to succeed.

Hanna, 20: Excellent mediator. Reads people easily. Original and opinionated. Romantic, sensual. Bold, courageous, a bit stubborn.

Hannah, 10: Sometimes a loner. Independent, critical of self and others. Creative, opinionated. Romantic, sensual. Bold, courageous, a bit stubborn. Self-reliant, successful.

Hans, 6: Creative in business. Pioneer and risk taker. Original and unconventional. Charming and devoted.

Hansel, 5: A passionate soul. Bright, adventuresome. Creative, opinionated. Charming and devoted. A free spirit, very adaptable. Strong verbal skills.

Hara, 10: Sometimes a loner. Independent, critical of self and others. Diligent, hardworking. Bold, courageous, a bit stubborn.

Harbin, 7: Perceptive, psychic. Not easily influenced. Gentle, kind, a hard worker. Friendly, but shy. Blessed in some ways. Original and unconventional.

Harden, 5: A passionate soul. Bright, adventuresome. Gentle, kind, a hard worker. Reliable, responsible. A free spirit, very adaptable. Original and unconventional.

Harding, 7: Perceptive, psychic. Not easily influenced. Spiritually motivated. Reliable, responsible. Blessed in some ways. Original, opinionated. Scientific and philosophical.

Hardy, 11: Self-reliant, successful. Intuitive, perceptive. Gentle, kind, a hard worker. Reliable, responsible. Needs a lot of freedom.

Hargrove, 4: Relies on own judgment. Natural teaching ability. Gentle, kind, a hard worker. Scientific and philosophical. Tendency to lose items. Nurturing, loving. Intuitive and inspired. A free spirit, very adaptable.

Harim, 4: Relies on own judgment. Natural teaching ability. Hardworking, idealistic. Blessed in some ways. Systematic, organized.

Harlan, 9: Likes helping others. Hardworking, sincere. Gentle, kind, very diligent. Strong verbal skills. Bold, courageous, a bit stubborn. Original and unconventional.

Harley, 6: Creative in business. Pioneer and risk taker. Gentle, kind, a hard worker. Strong verbal skills. A free spirit, very adaptable. Dislikes limitations.

Harlow, 5: A passionate soul. Bright, adventuresome. Hardworking, idealistic. Communicates skillfully. Natural counselor and healer. Likes to meet new people.

Harmony, 4: Relies on own judgment. Natural teaching ability. Gentle, kind, diligent. Domestic, hardworking. Nurturing, loving. Original and unconventional. Needs a lot of freedom.

Harod, 10: Sometimes a loner. Independent, critical of self and others. Gentle, kind, a hard worker. Natural counselor and healer. Systematic, organized.

Harold, 4: Relies on own judgment. Natural teaching ability. Gentle, kind, a hard worker. Nurturing, loving. Strong verbal skills. Reliable, responsible.

Harper, 3: Makes and loses money easily. Aims to please. Optimistic and kind. Intelligent and knowledgeable. A free spirit, very adaptable. Tendency to lose items.

Harriet, 7: Perceptive, psychic. Not easily influenced. Spiritual, idealistic. Tendency to lose items. Blessed in some ways. A free spirit, very adaptable. Dynamic, busy lifestyle.

Harris, 10: Sometimes a loner. Independent, critical of self and others. Gentle, kind, a hard worker. Tendency to lose items. Blessed in some ways. Charming and devoted.

Harrison, 3: Makes and loses money easily. Aims to please. Optimistic, very kind. Intense inner power. Artistic, having good taste. Natural counselor and healer. Original and opinionated.

Harry, 7: Perceptive, psychic. Not easily influenced. Gentle, kind, a hard worker. Tendency to lose items. Needs a lot of freedom.

Harv, 22: Self-reliant, successful. Ambitious leader, great vision. Gentle, kind, a hard worker. Intuitive and inspired.

Harvey, 7: Perceptive, psychic. Not easily influenced. Gentle, kind, a hard worker. Intuitive and inspired. A free spirit, very adaptable. Dislikes limitations.

Hasana, 8: Enjoys competition. Resolute and purposeful. Charismatic, loving. Independent, critical of self and others. Original and unconventional. Pioneer and risk taker.

Hasina, 7: Perceptive, psychic. Not easily influenced. Charming and devoted. Blessed in some ways. Original and unconventional. Bold, courageous, a bit stubborn.

Hassan, 8: Enjoys competition. Resolute and purposeful. Charming and devoted. Impulsive and extreme. Original and unconventional.

Hattie, 9: Likes helping others. Hardworking, sincere. Dynamic, busy lifestyle. Sensitive and easily hurt. Blessed in some ways. A free spirit, very adaptable.

Hatty, 20: Excellent mediator. Reads people easily. Socially active. Sensitive and easily hurt. Needs a lot of freedom.

Hawley, 11: Self-reliant, successful. Intuitive, perceptive. Likes to meet new people. Strong verbal skills. A free spirit, very adaptable. Dislikes limitations.

Hayden, 30: Makes and loses money easily. Aims to please. Needs a lot of freedom. Reliable, responsible. Loves adventure and excitement. Original and opinionated.

Hayes, 22: Self-reliant, successful. Ambitious leader, great vision. Needs a lot of freedom. Loves adventure and excitement. Charming and devoted.

Hayley, 4: Relies on own judgment. Natural teaching ability. Needs a lot of freedom. Strong verbal skills. Likes change and variety. Stylish and refined.

Hazel, 7: Perceptive, psychic. Not easily influenced. Uses common sense. A free spirit, very adaptable. Strong verbal skills.

Heath, 6: Creative in business. A step ahead of others. Pioneer and risk taker. Dynamic, busy lifestyle. Self-reliant, successful.

Heather, 11: Self-reliant, successful. Keenly perceptive. Independent, critical of self and others. Dynamic, busy lifestyle. Loves adventure and excitement. Gentle, kind, a hard worker.

Hector, 6: Creative in business. A step ahead of others. Self-expressive, cheerful. Dynamic, busy lifestyle. Natural counselor and healer. Gentle, kind, a hard worker.

Hedda, 22: Self-reliant, successful. Has big plans and ideas. Shrewd and determined. Down-to-earth, faithful. Ambitious leader, great vision.

Heddy, 10: Sometimes a loner. Likes change and variety. Reliable, responsible. Down-to-earth, faithful. Needs a lot of freedom.

Hedy, 6: Creative in business. A step ahead of others. Systematic, organized. Needs a lot of freedom.

Heidi, 8: Enjoys competition. Original and creative. Blessed in some ways. Reliable, responsible. Artistic, having good taste.

Helaine, 9: Likes helping others. Enjoys giving gifts. Frequent traveler. Independent, hardworking. Blessed in some ways. Original, creative. Physical and passionate.

Helen, 8: Enjoys competition. Original, creative, and unconventional. Strong verbal skills. Loves adventure and excitement.

Helena, 9: Likes helping others. Enjoys giving gifts. Strong verbal skills. Physical and passionate. Original, creative. Resolute and purposeful.

Helga, 6: Creative in business. A step ahead of others. Easygoing attitude. Scientific and philosophical. Independent, critical of self and others.

Helki, 9: Likes helping others. Enjoys giving gifts. Communicates skillfully. Strong desire to succeed. Blessed in some ways.

Henley, 6: Creative in business. A step ahead of others. Original and unconventional. Strong verbal skills. Physical and passionate. Dislikes limitations.

Henrietta, 10: Sometimes a loner. Likes change and variety. Creative, opinionated. Gentle, kind, a hard worker. Blessed in some ways. Loves adventure and excitement. Dynamic, busy lifestyle. Sensitive and easily hurt. Independent, critical of self and others.

Henry, 7: Perceptive, psychic. Not easily fooled. Original and unconventional. Gentle, kind, a hard worker. Needs a lot of freedom.

Herald, 30: Makes and loses money easily. A free spirit, very adaptable. Gentle, kind, a hard worker. Independent, critical of self and others. Strong verbal skills. Reliable, responsible.

Herb, 6: Creative in business. A step ahead of others. Generous, helpful. Friendly, but shy.

Herbert, 4: Relies on own judgment. Accesses quickly. Gentle, kind, a hard worker. Friendly, but shy. Loves adventure and excitement. Tendency to lose items. Dynamic, busy lifestyle.

Herm, 8: Enjoys competition. Original and creative. Intense inner power. Systematic, organized.

Herman, 5: A passionate soul. Adaptable to change. Gentle, kind, a hard worker. Systematic, organized. Bright, adventuresome. Original and unconventional.

Hermen, 9: Likes helping others. A free spirit, very adaptable. Gentle, kind, a hard worker. Systematic, organized. Tendency to overindulge. Original and unconventional.

Hermes, 5: A passionate soul. A free spirit, very adaptable. Intense inner power. Systematic, organized. Perceptive, reads people easily. Charming and devoted.

Hermie, 4: Relies on own judgment. Natural teaching ability. Diligent, helpful. Down-to-earth, faithful. Blessed in some ways. Loves adventure and excitement.

Hermosa, 7: Perceptive, psychic. Not easily fooled. Spiritually motivated. Systematic, organized. Natural counselor and healer. Charming and devoted. Independent, critical of self and others.

Hernando, 7: Perceptive, psychic. Not easily fooled. Spiritually motivated. Original and unconventional. Independent, self-reliant. Romantic, sensual. Reliable, responsible. Natural counselor and healer.

Herro, 10: Sometimes a loner. A free spirit, very adaptable. Gentle, kind, a hard worker. Tendency to lose items. Natural counselor and healer.

Herrod, 5: A passionate soul. Loves adventure and excitement. Intense inner power. Tendency to lose items. Natural counselor and healer. Reliable, responsible.

Hester, 30: Makes and loses money easily. A free spirit, very adaptable. Charming and devoted. Dynamic, busy lifestyle. Physical and passionate. Intense inner power.

Hetti, 8: Enjoys competition. Physical and passionate. Dynamic, busy lifestyle. Sensitive and easily hurt. Blessed in some ways.

Hettie, 4: Relies on own judgment. A free spirit, very adaptable. Busy family life. Sensitive and easily hurt. Blessed in some ways. Loves adventure and excitement.

Hetty, 6: Creative in business. A step ahead of others. Dynamic, busy lifestyle. Sensitive and easily hurt. Needs a lot of freedom.

Hewe, 5: A passionate soul. A free spirit, very adaptable. Likes to meet new people. Loves adventure and excitement.

Hewett, 9: Likes helping others. Enjoys giving gifts. Likes to meet new people. Physical and passionate. Dynamic, busy lifestyle. Sensitive and easily hurt.

Hiatt, 22: Self-reliant, successful. Blessed in some ways. Resolute and purposeful. Dynamic, busy lifestyle. Sensitive and easily hurt.

Hilary, 10: Sometimes a loner. Works for group effort. Strong verbal skills. Independent, critical of self and others. Gentle, kind, a hard worker. Needs a lot of freedom.

Hilda, 7: Perceptive, psychic. Needs alone time. Frequent traveler. Systematic, organized. Independent, critical of self and others.

Hildegard, 5: A passionate soul. Blessed in some ways. Communicates skillfully. Reliable, responsible. A free spirit, very adaptable. Scientific, philosophical. Independent, critical of self and others. Gentle, kind, a hard worker. Down-to-earth.

Hildie, 11: Self-reliant, successful. Idealistic, humanitarian. Strong verbal skills. Reliable, responsible. Artistic, having good taste. A free spirit, very adaptable.

Hildy, 4: Relies on own judgment. Blessed in some ways. Strong verbal skills. Reliable, responsible. Needs a lot of freedom.

Hillary, 4: Relies on own judgment. Blessed in some ways. Strong verbal skills. Frequent traveler. Resolute and purposeful. Gentle, kind, a hard worker. Needs a lot of freedom.

Hilton, 6: Creative in business. Artistic, having good taste. Communicates skillfully. Dynamic, busy lifestyle. Natural counselor and healer. Original and unconventional.

Hines, 10: Sometimes a loner. Respectful, kind. Original and unconventional. A free spirit, very adaptable. Charming and devoted.

Hiram, 4: Relies on own judgment. Blessed in some ways. Gentle, kind, a hard worker. Independent, critical of self and others. Systematic, organized.

Hobart, 10: Sometimes a loner. Natural counselor and healer. Friendly, but shy. Independent, critical of self and others. Gentle, kind, a hard worker. Dynamic, busy lifestyle.

Hogan, 9: Likes helping others. Creates group harmony. Scientific, philosophical. Independent, critical of self and others. Original and unconventional.

Holbrook, 6: Creative in business. Nurturing, loving. Communicates skillfully. Friendly, but shy. Gentle, kind, a hard worker. Musically talented. Magnetic personality. Strong desire to succeed.

Holden, 4: Relies on own judgment. Natural counselor and healer. Strong verbal skills. Reliable, responsible. A free spirit, very adaptable. Original and unconventional.

Holley, 5: A passionate soul. Natural counselor and healer. Strong verbal skills. Frequent traveler. Physical and passionate. Dislikes limitations.

Hollie, 7: Perceptive, psychic. Open to opportunities. Strong verbal skills. Frequent traveler. Blessed in some ways. A free spirit, very adaptable.

Hollis, 30: Makes and loses money easily. Has creative solutions. Communicates skillfully. Travels frequently. Artistic, having good taste. Charming and devoted.

Holly, 9: Likes helping others. Creates group harmony. Strong verbal skills. Frequent traveler. Needs a lot of freedom.

Holmes, 9: Likes helping others. Creates group harmony. Strong verbal skills. Domestic, hardworking. A free spirit, very adaptable. Charming and devoted.

Homa, 10: Sometimes a loner. Natural counselor and healer. Domestic, hardworking. Independent, critical of self and others.

Homer, 5: A passionate soul. Nurturing, loving. Systematic, organized. A free spirit, very adaptable. Gentle, kind, a hard worker.

Honey, 4: Relies on own judgment. Practical and duty-bound. Romantic, opinionated. Accesses quickly. Needs a lot of freedom.

Hong, 8: Enjoys competition. Natural counselor and healer. Original and unconventional. Scientific and philosophical.

Honoria, 8: Enjoys competition. Magnetic personality. Romantic, opinionated. Natural counselor and healer. Intense inner power. Blessed in some ways. Resolute and purposeful.

Hope, 8: Enjoys competition. Natural counselor and healer. Intelligent and knowledgeable. A free spirit, very adaptable.

Horace, 5: A passionate soul. Magnetic personality. Gentle, kind, a hard worker. Independent, critical of self and others. Self-expressive, cheerful. A free spirit, very adaptable.

Horatio, 5: A passionate soul. Natural counselor and healer. Intense inner power. Independent, critical of self and others. Dynamic, busy lifestyle. Blessed in some ways. May have musical abilities.

Hortense, 5: A passionate soul. Magnetic personality. Gentle, kind, a hard worker. Dynamic, busy lifestyle. A free spirit, very adaptable. Original and unconventional. Charming and devoted. Tendency to overindulge.

Horton, 9: Likes helping others. Creates group harmony. Gentle, kind, a hard worker. Dynamic, busy lifestyle. May have musical abilities. Original and unconventional.

Hoshi, 5: A passionate soul. Natural counselor and healer. Charming and devoted. Self-reliant, successful. Blessed in some ways.

Hoshie, 10: Sometimes a loner. Self-sacrificing, loving. Charming and devoted. Self-reliant, successful. Blessed in some ways. A free spirit, very adaptable.

Hoshiko, 4: Relies on own judgment. Natural counselor and healer. Charming and devoted. Self-reliant, successful. Blessed in some ways. Strong desire to succeed. May have musical abilities.

Hossain, 4: Relies on own judgment. Natural counselor and healer. Charming and devoted. Impulsive and extreme. Independent, critical of self and others. Blessed in some ways. Original and unconventional.

Houston, 4: Relies on own judgment. Responsible, duty-bound. Attractive and charming. Can be impulsive and extreme. Dynamic, busy lifestyle. May have musical abilities. Original and unconventional.

Howard, 6: Creative in business. Nurturing, loving. Likes to meet new people. Independent, critical of self and others. Gentle, kind, a hard worker. Reliable, responsible.

Howie, 6: Creative in business. Creates group harmony. Likes to meet new people. Blessed in some ways. A free spirit, very adaptable.

Hoyt, 5: A passionate soul. Natural counselor and healer. Needs a lot of freedom. Dynamic, busy lifestyle.

Hubert, 11: Self-reliant, successful. Attractive and charming. Friendly, but shy. A free spirit, very adaptable. Gentle, kind, a hard worker. Dynamic, busy lifestyle.

Huey, 5: A passionate soul. Fun, flirtatious. A free spirit, very adaptable. Dislikes limitations.

Hugh, 8: Enjoys competition. Attractive and charming. Scientific and philosophical. Self-reliant, successful.

Hughie, 4: Relies on own judgment. Attractive and charming. Scientific and philosophical. Self-reliant, successful. Blessed in some ways. A free spirit, very adaptable.

Hugo, 6: Creative in business. Charming, youthful. Scientific and philosophical. Natural counselor and healer.

Humbert, 6: Creative in business. Charming, youthful. Desires financial security. Friendly, but shy. A free spirit, very adaptable. Gentle, kind, a hard worker. Dynamic, busy lifestyle.

Hume, 20: Excellent mediator. Attractive and charming. Domestic, hardworking. Loves excitement and adventure.

Humfrey, 6: Creative in business. Charming, youthful. Domestic, hardworking. Self-sacrificing, loving. Intense inner power. A free spirit, very adaptable. Dislikes limitations.

Humphrey, 6: Creative in business. Charming, youthful. Desires financial security. Intelligent and knowledgeable. Self-reliant, successful. Intense inner power. A free spirit, very adaptable. Dislikes limitations.

Hunt, 9: Likes helping others. Attractive and charming. Original and unconventional. Dynamic, busy lifestyle.

Hunter, 5: A passionate soul. Attractive and charming. Creative, opinionated. Extremely social. A free spirit, very adaptable. Gentle, kind, a hard worker.

Huntington, 7: Perceptive, psychic. Attractive and charming. Original and unconventional. Dynamic, busy lifestyle. Blessed in some ways. Romantic, sensual. Extremely intelligent. Sensitive and easily hurt. Natural counselor and healer. Creative and opinionated.

Huntley, 6: Creative in business. Charming, youthful. Original and unconventional. Dynamic, busy lifestyle. Strong verbal skills. Likes change and variety. Needs a lot of freedom.

Hurley, 8: Enjoys competition. Attractive and charming. Gentle, kind, a hard worker. Strong verbal skills. A free spirit, very adaptable. Dislikes limitations.

Hutton, 8: Enjoys competition. Attractive and charming. Dynamic, busy lifestyle. Sensitive and easily hurt. Natural counselor and healer. Original and unconventional.

Huxford, 6: Creative in business. Charming, youthful. Artistic, sensual, perceptive. Self-sacrificing, loving. Natural counselor and healer. Gentle, kind, a hard worker. Reliable, responsible.

Huxley, 5: A passionate soul. Attractive and charming. Artistic, sensual, perceptive. Strong verbal skills. A free spirit, very adaptable. Dislikes limitations.

Hy, 6: Creative in business. Needs a lot of freedom. Nurturing, loving.

Hyacinth, 7: Perceptive, psychic. Needs a lot of freedom. Not easily fooled. Optimistic, outgoing. Blessed in some ways. Original and unconventional. Dynamic, busy lifestyle. Self-reliant, successful.

Hyatt, 20: Excellent mediator. Needs a lot of freedom. Independent, critical of self and others. Dynamic, busy lifestyle. Sensitive and easily hurt.

Hyde, 6: Creative in business. Dislikes limitations. Reliable, responsible. A free spirit, very adaptable.

Hyman, 7: Perceptive, psychic. Needs a lot of freedom. Domestic, hardworking. Independent, critical of self and others. Original and unconventional.

Hymen, 11: Self-reliant, successful. Needs a lot of freedom. Desires financial security. A free spirit, very adaptable. Original and unconventional.

Hymie, 6: Creative in business. Needs a lot of freedom. Domestic, hardworking. Blessed in some ways. Loves adventure and excitement.

Hyrum, 4: Relies on own judgment. Needs a lot of freedom. Gentle, kind, a hard worker. Attractive and charming. Domestic, goal-oriented.

I

If a name begins with I, has I as the first vowel, has more than one I, or ends with an I, this person is a humanitarian, blessed in some ways, and is artistic and creative. Those with the first letter of their name beginning with an I, or first vowel beginning with an I, tend to have good taste in décor. It's not surprising to find these individuals in artistic careers, especially since they aren't materialistic. Often they live in humble surroundings while they pursue artistic endeavors.

The letter I is the ninth letter of the alphabet and is influenced by the number 9 vibration. Its personality is similar to the astrological sign Sagittarius. Those with the letter I in their names have a generous, broad-minded attitude toward all of humanity. They tend to have friends and associates of all colors and backgrounds. The letter I is open-minded, spiritual, charitable, and tolerant of the differences of others. People with an I in the beginning of their names or as a first vowel are often recognized by their friendly, comfortable nature. Others feel safe when they're with an I person. They are the teachers and counselors that stay late to donate their time for the good of the whole. Often they are taken advantage of, but will be the last to say anything about it. God notices though, and that's why they are more blessed than the rest of us.

Whether their name begins with an I or they have an I first vowel, people often go up to the I person in a grocery store to ask where an item is located. I-named people somehow give the impression that they know everything. Life is much bigger and grander for an I person. It's difficult for I people to narrow their attention down to just one or two people when they are use to spreading themselves far and wide. So an I person can be a disappointment in a relationship, unless the other person also has an I or an R in their name. Another disappointment could be in their apparent lack of concern for material wealth. Spiritual development and greed don't go together in the mind of the I person.

Similar to Sagittarius, the I person is lucky. They often are blessed in some area of their lives. Although they are apparently immune to the call for materialism, they often are blessed enough to marry into money, as our late Princess Di, with I as the first vowel in her name. I types are often born into money. First I vowel Priscilla Presley, as well as Priscilla and Elvis's daughter, Lisa Marie Presley, were blessed by being born into money.

Sadly enough, this ninth letter of the alphabet usually suffers from the "poor little rich kid" syndrome. A sadness seems to be attached to those with an I influence. Although I first vowels and names are blessed in some ways, they often have old family pain that remains to haunt them. Many of them have "father issues." The I person will be happy if he or she can forgive offenses others have made against them. As spiritual as they are, forgiveness does not come easily for I individuals. As long as they are unable to forgive and forget, they will not truly be happy. They will remain tormented.

Often people will follow those with an I first vowel whether they are right or wrong. For some reason they seem to get away with more than the rest of us. Bill Clinton, Britney Spears, and Michael Jackson are forgiven. For example, Michael Jackson's bouncing back into the limelight right now with an updated *Thriller* album. I predict that Britney will be back—and forgiven—in a year or two. Somehow people tend to follow those with an I first vowel and overlook their faults, as if putting them on a pedestal.

Another I first vowel, Michelangelo, started his apprenticeship in the field of art at twelve years of age. Today he is regarded as one of the most famous artists ever born. His birthday, in the third month (March), on the sixth day, made him quite creative. In addition, those numbers add up to a 9 attitude number (3, 6, and 9 are the creative numbers). It's no wonder Michelangelo spent part of his youth and his entire adult life creating. It's the I in his name, however, that gave him natural artistic ability. The M influenced his work in sculpture, as it is a hardworking, harsh letter. Marble starts with the letter M, with which he worked most of his artistic career. To sculpt marble, one needs a hammer and chisel. The disciplined M in his name helped him to work tirelessly for many years on each masterpiece. The I as his first vowel, or heart's desire letter, led him to religious art work.

Bill O'Reilly of *The O'Reilly Factor* shows his humanitarianism by discussing world political affairs in his "fair and balanced" talk show. Bill's name sums up to an 8 power number, making him a little bit brutal, and the two Ls give him the edge in communication matters; still, he is a humanitarian by his heart's desire letter I. He invites people of all races and colors, and does not seem to discriminate. When he verbally thrashes someone, it doesn't seem to matter what color, race, religion, or political preference they are. This, brutal or not, makes him a humanitarian. Being color-blind and sticking with the issues are idealistic qualities of an I first vowel.

Another Fox News regular is Dr. Isadore Rosenfeld. This famous doctor has written numerous books and practiced medicine for many years. People tend to follow a person with an I first vowel. Not only is his first vowel an I, but the first letter of his name is an I. So Dr. Isadore Rosenfeld wears his heart's desire letter up front for everyone to see. He comes across as the kind of person one can trust and count on. He no doubt works hard for the good of the whole and is probably taken advantage of often, as are most 9-ruled individuals. He has such a kind and caring face. Isadore sums up to an 8 power number, so the good doctor is able to manage material success more easily than most with this much 9 vibration.

Diane Sawyer, currently with ABC News, *Primetime Thursday*, and co-anchor on *Good Morning America*, shows her humanitarianism through her work as well. The D in her name makes her systematic, organized, and up for any task. Her first vowel, I, conjuncts A, giving her leadership qualities in her efforts to be as humanitarian as possible. Since the A flavors her I heart's desire letter, she is a more daring and bold humanitarian type.

Those born with I anywhere in their name tend to work hard for the good of the whole. I is the ninth letter of the alphabet and 9 rules completions. Those with an I in their names are completing a stage of learning in this lifetime. They are farther along than the rest of us in God's eyes. They are the ones donating their time to help a good cause. Often they are taken advantage of as they are so charitable. They will do their own job and everyone else's without complaining. They have a special mission on earth. They're put here to do God's work, sort of like angels.

Some other famous names that begin with the letter I are: Ingrid Bergman, Indira Gandhi, Isaac Stern, Isaac Mizrahi, Isabella Rossellini, Isaac Newton, Ivana Trump, Ira Gershwin, Irving Berlin, Ian Fleming, Ione Skye, Imogene Coca, Ice-T, Iggy Pop, Ice Cube, and Isaac Hayes.

QUICK REFERENCE OF "I" NAMES

Ian, 6: Artistic, having good taste. Pioneer and risk taker. Romantic and creative.

Ibrahim, 6: Artistic, having good taste. Friendly, but shy. Gentle, kind, a hard worker. Pioneer and risk taker. Excellent judge of character. Artistic, having good taste. Desires financial security.

Ice, 8: Gives practical gifts. Optimistic and outspoken. Original and creative.

Ichabod, 6: Artistic, having good taste. Self-expressive, cheerful. Excellent judge of character. Pioneer and risk taker. Friendly, but shy. Natural counselor and healer. Reliable, responsible.

Ida, 5: Generous, thoughtful. Domestic, hardworking. Bright, adventuresome.

Idella, 7: Has spiritual undertones. Creative problem solver. A free spirit, very adaptable. Strong verbal skills. Frequent traveler. Not easily influenced.

Idelle, 11: Idealistic and humanitarian. Insightful, sensitive. Keenly perceptive. Strong verbal skills. Ups and downs financially. Loves adventure and excitement.

Iggy, 30: Communicates understanding. Scientific and philosophical. Stylish and refined. Needs a lot of freedom.

Ignacia, 8: Practical when giving. Creative opportunist. Romantic, sensual. Resolute and purposeful. Self-expressive, cheerful. Artistic, having good taste. Bold, courageous, a bit stubborn.

Ignacio, 4: Teaches kindness. Extremely intelligent. Original and unconventional. Resolute and purposeful. Great sense of humor. Artistic, having good taste. Natural counselor and healer.

Ignatia, 7: Has spiritual undertones. Scientific and philosophical. Original and unconventional. Not easily influenced. Dynamic, busy lifestyle. Artistic, having good taste. Bold, courageous, a bit stubborn.

Ignatius, 10: Works for group effort. Scientific and philosophical. Creative, opinionated. Independent, critical of self and others. Dynamic, busy lifestyle. Artistic, having good taste. Attractive and charming. Loving and devoted.

Ignatz, 5: Generous, thoughtful. Scientific and philosophical. Creative, opinionated. Bright, adventuresome. Dynamic, busy lifestyle. Uses common sense.

Igor, 4: Teaches kindness. A bit of a homebody. Natural counselor and healer. Gentle, kind, a hard worker.

Ike, 7: Has spiritual undertones. Strong desire to succeed. Not easily fooled.

Ilana, 10: Works for group effort. Strong verbal skills. Independent, critical of self and others. Original and unconventional. Bold, courageous, a bit stubborn.

Ilene, 9: Blessed in some ways. Communicates skillfully. Enjoys giving gifts. Creative and opinionated. Physical and passionate.

Ilenna, 10: Works for group effort. Strong verbal skills. Likes change and variety. Original and unconventional. Romantic, sensual. Independent, critical of self and others.

Iline, 4: Teaches kindness. Strong verbal skills. Artistic, having good taste. Original and unconventional. A free spirit, very adaptable.

Ilka, 6: Artistic, having good taste. Communicates well. Strong desire to succeed. Pioneer and risk taker.

Illene, 30: Communicates understanding. Ups and downs financially. Frequent traveler. A free spirit, very adaptable. Original and unconventional. Loves adventure and excitement.

Illona, 9: Blessed in some ways. Slow to make decisions. Frequent traveler. Natural counselor and healer. Original and unconventional. Independent, critical of self and others.

Ilona, 6: Artistic, having good taste. Strong verbal skills. Natural counselor and healer. Original and unconventional. Pioneer and risk taker.

Ilsa, 5: Generous, thoughtful. Communicates skillfully. Charming and devoted. Bright, adventuresome.

Ilse, 9: Blessed in some ways. Strong verbal skills. Charming and devoted. A free spirit, very adaptable.

Ima, 5: Generous, thoughtful. Domestic, hardworking. Bright, adventuresome.

Imer, 9: Blessed in some ways. Diligent, generous with time. A free spirit, very adaptable. Gentle, kind, very helpful.

Immanuel, 7: Has spiritual undertones. Must have faith. Systematic, organized. Not easily influenced. Original and unconventional. Attractive and charming. A free spirit, very adaptable. Strong verbal skills.

Imogene, 5: Generous, thoughtful. Domestic, hardworking. Natural counselor and healer. Scientific and philosophical. A free spirit, very adaptable. Original and unconventional. Physical and passionate.

Ina, 6: Artistic, having good taste. Creative and romantic. Pioneer and risk taker.

Inday, 8: Practical when giving. Romantic, sensual. Reliable, responsible. Resolute and purposeful. Needs a lot of freedom.

India, 10: Works for group effort. Friendly, likes people. Systematic, organized. Artistic, having good taste. Independent, critical of self and others.

Indiana, 7: Has spiritual undertones. Original and unconventional. Reliable, responsible. Blessed in some ways. Not easily influenced. Romantic, sensual. Bold, courageous, a bit stubborn.

Indigo, 4: Teaches kindness. Practical creativity. Reliable, responsible. Artistic, having good taste. Scientific and philosophical. Natural counselor and healer.

Indira, 10: Works for group effort. Friendly, likes people. A natural authority. Artistic, having good taste. Gentle, kind, a hard worker. Independent, critical of self and others.

Indra, 10: Works for group effort. Original and unconventional. Reliable, responsible. Gentle, kind, a hard worker. Independent, critical of self and others.

Indria, 10: (Same as Indira.)

Indy, 7: Has spiritual undertones. Original and unconventional. Reliable, responsible. Needs a lot of freedom.

Ines, 20: Emotional and considerate. Socially active. A free spirit, very adaptable. Charming and devoted.

Inessa, 22: Idealistic and humanitarian. Perceptive, intuitive. Enjoys giving gifts. Charming and devoted. Impulsive and extreme. Independent, critical of self and others.

Inez, 9: Blessed in some ways. Original and unconventional. A free spirit, very adaptable. Uses common sense.

Inga, 22: Idealistic and humanitarian. Intuitive and creative. Thinks on a large scale. Independent, critical of self and others.

Inge, 8: Gives practical gifts. Romantic, sensual. Scientific and philosophical. A free spirit, very adaptable.

Ingemar, 4: Teaches kindness. Original and unconventional. Scientific and philosophical. A free spirit, very adaptable. Desires financial security. Independent, critical of self and others. Gentle, kind, a hard worker.

Inglebert, 11: Idealistic and humanitarian. Intuitive and creative. Scientific and philosophical. Strong verbal skills. A free spirit, very adaptable. Friendly, but shy. Loves adventure and excitement. Gentle, kind, a hard worker. Dynamic, busy lifestyle.

Ingraham, 8: Gives practical gifts. Romantic, sensual. Scientific and philosophical. Gentle, kind, a hard worker. Resolute and purposeful. Excellent judge of character. Bold, courageous, a bit stubborn. Systematic, organized.

Ingram, 8: Gives practical gifts. Romantic, sensual. Scientific and philosophical. Intense inner power. Resolute and purposeful. Systematic, organized.

Ingred, 3: Communicates understanding. Creative, opinionated. Scientific and philosophical. Gentle, kind, a hard worker. A free spirit, very adaptable. Reliable, responsible.

Ingrid, 7: Has spiritual undertones. Original and unconventional. Scientific and philosophical. Gentle, kind, a hard worker. Artistic, having good taste. Reliable, responsible.

Inness, 8: Gives practical gifts. Creative, original. Romantic, sensual. A free spirit, very adaptable. Charming and devoted. Impulsive and extreme.

Innis, 11: Idealistic and humanitarian. Perceptive, opinionated. Romantic, sensual. Artistic, having good taste. Charming and devoted.

Iola, 10: Works for group effort. Natural counselor and healer. Strong verbal skills. Independent, critical of self and others.

Iona, 3: Communicates understanding. Creates group harmony. Creative, opinionated. Pioneer and risk taker.

Ione, 7: Has spiritual undertones. Natural counselor and healer. Original and unconventional. A free spirit, very adaptable.

Ira, 10: Works for group effort. Gentle, kind, a hard worker. Independent, critical of self and others.

Ireland, 9: Blessed in some ways. Diligent, helpful. A free spirit, very adaptable. Communicates skillfully. Respectful, kind. Original and unconventional. Reliable, responsible.

Irena, 11: Idealistic and humanitarian. Gentle, kind, a hard worker. Physical and passionate. Original and unconventional. Independent, critical of self and others.

Irene, 6: Artistic, having good taste. Helpful, generous with time. A step ahead of others. Creative and opinionated. Loves adventure and excitement.

Irina, 6: Artistic, having good taste. Helpful, generous with time. Artistic, having good taste. Creative and opinionated. Pioneer and risk taker.

Iris, 10: Works for group effort. Gentle, kind, a hard worker. Blessed in some ways. Charming and devoted.

Irma, 5: Generous, thoughtful. Intense inner power. Systematic, organized. Bright, adventuresome.

Irv, 22: Idealistic and humanitarian. Gentle, kind, a hard worker. Intuitive and inspired.

Irvin, 9: Blessed in some ways. Kind-hearted, helpful. Intuitive and inspired. Artistic, having good taste. Original and unconventional.

Irving, 7: Has spiritual undertones. Spiritually motivated. Intuitive and inspired. Blessed in some ways. Original and unconventional. Scientific and philosophical.

Irwin, 10: Works for group effort. Gentle, kind, a hard worker. Likes to meet new people. Artistic, having good taste. Original and unconventional.

Isaac, 6: Artistic, having good taste. Charming and devoted. Pioneer and risk taker. Bold, courageous, a bit stubborn. Self-expressive, cheerful.

Isabel, 3: Communicates understanding. Very charismatic. Aims to please. Friendly, but shy. A free spirit, very adaptable. Strong verbal skills.

Isabella, 7: Has spiritual undertones. Charming and devoted. Not easily influenced. Friendly, but shy. A free spirit, very adaptable. Strong verbal skills. Frequent traveler. Bold, courageous, a bit stubborn.

Isabelle, 11: Idealistic and humanitarian. Very charismatic. Intuitive, perceptive. Friendly, but shy. A free spirit, very adaptable. Strong verbal skills. Frequent traveler. Loves adventure and excitement.

Isadora, 4: Teaches kindness. Charming and devoted. Resolute and purposeful. Reliable, responsible. Natural counselor and healer. Gentle, kind, a hard worker. Bold, courageous, a bit stubborn.

Isadore, 8: Gives practical gifts. Passionate and loving. Resolute and purposeful. Reliable, responsible. Natural counselor and healer. Gentle, kind, a hard worker. A free spirit, very adaptable.

Isaiah, 11: Idealistic and humanitarian. Charming and devoted. Intuitive, perceptive. Artistic, having good taste. Bold, courageous, a bit stubborn. Self-reliant, successful.

Isham, 5: Generous, thoughtful. Charming and devoted. Excellent judge of character. Bright, adventuresome. Domestic, hardworking.

Ishaq, 9: Blessed in some ways. Charming and devoted. Self-reliant, successful. Helpful, sincere. Attracts wealth.

Ishmael, 4: Teaches kindness. Able to access quickly. Self-reliant, successful. Domestic, hardworking. Resolute and purposeful. A free spirit, very adaptable. Strong verbal skills.

Isidore, 7: Has spiritual undertones. Stylish and refined. Artistic, having good taste. Reliable, responsible. Natural counselor and healer. Gentle, kind, a hard worker. A free spirit, very adaptable.

Isis, 20: Emotional and considerate. Charming and devoted. Artistic, having good taste. Impulsive and extreme.

Ismael, 5: Generous, thoughtful. Passionate and loving. Domestic, hardworking. Bright, adventuresome. A free spirit, very adaptable. Strong verbal skills.

Ismail, 9: Blessed in some ways. Charming and devoted. Domestic, hardworking. Helpful, sincere. Artistic, having good taste. Strong verbal skills.

Isman, 20: Emotional and considerate. Charming and devoted. Domestic, hardworking. Reads people easily. Original and unconventional.

Isolde, 10: Works for group effort. Very charismatic. Natural counselor and healer. Strong verbal skills. Reliable, responsible. A free spirit, very adaptable.

Israel, 10: Works for group effort. Very charismatic. Gentle, kind, a hard worker. Independent, critical of self and others. A free spirit, very adaptable. Strong verbal skills.

Iva, 5: Generous, thoughtful. Eccentric or unpredictable. Bright, adventuresome.

Ivah, 22: Idealistic and humanitarian. Great potential for accomplishment. Resolute and purposeful. Self-reliant, successful.

Ivan, 10: Works for group effort. Intuitive and inspired. Independent, critical of self and others. Original and unconventional.

Ivana, 20: Emotional and considerate. Tactful and refined. Reads people easily. Original and unconventional. Bold, courageous, a bit stubborn.

Ivane, 6: Artistic, having good taste. Intuitive and inspired. Pioneer and risk taker. Original and unconventional. A free spirit, very adaptable.

Ivar, 5: Generous, thoughtful. Eccentric or unpredictable. Bright, adventuresome. Gentle, kind, a hard worker.

Iven, 5: Generous, thoughtful. Eccentric or unpredictable. Physical and passionate. Original and unconventional.

Ives, 10: Works for group effort. Intuitive and inspired. Likes change and variety. Charming and devoted.

Ivy, 20: Emotional and considerate. Intuitive and inspired. Needs a lot of freedom.

Izak, 20: Emotional and considerate. Uses common sense. Reads people easily. Strong desire to succeed.

J

If a name begins with J, has more than one J, or ends with a J, this person is clever, talented, honest, sincere, and tries hard to please everyone.

The letter J is the tenth letter of the alphabet. Since $1 + 0 = 1$, the tenth letter is similar to the first letter, A, which is ruled by the number 1 vibration. So J is co-ruled by 1. In fact, if a person has a J and an A in their name, like Jack or Janice, then the 1 vibration is even more evident in their personality than say a Joe or a Jill. It's as if they have a double dose of the first vibration with two 1-ruled letters in the beginning of their name.

Although mathematically the zero in the tenth letter adds up to nothing, in numerology, the zero means "assistance from God." The influence of a zero can mean everything happening all at once (all hell breaking loose), or nothing happening at all (hearing crickets). Consequently, the J-named person seems to either have a lot going on, or nothing much going on at all! Most of us know someone with a name beginning with J who doesn't seem to have anything going on in their life—or too much going on all at once. Even months of the year that begin with J (January, June, and July), are all or nothing months for some businesses and many people.

The letter A, ruled by 1, means beginnings; the letter J, ruled by 10, means beginnings with assistance from God. So these individuals often receive assistance from God at just the right moment. God tends not to be very far away from the J-named.

Speaking of God, in the Bible there are many J names. Jehovah, Jesus, Joseph, John, James, Judas, Joel, Job, Jacob, Joshah, Jeremiah, Jesse, Jonah, Jonathan, Johanan, Joah, and Joanna are only some of the J names found in the Bible. The Bible also refers to cities where important biblical events took place that began with the letter J, such as Jerusalem, Judah, Jordan, and Jericho.

Those whose names begin with J often choose to be single. J shares the need to be independent along with the letters A and S. It's no wonder Jesus Christ chose to stay single with three letters in his name ruled by the independent number 1. Jesus also had a freedom-loving E for his first vowel. E first vowels like to change the existing order of things. His first two letters added up to a hidden 6, the "counselor and healer." Also 6 is magnetic, which explains why so many were drawn to him. With both an intensity number 1 in his name and the assistance of God, he began the Christian movement as we know it today. Jesus ushered in the age of Pisces, the fish, which rules Christianity. Even today the fish symbolizes Christian faith. J names are leaders; they're bold and courageous, similar to the letter A. It's also worth mentioning that his name summed up to an 11 power number, since 11 is one of the master numbers. Many referred to him as "Master." His accomplishments were great for such a short time on earth. He definitely was and still is a master teacher.

J-named individuals want to improve the lives of others. They are clever, bright as a penny, and as a rule very talented. However, they might need a little push in the motivation department. Sometimes they suffer from "procrastinitis." Some J names need "assistance from God" to help motivate them off the recliner.

J names want to please others. Many are amazingly keen with electronics and machinery. They often amaze others with their talents and abilities. All 1 vibration letters must learn to stand on their own two feet and not lean on others too much. If they are trying to be independent, then they are on the right path. Encourage their independence and they'll come back to you, happy.

Although Jodie Foster's birth name is Alicia, J and A are both ruled by the number 1, giving her that independent, bold, and courageous personality. Both her names have influenced her. Alicia has two letters ruled by the number 3: L and C. The intensity 3 in her birth name gives her the ability to master the art of communication. In fact, it's been said she speaks flawless French. With the name Jodie, her heart's desire letter is the loving, nurturing letter O. She's magnetic and has to have someone to love. Yet the J and E make her crave independence and freedom. She needs to be on her own, yet she has to be responsible for others to make herself happy. What a dilemma. The duty-bound O in Jodie makes her self-sacrificing and responsible. She sacrificed her childhood to take care of her family. Her ability to memorize scripts at an early age landed her first in commercials, then in movies. Her paychecks put food on the table for her and her family. The O and D are businesslike. The I helps to bless her in some ways. Jodie adds up to a 7 power number, which is why she looks so good on the silver screen. The J and O add up to a hidden 7, so if she doesn't like someone they know it. She either likes a person or not—there's no gray area with her. She can act, but pretending in real life is a different story for a 7 power number.

What about the nickname Jack for John? The late great President John F. Kennedy's nickname while growing up was Jack. Both names numerologically fit his personality. The C in Jack is a youthful letter; it's Gemini-like. In fact, his astrological sign was Gemini. The K can be a bit high-strung and sickly. History shows he was a sickly child. Jack has a power number 7. With the I-ruled J and A this name is very intelligent. John has a power number 20, reflected in his years in the presidency as partnership with assistance from God. The number 20 is sensitive, dynamic, and social, just as he was.

Another independent J name who received assistance from God was Joan of Arc. At the young age of sixteen she led an army of men to free her beloved country, France. It was thought she was guided by angels or spirits. She had a hidden 7 in the beginning of her name which is the number for faith. Unfortunately her name adds up to a power number 13 which, as we all know, can be unlucky. That "cursed" number may have been her downfall.

Some other famous J names are: Jason Robards, John Travolta, Julia Roberts, Jim Carrey, Jane Fonda, James Earl Jones, Jennifer Lopez, Jessica Simpson, Johnny Depp, Jamie Lee Curtis, James Taylor, Justin Timberlake, Jennifer Aniston, John Mayer, Jerry Seinfeld, Jason Alexander, Julia Louis-Dreyfus, Jackie Chan, Jessica Lange, Jackson Browne, Jesse James, Jimi Hendrix, Janet Jackson, Jessica Walter, John Stamos, Jennifer Garner, Jack Nicholson, Jessica Biel, and Jacqueline Bouvier Kennedy.

QUICK REFERENCE OF "J" NAMES

Jacinda, 6: Quick to service. Pioneer and risk taker. Self-expressive, cheerful. Blessed in some ways. Original and unconventional. Reliable, responsible. Bold, courageous, a bit stubborn.

Jacinta, 22: Improves the lives of others. Ambitious leader, great vision. Inspiring, creative. Blessed in some ways. Original and unconventional. Dynamic, busy lifestyle. Bold, courageous, a bit stubborn.

Jack, 7: For truth and justice. Not easily influenced. Optimistic, outspoken. Strong desire to succeed.

Jackee, 8: Accepts responsibility. Resolute and purposeful. Self-expressive, cheerful. Has a powerful presence. A free spirit, very adaptable. Loves adventure and excitement.

Jackie, 3: Cheerful and sincere. Aims to please. Youthful, outspoken. Enthusiastic, quick:witted. Blessed in some ways. A free spirit, very adaptable.

Jackson, 10: Extremely talented. Independent, critical of self and others. Optimistic, outspoken. Strong desire to succeed. Charismatic leader. Magnetic personality. Original and romantic.

Jacob, 4: Honest and reliable. Natural teaching ability. Self-expressive, cheerful. Natural counselor and healer. Friendly, but shy.

Jacqueline, 7: For truth and justice. Not easily influenced. Sees the irony in situations. Attracts wealth. Attractive and charming. A free spirit, very adaptable. Strong verbal skills. Blessed in some ways. Original and unconventional. Loves adventure and excitement.

Jacques, 22: Improves the lives of others. Ambitious leader, great vision. Self-expressive, cheerful. Attracts wealth. Youthful, appealing. A free spirit, very adaptable. Impulsive and extreme.

Jacqui, 7: For truth and justice. Not easily influenced. Sees the irony in situations. Attracts wealth. Attractive and charming. Blessed in some ways.

Jade, 11: Improves the lives of others. Intuitive, perceptive. Reliable, responsible. A free spirit, very adaptable.

Jaden, 7: For truth and justice. Not easily influenced. Systematic, organized. Physical, passionate. Creative, opinionated.

Jag, 9: Generous and helpful. Hardworking, sincere. Scientific and philosophical.

Jagger, 30: Cheerful and sincere. Aims to please. Scientific and philosophical. Extremely intelligent. A free spirit, very adaptable. Gentle, kind, a hard worker.

Jaime, 20: Wants to please everyone. Reads people easily. Emotional, considerate. Domestic, hardworking. A free spirit, very adaptable.

Jaimi, 6: Quick to service. Pioneer and risk taker. Blessed in some ways. Domestic, hardworking. Artistic, having good taste.

Jairo, 8: Accepts responsibility. Resolute and purposeful. Generous in a practical way. Intense inner power. Natural counselor and healer.

Jakeem, 9: Generous and helpful. Hardworking, sincere. Sees the big picture. A free spirit, very adaptable. Loves adventure and excitement. Domestic and practical.

Jakob, 3: Cheerful and sincere. Aims to please. Strong desire to succeed. Natural counselor and healer. Friendly, but shy.

Jalil, 8: Accepts responsibility. Resolute and purposeful. Communicates skillfully. Blessed in some ways. Frequent traveler.

Jamal, 10: Extremely talented. Independent, critical of self and others. Systematic, organized. Bold, courageous, a bit stubborn. Strong verbal skills.

Jamar, 7: For truth and justice. Not easily influenced. Systematic, organized. Gentle, kind, a hard worker.

James, 3: Cheerful and sincere. Aims to please. Systematic, organized. A free spirit, very adaptable. Charming and devoted.

Jami, 6: Quick to service. Pioneer and risk taker. Domestic and hardworking. Blessed in some ways.

Jamie, 20: Wants to please everyone. Reads people easily. Domestic and hardworking. Blessed in some ways. A free spirit, very adaptable.

Jamil, 9: Generous, helpful, and sincere. Domestic and hardworking. Blessed in some ways. Strong verbal skills.

Jan, 7: For truth and justice. Not easily influenced. Original and unconventional.

Janae, 4: Honest and reliable. Natural teaching ability. Unconventional, opinionated. Independent, critical of self and others. A free spirit, very adaptable.

Jane, 3: Cheerful and sincere. Aims to please. Romantic, sensual. Loves adventure and excitement.

Janel, 6: Quick to service. Pioneer and risk taker. Puts the needs of others first. A step ahead of others. Communicates skillfully.

Janessa, 6: Quick to service. Pioneer and risk taker. Original and unconventional. A step ahead of others. Charming and devoted. Intense and extreme. Bold, courageous, a bit stubborn.

Janet, 5: Has a clever mind. Bright, adventuresome. Creative, opinionated. Physical and passionate. Dynamic, busy lifestyle.

Janette, 3: Cheerful and sincere. Aims to please. Original and unconventional. A free spirit, very adaptable. Dynamic, busy lifestyle. Sensitive and easily hurt. Loves adventure and excitement.

Janeva, 8: Accepts responsibility. Resolute and purposeful. Romantic, sensual. A free spirit, very adaptable. Intuitive and inspired. Bold, courageous, a bit stubborn.

Janice, 6: Quick to service. Pioneer and risk taker. Creative, opinionated. Artistic, having good taste. Self-expressive, cheerful. A free spirit, very adaptable.

Janie, 3: Cheerful and sincere. Aims to please. Original and unconventional. Blessed in some ways. Physical and passionate.

Janine, 8: Accepts responsibility. Resolute and purposeful. Original and unconventional. Blessed in some ways. Romantic and sensual. A free spirit, very adaptable.

Jared, 20: Wants to please everyone. Reads people easily. Gentle, kind, a hard worker. A free spirit, very adaptable. Reliable, responsible.

Jarell, 22: Improves the lives of others. Ambitious leader, great vision. Diligent, hardworking. A free spirit, very adaptable. Strong verbal skills. Frequent traveler.

Jarrell, 4: Honest and reliable. Natural teaching ability. Diligent, hardworking. Tendency to lose items. A free spirit, very adaptable. Strong verbal skills. Frequent traveler.

Jarvis, 7: For truth and justice. Not easily influenced. Gentle, kind, a hard worker. Intuitive and inspired. Blessed in some ways. Charming and devoted.

Jasmin, 3: Cheerful and sincere. Aims to please. Charming and devoted. Domestic and hardworking. Blessed in some ways. Original and unconventional.

Jasmina, 22: Improves the lives of others. Ambitious leader, great vision. Charming and devoted. Domestic and hardworking. Blessed in some ways. Original and unconventional. Bold, courageous, a bit stubborn.

Jasmine, 8: Accepts responsibility. Resolute and purposeful. Passionate and loving. Domestic and hardworking. Blessed in some ways. Original and unconventional. A free spirit, very adaptable.

Jason, 5: Has a clever mind. Bright, adventuresome. Very charismatic. Natural counselor and healer. Original and unconventional.

Jasper, 6: Quick to service. Pioneer and risk taker. Charming and devoted. Intelligent and knowledgeable. A free spirit, very adaptable. Gentle, kind, a hard worker.

Javier, 11: Improves the lives of others. Intuitive, perceptive, and inspired. Blessed in some ways. A free spirit, very adaptable. Gentle, kind, a hard worker.

Javon, 8: Accepts responsibility. Resolute and purposeful. Intuitive and inspired. Natural counselor and healer. Original and unconventional.

Javonne, 9: Generous and helpful. Hardworking, sincere. Intuitive and inspired. Natural counselor and healer. Original and unconventional. Romantic, sensual. A free spirit, very adaptable.

Jax, 10: Extremely talented. Independent, critical of self and others. Artistic, sensual, and perceptive.

Jay, 9: Generous and helpful. Hardworking, sincere. Needs a lot of freedom.

Jayme, 9: Generous, helpful, and sincere. Dislikes restrictions. Domestic, hardworking. Loves adventure and excitement.

Jayne, 10: Extremely talented. Independent, critical of self and others. Needs a lot of freedom. Original and unconventional. Loves adventure and excitement.

Jazztine, 3: Cheerful and sincere. Aims to please. Uses common sense. Impatient and stubborn. Dynamic, busy lifestyle. Blessed in some ways. Original and unconventional. A free spirit, very adaptable.

Jean, 3: Cheerful and sincere. Aims to please. Pioneer and risk taker. Original and unconventional.

Jeane, 8: Accepts responsibility. Original and creative. Resolute and purposeful. Opinionated and unconventional. Physical and passionate.

Jeanette, 8: Accepts responsibility. Original, creative and unconventional. Resolute and purposeful. Physical and passionate. Dynamic, busy lifestyle. Sensitive and easily hurt. A free spirit, very adaptable.

Jeanne, 22: Improves the lives of others. Has big plans and ideas. Ambitious leader, great vision. Unconventional and original. Romantic, sensual. Needs change and variety.

Jeannine, 9: Generous and helpful. Enjoys giving gifts. Hardworking and sincere. Original and unconventional. Romantic, sensual. Blessed in some ways. Creative, opinionated. Tendency to overindulge.

Jeb, 8: Accepts responsibility. Original and creative. Friendly, but shy.

Jed, 10: Extremely talented. Likes change and variety. Workaholic, shrewd, and determined.

Jedediah, 10: Extremely talented. Likes change and variety. Systematic, organized. Loves adventure and excitement. Down-to-earth, faithful. Blessed in some ways. Independent, critical of self and others. Great judge of character.

Jedidiah, 5: Has a clever mind. Physical and passionate. Reliable, responsible. Blessed in some ways. Down-to-earth, faithful. Artistic, having good taste. Independent, critical of self and others. Great judge of character.

Jeff, 9: Generous and helpful. Enjoys giving gifts. Self-sacrificing, loving. Easygoing nature.

Jefferson, 8: Accepts responsibility. Original, creative, and unconventional. Self-sacrificing, loving. Likes competition. Physical and passionate. Gentle, kind, a hard worker. Charming and devoted. Natural counselor and healer.

Jeffrey, 3: Cheerful and sincere. A free spirit, very adaptable. Self-sacrificing, loving. Great with plants, kids, and animals. Gentle, kind, a hard worker. Loves adventure and excitement. Dislikes limitations.

Jelani, 6: Quick to service. A step ahead of others. Strong verbal skills. Independent, critical of self and others. Original and unconventional. Blessed in some ways.

Jem, 10: Extremely talented. Likes variety and change. Systematic, organized.

Jemima, 6: Quick to service. A step ahead of others. Domestic, hardworking. Blessed in some ways. Systematic, organized. Independent, critical of self and others.

Jemimah, 5: Has a clever mind. Physical and passionate. Domestic, hardworking. Blessed in some ways. Systematic, organized. Independent, critical of self and others. Great judge of character.

Jen, 11: Improves the lives of others. Keenly perceptive. Creative, opinionated.

Jeneesa, 5: Has a clever mind. A free spirit, very adaptable. Original and unconventional. Loves adventure and excitement. Physical and passionate. Charming and devoted. Independent, critical of self and others.

Jeni, 20: Wants to please everyone. A free spirit, very adaptable. Original and unconventional. Blessed in some ways.

Jenna, 8: Accepts responsibility. Original and creative. Opinionated and unconventional. Romantic, sensual. Independent, critical of self and others.

Jennie, 30: Cheerful and sincere. A free spirit, very adaptable. Original and unconventional. Romantic, sensual. Blessed in some ways. Loves adventure and excitement.

Jennifer, 9: Generous and helpful. A true humanitarian. Original and unconventional. Romantic, sensual. Blessed in some ways. Self-sacrificing, loving. Loves adventure and excitement. Gentle, kind, a hard worker.

Jenny, 5: Has a clever mind. Physical and passionate. Original and unconventional. Creative, opinionated. Needs a lot of freedom.

Jeong:hee, 6: Quick to service. A step ahead of others. Natural counselor and healer. Original and unconventional. Scientific and philosophical. Great judge of character. Tendency to overindulge. Loves adventure and excitement.

Jeraldine, 6: Quick to service. A step ahead of others. Intense inner power. Independent, critical of self and others. Strong verbal skills. Reliable, responsible. Blessed in some ways. Original and unconventional. Loves adventure and excitement.

Jeralyn, 4: Honest and reliable. Accesses quickly. Gentle, kind, a hard worker. Independent, critical of self and others. Strong verbal skills. Dislikes limitations. Original and unconventional.

Jerelyn, 8: Accepts responsibility. Physical and passionate. Intense inner power. Loves adventure and excitement. Strong verbal skills. Dislikes limitations. Original and unconventional.

Jeremiah, 6: Quick to service. A step ahead of others. Intense inner power. Loves adventure and excitement. Systematic, organized. Blessed in some ways. Independent, critical of self and others. Great judge of character.

Jeremy, 4: Honest and reliable. Accesses quickly. Healthy, strong. Loves adventure and excitement. Systematic, organized. Dislikes limitations.

Jeri, 6: Quick to service. A step ahead of others. Gentle, kind, a hard worker. Artistic, having good taste.

Jerilyn, 3: Cheerful and sincere. A free spirit, very adaptable. Kind and considerate. Blessed in some ways. Strong verbal skills. Dislikes limitations. Original and unconventional.

Jerina, 30: Cheerful and sincere. Likes change and variety. Intense inner power. Artistic, having good taste. Romantic and opinionated. Independent, self-motivated.

Jermaine, 3: Cheerful and sincere. A free spirit, very adaptable. Gentle, kind, a hard worker. Systematic, organized. Independent, critical of self and others. Blessed in some ways. Original and unconventional. Loves adventure and excitement.

Jermyn, 6: Quick to service. A step ahead of others. Gentle, kind, a hard worker. Systematic, organized. Dislikes limitations. Original and unconventional.

Jerold, 10: Extremely talented. Likes change and variety. Gentle, kind, a hard worker. Natural counselor and healer. Strong verbal skills. Reliable, responsible.

Jerome, 30: Cheerful and sincere. A free spirit, very adaptable. Gentle, kind, a hard worker. Natural counselor and healer. Systematic, organized. Loves adventure and excitement.

Jerrell, 8: Accepts responsibility. Original and creative. Intense inner power. Diligent, helpful. Loves adventure and excitement. Strong verbal skills. Financial ups and downs.

Jerri, 6: Quick to service. A step ahead of others. Gentle, kind, a hard worker. Diligent, helpful. Blessed in some ways.

Jerrick, 11: Improves the lives of others. Keenly perceptive. Gentle, kind, a hard worker. Tendency to lose items. Blessed in some ways. Self-expressive, cheerful. Strong desire to succeed.

Jerrie, 11: Improves the lives of others. Keenly perceptive. Gentle, kind, a hard worker. Tendency to lose items. Blessed in some ways. Loves adventure and excitement.

Jerrold, 10: Extremely talented. Likes change and variety. Gentle, kind, a hard worker. Diligent, helpful. Natural counselor and healer. Strong verbal skills. Reliable, responsible.

Jerry, 4: Honest and reliable. Accesses quickly. Gentle, kind, a hard worker. Tendency to lose items. Dislikes limitations.

Jervis, 11: Improves the lives of others. Keenly perceptive. Gentle, kind, a hard worker. Intuitive and inspired. Blessed in some ways. Charming and devoted.

Jess, 8: Accepts responsibility. Original and creative. Very charismatic. Intense and extreme.

Jessa, 9: Generous and helpful. Enjoys giving gifts. Charming and devoted. Intense and extreme. Independent, critical of self and others.

Jesse, 4: Honest and reliable. Accesses quickly. Charming and devoted. Intense and extreme. Loves adventure and excitement.

Jessenia, 10: Extremely talented. Likes change and variety. Needs to be independent. Intense and extreme. Loves adventure and excitement. Original and unconventional. Blessed in some ways. Critical of self and others.

Jessica, 3: Cheerful, sincere, and self-expressive. A free spirit, very adaptable. Charming and devoted. Intense and extreme. Blessed in some ways. Independent, critical of self and others.

Jessie, 22: Improves the lives of others. Keenly perceptive. Very charismatic. Intense and extreme. Blessed in some ways. Loves adventure and excitement.

Jessyca, 10: Extremely talented. Likes change and variety. Needs to be independent. Intense and extreme. Dislikes limitations. Self-expressive, cheerful. Critical of self and others.

Jesus, 11: Improves the lives of others. Intuitive, perceptive. Charming and devoted. Creative and inspiring. Intense and extreme.

Jethro, 4: Honest and reliable. Accesses quickly. Dynamic, busy lifestyle. Great judge of character. Gentle, kind, a hard worker. Natural counselor and healer.

Jevon, 3: Cheerful and sincere. A free spirit, very adaptable. Intuitive and inspired. Natural counselor and healer. Original and unconventional.

Jewel, 10: Extremely talented. Needs change and variety. Likes to meet new people. Loves adventure and excitement. Communicates skillfully.

Jezebel, 11: Improves the lives of others. Keenly perceptive. Able to achieve greatness. Physical and passionate. Good business partner. A free spirit, very adaptable. Strong verbal skills.

Jhamal, 9: Generous and helpful. Great judge of character. Independent, critical of self and others. Domestic, hardworking. Bold, courageous, a bit stubborn. Strong verbal skills.

Jill, 7: Scientific aptitude. Blessed in some ways. Communicates skillfully. Slow to make decisions.

Jillian, 4: Sincere and reliable. Natural teacher. Strong verbal skills. Slow to make decisions. Artistic, having good taste. Independent, critical of self and others. Original and unconventional.

Jim, 5: Has a clever mind. Blessed in some ways. Systematic, organized.

Jimbo, 22: Improves the lives of others. Idealistic, humanitarian. Domestic, hardworking. Friendly, but shy. Natural counselor and healer.

Jimi, 5: Has a clever mind. Blessed in some ways. Creative entrepreneur. Artistic, having good taste.

Jimmy, 7: For truth and justice. Spiritually motivated. Domestic, hardworking. Desires financial security. Needs a lot of freedom.

Jina, 7: For truth and justice. Spiritually motivated. Original and unconventional. Independent, critical of self and others.

Jo, 7: For truth and justice. Natural counselor and healer. Must have faith to be happy.

Joachim, 5: Has a clever mind. Versatile in service. Independent, critical of self and others. Self-expressive, cheerful. Great judge of character. Blessed in some ways. Domestic, hardworking.

Joan, 4: Sincere and reliable. Nurturing, loving. Natural teaching ability. Creative and opinionated.

Joann, 9: Generous and helpful. Creates group harmony. Hardworking, sincere. Creative and romantic. Unassuming, naive.

Joanna, 10: Extremely talented. Ambitious and innovative. Independent, critical of self and others. Original and unconventional. Creative, opinionated. Bold, courageous, a bit stubborn.

Joanne, 5: Has a clever mind. Versatile in service. Bold, adventure-some. Original and unconventional. Creative, opinionated. Physical and passionate.

Job, 9: Generous and helpful. Creates group harmony. Friendly, but shy.

Joby, 7: For truth and justice. Natural counselor and healer. Friendly, but shy. Needs a lot of freedom.

Jocelyn, 3: Cheerful, sincere, and self-expressive. Has creative solutions. A free spirit, very adaptable. Strong verbal skills. Dislikes limitations. Original and unconventional.

Jodi, 20: Wants to please everyone. Natural counselor and healer. Reliable, responsible. Blessed in some ways.

Jodie, 7: For truth and justice. Open to opportunities. Domestic, responsible. Blessed in some ways. Loves adventure and excitement.

Jodina, 8: Accepts responsibility. Competitive in business. Systematic, organized. Blessed in some ways. Romantic, sensual. Resolute and purposeful.

Jody, 9: Generous and helpful. Creates group harmony. Reliable, responsible. Needs a lot of freedom.

Joe, 3: Cheerful and sincere. Natural counselor and healer. A free spirit, very adaptable.

Joel, 6: Quick to service. Assumes responsibility. A free spirit, very adaptable. Strong verbal skills.

Joella, 10: Extremely talented. Ambitious, innovative. A free spirit, very adaptable. Strong verbal skills. Financial ups and downs. Independent, critical of self and others.

Joelle, 5: Has a clever mind. Natural counselor and healer. A free spirit, very adaptable. Strong verbal skills. Financial ups and downs. Physical and passionate.

Joely, 22: Improves the lives of others. Respects rules. Likes to entertain. Frequent traveler. Needs a lot of freedom.

Joey, 10: Extremely talented. Ambitious, innovative. A free spirit, very adaptable. Dislikes limitations.

Johan, 3: Cheerful and sincere. Natural counselor and healer. Great judge of character. Independent, critical of self and others. Original and unconventional.

Johann, 8: Accepts responsibility. Competitive in business. Self-reliant, successful. Resolute and purposeful. Original and unconventional. Romantic, sensual.

Johanna, 9: Generous and helpful. Creates group harmony. Great judge of character. Independent, critical of self and others. Original and unconventional. Romantic, sensual. Bold, courageous, a bit stubborn.

Johannes, 5: Has a clever mind. Versatile in service. Great judge of character. Independent, critical of self and others. Original, unconventional. Creative, opinionated. Physical, passionate. Charming and devoted.

John, 20: Wants to please everyone. Natural counselor and healer. Great judge of character. Original and unconventional.

Johnny, 5: Has a clever mind. Versatile in service. Great judge of character. Original and unconventional. Creative and opinionated. Needs a lot of freedom.

Jolie, 6: Quick to service. Nurturing, loving. Strong verbal skills. Blessed in some ways. A free spirit, very adaptable.

Jomana, 9: Generous, helpful, and sincere. Creates group harmony. Domestic, hardworking. Independent, critical of self and others. Creative, original.

Jomei, 7: For truth and justice. Open to opportunities. Domestic, hardworking. A free spirit, very adaptable. Blessed in some ways.

Jon, 3: Cheerful and sincere. Natural counselor and healer. Romantic, opinionated.

Jonah, 3: Cheerful and sincere. Natural counselor and healer. Romantic, opinionated. Independent, critical of self and others. Great judge of character.

Jonas, 5: Has a clever mind. Versatile in service. Original and unconventional. Independent, critical of self and others. Charming and devoted.

Jonathan, 11: Improves the lives of others. Creates group harmony. Original and unconventional. Intuitive, perceptive. Dynamic, busy lifestyle. Great judge of character. Bold, courageous, a bit stubborn. Romantic, sensual.

Jonathon, 7: Clever and talented. Open to opportunities. Original and unconventional. Not easily influenced. Dynamic, busy lifestyle. Great judge of character. Natural counselor and healer. Romantic, sensual.

Jonette, 8: Accepts responsibility. Competitive in business. Original, opinionated. Physical and passionate. Dynamic, busy lifestyle. Natural mediator. A free spirit, very adaptable.

Jordan, 8: Accepts responsibility, reliable. Competitive in business. Intense inner power. Independent, critical of self and others. Original and unconventional.

Jordana, 9: Generous and helpful. Creates group harmony. Gentle, kind, a hard worker. Reliable, responsible. Independent, critical of self and others. Original and unconventional. Bold, courageous, a bit stubborn.

Jordy, 9: Generous and helpful. Creates group harmony. Gentle, kind, a hard worker. Reliable, responsible. Needs a lot of freedom.

Jorge, 10: Extremely talented. Ambitious, innovative. Diligent, hardworking. Scientific and philosophical. A free spirit, very adaptable.

Jose, 4: Honest and reliable. Natural counselor and healer. Charming and devoted. A free spirit, very adaptable.

Joseph, 10: Extremely talented. Ambitious, innovative. Charming and devoted. A free spirit, very adaptable. Intelligent and knowledgeable. Great judge of character.

Josephine, 11: Improves the lives of others. Natural counselor and healer. Very charismatic. A free spirit, very adaptable. Intelligent and knowledgeable. Great judge of character. Blessed in some ways. Original and unconventional. Loves adventure and excitement.

Joshua, 20: Wants to please everyone. Natural counselor and healer. Charming and devoted. Great judge of character. Creative, intuitive. Independent, critical of self and others.

Josiah, 8: Accepts responsibility. Competitive in business. Loving and devoted. Blessed in some ways. Independent, critical of self and others. Great judge of character.

Josie, 22: Improves the lives of others. Creates group harmony. Very charismatic. Blessed in some ways. A free spirit, very adaptable.

Jova, 3: Cheerful and sincere. Natural counselor and healer. Intuitive and inspired. Independent, critical of self and others.

Jovani, 8: Accepts responsibility. Competitive in business. Intuitive and inspired. Resolute and purposeful. Romantic, sensual. Blessed in some ways.

Joy, 5: Has a clever mind. Natural counselor and healer. Needs a lot of freedom.

Joyce, 22: Improves the lives of others. Creates group harmony. Needs a lot of freedom. Self-expressive, cheerful. Loves adventure and excitement.

Joyita, 8: Accepts responsibility. Competitive in business. Needs a lot of freedom. Blessed in some ways. Dynamic, busy lifestyle. Independent, critical of self and others.

Juan, 10: Extremely talented. Optimistic, outgoing. Independent, critical of self and others. Original and unconventional.

Juana, 11: Improves the lives of others. Creative and inspiring. Independent, critical of self and others. Original and unconventional. Intuitive, perceptive.

Juanita, 22: Improves the lives of others. Creative and inspiring. Independent, critical of self and others. Original and unconventional. Blessed in some ways. Dynamic, busy lifestyle. Bold, courageous, a bit stubborn.

Juanito, 9: Generous and helpful. Attractive and charming. Independent, critical of self and others. Original and unconventional. Blessed in some ways. Dynamic, busy lifestyle. Natural counselor and healer.

Jud, 8: Accepts responsibility. Usually very lucky. Down-to-earth, practical.

Judah, 8: Accepts responsibility. Usually very lucky. Down-to-earth, practical. Resolute and purposeful. Excellent judge of character.

Jude, 4: Honest and reliable. Quickly sizes up situations. Systematic, organized. A free spirit, very adaptable.

Judi, 8: Accepts responsibility. Usually very lucky. Down-to-earth, practical. Blessed in some ways.

Judith, 9: Generous and helpful. Attractive and charming. Reliable, responsible. Blessed in some ways. Dynamic, busy lifestyle. Great judge of character.

Judy, 6: Quick to service. Attractive and charming. Reliable, responsible. Needs a lot of freedom.

Juelz, 20: Wants to please everyone. Attractive and charming. Physical and passionate. Communicates skillfully. An excellent mediator.

Jules, 4: Honest and reliable. Quickly sizes up situations. Strong verbal skills. A free spirit, very adaptable. Intense and extreme.

Juli, 7: For truth and justice. Stylish and refined. Communicates skillfully. Needs alone time.

Julia, 8: Accepts responsibility. Attractive and charming. Doesn't mince words. Blessed in some ways. Independent, critical of self and others.

Julian, 22: Improves the lives of others. Creative and inspiring. Strong verbal skills. Idealistic, humanitarian. Independent, critical of self and others. Original and unconventional.

Julie, 3: Cheerful and sincere. Attractive and charming. Communicates skillfully. Blessed in some ways. A free spirit, very adaptable.

Juliet, 5: Has a clever mind. Fun, flirtatious. Strong verbal skills. Generous, thoughtful. A free spirit, very adaptable. Dynamic, busy lifestyle.

Julieta, 6: Quick to service. Attractive and charming. Strong verbal skills. Blessed in some ways. A free spirit, very adaptable. Dynamic, busy lifestyle. Independent, critical of self and others.

Juliette, 30: Cheerful and sincere. Youthful, appealing. Strong verbal skills. Blessed in some ways. A free spirit, very adaptable. Dynamic, busy lifestyle. Sensitive, easily hurt. Loves adventure and excitement.

Julio, 22: Improves the lives of others. Creative and inspiring. Strong verbal skills. Blessed in some ways. Natural counselor and healer.

Julius, 20:Wants to please everyone. Attractive and charming. Strong verbal skills. Blessed in some ways. Creative, intuitive. Intense and extreme.

Jun, 9: Generous and helpful. Attractive and charming. Original and unconventional.

Juna, 10: Extremely talented. Attractive and charming. Original and unconventional. Independent, critical of self and others.

June, 5: Has a clever mind. Great social skills. Creative and opinionated. A free spirit, very adaptable.

Junie, 5: Has a clever mind. Great social skills. Creative and opinionated. Blessed in some ways. A free spirit, very adaptable.

Juno, 6: Quick to service. Attractive and charming. Original and unconventional. Natural counselor and healer.

Justin, 3: Cheerful and sincere. Youthful, appealing. Intense and extreme. Dynamic, busy lifestyle. Blessed in some ways. Original and unconventional.

Justina, 22: Improves the lives of others. Creative and inspiring. Intense and extreme. Dynamic, busy lifestyle. Blessed in some ways. Original and unconventional. Independent, critical of self and others.

Justine, 8: Accepts responsibility. Attractive and charming. Intense and extreme. Dynamic, busy lifestyle. Blessed in some ways. Original and unconventional. A free spirit, very adaptable.

Justis, 8: Accepts responsibility. Attractive and charming. Intense and extreme. Dynamic, busy lifestyle. Blessed in some ways. Passionate and loving.

Jynx, 10: Extremely talented. Needs a lot of freedom. Creative, original. Artistic, perceptive, and sensual.

K

If a name begins with K, has more than one K, or ends with a K, this person is highly creative, sensitive, perceptive, and intuitive with a strong desire to succeed.

The letter K is the 11th letter of the alphabet. The number 11 is one of the master numbers (22 is the other). We have only two master numbers in numerology. When a person is born with a letter K anywhere in their name, they are meant to accomplish something worthwhile this lifetime. Those whose names begin with K are special. Maybe we should call them "Special K." We can learn from them. K is the lightning rod of letters. In astrology, the 11th house is ruled by Aquarius. This is the sign of genius and inspiration. K people seem driven toward their goals and aspirations. Occasionally we have the dreamer type, which is very spiritual and idealistic, but never seems to accomplish much of anything. The average K personality can be quite forceful as well as multifaceted. At the very least, they are different. Some are high-strung and exhibit nervous energy. Someone named Kirk will have a double dose of this energy and could be even more driven to succeed in their chosen fields. This letter seems in its element when with friends, groups, organizations, and governmental positions. Some careers tend to fall into the field of electricity and modern technology. These individuals are prone to flashes of inspiration and are quite ingenious and creative.

In numerology we condense numbers down to one digit. Sometimes we add the 11, as 1 + 1 = 2, so this number is co-ruled by the number 2. As a rule, we do not condense 11 to 2. However, when initially adding a name, if there is an 11 we count it as a 2, then we keep adding all the letters until the name condenses to one digit, unless it condenses to an 11 or 22. At any rate, we cannot rule out this 2 energy. Similar to the 2 vibration, the 11 is emotional and partnership-oriented. Most K-named people prefer to be in a partnership, romantic or business, unless their name is Jack or Kasey, with two independent I-ruled letters in the beginning of their names. The average Katie or Kevin make wonderful partners. They will be focused on their goals. Similar to the II, or two Is which means beginning and beginning, the typical K-named person can handle two beginnings—the career and family—quite well.

Since this letter is extremely social or partnership-oriented, it would seem they would put on weight more easily. Often socializing involves food and drink and calories galore. The Ks social siblings, B and T, often struggle with the extra pounds. But, unless the K name has escapist letters in it, often they are a little on the lean side. Perhaps it's because they often run on nervous energy. This is why a good night's sleep and plenty of exercise will keep our special Ks happy and healthy. The II of K is really double Is, so exercise is important to the K-named. Those ruled by I tend to have a bully in their heads. Imagine with double Is, it's a double dose of this bully in the head. Exercise helps the K-named get out of their heads; otherwise they tend to beat themselves up twice as much as our A, J, or S friends do. Their brains seem to get a continual workout, but more often than not, their bodies need a strong push. Exercise can help defuse much of the nervous energy this letter seems to have.

One famous K-named person is American Daytime Emmy Award-winning actress, television personality, and talk show host, Kelly Ripa. Since February 2001, she has served as the cohost of *Live with Regis and Kelly*. Earlier in her career, Ripa acted in television series on ABC. She played Hayley Vaughan Santos on *All My Children* and Faith Fairfield on *Hope and Faith*. Kelly exhibits her strong desire to succeed by holding down many jobs. Not only does she cohost with Regis, but she also does commercials and acts occasionally in movies, all while being an active wife and mother of three. Whew! Good thing her name starts with a K or she might not be able to handle all that! Her ability to make others laugh can be attributed to the double Ls in her name. Also, the Ls give her the gift of gab as they are ruled by the number 3, which governs communication and transportation. She no doubt makes many short trips around town with her busy schedule. With a power number 20, and two Ls in her name, it's no wonder she is so busy. Interestingly enough, she's a Libra which is ruled by the partnership-oriented number 2. K is co-ruled by 2; it's social as well as partnership-oriented, just like a Libra.

Singer, songwriter, and guitarist Kenny Loggins achieved fame by writing such popular songs as "House at Pooh Corner" and "Celebrate Me Home." His cheerful, sensitive style in the late '70s made him the king of movie soundtracks with hit songs in *Caddyshack, Footloose,* and *Top Gun.* This famous K-named person was especially creative with an E first vowel and two Ns, giving him an intensity number 5 and power number 6. Kenny is a freedom-loving name. Not only does he have all that 5 vibration urging him to be free, but the Y at the end of his name makes him dislike restrictions. His 6 power number helps him on the business aspect of his musical career. Those with 6 power numbers like to be their own boss. It is ultimately the K in the beginning of his name that opened doors with friends, groups, and organizations. This letter is sensitive, unusual, and finely tuned.

Another musically talented individual with the same name is Kenny Gorelick, better known as Kenny G. This musician is slightly controversial, not uncommon with a 5 intensity number. He's known as the musician jazz listeners love to hate, annoying jazz purists with his "smooth jazz" and "crossover jazz" style. He's a phenomenally successful instrumentalist whose recordings made the pop charts in the '80s and '90s. Kenny puts a lot of emotion in his solos. His music reflects the sensitive emotional side of his K first letter. Both Kenny G and Kenny Loggins exhibit their musical talents through socially acceptable modes of expression. Both performers are sensitive, emotional, and personal in their delivery. This letter leaves an impression that doesn't go away. Furthermore, with a 6 power number, both Kennys tend to have a magnetic quality about them.

Notice the list of K names is shorter than most. This letter is for those who must accomplish something worthwhile. K names are unusual, uncommon, and only meant for those with a master lesson to achieve excellence during their short time on earth. Those born with this letter are unique and have a special mission in life. They are our "special Ks."

More famous people with K first names are: Karl Strauss, Kiefer Sutherland, Kate Beckinsale, Kelsey Grammer, Kermit the Frog, Kate Hudson, Kim Basinger, Kevin Bacon, Keira Knightley, Keanu Reeves, Katharine Hepburn, Kirstie Alley, Kevin Spacey, Kobe Bryant, Kurt Russell, Kelly Clarkson, Kirk Douglas, Kris Kristofferson, Kevin Costner, Kathleen Quinlan, Kenny Rogers, Kanye West, and Kirsten Dunst.

QUICK REFERENCE OF "K" NAMES

Kacey, 9: Sees the big picture. Hardworking and sincere. Self-expressive, cheerful. Loves adventure and excitement. Needs a lot of freedom.

Kacie, 20: Sensitive and diplomatic. Reads people easily. Self-expressive, cheerful. Blessed in some ways. A free spirit, very adaptable.

Kadeem, 3: Enthusiastic and quick-witted. Aims to please. Reliable, responsible. A free spirit, very adaptable. Loves adventure and excitement. Domestic, hardworking.

Kahlil, 8: Has a powerful presence. Resolute and purposeful. Great judge of character. Good verbal skills. Blessed in some ways. Frequent traveler.

Kai, 3: Enthusiastic and quick-witted. Aims to please. Blessed in some ways.

Kalee, 7: Multifaceted and disciplined. Not easily influenced. Frequent traveler. A free spirit, very adaptable. Loves adventure and excitement.

Kaleena, 22: Strong desire to succeed. Ambitious leader, great vision. Communicates skillfully. A free spirit, very adaptable. Physical and passionate. Original and unconventional. Bold, courageous, a bit stubborn.

Kalei, 20: Sensitive and diplomatic. Reads people easily. Communicates skillfully. A free spirit, very adaptable. Blessed in some ways.

Kalil, 9: Sees the big picture. Hardworking and sincere. Strong verbal skills. Blessed in some ways. Frequent traveler.

Kalina, 3: Enthusiastic and quick-witted. Aims to please. Communicates skillfully. Blessed in some ways. Original and unconventional. Bold, courageous, a bit stubborn.

Kalinda, 7: Multifaceted and disciplined. Not easily influenced. Frequent traveler. Blessed in some ways. Original and unconventional. Reliable, responsible. Bold, courageous, a bit stubborn.

Kalli, 9: Empathetic, sees the big picture. Hardworking and sincere. Strong verbal skills. Frequent traveler. Blessed in some ways.

Kallie, 5: Energetic, forceful. Bright, adventuresome. Communicates skillfully. Frequent traveler. Blessed in some ways. A free spirit, very adaptable.

Kalynn, 5: Energetic, forceful. Bright, adventuresome. Communicates skillfully. Needs a lot of freedom. Original and unconventional. Romantic, sensual.

Kam, 7: Multifaceted and disciplined. Not easily influenced. Domestic, hardworking.

Kamal, 11: Strong desire to succeed. Intuitive, perceptive. Domestic, hardworking. Bold, courageous, a bit stubborn. Good verbal skills.

Kameko, 20:Sensitive and diplomatic. Reads people easily. Domestic, hardworking. A free spirit, very adaptable. Forceful at times. Natural counselor and healer.

Kane, 4: Practical imagination. Natural teaching ability. Original and unconventional. A free spirit, very adaptable.

Kanye, 20: Sensitive and diplomatic. Reads people easily. Needs a lot of freedom. Original and unconventional. Loves adventure and excitement.

Kareem, 8: Has a powerful presence. Resolute and purposeful. Intense inner power. A free spirit, very adaptable. Loves adventure and excitement. Systematic, organized.

Karen, 22: Strong desire to succeed. Ambitious leader, great vision. Gentle, kind, a hard worker. A free spirit, very adaptable. Creative and opinionated.

Kari, 3: Enthusiastic and quick-witted. Aims to please. Sympathetic, kind. Blessed in some ways.

Karim, 7: Multifaceted and disciplined. Not easily influenced. Gentle, kind, a hard worker. Blessed in some ways. Systematic, organized.

Karin, 8: Has a powerful presence. Resolute and purposeful. Intense inner power. Blessed in some ways. Original and unconventional.

Karina, 9: Sees the big picture. Hardworking and sincere. Sympathetic, kind. Artistic, having good taste. Original and unconventional. Bold, courageous, a bit stubborn.

Karis, 22: Strong desire to succeed. Ambitious leader, great vision. Gentle, kind, a hard worker. Blessed in some ways. Charming and devoted.

Karissa, 6: Creatively inspired. Pioneer and risk taker. Gentle, kind, a hard worker. Blessed in some ways. Charming and devoted. Intense and extreme. Bold, courageous, a bit stubborn.

Karl, 6: Creatively inspired. Pioneer and risk taker. Gentle, kind, a hard worker. Communicates skillfully.

Karla, 7: Multifaceted and disciplined. Not easily influenced. Gentle, kind, a hard worker. Strong verbal skills. Bold, courageous, a bit stubborn.

Karmen, 8: Has a powerful presence. Resolute and purposeful. Intense inner power. Systematic, organized. A free spirit, very adaptable. Original and unconventional.

Karol, 3: Enthusiastic and quick-witted. Aims to please. Gentle, kind, hard worker. Natural counselor and healer. Communicates skillfully.

Karolina, 9: Sees the big picture. Hardworking, sincere. Intense inner power. Natural counselor and healer. Strong verbal skills. Blessed in some ways. Original and unconventional. Bold, courageous, a bit stubborn.

Karoline, 4: Practical imagination. Natural teaching ability. Gentle, kind, a hard worker. Nurturing, loving. Strong verbal skills. Blessed in some ways. Original and unconventional. A free spirit, very adaptable.

Karolyn, 6: Creatively inspired. Pioneer and risk taker. Gentle, kind, a hard worker. Natural counselor and healer. Strong verbal skills. Needs a lot of freedom. Original and unconventional.

Karyn, 8: Has a powerful presence. Resolute and purposeful. Intense inner power. Needs a lot of freedom. Original and unconventional.

Kasmira, 9: Sees the big picture. Hardworking, sincere. Loving and devoted. Domestic, helpful. Blessed in some ways. Intense inner power. Bold, courageous, a bit stubborn.

Kaspar, 3: Enthusiastic and quick-witted. Aims to please. Attractive and charming. Levelheaded. Bold, courageous, a bit stubborn. Gentle, kind, a hard worker.

Kasseem, 10: Exercise very beneficial. Independent, critical of self and others. Charming and devoted. Impulsive and extreme. A free spirit, adaptable. Loves adventure and excitement. Domestic and hardworking.

Kassidy, 7: Multifaceted and disciplined. Not easily influenced. Charming and devoted. Impulsive and extreme. Blessed in some ways. Reliable, responsible. Needs a lot of freedom.

Kata, 6: Creatively inspired. Pioneer and risk taker. Dynamic, busy lifestyle. Independent, self-motivated.

Kate, 10: Exercise very beneficial. Independent, critical of self and others. Energetic, highly charged. A free spirit, very adaptable.

Katerina, 7: Multifaceted and disciplined. Not easily influenced. Dynamic, busy lifestyle. A free spirit, very adaptable. Gentle, kind, a hard worker. Artistic, having good taste. Original, unconventional. Bold, courageous, a bit stubborn.

Katharine, 6: Creatively inspired. Pioneer and risk taker. Dynamic, busy lifestyle. Self-reliant, successful. Bold, courageous, a bit stubborn. Diligent, helpful. Artistic, having good taste. Original and unconventional. Physical and passionate.

Katherine, 10: Exercise very beneficial. Independent, critical of self and others. Energetic, highly charged. Great judge of character. A free spirit, very adaptable. Gentle, kind, a hard worker. Blessed in some ways. Original and unconventional. Loves adventure and excitement.

Kathie, 9: Sees the big picture. Hardworking and helpful. Dynamic, busy lifestyle. Original and creative. Artistic, having good taste. Physical and passionate.

Kathleen, 4: Practical imagination. Natural teaching ability. Dynamic, busy lifestyle. Great judge of character. Good verbal skills. A free spirit, very adaptable. Loves adventure and excitement. Original and unconventional.

Kathlene, 4: (Same as Kathleen.)

Kathryn, 7: Multifaceted and disciplined. Not easily influenced. Dynamic, busy lifestyle. Self-reliant, successful. Gentle, kind, a hard worker. Needs a lot of freedom. Original and unconventional.

Kathy, 20: Sensitive and diplomatic. Reads people easily. Energetic, highly charged. Great judge of character. Needs a lot of freedom.

Katrina, 11: Strong desire to succeed. Intuitive, perceptive. Energetic, highly charged. Intense inner power. Artistic, having good taste. Original and unconventional. Bold, courageous, a bit stubborn.

Kay, 10: Exercise very beneficial. Independent, critical of self and others. Needs a lot of freedom.

Kaycee, 5: Energetic, forceful. Bright, adventuresome. Dislikes restrictions. Self-expressive, cheerful. Physical and passionate. A free spirit, very adaptable.

Kayla, 5: Energetic, forceful. Bright, adventuresome. Needs a lot of freedom. Communicates skillfully. Bold, courageous, a bit stubborn.

Kaylynn, 30: Enthusiastic and quick-witted. Aims to please. Needs a lot of freedom. Strong verbal skills. Highly perceptive. Original and unconventional. Romantic, sensual.

Kayne, 20: Sensitive and diplomatic. Reads people easily. Needs a lot of freedom. Original and unconventional. Loves adventure and excitement.

Kazuki, 7: Multifaceted and disciplined. Not easily influenced. Excellent mediator. Attractive and charming. A bit high-strung. Blessed in some ways.

Keane, 9: Sees the big picture. Enjoys giving gifts. Hardworking, sincere. Original and unconventional. Physical and passionate.

Keanu, 7: Multifaceted and disciplined. Perceptive, not easily fooled. Romantic, sensual. Attractive and charming.

Keaton, 3: Enthusiastic and quick-witted. A free spirit, very adaptable. Independent, critical of self and others. Dynamic, busy lifestyle. Natural counselor and healer. Original and unconventional.

Keefe, 5: Energetic, forceful. Physical and passionate. Loves adventure and excitement. Self-sacrificing, loving. Enjoys meeting new people.

Keegan, 7: Multifaceted and disciplined. Not easily fooled. Loves adventure and excitement. Scientific and philosophical. Independent, critical of self and others. Original and unconventional.

Keeley, 9: Sees the big picture. Enjoys giving gifts. Loves adventure and excitement. Communicates skillfully. Physical and passionate. Needs a lot of freedom.

Keely, 22: Strong desire to succeed. Has big plans and ideas. Loves adventure and excitement. Strong verbal skills. Dislikes limitations.

Keenan, 5: Energetic, forceful. Physical and passionate. Enjoys meeting new people. Original and unconventional. Independent, critical of self and others. Creative and opinionated.

Keifer, 9: Sees the big picture. Enjoys giving gifts. Blessed in some ways. Self-sacrificing, loving. Loves adventure and excitement. Gentle, kind, a hard worker.

Keir, 7: Multifaceted and disciplined. Not easily fooled. Blessed in some ways. Gentle, kind, a hard worker.

Keira, 8: Has a powerful presence. Original and creative. Artistic, having good taste. Intense inner power. Resolute and purposeful.

Keisha, 8: Has a powerful presence. Original and creative. Blessed in some ways. Charming and devoted. Great judge of character. Independent, critical of self and others.

Keith, 8: Has a powerful presence. Original and creative. Blessed in some ways. Dynamic, busy lifestyle. Great judge of character.

Kel, 10: Exercise very beneficial. Likes change and variety. Strong verbal skills.

Kelby, 10: Exercise very beneficial. Likes change and variety. Strong verbal skills. Friendly, but shy. Dislikes limitations.

Keli, 10: Exercise very beneficial. Likes change and variety. Frequent traveler. Blessed in some ways.

Keller, 9: Sees the big picture. Enjoys giving gifts. Strong verbal skills. Frequent traveler. Loves adventure and excitement. Gentle, kind, a hard worker.

Kelli, 22: Strong desire to succeed. Has big plans and ideas. Communicates skillfully. Travels frequently. Blessed in some ways.

Kellie, 9: Sees the big picture. Enjoys giving gifts. Strong verbal skills. Frequent traveler. Blessed in some ways. Loves adventure and excitement.

Kelly, 20: Sensitive and diplomatic. Social and entertaining. Communicates skillfully. Travels frequently. Needs a lot of freedom.

Kelsey, 5: Energetic, forceful. Physical and passionate. Communicates skillfully. Charming and devoted. Loves adventure and excitement. Needs a lot of freedom.

Kelsy, 9: Sees the big picture. Enjoys giving gifts. Strong verbal skills. Charming and devoted. Needs a lot of freedom.

Kelvin, 10: Exercise very beneficial. Likes change and variety. Strong verbal skills. Intuitive and inspired. Blessed in some ways. Original and unconventional.

Ken, 3: Enthusiastic and quick-witted. A free spirit, very adaptable. Romantic, opinionated.

Kendall, 5: Energetic, forceful. Physical and passionate. Creative, opinionated. Reliable, responsible. Bright, adventuresome. Communicates skillfully. Frequent traveler.

Kendra, 8: Has a powerful presence. Original and creative. Romantic, opinionated. Systematic, organized. Intense inner power. Resolute and purposeful.

Kendrick, 3: Enthusiastic and quick-witted. A free spirit, very adaptable. Original and unconventional. Reliable, responsible. Gentle, kind, a hard worker. Blessed in some ways. Self-expressive, cheerful. A bit forceful at times.

Kenisha, 4: Practical imagination. Accesses quickly. Creative and original. Blessed in some ways. Charming and devoted. Great judge of character. Natural teaching abilities.

Kenji, 22: Strong desire to succeed. Has big plans and ideas. Romantic, opinionated. Wants to please everyone. Idealistic and humanitarian.

Kenley, 9: Sees the big picture. Enjoys giving gifts. Original and unconventional. Communicates skillfully. Physical and passionate. Needs a lot of freedom.

Kennedy, 6: Creatively inspired. A step ahead of others. Original and unconventional. Romantic, opinionated. Likes change and variety. Natural authority. Needs a lot of freedom.

Kenneth, 5: Energetic, forceful. A free spirit, very adaptable. Creative and opinionated. Romantic, sensual. Loves adventure and excitement. Dynamic, busy lifestyle. Great judge of character.

Kenney, 11: Strong desire to succeed. Physical and passionate. Original and unconventional. Creative, opinionated. Likes change and variety. Needs a lot of freedom.

Kenny, 6: Creatively inspired. A step ahead of others. Opinionated, original. Romantic, sensual. Needs a lot of freedom.

Kenric, 6: Creatively inspired. A step ahead of others. Original and unconventional. Gentle, kind, a hard worker. Blessed in some ways. Self-expressive, cheerful.

Kent, 5: Energetic, forceful. Physical and passionate. Original and unconventional. Dynamic, busy lifestyle.

Kenton, 7: Multifaceted and disciplined. Perceptive, not easily fooled. Original and unconventional. Dynamic, busy lifestyle. Natural counselor and healer. Romantic, sensual.

Kenway, 7: Multifaceted and disciplined. Perceptive, not easily fooled. Original and unconventional. Likes to meet new people. Independent, critical of self and others. Needs a lot of freedom.

Kenyon, 30: Enthusiastic and quick-witted. A free spirit, very adaptable. Original and unconventional. Dislikes limitations. Natural counselor and healer. Romantic, sensual.

Kerby, 7: Multifaceted and disciplined. Perceptive, not easily fooled. Gentle, kind, a hard worker. Friendly, but shy. Dislikes limitations.

Kermit, 4: Practical imagination. Accesses quickly. Gentle, kind, a hard worker. Systematic, organized. Blessed in some ways. Dynamic, busy lifestyle.

Keri, 7: Multifaceted and disciplined. Perceptive, not easily fooled. Gentle, kind, a hard worker. Blessed in some ways.

Kern, 3: Enthusiastic and quick-witted. A free spirit, very adaptable. Sympathetic, kind. Original and unconventional.

Kerri, 7: Multifaceted and disciplined. Perceptive, not easily fooled. Gentle, kind, a hard worker. Tendency to lose items. Blessed in some ways.

Kerrie, 3: Enthusiastic and quick-witted. A free spirit, very adaptable. Gentle, kind, a hard worker. Tendency to lose items. Blessed in some ways. Loves adventure and excitement.

Kerry, 5: Energetic, forceful. Perceptive, socially adept. Gentle, kind, a hard worker. Tendency to lose items. Needs a lot of freedom.

Kerwin, 8: Has a powerful presence. Original and creative. Intense inner power. Likes to meet new people. Blessed in some ways. Romantic, sensual.

Kesha, 8: Has a powerful presence. Original and creative. Charming and devoted. Great judge of character. Resolute and purposeful.

Ketti, 20: Perceptive and diplomatic. Social and entertaining. Dynamic, busy lifestyle. Sensitive and easily hurt. Blessed in some ways.

Ketura, 22: Strong desire to succeed. Has big plans and ideas. Energetic, highly charged. Attractive and charming. Gentle, kind, a hard worker. Independent, critical of self and others.

Ketzia, 9: Sees the big picture. Enjoys giving gifts. Dynamic, busy lifestyle. Uses common sense. Blessed in some ways. Independent, critical of self and others.

Keven, 3: Enthusiastic and quick-witted. A free spirit, very adaptable. Intuitive and inspired. Likes to entertain. Romantic and sensual.

Kevin, 7: Multifaceted and disciplined. Not easily fooled. Intuitive and inspired. Blessed in some ways. Original and unconventional.

Keyla, 9: Sees the big picture. Enjoys giving gifts. Needs a lot of freedom. Strong verbal skills. Independent, critical of self and others.

Keyton, 9: Sees the big picture. Enjoys giving gifts. Needs a lot of freedom. Dynamic, busy lifestyle. Natural counselor and healer. Romantic, opinionated.

Kezi, 6: Creatively inspired. A step ahead of others. Uses common sense. Blessed in some ways.

Khadeem, 11: Strong desire to succeed. Great judge of character. Intuitive and perceptive. Reliable, responsible. A free spirit, very adaptable. Loves adventure and excitement. Systematic, organized.

Khamis, 7: Multifaceted and disciplined. Great judge of character. Not easily influenced. Domestic, hardworking. Blessed in some ways. Charming and devoted.

Kidae, 3: Enthusiastic and quick-witted. Blessed in some ways. Domestic, hardworking. Aims to please. A free spirit, very adaptable.

Kiefer, 9: Sees the big picture. Enjoys giving gifts. Blessed in some ways. Self-sacrificing, loving. Loves adventure and excitement. Gentle, kind, a hard worker.

Kieran, 4: Practical imagination. Devoted to family. Accesses quickly. Gentle, kind, a hard worker. Independent, critical of self and others. Original and unconventional.

Kieron, 9: Sees the big picture. Blessed in some ways. A free spirit, very adaptable. Gentle, kind, a hard worker. Natural counselor and healer. Original and unconventional.

Kiesha, 8: (Same as Keisha.)

Kiki, 22: Strong desire to succeed. Blessed in some ways. A bit forceful at times. Idealistic and humanitarian.

Kiko, 10: Exercise very beneficial. Respectful, kind. A bit forceful at times. Natural counselor and healer.

Kile, 10: Exercise very beneficial. Respectful, kind. Travels frequently. A free spirit, very adaptable.

Killian, 5: Energetic, forceful. Generous and thoughtful. Great verbal skills. Frequent traveler. Artistic, having good taste. Independent, critical of self and others. Original and unconventional.

Kim, 6: Creatively inspired. Artistic, having good taste. Domestic, hardworking.

Kimba, 9: Sees the big picture. Blessed in some ways. Domestic, hardworking. Friendly, but shy. Independent, critical of self and others.

Kimbal, 3: Enthusiastic and quick-witted. Blessed in some ways. Domestic, hardworking. Friendly, but shy. Independent, critical of self and others. Communicates skillfully.

Kimball, 6: Creatively inspired. Artistic, having good taste. Domestic, hardworking. Friendly, but shy. Independent, critical of self and others. Great verbal skills. Frequent traveler.

Kimberlee, 8: Has a powerful presence. Blessed in some ways. Domestic, hardworking. Friendly, but shy. Physical and passionate. Gentle, kind, humanitarian. Great verbal skills. Loves adventure and excitement. A free spirit, very adaptable.

Kimberly, 5: Energetic, forceful. Generous, thoughtful. Domestic, hardworking. Friendly, but shy. A free spirit, very adaptable. Gentle, kind, humanitarian. Communicates skillfully. Dislikes limitations.

Kimi, 6: Creatively inspired. Blessed in some ways. Domestic, hardworking. Artistic, having good taste.

Kimiko, 5: Energetic, forceful. Generous, thoughtful. Domestic, hardworking. Artistic, having good taste. Strong desire to succeed. Natural counselor and healer.

Kimiyo, 10: Exercise very beneficial. Blessed in some ways. Domestic, hardworking. Artistic, having good taste. Needs a lot of freedom. Natural counselor and healer.

Kimmi, 10: Exercise very beneficial. Respectful, kind. Domestic, hardworking. Desires financial security. Artistic, having good taste.

Kimmy, 8: Has a powerful presence. Blessed in some ways. Domestic, hardworking. Desires financial security. Needs a lot of freedom.

Kincaid, 6: Creatively inspired. Blessed in some ways. Original and unconventional. Self-expressive, cheerful. Independent, critical of self and others. Artistic, having good taste. Reliable, responsible.

Kindra, 30: Enthusiastic and quick-witted. Understanding, kind. Original and unconventional. Reliable, responsible. Gentle, kind, a hard worker. Independent, critical of self and others.

Kiné, 3: Enthusiastic and quick-witted. Blessed in some ways. Romantic, opinionated. A free spirit, very adaptable.

King, 5: Energetic, forceful. Generous, thoughtful. Creative, romantic. Scientific and philosophical.

Kingsley, 3: Enthusiastic and quick-witted. Blessed in some ways. Original and unconventional. Scientific and philosophical. Charming and devoted. Strong verbal skills. A free spirit, very adaptable. Dislikes limitations.

Kingston, 10: Exercise very beneficial. Respectful, kind. Romantic, original. Scientific and philosophical. Charming and devoted. Dynamic, busy lifestyle. Natural counselor and healer. Creative and opinionated.

Kino, 22: Strong desire to succeed. Idealistic, humanitarian. Intuitive and creative. Natural counselor and healer.

Kinsey, 11: Strong desire to succeed. Idealistic, humanitarian. Original and unconventional. Charming and devoted. Loves adventure and excitement. Needs a lot of freedom.

Kion, 22: (Same as Kino.)

Kip, 9: Sees the big picture. Blessed in some ways. Levelheaded, secretive.

Kirby, 11: Strong desire to succeed. Idealistic, humanitarian. Gentle, kind, a hard worker. Friendly, but shy. Needs a lot of freedom.

Kirill, 8: Has a powerful presence. Blessed in some ways. Intense inner power. Artistic, having good taste. Great verbal skills. Many financial ups and downs.

Kirk, 22: Strong desire to succeed. Idealistic, humanitarian. Gentle, kind, a hard worker. A bit forceful at times.

Kirsten, 6: Creatively inspired. Artistic, having good taste. Gentle, kind, a hard worker. Charming and devoted. Dynamic, busy lifestyle. A free spirit, very adaptable. Original and unconventional.

Kirstie, 10: Exercise very beneficial. Respectful, kind. Diligent, hardworking. Charming and devoted. Dynamic, busy lifestyle. Artistic, having good taste. A free spirit, very adaptable.

Kirstin, 10: Exercise very beneficial. Respectful, kind. Diligent, hardworking. Charming and devoted. Dynamic, busy lifestyle. Artistic, having good taste.

Kirsty, 30: Enthusiastic and quick-witted. Blessed in some ways. Gentle, kind, a hard worker. Charming and devoted. Dynamic, busy lifestyle. Needs a lot of freedom.

Kisha, 3: Enthusiastic and quick-witted. Blessed in some ways. Charming and devoted. Great judge of character. Independent, critical of self and others.

Kit, 4: Practical imagination. Blessed in some ways. Dynamic, busy lifestyle.

Kitty, 22: Strong desire to succeed. Idealistic, humanitarian. Dynamic, busy lifestyle. Sensitive and easily hurt. Needs a lot of freedom.

Kizzy, 7: Multifaceted and disciplined. Blessed in some ways. Uses common sense. Impatient and stubborn. Needs a lot of freedom.

Knox, 10: Exercise very beneficial. Original and unconventional. Natural counselor and healer. Artistic, sensual, perceptive.

Knute, 8: Has a powerful presence. Creative, original. Attractive and charming. Dynamic, busy lifestyle. A free spirit, very adaptable.

Kobe, 6: Creatively inspired. Magnetic personality. Friendly, but shy. Physical and passionate.

Koko, 7: Multifaceted and disciplined. Respects rules. Nervous, high-strung. Musically inclined.

Konrad, 9: Sees the big picture. Natural counselor and healer. Original and unconventional. Gentle, kind, a hard worker. Independent, critical of self and others. Reliable, responsible.

Kori, 8: Has a powerful presence. Competitive in business. Gentle, kind, a hard worker. Blessed in some ways.

Kory, 6: Creatively inspired. Magnetic personality. Gentle, kind, a hard worker. Needs a lot of freedom.

Krishna, 8: Has a powerful presence. Intense inner power. Blessed in some ways. Charming and devoted. Great judge of character. Original and unconventional. Independent, critical of self and others.

Kriss, 22: Strong desire to succeed. Gentle, kind, a hard worker. Blessed in some ways. Charming and devoted. Intense and extreme.

Kristiana, 3: Enthusiastic and quick-witted. Gentle, kind, a hard worker. Blessed in some ways. Charming and devoted. Dynamic, busy lifestyle. Artistic, having good taste. Independent, critical of self and others. Original and unconventional. Bold, courageous, a bit stubborn.

Kristin, 10: Exercise very beneficial. Diligent, hardworking. Blessed in some ways. Charming and devoted. Dynamic, busy lifestyle. Artistic, having good taste. Original and unconventional.

Kristina, 11: Strong desire to succeed. Gentle, kind, a hard worker. Idealistic, humanitarian. Charming and devoted. Dynamic, busy lifestyle. Artistic, having good taste. Original and unconventional. Independent, critical of self and others.

Kristine, 6: Creatively inspired. Kindhearted, helpful. Blessed in some ways. Completely devoted. Dynamic, busy lifestyle. Artistic, having good taste. Original and unconventional. A free spirit, very adaptable.

Kristoffer, 10: Exercise very beneficial. Diligent, hardworking. Blessed in some ways. Charming and devoted. Dynamic, busy lifestyle. Assumes responsibility easily. Strong family ties. Nurturing, protective. Physical, passionate. Tendency to lose items.

Krysta, 22: Strong desire to succeed. Gentle, kind, a hard worker. Needs a lot of freedom. Charming and devoted. Dynamic, busy lifestyle. Independent, critical of self and others.

Kultida, 6: Creatively inspired. Attractive and charming. Excellent verbal skills. Dynamic, busy lifestyle. Blessed in some ways. Reliable, responsible. Independent, critical of self and others.

Kumiko, 8: Has a powerful presence. Usually very lucky. Domestic, hardworking. Artistic, having good taste. A bit forceful at times. Natural counselor and healer.

Kurt, 7: Multifaceted and disciplined. Attractive and charming. Gentle, kind, a hard worker. Dynamic, busy lifestyle.

Kwame, 8: Has a powerful presence. Likes to meet new people. Resolute and purposeful. Domestic, hardworking. A free spirit, very adaptable.

Kwan, 4: Practical imagination. Likes meeting new people. Resolute and purposeful. Romantic, opinionated.

Kwang:soo, 6: Creatively inspired. Likes to meet new people. Independent, critical of self and others. Original and unconventional. Scientific and philosophical. Charming and devoted. Natural counselor and healer. Has musical abilities.

Kyasha, 20: Sensitive and diplomatic. Needs a lot of freedom. Independent, critical of self and others. Charming and devoted. Great judge of character. Bold, courageous, a bit stubborn.

Kye, 5: Energetic, forceful. Needs a lot of freedom. Loves adventure and excitement.

Kyla, 4: Practical imagination. Finds shortcuts. Good verbal skills. Independent, critical of self and others.

Kylah, 3: Enthusiastic and quick-witted. Needs a lot of freedom. Good verbal skills. Independent, critical of self and others. Great judge of character.

Kyle, 8: Has a powerful presence. Strong intuition. Good verbal skills. Physical and passionate.

Kylie, 8: Has a powerful presence. Strong intuition. Good verbal skills. Blessed in some ways. Physical and passionate.

Kym, 4: Practical imagination. Finds shortcuts. Domestic, hardworking.

Kynan, 20: Sensitive and diplomatic. Needs a lot of freedom. Original and unconventional. Independent, critical of self and others. Romantic, sensual.

Kyne, 10: Exercise very beneficial. Needs a lot of freedom. Original and unconventional. Loves adventure and excitement.

Kyra, 10: Exercise very beneficial. Needs a lot of freedom. Gentle, kind, a hard worker. Independent, critical of self and others.

L

If a name begins with L, has more than one L, or ends with an L, this person is lucky, good-natured in disposition, travels and moves frequently, and is slow to make decisions.

The letter L is the 12th letter in the alphabet. Since 1 + 2 = 3, the 12th letter has a 3 vibration influence. This same vibration also rules the letters C and U. The 1 rules beginnings and the 2 rules partnerships; together they equal 3 which rules balance. So quite often the L-named individual is learning to be in a partnership and must learn to be in balance with it. When L people are emotionally stressed, they tend to be accident-prone. They can be literally thrown off balance easily. It's important for the L-named to maintain balance in all areas of life.

Persons with double Ls in their names, for example, Bill or Kelly, tend to be good conversationalists. They seem to possess a high degree of creative self-expression and sociability. Kelly Ripa of *Live with Regis and Kelly* and Bill O'Reilly of *The O'Reilly Factor* have found themselves quite at home on talk shows. L-named people like to communicate almost as much as Cs. The Ls know how to make others feel at home. They are a welcome addition to any social situation.

The L can soften any name with A as their first vowel. Although Laura is an ambitious name with two As in it, the L gives Laura a sense of humor; coupled with the U, she is easygoing and youthful no matter how ambitious she is. Larry can be intimidating with the double Rs. Double Rs sometimes enjoy bullying others around, but with an L in the beginning of his name, he most likely will be a showman about it, acting as if on stage to get a laugh. L types, similar to C types, will be the first to crack a joke when things get a little quiet. They are warm, friendly, social, and tend to express an air of openness.

L is a lovely letter to have anywhere in a name. The L influence is one of cheerfulness, creativity, social ability, and excellent communication skills. It's a warm, go-with-the-flow letter that is forever youthful and happy, no matter the age of the person.

Similar to the letters C and U, this 3-ruled letter is quite resilient and bounces back from illness better than the other letters. It has a strong constitution and won't stay down. Lance Armstrong, national and world champion cyclist, two time Olympian, renowned humanitarian, role model, and cancer survivor, is a good example of the power of the L. Lance, seven-time winner of the Tour de France, has two 3-ruled letters in his first name. The number 3 is the communicator and is gifted in the area of writing. Lance has written two books so far. Cancer left him scarred physically and emotionally, but he now maintains it was an unexpected gift—a viewpoint shared by many cancer survivors. Getting cancer was "…the best thing that ever happened to me," Lance said, in relation to the direction this disease forced him to face. This is the optimistic, cheerfulness of the letter L. Lance Armstrong made the most stunning comeback ever in the history of sports. His chances of recovery were far less than 50/50 when he began an aggressive form of chemotherapy. He began riding and training only five months after his diagnosis. His strength and courage must in part be credited to his name summing up to an 8 power number. 8 is the survivor of numbers. He gives a lot of credit to his mother for the support she gave him; his mother's name also begins with the letter L. Her name is Linda. Lance no doubt inherited his cheerful, optimistic attitude from his L-named mother.

Actor Leonardo DiCaprio knows how to bring emotional reality to his roles. He has touched the hearts of millions all over the world, especially in the blockbuster movie, *Titanic.* Leonardo's power number is 3, the same number that rules the letter L. It's no wonder he became successful during his adolescence, as the number 3 rules adolescence along with the third astrological sign, Gemini. He has two Os in his name which give him a magnetic quality. Later the Os will lend a nurturing ability. No doubt he will want children some day, as he has a lot of love to give. He is a free spirit with an E first vowel, but just like his father, George, his E conjuncts the duty-bound O vowel. Although he loves freedom and adventure, he is also service-oriented and cannot help but work tirelessly in any field he chooses. This is what he inherited from his father.

Another youthful famous person whose name starts with the letter L is Liv Tyler. Although she is no longer an adolescent, she appears very young on screen. Her first name sums up to a 7 power number. This number performs well in front of a camera. While still a teenager, a friend talked her into modeling—her career skyrocketed. A few years later she decided to try acting—she took to it like a fish takes to water, even without acting lessons. Of course she is blessed with an I first vowel. The 7 and 9 influence gives her an ethereal quality, which was beneficial for her role in *The Lord of the Rings* films. She also inherited the V from her famous father, Steven Tyler, member of the rock band Aerosmith. V is an international letter ruled by the master number 22. Those with a V anywhere in their names tend to be tenacious about reaching goals. Still, she seems easygoing and easy to talk to. The L in the beginning of her name gives her a cheerful, optimist's youthful appearance. She is tenacious about reaching her goals, but she's as smooth as whipped cream about it.

L is for lucky! The Lewis and Clark expedition had an L in each name. This dangerous expedition started in May 1804 in St. Louis, Missouri, and ended two years later back in St. Louis. The group traveled by foot, horseback, and boat across the vast wilderness of the Northwest United States to the Pacific Ocean. Interestingly enough, despite the scorching and freezing weather, swift river currents, rugged mountain trails, dangerous animals, Indian tribes, hunger, and exhaustion, the group didn't quarrel and they had no serious casualties during the entire expedition! This lucky, cheerful, optimistic letter L seems to have played an important role in this expedition. No other expedition has the claim to fame this one does for everyone getting along so well in spite of their adversities. Never underestimate the power of the letter L!

Some more famous L people are: Lucille Ball, Laurence Olivier, Lee Majors, Lionel Ritchie, Leif Erikson, Louis Armstrong, LeAnn Rimes, Linda Blair, Liam Neeson, Laura Dern, Lea Thompson, Lisa Marie Presley, Laurence Fishburne, Lana Turner, Laura Linney, Lucy Liu, Lauren Hutton, Linda Hamilton, Lenny Kravitz, Lee Remick, Levi

Strauss, Leon Spinks, Leonard Nimoy, Larry Hagman, Liberace, LaToya Jackson, Lil Romeo, Lauren Bacall, Lou Ferrigno, Lawrence Welk, Little Richard, Luke Perry, Lyle Lovett, and Larry King.

QUICK REFERENCE OF "L" NAMES

Lachlan, 6: Easygoing attitude. Pioneer and risk taker. A sense of humor. Great judge of character. Slow to make decisions. Bold, courageous, a bit stubborn. Creative and original.

Laila, 8: Recuperates quickly. Resolute and purposeful. Blessed in many ways. Slow to make decisions. Bold, courageous, a bit stubborn.

Laine, 5: Moves and travels often. Bright, adventuresome. Blessed in many ways. Original and unconventional. A free spirit, very adaptable.

Laird, 8: Recuperates quickly. Resolute and purposeful. Artistic, having good taste. Gentle, kind, a hard worker. Problem solver and natural authority.

Lakeesha, 8: Recuperates quickly. Resolute and purposeful. Desire to succeed. Physical and passionate. Loves adventure and excitement. Charming and devoted. Self-reliant, successful. Bold, courageous, a bit stubborn.

Lakeisha, 30: Slow to make decisions. Aims to please. Strong desire to succeed. A free spirit, very adaptable. Blessed in some ways. Charming and devoted. Great judge of character. Bold, courageous, a bit stubborn.

Lakisha, 7: Intellectually sound. Not easily fooled. Strong desire to succeed. Blessed in some ways. Charming and devoted. Great judge of character. Bold, courageous, a bit stubborn.

Lalaine, 9: Benefits from meditation. Helpful, sincere. Communicates skillfully. Bold, courageous, a bit stubborn. Blessed in some ways. Original and unconventional. A free spirit, very adaptable.

Lamar, 9: Benefits from meditation. Helpful, sincere. Domestic, hardworking. Bold, courageous, a bit stubborn. Gentle, kind, diligent.

LaMarr, 9: Benefits from meditation. Helpful, sincere. Domestic, hardworking. Bold, courageous, a bit stubborn. Gentle, kind, diligent. Could be forgetful.

Lambert, 8: Recuperates quickly. Resolute and purposeful. Domestic, hardworking. Friendly, but shy. A free spirit, very adaptable. Gentle, kind, diligent. Dynamic, busy lifestyle.

Lamont, 3: Slow to make decisions. Aims to please. Domestic, hardworking. Natural counselor and healer. Original and unconventional. Dynamic, busy lifestyle.

Lana, 10: Strong verbal skills. Independent, critical of self and others. Original and unconventional. Bold, courageous, a bit stubborn.

Lance, 8: Recuperates quickly. Resolute and purposeful. Creative, romantic. Self-expressive, cheerful. A free spirit, very adaptable.

Lancelot, 10: Strong verbal skills. Independent, critical of self and others. Creative, romantic. Self-expressive, cheerful. A free spirit, very adaptable. Frequent traveler. A natural counselor and healer. Dynamic, busy lifestyle.

Lander, 9: Benefits from meditation. Helpful, sincere. Creative, opinionated. Reliable, responsible. A free spirit, very adaptable. Gentle, kind, a hard worker.

Landon, 6: Easygoing attitude. Pioneer and risk taker. Creative, opinionated. Reliable, responsible. Natural counselor and healer. Romantic, sensual.

Lane, 5: Moves and travels frequently. Bright, adventuresome. Romantic, sensual. A free spirit, very adaptable.

Lanette, 5: Moves and travels frequently. Bright, adventuresome. Creative, opinionated. A free spirit, very adaptable. Dynamic, busy lifestyle. Sensitive and easily hurt. Physical and passionate.

Lang, 7: Intellectually sound. Not easily influenced. Original and unconventional. Has willpower and determination.

Langdon, 4: Domestically creative. Natural teaching ability. Original and unconventional. Scientific and philosophical. Reliable, responsible. Nurturing, loving. Romantic, opinionated.

Langford, 5: Moves and travels frequently. Bright, adventuresome. Original and unconventional. Scientific and philosophical. Self-sacrificing, loving. Natural counselor and healer. Gentle, kind, a hard worker. Reliable, responsible.

Langley, 4: Domestically creative. Natural teaching ability. Original and unconventional. Scientific and philosophical. Frequent traveler. Loves adventure and excitement. Needs a lot of freedom.

Langston, 30: Slow to make decisions. Aims to please. Original and unconventional. Scientific and philosophical. Charming and devoted. Dynamic, busy lifestyle. Natural counselor and healer. Romantic, sensual.

Lani, 9: Benefits from meditation. Helpful, sincere. Original and unconventional. Blessed in some ways.

Lara, 5: Moves and travels frequently. Bright, adventuresome. Gentle, kind, a hard worker. Bold, courageous, a bit stubborn.

Laraine, 6: Easygoing attitude. Pioneer and risk taker. Diligent, hardworking. Bold, courageous, a bit stubborn. Blessed in some ways. Original and unconventional. A free spirit, very adaptable.

Larissa, 7: Intellectually sound. Not easily influenced. Gentle, kind, a hard worker. Blessed in some ways. Charming and devoted. Impulsive and extreme. Bold, courageous, a bit stubborn.

Lark, 6: Easygoing attitude. Pioneer and risk taker. Diligent, hardworking. Desires to succeed.

LaRoux, 10: Strong verbal skills. Independent, critical of self and others. Gentle, kind, a hard worker. Natural counselor and healer. Attractive and charming. Artistic, sensual, perceptive.

Larry, 11: Travels frequently. Intuitive, perceptive. Gentle, kind, a hard worker. Tendency to lose items. Needs a lot of freedom.

Lars, 5: Moves and travels often. Bright, adventuresome. Intense inner power. Charming and devoted.

Larson, 7: Intellectually sound. Not easily influenced. Intense inner power. Charming and devoted. Natural counselor and healer. Original and unconventional.

Larz, 3: Slow to make decisions. Aims to please. Gentle, kind, a hard worker. Uses common sense.

Lassie, 20: Honest and sincere. Reads people easily. Charming and devoted. Impulsive and extreme. Blessed in some ways. A free spirit, very adaptable.

Latania, 22: Travels frequently. Ambitious leader, great leader. Dynamic, busy lifestyle. Bold, courageous, a bit stubborn. Original and unconventional. Blessed in some ways. Pioneer and risk taker.

Latanya, 20: Honest and sincere. Independent, critical of self and others. Energetic, highly charged. Bold, courageous, a bit stubborn. Original and unconventional. Needs a lot of freedom. Pioneer and risk taker.

Lateefah, 4: Domestically creative. Natural teaching ability. Dynamic, busy lifestyle. A free spirit, very adaptable. Loves adventure and excitement. Self-sacrificing, loving. Bold, courageous, a bit stubborn. Great judge of character.

Latham, 10: Strong verbal skills. Independent, critical of self and others. Energetic, highly charged. Great judge of character. Bold, courageous, a bit stubborn. Domestic, hardworking.

Lathrop, 9: Benefits from meditation. Helpful, sincere. Dynamic, busy lifestyle. Great judge of character. Gentle, kind, hard worker. Natural counselor and healer. Intelligent and knowledgeable.

Latimer, 6: Easygoing attitude. Natural teaching ability. Dynamic, busy lifestyle. Blessed in some ways. Domestic, hardworking. A free spirit, very adaptable. Tendency to lose items.

Latoya, 20: Honest and sincere. Reads people easily. Energetic, highly charged. Natural counselor and healer. Needs a lot of freedom. Bold, courageous, a bit stubborn.

Launce, 20: Honest and sincere. Reads people easily. Socially charming. Original and unconventional. Self-expressive, cheerful. A free spirit, very adaptable.

Launcelot, 4: Domestically creative. Natural teaching ability. Attractive and charming. Original and unconventional. Self-expressive, cheerful. A free spirit, very adaptable. Frequent traveler. Natural counselor and healer. Dynamic, busy lifestyle.

Laura, 8: Recuperates quickly. Resolute and purposeful. Attractive and charming. Intense inner power. Bold, courageous, a bit stubborn.

Laureen, 4: Domestically creative. Natural teaching ability. Attractive and charming. Gentle, kind, a hard worker. A free spirit, very adaptable. Loves adventure and excitement. Original and unconventional.

Laurel, 6: Easygoing attitude. Natural teaching ability. Youthful and appealing. Gentle, kind, a hard worker. A free spirit, very adaptable. Frequent traveler.

Lauren, 8: Recuperates quickly. Resolute and purposeful. Attractive and charming. Intense inner power. A free spirit, very adaptable. Original and unconventional.

Laurence, 7: Intellectually sound. Not easily influenced. Attractive and charming. Gentle, kind, a hard worker. A free spirit, very adaptable. Original and unconventional. Self-expressive, cheerful. Loves adventure and excitement.

Laurent, 10: Strong verbal skills. Independent, critical of self and others. Attractive and charming. Gentle, kind, a hard worker. A free spirit, very adaptable. Original and unconventional. Dynamic, busy lifestyle.

Lauretta, 8: Recuperates quickly. Resolute and purposeful. Attractive and charming. Intense inner power. A free spirit, very adaptable. Dynamic, busy lifestyle. Sensitive and easily hurt. Bold, courageous, a bit stubborn.

Laurette, 30: Slow to make decisions. Aims to please. Youthful and appealing. Gentle, kind, a hard worker. A free spirit, very adaptable. Dynamic, busy lifestyle. Sensitive and easily hurt. Loves adventure and excitement.

Laurie, 30: Slow to make decisions. Aims to please. Youthful and appealing. Gentle, kind, a hard worker. Blessed in some ways. A free spirit, very adaptable.

LaVerne, 5: Moves and travels often. Bright, adventuresome. Intuitive and inspired. A free spirit, very adaptable. Gentle, kind, a hard worker. Original and unconventional. Tendency to overindulge.

Laverne, 5: (Same as LaVerne.)

Lavinia, 5: Moves and travels often. Bright, adventuresome. Intuitive and inspired. Blessed in some ways. Romantic and sensual. Artistic, having good taste. Independent, critical of self and others.

Lawford, 7: Intellectually sound. Not easily influenced. Likes to meet new people. Self-sacrificing, loving. Natural counselor and healer. Gentle, kind, a hard worker. Reliable, responsible.

Lawrence, 9: Benefits from meditation. Helpful, sincere. Likes to meet new people. Gentle, kind, a hard worker. A free spirit, very adaptable. Original and unconventional. Self-expressive, cheerful. Loves adventure and excitement.

Lawson, 3: Slow to make decisions. Aims to please. Likes to meet new people. Charming and devoted. Natural counselor and healer. Original and unconventional.

Lawton, 22: Travels frequently. Ambitious leader, great vision. Likes to meet new people. Dynamic, busy lifestyle. Natural counselor and healer. Original and unconventional.

Layla, 6: Easygoing attitude. Pioneer and risk taker. Needs a lot of freedom. Frequent traveler. Bold, courageous, a bit stubborn.

Laylah, 5: Moves and travels often. Bright, adventuresome. Needs a lot of freedom. Bold, courageous, a bit stubborn. Great judge of character.

Lazarus, 8: Recuperates quickly. Resolute and purposeful. Uses common sense. Bold, courageous, a bit stubborn. Gentle, kind, a hard worker. Attractive and charming. Intense and extreme.

Lea, 9: Benefits from meditation. Enjoys giving gifts. Helpful and sincere.

Leah, 8: Recuperates quickly. Original and creative. Resolute and purposeful. Great judge of character.

Leander, 5: Moves and travels often. Physical and passionate. Bright, adventuresome. Original and unconventional. Reliable, responsible. Likes change and variety. Gentle, kind, a hard worker.

Leann, 10: Strong verbal skills. Likes change and variety. Independent, critical of self and others. Original and unconventional. Romantic, sensual.

Leanna, 20: Honest and sincere. Social and entertaining. Reads people easily. Original and unconventional. Romantic, sensual. Bold, courageous, a bit stubborn.

Leanne, 6: Easygoing attitude. A step ahead of others. Pioneer and risk taker. Original and unconventional. Romantic, sensual. A free spirit, adaptable to change.

Lee, 4: Domestically creative. Accesses quickly. Loves adventure and excitement.

Leif, 5: Moves and travels often. Physical and passionate. Generous, thoughtful. Self-sacrificing, loving.

Leigh, 5: Moves and travels often. Physical and passionate. Generous, thoughtful. Scientific and philosophical. Great judge of character.

Leighton, 9: Benefits from meditation. Enjoys giving gifts. Blessed in some ways. Scientific and philosophical. Great judge of character. Dynamic, busy lifestyle. Natural counselor and healer. Original and unconventional.

Leila, 3: Slow to make decisions. A free spirit, very adaptable. Blessed in some ways. Frequent traveler. Independent, critical of self and others.

Leilani, 8: Recuperates quickly. Original and creative. Blessed in some ways. Frequent traveler. Resolute and purposeful. Romantic, sensual. Artistic, having good taste.

Lekisha, 11: Travels frequently. Has big plans and ideas. Strong desire to succeed. Blessed in some ways. Charming and devoted. Great judge of character. Independent, critical of self and others.

Lela, 3: Slow to make decisions. A free spirit, very adaptable. Frequent traveler. Independent, critical of self and others.

Leland, 3: Slow to make decisions. A free spirit, very adaptable. Frequent traveler. Aims to please. Original and unconventional. Reliable, responsible.

Lena, 5: Moves and travels often. Physical and passionate. Original and unconventional. Independent, critical of self and others.

Lennie, 5: Moves and travels often. Physical and passionate. Original and unconventional. Creative, opinionated. Blessed in some ways. A free spirit, very adaptable.

Lenny, 7: Intellectually sound. Not easily fooled. Original and unconventional. Romantic, sensual. Needs a lot of freedom.

Lenora, 11: Travels frequently. Keenly perceptive. Creative, romantic. Natural counselor and healer. Gentle, kind, a hard worker. Independent, critical of self and others.

Lenore, 6: Easygoing attitude. A step ahead of others. Romantic, sensual. Natural counselor and healer. Gentle, kind, a hard worker. Loves adventure and excitement.

Leo, 5: Moves and travels often. Physical and passionate. Natural counselor and healer.

Leon, 10: Strong verbal skills. Likes change and variety. Self-sacrificing, devoted. Romantic, opinionated.

Leona, 20: Honest and sincere. Social and entertaining. Natural counselor and healer. Original and unconventional. Independent, critical of self and others.

Leonard, 6: Easygoing attitude. A step ahead of others. Nurturing, loving. Original and unconventional. Independent, critical of self and others. Gentle, kind, a hard worker. Reliable, responsible.

Leonardo, 30: Slow to make decisions. A free spirit, very adaptable. Natural counselor and healer. Original and unconventional. Independent, critical of self and others. Gentle, kind, a hard worker. Reliable, responsible. Good parental skills.

Leonides, 11: Travels frequently. Keenly perceptive. Creates group harmony. Creative, opinionated. Blessed in some ways. Natural authority. Physical and passionate. Charming and devoted.

Leonora, 8: Recuperates quickly. Original and unconventional. Natural counselor and healer. Creative, opinionated. Good parental skills. Gentle, kind, a hard worker. Independent, critical of self and others.

Leonore, 3: Slow to make decisions. A free spirit, very adaptable. Natural counselor and healer. Original and unconventional. Good parental skills. Gentle, kind, a hard worker. Tendency to overindulge.

Leontyne, 11: Travels frequently. Keenly perceptive. Creates group harmony. Creative, opinionated. Dynamic, busy lifestyle. Dislikes limitations. Romantic, sensual. Loves adventure and excitement.

Leony, 8: Recuperates quickly. Original and creative. Competitive in business. Romantic, sensual. Dislikes limitations.

Leopold, 7: Intellectually sound. Not easily fooled. Natural counselor and healer. Intelligent and knowledgeable. May have musical abilities. Slow to make decisions. Reliable, responsible.

Leroy, 30: Slow to make decisions. A free spirit, very adaptable. Gentle, kind, a hard worker. Natural counselor and healer. Needs a lot of freedom.

Les, 9: Benefits from meditation. Enjoys giving gifts. Charming and devoted.

Lesley, 6: Easygoing attitude. A step ahead of others. Devoted and loving. Frequent traveler. Loves adventure and excitement. Needs a lot of freedom.

Lesli, 3: Slow to make decisions. A free spirit, very adaptable. Charming and devoted. Blessed in some ways.

Leslie, 8: Recuperates quickly. Original and creative. Passionate and loving. Slow to make decisions. Blessed in some ways. Loves adventure and excitement.

Lester, 7: Intellectually sound. Not easily fooled. Charming and devoted. Dynamic, busy lifestyle. Tendency to overindulge. Gentle, kind, a hard worker.

Leticia, 5: Moves and travels often. Physical and passionate. Dynamic, busy lifestyle. Blessed in some ways. Self-expressive, cheerful. Artistic, having good taste. Independent, critical of self and others.

Lettie, 8: Recuperates quickly. Original and creative. Dynamic, busy lifestyle. Sensitive and easily hurt. Blessed in some ways. Loves adventure and excitement.

Letty, 10: Strong verbal skills. Likes change and variety. Dynamic, busy lifestyle. Sensitive and easily hurt. Needs a lot of freedom.

Levi, 3: Slow to make decisions. A free spirit, very adaptable. Intuitive and inspired. Blessed in some ways.

Levy, 10: Strong verbal skills. Likes change and variety. Intuitive and inspired. Dislikes limitations.

Lew, 4: Domestically creative. Accesses quickly. Likes to meet new people.

Lewis, 5: Moves and travels often. Physical and passionate. Likes to meet new people. Blessed in some ways. Charming and devoted.

Lexie, 10: Strong verbal skills. Likes change and variety. Artistic, sensual, perceptive. Blessed in some ways. Tendency to overindulge.

Li, 3: Slow to make decisions. Blessed in some ways. Inspiring and creative.

Lia, 4: Domestically creative. Blessed in some ways. Independent, critical of self and others.

Liam, 8: Recuperates quickly. Blessed in some ways. Independent, critical of self and others. Domestic, hardworking.

Liana, 10: Strong verbal skills. Respectful and kind. Independent, critical of self and others. Original and unconventional. Bold, courageous, a bit stubborn.

Lianne, 10: Strong verbal skills. Respectful and kind. Independent, critical of self and others. Original and unconventional. Romantic, sensual. A free spirit, very adaptable.

Libbie, 30: Slow to make decisions. Blessed in some ways. Affectionate, social. Emotional and sensitive. Artistic, having good taste. A free spirit, very adaptable.

Libby, 5: Moves and travels often. Generous and thoughtful. Friendly, but shy. Emotional, sensitive. Needs a lot of freedom.

Lida, 8: Recuperates quickly. Blessed in some ways. Reliable, responsible. Independent, critical of self and others.

Liddy, 9: Benefits from meditation. Idealistic and humanitarian. Reliable, responsible. Down-to-earth, faithful. Needs a lot of freedom.

Liene, 9: Benefits from meditation. Idealistic and humanitarian. A free spirit, very adaptable. Original and unconventional. Enjoys giving gifts.

Lil, 6: Easygoing attitude. Artistic, having good taste. Communicates skillfully.

Lila, 7: Intellectually sound. Stylish and refined. Great verbal skills. Independent, critical of self and others.

Lilac, 10: Strong verbal skills. Respectful and kind. Slow to make decisions. Independent, critical of self and others. Self-expressive, cheerful.

Lilith, 7: Intellectually sound. Stylish and refined. Communicates skillfully. Artistic, having good taste. Dynamic, busy lifestyle. Great judge of character.

Lillian, 6: Easygoing attitude. Artistic, having good taste. Slow to make decisions. Communicates skillfully. Independent, critical of self and others. Original and unconventional.

Lillie, 5: Moves and travels often. Generous and thoughtful. Slow to make decisions. Great verbal skills. Artistic, having good taste. A free spirit, very adaptable.

Lilly, 7: Intellectually sound. Stylish and refined. Slow to make decisions. Communicates skillfully. Needs a lot of freedom.

Lily, 22: Travels frequently. Blessed in some ways. Great verbal skills. Needs a lot of freedom.

Lincoln, 7: Intellectually sound. Stylish and refined. Original and unconventional. Self-expressive, cheerful. Natural counselor and healer. Frequent traveler. Romantic, sensual.

Lind, 3: Slow to make decisions. Blessed in some ways. Original and unconventional. Reliable, responsible.

Linda, 22: Travels frequently. Respectful and kind. Original and unconventional. Reliable, responsible. Independent, critical of self and others.

Lindell, 5: Moves and travels often. Generous and thoughtful. Original and unconventional. Reliable, responsible. A free spirit, very adaptable. Communicates skillfully. Slow to make decisions.

Linder, 8: Recuperates quickly. Blessed in some ways. Romantic, sensual. Reliable, responsible. A free spirit, very adaptable. Gentle, kind, a hard worker.

Lindie, 8: Recuperates quickly. Blessed in some ways. Romantic, sensual. Reliable, responsible. Artistic, having good taste. A free spirit, very adaptable.

Lindley, 9: Benefits from meditation. Idealistic, humanitarian. Original and unconventional. Reliable, responsible. Frequent traveler. A free spirit, very adaptable. Dislikes restrictions.

Lindsay, 30: Slow to make decisions. Blessed in some ways. Creative, romantic. Reliable, responsible. Charming and devoted. Aims to please. Needs a lot of freedom.

Lindsey, 7: Intellectually sound. Stylish and refined. Original and unconventional. Reliable, responsible. Charming and devoted. A free spirit, very adaptable. Dislikes limitations.

Lindy, 10: Strong verbal skills. Respectful and kind. Original and unconventional. Reliable, responsible. Needs a lot of freedom.

Linette, 4: Domestically creative. Blessed in some ways. Original and unconventional. A free spirit, very adaptable. Dynamic, busy lifestyle. Sensitive and easily hurt. Tendency to overindulge.

Link, 10: Frequent traveler. A gentle leader. Original and unconventional. Desires to be successful.

Linley, 5: Moves and travels often. Generous and thoughtful. Original and unconventional. A free spirit, very adaptable. Dislikes limitations.

Linne, 9: Benefits from meditation. Idealistic, humanitarian. Original and unconventional. Opinionated and creative. Physical and passionate.

Linsey, 30: Slow to make decisions. Blessed in some ways. Creative and romantic. Charming and devoted. A free spirit, very adaptable. Dislikes limitations.

Linus, 3: Slow to make decisions. Blessed in some ways. Creative and romantic. Attractive and lucky. Charming and devoted.

Lionel, 4: Domestically creative. Blessed in some ways. Natural counselor and healer. Original and unconventional. A free spirit, very adaptable. Frequent traveler.

Lisa, 5: Moves and travels often. Generous and thoughtful. Charming and devoted. Independent, critical of self and others.

Lisette, 9: Benefits from meditation. Idealistic, humanitarian. Angelic leanings. A free spirit, very adaptable. Dynamic, busy lifestyle. Sensitive and easily hurt. Tendency to overindulge.

Lisle, 3: Slow to make decisions. Blessed in some ways. Charming and devoted. Frequent traveler. A free spirit, very adaptable.

Lissa, 6: Easygoing attitude. Artistic, having good taste. Charming and devoted. Impulsive and extreme. Independent, critical of self and others.

Litton, 9: Benefits from meditation. Idealistic, humanitarian. Dynamic, busy lifestyle. Sensitive and easily hurt. Natural counselor and healer. Original and unconventional.

Liu, 6: Easygoing attitude. Artistic, having good taste. Attractive and charming.

Liv, 7: Intellectually sound. Stylish and refined. Intuitive and inspired.

Livia, 8: Recuperates quickly. Blessed in some ways. Intuitive and inspired. Artistic, having good taste. Independent, critical of self and others.

Livya, 6: Easygoing attitude. Artistic, having good taste. Intuitive and inspired. Needs a lot of freedom. Independent, critical of self and others.

Liz, 20: Honest and sincere. Emotional and considerate. Tendency to look at the bright side.

Liza, 3: Slow to make decisions. Blessed in some ways. Uses common sense. Independent, critical of self and others.

Llewellyn, 3: Slow to make decisions. Frequent traveler. A free spirit, very adaptable. Likes to meet new people. Tendency to overindulge. Great verbal skills. Inspiring, very creative. Dislikes limitations. Original and unconventional.

Lloyd, 5: Moves and travels often. Communicates skillfully. Natural counselor and healer. Needs a lot of freedom. Reliable, responsible.

Loelia, 9: Benefits from meditation. Artistic, creative. A free spirit, very adaptable. Frequent traveler. Blessed in some ways. Independent, critical of self and others.

Logan, 22: Travels frequently. Creates group harmony. Scientific and philosophical. Ambitious leader, great vision. Original and unconventional.

Lois, 10: Strong verbal skills. Self-sacrificing, loving. Blessed in some ways. Charming and devoted.

Lokelani, 7: Intellectually sound. Open to opportunities. Desire to succeed. A free spirit, very adaptable. Frequent traveler. Not easily influenced. Original and unconventional. Blessed in some ways.

Lola, 4: Domestically creative. Assumes responsibility. Communicates skillfully. Natural teaching ability.

Lolita, 6: Easygoing attitude. Magnetic personality. Great verbal skills. Blessed in some ways. Dynamic, busy lifestyle. Independent, critical of self and others.

Lombard, 11: Travels frequently. Creates group harmony. Domestic, hardworking. Friendly, but shy. Independent, critical of self and others. Gentle, kind, diligent. Reliable, responsible.

Lon, 5: Moves and travels often. Natural counselor and healer. Original and unconventional.

Lona, 6: Easygoing attitude. Magnetic personality. Creative, opinionated. Self-motivated, independent.

Lonnie, 6: Easygoing attitude. Magnetic personality. Creative, opinionated. Romantic, sensual. Blessed in some ways. A free spirit, very adaptable.

Lonny, 8: Recuperates quickly. Competitive in business. Original and unconventional. Romantic, sensual. Needs a lot of freedom.

Lora, 10: Strong verbal skills. Self-sacrificing, devoted. Diligent, helpful. Independent, critical of self and others.

Loraine, 11: Travels frequently. Creates group harmony. Gentle, kind, a hard worker. Intuitive, perceptive. Blessed in some ways. Original and unconventional. A free spirit, very adaptable.

Loralie, 9: Benefits from meditation. Artistically creative. Idealistic, humanitarian. Independent, critical of self and others. Frequent traveler. Blessed in some ways. A free spirit, very adaptable.

Lorelei, 4: Domestically creative. Assumes responsibility. Gentle, kind, a hard worker. Accesses quickly. Frequent traveler. Tendency to overindulge. Blessed in some ways.

Loren, 10: Strong verbal skills. Self-sacrificing, devoted. Diligent, helpful. Likes variety and change. Original and unconventional.

Lorena, 11: Travels frequently. Creates group harmony. Gentle, kind, a hard worker. Keenly perceptive. Original and unconventional. Self-motivated, independent.

Lorenzo, 6: Easygoing attitude. Magnetic personality. Gentle, kind, a hard worker. A step ahead of others. Original and unconventional. Uses common sense. Nurturing, loving.

Loretta, 10: Strong verbal skills. Self-sacrificing, devoted. Diligent, helpful. Likes change and variety. Dynamic, busy lifestyle. Sensitive and easily hurt. Independent, critical of self and others.

L'Oretta, 10: (Same as Loretta.)

Lorette, 5: Moves and travels often. Natural counselor and healer. Intense inner power. A free spirit, very adaptable. Dynamic, busy lifestyle. Sensitive and easily hurt. Tendency to overindulge.

Lori, 9: Benefits from meditation. Artistic and creative. Gentle, kind, a hard worker. Blessed in some ways.

Lorie, 5: Moves and travels often. Natural counselor and healer. Intense inner power. Good deed doer. A free spirit, very adaptable.

Lorimer, 9: Benefits from meditation. Artistic and creative. Gentle, kind, a hard worker. Blessed in some ways. Systematic, organized. A free spirit, very adaptable. Tendency to lose items.

Lorin, 5: Moves and travels often. Natural counselor and healer. Intense inner power. Good deed doer. Original and unconventional.

Loring, 3: Slow to make decisions. Has creative solutions. Gentle, kind, a hard worker. Blessed in some ways. Original and unconventional. Scientific, philosophical.

Loris, 10: Strong verbal skills. Self-sacrificing, loving. Diligent, hardworking. Respectful, kind. Charming and devoted.

Lorna, 6: Easygoing attitude. Magnetic personality. Self-sacrificing and duty-bound. Original and unconventional. Independent, critical of self and others.

Lorne, 10: Strong verbal skills. Self-sacrificing, devoted. Diligent, hardworking. Creative, opinionated. Physical and passionate.

Lorraine, 11: Travels frequently. Creates group harmony. Gentle, kind, a hard worker. Tendency to lose items. Independent, critical of self and others. Blessed in some ways. Original and unconventional. A free spirit, very adaptable.

Lorrie, 5: Moves and travels often. Natural counselor and healer. Intense inner power. Tendency to lose items. Blessed in some ways. A free spirit, very adaptable.

Lorry, 7: Intellectually sound. Open to opportunities. Gentle, kind, a hard worker. Tendency to lose items. Needs a lot of freedom.

Lot, 11: Travels frequently. Creates group harmony. Dynamic, busy lifestyle.

Lothario, 8: Recuperates quickly. Competitive in business. Dynamic, busy lifestyle. Great judge of character. Independent, critical of self and others. Gentle, kind, a hard worker. Blessed in some ways. Nurturing, loving.

Lottie, 9: Benefits from meditation. Artistic and creative. Dynamic, busy lifestyle. Needs to slow down. A free spirit, very adaptable.

Lou, 3: Slow to make decisions. Has creative solutions. Attractive and charming.

Louella, 6: Easygoing attitude. Magnetic personality. Attractive and charming. A free spirit, very adaptable. Strong verbal skills. Ups and downs financially. Independent and self-motivated.

Louie, 8: Recuperates quickly. Competitive in business. Attractive and charming. Blessed in some ways. A free spirit, very adaptable.

Louis, 22: Travels frequently. Creates group harmony. Creative and inspiring. Blessed in some ways. Charming and devoted.

Louisa, 5: Moves and travels often. Natural counselor and healer. Fun, attractive. Generous, thoughtful. Charming and devoted. Bright, adventuresome.

Louise, 9: Benefits from meditation. Artistic and creative. Easygoing manner. Blessed in some ways. Charming and devoted. A free spirit, very adaptable.

Lourdes, 4: Domestically creative. Assumes responsibility. Gracious, well-mannered. Gentle, kind, a hard worker. Reliable, responsible. A free spirit, very adaptable. Charming and devoted.

Love, 9: Benefits from meditation. Artistic and creative. Intuitive and inspired. A free spirit, very adaptable.

Lowell, 7: Intellectually sound. Open to opportunities. Likes to meet new people. A free spirit, very adaptable. Frequent traveler. Many ups and downs financially.

Loyal, 20: Honest and sincere. Natural counselor and healer. Needs a lot of freedom. Reads people easily. Communicates skillfully.

L'Toya, 10: Strong verbal skills. Dynamic, busy lifestyle. Natural counselor and healer. Needs a lot of freedom. Independent, critical of self and others.

Lu, 6: Easygoing attitude. Attractive and charming. Self-sacrificing and devoted.

Luana, 4: Domestically creative. Gracious, well-mannered. Independent, critical of self and others. Original and unconventional. Bold, courageous, a bit stubborn.

Luanne, 22: Travels frequently. Gracious, well-mannered. Independent, critical of self and others. Original and unconventional. Romantic, sensual. A free spirit, very adaptable.

Lucas, 11: Travels frequently. Creative and inspiring. Cheerful, light-hearted. Independent, critical of self and others. Charming and devoted. A bit forceful.

Luci, 9: Benefits from meditation. Easygoing manner. Self-expressive, cheerful. Blessed in some ways.

Lucia, 10: Strong verbal skills. Attractive and charming. Optimistic, outspoken. Blessed in some ways. Independent, critical of self and others.

Lucian, 6: Easygoing attitude. Lovely, attractive. Cheerful, optimistic. Artistic, having good taste. Independent, self-motivated. Creative and opinionated.

Luciana, 7: Intellectually sound. Stylish and refined. Self-expressive, cheerful. Blessed in some ways. Independent, critical of self and others. Original and unconventional. Bold, courageous, a bit stubborn.

Lucille, 11: Travels frequently. Creative and inspiring. Cheerful, light-hearted. Blessed in some ways. Frequent traveler. Many ups and downs financially. A free spirit, very adaptable.

Lucinda, 10: Strong verbal skills. Attractive and charming. Self-expressive, cheerful. Blessed in some ways. Original and unconventional. Reliable, responsible. Independent, critical of self and others.

Lucio, 6: Easygoing attitude. Lovely and attractive. Self-expressive, cheerful. Artistic, having good taste. Natural counselor and healer.

Lucius, 22: Travels frequently. Creative and inspiring. Optimistic, outspoken. Blessed in some ways. Difficulty making decisions. Many mood swings.

Lucretia, 8: Recuperates quickly. Attractive and charming. Self-expressive, cheerful. Gentle, kind, a hard worker. A free spirit, very adaptable. Dynamic, busy lifestyle. Blessed in some ways. Independent, critical of self and others.

Lucy, 7: Intellectually sound. Stylish and refined. Self-expressive, cheerful. Needs a lot of freedom.

Ludlow, 6: Easygoing attitude. Lovely and attractive. Systematic, organized. Frequent traveler. Natural counselor and healer. Likes to meet new people.

Ludovick, 7: Intellectually sound. Stylish and refined. Reliable, responsible. Natural counselor and healer. Intuitive and inspired. Blessed in some ways. Self-expressive, cheerful. Desire to succeed.

Ludvig, 30: Slow to make decisions. Youthful, appealing. Reliable, responsible. Intuitive and inspired. Blessed in some ways. Scientific and philosophical.

Ludwig, 4: Domestically creative. Gracious, well-mannered. Systematic, organized. Likes to meet new people. Blessed in some ways. Scientific and philosophical.

Luella, 9: Benefits from meditation. Attractive and charming. A free spirit, very adaptable. Frequent traveler. Many ups and downs financially. Independent, critical of self and others.

Luigi, 4: Domestically creative. Gracious, well-mannered. Blessed in some ways. Scientific and philosophical. Artistic, having good taste.

Luis, 7: Intellectually sound. Stylish and refined. Blessed in some ways. Impulsive and extreme.

Luke, 4: Domestically creative. Gracious, well-mannered. Strong desire to succeed. A free spirit, very adaptable.

Lulu, 3: Slow to make decisions. Youthful, appealing. Great verbal skills. Ups and downs financially.

Luna, 3: Slow to make decisions. Youthful, appealing. Romantic, original. Aims to please.

Lundy, 22: Travels frequently. Gracious, well-mannered. Original and unconventional. Reliable, responsible. Needs a lot of freedom.

Lunette, 7: Intellectually sound. Stylish and refined. Original and unconventional. A free spirit, very adaptable. Dynamic, busy lifestyle. Sensitive and easily hurt. Likes change and variety.

Lupe, 9: Benefits from meditation. Attractive and charming. Intelligent and knowledgeable. A free spirit, very adaptable.

Lupita, 7: Intellectually sound. Stylish and refined. Levelheaded, knowledgeable. Blessed in some ways. Dynamic, busy lifestyle. Not easily fooled.

Luther, 30: Slow to make decisions. Attractive and charming. Dynamic, busy lifestyle. Great judge of character. A free spirit, very adaptable. Gentle, kind, a hard worker.

Lydia, 6: Easygoing attitude. Needs a lot of freedom. Reliable, responsible. Blessed in some ways. Independent, critical of self and others.

Lyell, 3: Slow to make decisions. Freedom-loving. A free spirit, very adaptable. Frequent traveler. Many ups and downs financially.

Lyle, 9: Benefits from meditation. Dislikes limitations. Many ups and downs financially. A free spirit, very adaptable.

Lyman, 20: Honest and sincere. Perceptive, psychic. Domestic, hardworking. Independent, critical of self and others. Original and unconventional.

Lyn, 6: Easygoing attitude. Needs a lot of freedom. Creative, original.

Lynda, 20: Honest and sincere. Perceptive, psychic. Original and unconventional. Reliable, responsible. Independent, critical of self and others.

Lyndon, 30: Slow to make decisions. Freedom-loving. Creative, original. Reliable, responsible. Natural counselor and healer. Romantic, sensual.

Lynette, 11: Travels frequently. A truth seeker. Original and unconventional. A free spirit, very adaptable. Dynamic, busy lifestyle. Sensitive and easily hurt. Tendency to overindulge.

Lynn, 20: Honest and sincere. Needs a lot of freedom. Original and unconventional. Romantic, sensual.

Lynne, 7: Intellectually sound. Stylish and refined. Original and unconventional. Romantic, sensual. A free spirit, very adaptable.

Lyon, 3: Slow to make decisions. Freedom loving. Natural counselor and healer. Original and unconventional.

Lyssa, 4: Domestically creative. Needs a lot of freedom. Charming and devoted. Many mood swings. Independent, critical of self and others.

M

If a name begins with M, has more than one M, or ends with an M, this person is domestic, hardworking, energetic, and has a strong physical constitution.

The letter M is the 13th letter of the alphabet. Since 1 + 3 = 4, the 13th letter of the alphabet has the same vibrational influence as the number 4. The 1 rules beginnings, 3 rules balance, and 4 rules work and family. So people whose names begin with M are often beginning to balance work and family. They've been blessed with an extra strong physical constitution to handle the demands of this lifetime.

The 13th letter is a "karmic debt" letter. Most of us grew up hearing that the number 13 is an unlucky number. The curse of this 13th letter M is that we often learn lessons the hard way in some area of our life. Actually, the reason it's unlucky is because it adds up to a 4. A square has four sides; in astrology, "squares" mean "difficulty." Those with this letter anywhere in their name must work very hard to accomplish their task at hand. Obstacles seem to get in the way and challenges must be overcome time and again. M is for messy! Some with this letter in their name will give in to laziness or negativity. Some may easily give up on their goals. The key to success for an M person is to focus on one thing at a time, as opposed to wasting time scattering energies over many different projects. The lesson of the M is simply to work hard and stay on task. That's why Moms work so hard and have so much to do. If Mommy didn't have so many Ms in her name, she probably wouldn't have so many messes to clean up!

Those with M as the first letter of their name and A as the first vowel can be quite ambitious. If they don't accomplish much by the end of the day, they will beat themselves up over it. M names, similar to D names, are list keepers. Most top executives keep a list of tasks to accomplish for the day. A successful M will learn to write a list every day. The 4 vibration rings through the letter M, coloring it with work and family. Therefore, M is very domestic. Cooking and cleaning come easily with this letter. Similar to the letter D, M doesn't mind doing the chores most of us hate doing. If the M person gives in to alcohol, it's to escape the bully in his or her head. They are their own worst critic! Also, similar to D and V, those with this letter will often say they don't want to argue, but end up arguing anyway. An hour after they've said they don't want to argue, they are still arguing.

The most important lesson for the M-named person is to finish one task at a time to completion. Keeping a list might be the single most important piece of advice for anyone with an M in his or her name. Achieving their goals will make them happy, and completing each task one at a time will help them reach their goals. Then they'll be happy campers.

Similar to Ds, the typical M person doesn't feel comfortable being unfaithful. This letter also likes financial security; the sound of rustling dollars soothes their nerves somehow. As a general rule, names that begin with M can be counted on to pay the bills on time and handle chores without complaining. All in all, those of us looking for some stability in our lives can turn to the M. They'll be right there, paying the bills and taking care of life's little burdens so we don't have to.

Martha Stewart is a prime example of the domestic type M. This domestic goddess is best known as an entrepreneur. The intensity I, from the two As in her name, makes her quite a pioneer woman. With a hidden 5 in the beginning of her name, she loves adventure. This 5 coupled with the two As makes her bold and daring too. Many entrepreneurs have at least one A in their name. Martha heads her own magazine and television show. She makes cooking, gardening, cleaning, organizing, and refinishing furniture not only look easy, but fun too! Still, that unlucky 13th letter has gotten her into some difficult situations. The 2004 jury of the "insider trading" scandal found her guilty of obstructing justice. As mentioned before, M is for messy. The combination of her two As and power number 7 sometimes make it difficult for her to get along with others. Similar to Simon Cowell, she can't pretend to like someone she doesn't like due to her power number 7. On the other hand, with two

I-ruled letters and a 2-ruled letter T in her name, she is a baby in some areas of her life. Her name is made up of very young and very old numbers. The center of her name is a hardworking, gentle, kind R, coupled with a very social and sensitive T. The outer part of her name has enough strength to carry her to any goal she undertakes. The material lessons of her H plus the first letter M have caused her to learn lessons the hard way. Hs usually have many financial ups and downs. Many of the letters in her name are harsh, except the vulnerable and sensitive T in the middle. Her name is built like a Sherman tank on the outside, but vulnerable on the inside. Only those close to her really know her because she doesn't let very many people in.

Madonna is another famous ambitious M person with her three children and busy career schedule. Born a Leo, she desires to create children of her body and mind as well. She has three intensity numbers in her name: 1, 4, and 5. The 1 makes her bold and courageous, and also a pioneer; the 4 makes her hardworking and domestic; and the 5 gives her wild tendencies. Many rock stars have an intensity 5 in their names. Madonna does seem a bit intense, but it's her power number 8 that makes her the "material girl." With all this intensity, will she ever burn out? Probably not; she has a strong constitution with the M and D in her name. Notice the O in the middle of her name? Deep down in the middle is a nurturer. She may not be done raising children yet. Or else she will find a business or an organization to nurture and love. Her name is methodical, disciplined, and service-oriented. With the 8 power number, the same as Lance Armstrong, she's a survivor and in complete control.

The late Martin Luther King, Jr., was a civil rights leader who worked to bring about equal rights for black people. He was a Baptist minister who preached "nonviolent resistance." The intensity 9, from the R and I in his name, made him a humanitarian. He liked people of all race and color. This trait helped him with his "I have a dream…" speech which rang out his futuristic vision of people not being "judged by the color of their skin, but by the content of their character." With a 30 power number, he was able to help others through communicating, counseling, and advice, with assistance from God. Although the M in his name made him systematic, disciplined, and organized, it's ruled by that unlucky 4 vibration, which may be why he did not live long enough to see his dream come true. On April 4, 1968, he died from a violent act.

Some other famous people whose names start with M are: Mae West, Mary Tyler Moore, Macaulay Culkin, Matthew Broderick, Madeleine Stowe, Mel Gibson, Maia Morgenstern, Mikhail Baryshnikov, Margot Kidder, Michael Douglas, Meg Ryan, Michael Keaton, Meryl Streep, Michael Jackson, Morgan Freeman, Michelle Pfeiffer, Michael J. Fox, Muhammad Ali, Mel Brooks, Morgan Fairchild, Mike Myers, Mary-Kate Olsen, Matt Damon, Margaret O'Brien, Mariah Carey, Mark Twain, Marlon Brando, Martin Sheen, Michael Caine, Martin Short, Mick Jagger, and Maya Angelou.

QUICK REFERENCE OF "M" NAMES

Mabel, 6: Creative entrepreneur. Pioneer and risk taker. Friendly, but shy. A free spirit, very adaptable. Strong verbal skills.

Mac, 8: Patient, tolerant. Resolute and purposeful. Self-expressive, cheerful.

Macaulay, 5: Entertains at home. Bright, adventuresome. Self-expressive, cheerful. Bold, courageous, a bit stubborn. Charming and attractive. Strong verbal skills. Pioneer, risk:taker. Needs a lot of freedom.

Macauley, 9: Works hard, devoted. Helpful, sincere. Self-expressive, cheerful. Bold, courageous, a bit stubborn. Attractive and charming. Strong verbal skills. A free spirit, very adaptable. Dislikes restrictions.

Machiko, 6: Creative entrepreneur. Pioneer and risk taker. Self-expressive, cheerful. Great judge of character. Blessed in some ways. Strong desire to succeed. Natural counselor and healer.

Mack, 10: Steadfast and determined. Independent, critical of self and others. Self-expressive, cheerful. Strong desire to succeed.

Mackenzie, 6: Creative entrepreneur. Pioneer and risk taker. Self-expressive, cheerful. Strong desire to succeed. A free spirit, very adaptable. Original and unconventional. Uses common sense. Blessed in some ways. Loves adventure and excitement.

Macy, 6: Creative entrepreneur. Pioneer and risk taker. Self-expressive, cheerful. Needs a lot of freedom.

Maddock, 6: Creative entrepreneur. Pioneer and risk taker. Domestic, hardworking. Workaholic, determined. Natural counselor and healer. Self-expressive, cheerful. Strong desire to succeed.

Maddox, 7: Must have faith. Not easily influenced. Reliable, responsible. Workaholic, determined. Natural counselor and healer. Artistic, sensual, perceptive.

Madeleine, 5: Entertains at home. Bright, adventuresome. Reliable, responsible. A free spirit, very adaptable. Strong verbal skills. Likes change and variety. Blessed in some ways. Original and unconventional. Physical and passionate.

Madeline, 9: Works hard, devoted. Helpful, sincere. Reliable, responsible. A free spirit, very adaptable. Strong verbal skills. Blessed in some ways. Original and unconventional. Loves adventure and excitement.

Madelyn, 11: Insightful, sensitive. Independent, self-motivated. Domestic, hardworking. A free spirit, very adaptable. Strong verbal skills. Dislikes limitations. Original and unconventional.

Madge, 3: Family communicator. Aims to please. Serious, yet fun:loving. Scientific and philosophical. A free spirit, very adaptable.

Madison, 30: Family communicator. Aims to please. Serious, yet fun:loving. Blessed in some ways. Charming and devoted. Natural counselor and healer. Original and unconventional.

Madonna, 8: Patient, tolerant. Resolute and purposeful. Domestic, hardworking. Natural counselor and healer. Original and unconventional. Romantic, sensual. Bold, courageous, a bit stubborn.

Mae, 10: Steadfast and determined. Independent, critical of self and others. A free spirit, very adaptable.

Maelyne, 30: Family communicator. Aims to please. A free spirit, very adaptable. Strong verbal skills. Dislikes limitations. Original and unconventional. Tendency to overindulge.

Magdelaine, 8: Patient, tolerant. Resolute and purposeful. Willpower and determination. Problem solver. A free spirit, very adaptable. Strong verbal skills. Not easily influenced. Artistic, having good taste. Creative, opinionated. Physical and passionate.

Maggie, 6: Creative entrepreneur. Pioneer and risk taker. Scientific and philosophical. Levelheaded. Blessed in some ways. A free spirit, very adaptable.

Magnolia, 9: Works hard, devoted. Helpful, sincere. Gracious, well-mannered. Original and unconventional. Natural counselor and healer. Strong verbal skills. Blessed in some ways. Bold, courageous, a bit stubborn.

Magnus, 3: Family communicator. Aims to please. Gracious, well-mannered. Original and unconventional. Very lucky. Charming and devoted.

Maguire, 11: Insightful, sensitive. Independent, self-motivated. Scientific and philosophical. Attractive and charming. Blessed in some ways. Gentle, kind, very diligent. A free spirit, very adaptable.

Mahalia, 9: Works hard, devoted. Helpful, sincere. Great judge of character. Critical of self and others. Strong verbal skills. Blessed in some ways. Pioneer and risk taker.

Mahina, 10: Steadfast and determined. Independent, critical of self and others. Great judge of character. Blessed in some ways. Original and unconventional. Bold, courageous, a bit stubborn.

Mai, 5: Entertains at home. Bright, adventuresome. Blessed in some ways.

Maia, 6: Creative entrepreneur. Pioneer and risk taker. Artistic, having good taste. Independent, a bit stubborn.

Maisie, 11: Insightful, sensitive. Independent, self-motivated. Blessed in some ways. Charming and devoted. Artistic, having good taste. A free spirit, very adaptable.

Maja, 7: Must have faith. Not easily influenced. Very clever and talented. Bold, courageous, a bit stubborn.

Major, 3: Family communicator. Aims to please. Very clever and talented. Natural counselor and healer. Gentle, kind, very diligent.

Makaila, 3: Family communicator. Aims to please. Strong desire to succeed. Critical of self and others. Blessed in some ways. Slow to make decisions. Not easily influenced.

Makayla, 10: Steadfast and determined. Independent, critical of self and others. Strong desire to succeed. Bright, adventuresome. Needs a lot of freedom. Communicates skillfully. Pioneer and risk taker.

Mala, 9: Works hard, devoted. Helpful, sincere. Strong verbal skills. Bold, courageous, a bit stubborn.

Malachai, 30: Family communicator. Aims to please. Great verbal skills. Independent, a bit stubborn. Self-expressive, cheerful. Great judge of character. Pioneer and risk taker. Blessed in some ways.

Malachi, 11: Insightful, sensitive. Independent, self-motivated. Communicates skillfully. Bold, courageous, a bit stubborn. Self-expressive, cheerful. Great judge of character. Blessed in some ways.

Malcolm, 6: Creative entrepreneur. Pioneer and risk taker. Strong verbal skills. Optimistic, outspoken. Nurturing, loving. Frequent traveler. Desires financial security.

Mali, 8: Patient, tolerant. Resolute and purposeful. Great verbal skills. Blessed in some ways.

Malina, 5: Entertains at home. Bright, adventuresome. Travels frequently. Blessed in some ways. Original and unconventional. Bold, courageous, a bit stubborn.

Malinda, 9: Works hard, devoted. Helpful, sincere. Communicates skillfully. Blessed in some ways. Original and unconventional. Reliable, responsible. Pioneer and risk taker.

Mallory, 6: Creative entrepreneur. Pioneer and risk taker. Travels frequently. Communicates skillfully. Natural counselor and healer. Gentle, kind, diligent. Needs a lot of freedom.

Malorie, 10: Steadfast and determined. Independent, critical of self and others. Strong verbal skills. Natural counselor and healer. Gentle, kind, very diligent. Blessed in some ways. A free spirit, very adaptable.

Malory, 30: Family communicator. Aims to please. Great verbal skills. Natural counselor and healer. Gentle, kind, very diligent. Needs a lot of freedom.

Malven, 22: A workaholic, focused. Ambitious leader, great vision. Travels frequently. Intuitive and inspired. A free spirit, very adaptable. Original and unconventional.

Malvina, 9: Works hard, devoted. Helpful, sincere. Strong verbal skills. Intuitive and inspired. Blessed in some ways. Original and unconventional. Pioneer and risk taker.

Mamie, 5: Entertains at home. Bright, adventuresome. Domestic, hardworking. Artistic, having good taste. Physical and passionate.

Mamood, 7: Must have faith. Not easily influenced. Desires financial security. Natural counselor and healer. Strong parental skills. Reliable, responsible.

Manda, 6: Creative entrepreneur. Pioneer and risk taker. Original and unconventional. Reliable, responsible. Bold, courageous, a bit stubborn.

Mandel, 22: A workaholic, focused. Ambitious leader, great vision. Romantic, opinionated. Domestic, responsible. A free spirit, very adaptable. Strong verbal skills.

Mandie, 10: Steadfast and determined. Independent, critical of self and others. Original and unconventional. Reliable, responsible. Blessed in some ways. A free spirit, very adaptable.

Mandy, 3: Family communicator. Aims to please. Romantic, creative. Reliable, responsible. Needs a lot of freedom.

Manfred, 7: Must have faith. Not easily influenced. Original and unconventional. Self-sacrificing, loving. Gentle, kind, very diligent. A free spirit, very adaptable. Reliable, responsible.

Manning, 9: Works hard, devoted. Helpful, sincere. Creative, opinionated. Romantic, sensual. Blessed in some ways. Scientific and philosophical.

Manny, 22: A workaholic, focused. Ambitious leader, great vision. Original and opinionated. Romantic, sensual. Needs a lot of freedom.

Manrique, 8: Patient, tolerant. Resolute and purposeful. Creative and original. Gentle, kind, very helpful. Blessed in some ways. Influential, a natural leader. Attractive and charming. A free spirit, very adaptable.

Mansoor, 5: Entertains at home. Bright, adventuresome. Original and unconventional. Charming and devoted. Natural counselor and healer. Enjoys working. Gentle, kind, very diligent.

Manuel, 3: Family communicator. Aims to please. Creative, original. Attractive and charming. Physical and passionate. Slow to make decisions.

Manuela, 22: A workaholic, focused. Ambitious leader, great vision. Original and unconventional. Attractive and charming. A free spirit, very adaptable. Strong verbal skills. Bold, courageous, a bit stubborn.

Mara, 6: Creative entrepreneur. Pioneer and risk taker. Duty-bound, self-sacrificing. Bold, courageous, a bit stubborn.

Marbin, 30: Family communicator. Aims to please. Sympathetic, kind. Friendly, but shy. Blessed in some ways. Original and unconventional.

Marc, 8: Patient, tolerant. Resolute and purposeful. Intense inner power. Self-expressive, cheerful.

Marcel, 7: Must have faith. Not easily influenced. Gentle, kind, very diligent. Self-expressive, cheerful. A free spirit, very adaptable. Strong verbal skills.

Marcela, 8: Patient, tolerant. Resolute and purposeful. Intense inner power. Self-expressive, cheerful. A free spirit, very adaptable. Strong verbal skills. Bold, courageous, a bit stubborn.

Marcella, 11: Insightful, sensitive. Independent, self-motivated. Gentle, kind, very diligent. Self-expressive, cheerful. A free spirit, very adaptable. Strong verbal skills. Ups and downs financially. Bold, courageous, a bit stubborn.

Marcelle, 6: Creative entrepreneur. Pioneer and risk taker. Duty-bound, self-sacrificing. Self-expressive, cheerful. A free spirit, very adaptable. Strong verbal skills. Ups and downs financially. Loves adventure and excitement.

Marcelo, 4: Strong physical constitution. Resolute, purposeful. Gentle, kind, very diligent. Self-expressive, cheerful. Sensual, passionate. Strong verbal skills. Natural counselor and healer.

Marci, 8: Patient, tolerant. Resolute and purposeful. Intense inner power. Self-expressive, cheerful. Blessed in some ways.

Marcia, 9: Works hard, devoted. Helpful, sincere. Humanitarian, idealistic. Self-expressive, cheerful. Blessed in some ways. Bold, courageous, a bit stubborn.

Marcie, 4: Strong physical constitution. Natural teaching ability. Gentle, kind, very diligent. Self-expressive, cheerful. Blessed in some ways. A free spirit, very adaptable.

Marco, 5: Entertains at home. Bright, adventuresome. Good deed doer. Self-expressive, cheerful. Natural counselor and healer.

Marcos, 6: Creative entrepreneur. Pioneer and risk taker. Duty-bound, self-sacrificing. Self-expressive, cheerful. Natural counselor and healer. Charming and devoted.

Marcus, 3: Family communicator. Aims to please. Sympathetic, kind. Self-expressive, cheerful. Attractive and charming. Very devoted.

Marcy, 6: Creative entrepreneur. Pioneer and risk taker. Duty-bound, self-sacrificing. Cheerful, great sense of humor. Needs a lot of freedom.

Margaret, 11: Insightful, sensitive. Independent, self-motivated. Gentle, kind, very diligent. Scientific and philosophical. Bold, courageous, a bit stubborn. Could be forgetful. A free spirit, very adaptable. Dynamic, busy lifestyle.

Margarita, 7: Must have faith. Not easily influenced. Diligent, helpful. Extremely intelligent. Resolute and purposeful. Tendency to lose items. Blessed in some ways. Dynamic, busy lifestyle. Independent, critical of self and others.

Margarite, 11: Insightful, sensitive. Independent, self-motivated. Gentle, kind, very diligent. Scientific and philosophical. Bold, courageous, a bit stubborn. Could be forgetful. Blessed in some ways. Dynamic, busy lifestyle. A free spirit, very adaptable.

Margarito, 3: Family communicator. Aims to please. Sympathetic, kind. Has willpower and determination. Bold, courageous, a bit stubborn. Diligent, helpful. Blessed in some ways. Dynamic, busy lifestyle. Natural counselor and healer.

Margaux, 4: Strong physical constitution. Natural teaching ability. Gentle, kind, a hard worker. Scientific and philosophical. Bold, courageous, a bit stubborn. Attractive and charming. Artistic, sensual, perceptive.

Marge, 8: Patient, tolerant. Resolute and purposeful. Intense inner power. Scientific and philosophical. A free spirit, very adaptable.

Margery, 6: Creative entrepreneur. Pioneer and risk taker. Duty-bound, self-sacrificing. Scientific and philosophical. A step ahead of others. Tendency to lose items. Needs a lot of freedom.

Margo, 9: Works hard, devoted. Helpful, sincere. Humanitarian, idealistic. Scientific and philosophical. Natural counselor and healer.

Margot, 11: Insightful, sensitive. Independent, self-motivated. Gentle, kind, very diligent. Scientific and philosophical. Natural counselor and healer. Dynamic, busy lifestyle.

Mari, 5: Entertains at home. Bright, adventuresome. Good deed doer. Blessed in some ways.

Maria, 6: Creative entrepreneur. Pioneer and risk taker. Duty-bound, self-sacrificing. Artistic, having good taste. Bold, courageous, a bit stubborn.

Mariah, 5: Entertains at home. Bright, adventuresome. Good deed doer. Blessed in some ways. Bold, courageous, a bit stubborn. Great judge of character.

Mariam, 10: Steadfast and determined. Independent, critical of self and others. Gentle, kind, very diligent. Blessed in some ways. Bold, courageous, a bit stubborn. Desires financial security.

Marian, 11: Insightful, sensitive. Independent, self-motivated. Gentle, kind, very diligent. Blessed in some ways. Bold, courageous, a bit stubborn. Original and unconventional.

Mariana, 30: Family communicator. Aims to please. Sympathetic, kind. Blessed in some ways. Bold, courageous, a bit stubborn. Original and unconventional. Pioneer and risk taker.

Marianne, 3: Family communicator. Aims to please. Sympathetic, kind. Blessed in some ways. Bold, courageous, a bit stubborn. Original and unconventional. Creative and opinionated. Physical and passionate.

Mariano, 8: Patient, tolerant. Resolute and purposeful. Intense inner power. Blessed in some ways. Bold, courageous, a bit stubborn. Original and unconventional. Natural counselor and healer.

Maricar, 9: Works hard, devoted. Helpful, sincere. Humanitarian, idealistic. Blessed in some ways. Self-expressive, cheerful. Bold, courageous, a bit stubborn. Tendency to lose items.

Maricella, 11: Insightful, sensitive. Independent, self-motivated. Gentle, kind, very diligent. Blessed in some ways. Self-expressive, cheerful. A free spirit, very adaptable. Great verbal skills. Ups and downs financially. Bold, courageous, a bit stubborn.

Marie, 10: Steadfast and determined. Independent, critical of self and others. Gentle, kind, very diligent. Blessed in some ways. A free spirit, very adaptable.

Mariela, 5: Entertains at home. Bright, adventuresome. Good deed doer. Blessed in some ways. A free spirit, very adaptable. Strong verbal skills. Bold, courageous, a bit stubborn.

Marietta, 6: Creative entrepreneur. Pioneer and risk taker. Duty-bound, self-sacrificing. Artistic, having good taste. A free spirit, very adaptable. Dynamic, busy lifestyle. Sensitive and easily hurt. Bold, courageous, a bit stubborn.

Mariette, 10: Steadfast and determined. Independent, critical of self and others. Gentle, kind, very diligent. Blessed in some ways. A free spirit, very adaptable. Dynamic, busy lifestyle. Sensitive and easily hurt. Loves adventure and excitement.

Marili, 8: Patient, tolerant. Resolute and purposeful. Intense inner power. Blessed in some ways. Strong verbal skills. Artistic, having good taste.

Marilu, 11: Insightful, sensitive. Independent, self-motivated. Gentle, kind, very diligent. Blessed in some ways. Strong verbal skills. Attractive and charming.

Mariluz, 10: Steadfast and determined. Independent, critical of self and others. Gentle, kind, very diligent. Blessed in some ways. Strong verbal skills. Attractive and charming. Uses common sense.

Marilyn, 11: Insightful, sensitive. Independent, self-motivated. Gentle, kind, very diligent. Blessed in some ways. Strong verbal skills. Needs a lot of freedom. Original and unconventional.

Marina, 11: Insightful, sensitive. Independent, self-motivated. Gentle, kind, very diligent. Blessed in some ways. Original and unconventional. Bold, courageous, a bit stubborn.

Marini, 10: Steadfast and determined. Independent, critical of self and others. Gentle, kind, very diligent. Blessed in some ways. Original and unconventional. Artistic, having good taste.

Mario, 11: Insightful, sensitive. Independent, self-motivated. Gentle, kind, very diligent. Blessed in some ways. Natural counselor and healer.

Marion, 7: Must have faith. Not easily influenced. Gentle, kind, very diligent. Blessed in some ways. Natural counselor and healer. Original and unconventional.

Marisol, 6: Creative entrepreneur. Pioneer and risk taker. Duty-bound, self-sacrificing. Artistic, having good taste. Charming and devoted. Natural counselor and healer. Strong verbal skills.

Marissa, 8: Patient, tolerant. Resolute and purposeful. Intense inner power. Blessed in some ways. Charming and devoted. Impulsive and extreme. Bold, courageous, a bit stubborn.

Maritza, 7: Must have faith. Not easily fooled. Gentle, kind, a hard worker. Artistic, having good taste. Dynamic, busy lifestyle. Great judge of character. Independent, critical of self and others.

Marjo, 3: Family communicator. Pioneer and risk taker. Sympathetic, kind. Clever and talented. Natural counselor and healer.

Marjorie, 8: Patient, tolerant. Resolute and purposeful. Intense inner power. Very clever and talented. Natural counselor and healer. Tendency to lose items. Blessed in some ways. A free spirit, very adaptable.

Mark, 7: Must have faith. Not easily influenced. Gentle, kind, a hard worker. Strong desire to succeed.

Marla, 9: Works hard, devoted. Helpful, sincere. Humanitarian, idealistic. Strong verbal skills. Bold, courageous, a bit stubborn.

Marleen, 5: Entertains at home. Bright, adventuresome. Good deed doer. Communicates skillfully. A free spirit, very adaptable. Physical and passionate. Original and unconventional.

Marlene, 5: (Same as Marleen.)

Marley, 11: Insightful, sensitive. Independent, self-motivated. Gentle, kind, a hard worker. Great verbal skills. A free spirit, very adaptable. Dislikes limitations.

Marlo, 5: Entertains at home. Pioneer and risk taker. Good deed doer. Strong verbal skills. Natural counselor and healer.

Marlow, 10: Steadfast and determined. Independent, critical of self and others. Gentle, kind, a hard worker. Strong verbal skills. Natural counselor and healer. Likes to meet new people.

Marly, 6: Creative entrepreneur. Pioneer and risk taker. Duty-bound, self-sacrificing. Strong verbal skills. Needs a lot of freedom.

Marney, 4: Strong physical constitution. Natural teaching ability. Gentle, kind, very diligent. Original and unconventional. A free spirit, very adaptable. Dislikes limitations.

Marni, 10: Steadfast and determined. Independent, critical of self and others. Gentle, kind, very diligent. Original and unconventional. Blessed in some ways.

Marnie, 6: Creative entrepreneur. Pioneer and risk taker. Duty-bound, self-sacrificing. Original and unconventional. Blessed in some ways. A free spirit, very adaptable.

Marquita, 10: Steadfast and determined. Independent, critical of self and others. Gentle, kind, a hard worker. Influential, a natural leader. Attractive and charming. Blessed in some ways. Dynamic, busy lifestyle. Bold, courageous, a bit stubborn.

Marsh, 5: Entertains at home. Bright, adventuresome. Good deed doer. Charming and devoted. Great judge of character.

Marsha, 6: Creative entrepreneur. Pioneer and risk taker. Duty-bound, self-sacrificing. Charming and devoted. Great judge of character. Bold, courageous, a bit stubborn.

Marshall, 30: Family communicator. Aims to please. Sympathetic, kind. Charming and devoted. Great judge of character. Bold, courageous, a bit stubborn. Strong verbal skills. Financial ups and downs.

Marsi, 6: Creative entrepreneur. Pioneer and risk taker. Duty-bound, self-sacrificing. Charming and devoted. Artistic, having good taste.

Mart, 7: Must have faith. Not easily influenced. Gentle, kind, very diligent. Dynamic, busy lifestyle.

Marta, 8: Patient, tolerant. Resolute and purposeful. Intense inner power. Dynamic, busy lifestyle. Bold, courageous, a bit stubborn.

Marten, 8: Patient, tolerant. Resolute and purposeful. Intense inner power. Dynamic, busy lifestyle. A free spirit, very adaptable. Original and unconventional.

Martha, 7: Must have faith. Not easily influenced. Gentle, kind, very diligent. Dynamic, busy lifestyle. Great judge of character. Bold, courageous, a bit stubborn.

Marthe, 11: Insightful, sensitive. Independent, self-motivated. Gentle, kind, very diligent. Dynamic, busy lifestyle. Great judge of character. A free spirit, very adaptable.

Marti, 7: Must have faith. Not easily influenced. Gentle, kind, very diligent. Dynamic, busy lifestyle. Blessed in some ways.

Martie, 30: Family communicator. Aims to please. Sympathetic, kind. Dynamic, busy lifestyle. Blessed in some ways. A free spirit, very adaptable.

Martin, 30: Family communicator. Aims to please. Sympathetic, kind. Dynamic, busy lifestyle. Blessed in some ways. Original and unconventional.

Martina, 4: Strong physical constitution. Natural teaching ability. Gentle, kind, very diligent. Dynamic, busy lifestyle. Blessed in some ways. Original and unconventional. Bold, courageous, a bit stubborn.

Martine, 8: Patient, tolerant. Resolute and purposeful. Intense inner power. Dynamic, busy lifestyle. Blessed in some ways. Original and unconventional. A free spirit, very adaptable.

Marty, 5: Entertains at home. Bright, adventuresome. Good deed doer. Dynamic, busy lifestyle. Needs a lot of freedom.

Martyne, 6: Creative entrepreneur. Pioneer and risk taker. Duty-bound, self-sacrificing. Dynamic, busy lifestyle. Needs a lot of freedom. Original and unconventional. A free spirit, very adaptable.

Marv, 9: Works hard, devoted. Helpful, sincere. Humanitarian, idealistic. Intuitive and inspired.

Marvel, 8: Patient, tolerant. Resolute and purposeful. Intense inner power. Intuitive and inspired. A free spirit, very adaptable. Communicates skillfully.

Marvin, 5: Entertains at home. Bright, adventuresome. Good deed doer. Intuitive and inspired. Blessed in some ways. Original and unconventional.

Marwa, 20: Domestically social. Reads people easily. Gentle, kind, very diligent. Likes to meet new people. Bold, courageous, a bit stubborn.

Mary, 3: Family communicator. Aims to please. Sympathetic, kind. Needs a lot of freedom.

Maryam, 8: Patient, tolerant. Resolute and purposeful. Intense inner power. Needs a lot of freedom. Bold, courageous, a bit stubborn. Desires financial security.

Maryann, 5: Entertains at home. Bright, adventuresome. Good deed doer. Needs a lot of freedom. Bold, courageous, a bit stubborn. Original and unconventional. Romantic, sensual.

Marye, 8: Patient, tolerant. Resolute and purposeful. Intense inner power. Needs a lot of freedom. Physical and passionate.

Marylou, 6: Creative entrepreneur. Pioneer and risk taker. Duty-bound, self-sacrificing. Dislikes limitations. Strong verbal skills. Natural counselor and healer. Attractive and charming.

Marylyn, 9: Works hard, devoted. Helpful and sincere. Should practice tolerance. Needs a lot of freedom. Strong verbal skills. Highly perceptive. Creative, opinionated.

Mashka, 8: Patient, tolerant. Resolute and purposeful. Passionate and loving. Great judge of character. Strong desire to succeed. Bold, courageous, a bit stubborn.

Masika, 9: Works hard, diligent. Helpful, sincere. Charming and devoted. Blessed in some ways. Strong desire to succeed. Bold, courageous, a bit stubborn.

Mason, 8: Patient, tolerant. Resolute and purposeful. Passionate and loving. Natural counselor and healer. Original and unconventional.

Mateo, 9: Works hard, devoted. Helpful and sincere. Dynamic, busy lifestyle. A free spirit, very adaptable. Natural counselor and healer.

Mathew, 7: Must have faith. Not easily influenced. Dynamic, busy lifestyle. Great judge of character. A free spirit, very adaptable. Likes to meet new people.

Mathilda, 5: Entertains at home. Bright, adventuresome. Energetic, highly charged. Great judge of character. Blessed in some ways. Strong verbal skills. Reliable, responsible. Bold, courageous, a bit stubborn.

Matilda, 6: Creative entrepreneur. Pioneer and risk taker. Dynamic, busy lifestyle. Blessed in some ways. Strong verbal skills. Reliable, responsible. Bold, courageous, a bit stubborn.

Matis, 8: Patient, tolerant. Resolute and purposeful. Energetic, highly charged. Blessed in some ways. Charming and devoted.

Matt, 9: Works hard, devoted. Helpful and sincere. Dynamic, busy lifestyle. Sensitive and easily hurt.

Matthew, 9: Works hard, devoted. Helpful and sincere. Dynamic, busy lifestyle. Sensitive and easily hurt. Great judge of character. A free spirit, very adaptable. Likes to meet new people.

Matti, 9: Works hard, devoted. Helpful and sincere. Dynamic, busy lifestyle. Sensitive and easily hurt. Blessed in some ways.

Mattie, 5: Entertains at home. Bright, adventuresome. Energetic, highly charged. Sensitive and easily hurt. Blessed in some ways. A free spirit, very adaptable.

Maud, 3: Family communicator. Aims to please. Youthful, attractive. Domestic, responsible.

Maude, 8: Patient, tolerant. Resolute and purposeful. Attractive and charming. Domestic, responsible. A free spirit, very adaptable.

Maura, 9: Works hard, devoted. Helpful, sincere. Attractive and charming. Gentle, kind, very diligent. Bold, courageous, a bit stubborn.

Maureen, 5: Entertains at home. Bright, adventuresome. Youthful, attractive. Gentle, kind, very diligent. A free spirit, very adaptable. Tendency to overindulge. Original and unconventional.

Maurey, 11: Insightful, sensitive. Independent, self-motivated. Attractive and charming. Gentle, kind, very diligent. A free spirit, very adaptable. Dislikes limitations.

Maurice, 7: Must have faith. Not easily influenced. Attractive and charming. Gentle, kind, very diligent. Blessed in some ways. Self-expressive, cheerful. A free spirit, very adaptable.

Mauricio, 8: Patient, tolerant. Resolute and purposeful. Attractive and charming. Gentle, kind, a hard worker. Blessed in some ways. Cheerful, optimistic. Artistic, having good taste. Natural counselor and healer.

Maury, 6: Creative entrepreneur. Pioneer and risk taker. Attractive and charming. Gentle, kind, very diligent. Dislikes limitations.

Mavis, 10: Steadfast and determined. Independent, critical of self and others. Intuitive and inspired. Blessed in some ways. Charming and devoted.

Max, 11: Insightful, sensitive. Independent, self-motivated. Artistic, sensual, perceptive.

Maximillian, 9: Works hard, devoted. Helpful, sincere. Artistic, sensual, perceptive. Blessed in some ways. Desires financial security. Strong verbal skills. Financial ups and downs. Idealistic, humanitarian. Bold, courageous, a bit stubborn. Original and unconventional.

Maxine, 30: Family communicator. Aims to please. Artistic, sensual, perceptive. Blessed in some ways. Original and unconventional. A free spirit, very adaptable.

Maxwell, 9: Works hard, devoted. Helpful, sincere. Artistic, sensual, perceptive. Likes to meet new people. A free spirit, very adaptable. Strong verbal skills. Financial ups and downs.

May, 3: Family communicator. Aims to please. Needs a lot of freedom.

Maya, 4: Strong physical constitution. Natural teaching ability. Needs a lot of freedom. Bold, courageous, a bit stubborn.

Mayeen, 9: Works hard, devoted. Helpful, sincere. Dislikes limitations. A free spirit, very adaptable. Tendency to overindulge. Original and unconventional.

Mayer, 8: Patient, tolerant. Resolute and purposeful. Needs a lot of freedom. Loves adventure and excitement. Gentle, kind, very diligent.

Mayfield, 3: Family communicator. Aims to please. Needs a lot of freedom. Self-sacrificing, loving. Blessed in some ways. Loves adventure and excitement. Strong verbal skills. Reliable, responsible.

Maynard, 4: Strong physical constitution. Natural teaching ability. Dislikes restrictions. Original and unconventional. Bold, courageous, a bit stubborn. Gentle, kind, very diligent. Reliable, responsible.

Mayra, 22: A workaholic, focused. Ambitious leader, great vision. Dislikes restrictions. Gentle, kind, very diligent. Bold, courageous, a bit stubborn.

Mead, 5: Entertains at home. Physical and passionate. Independent, critical of self and others. Reliable, responsible.

Mec, 3: Family communicator. A free spirit, very adaptable. Cheerful, optimistic.

Mecauley, 4: Strong physical constitution. Accesses quickly. Self-expressive, cheerful. Independent, critical of self and others. Attractive and charming. Strong verbal skills. Loves adventure and excitement. Dislikes limitations.

Meg, 7: Must have faith. Not easily fooled. Scientific and philosophical.

Megan, 22: A workaholic, focused. Has big plans and ideas. Scientific and philosophical. Independent, self-motivated. Creative, opinionated.

Meghan, 30: Family communicator. A free spirit, very adaptable. Scientific and philosophical. Great judge of character. Independent, critical of self and others. Original and unconventional.

Melanie, 9: Works hard, devoted. A true humanitarian. Great verbal skills. Independent, critical of self and others. Original and unconventional. Blessed in some ways. Loves adventure and excitement.

Melba, 6: Creative entrepreneur. A step ahead of others. Communicates skillfully. Friendly, but shy. Independent, critical of self and others.

Melbourne, 6: Creative entrepreneur. A step ahead of others. Communicates skillfully. Friendly, but shy. Natural counselor and healer. Attractive and charming. Gentle, kind, very diligent. Original and unconventional. Loves adventure and excitement.

Melina, 9: Works hard, devoted. A true humanitarian. Strong verbal skills. Blessed in some ways. Original and unconventional. Independent, critical of self and others.

Melinda, 4: Strong physical constitution. Accesses quickly. Travels frequently. Blessed in some ways. Original and unconventional. Reliable, responsible. Independent, critical of self and others.

Melissa, 6: Creative entrepreneur. A step ahead of others. Communicates skillfully. Blessed in some ways. Charming and devoted. Impulsive and extreme. Independent, critical of self and others.

Melodie, 9: Works hard, devoted. A true humanitarian. Great verbal skills. Natural counselor and healer. Reliable, responsible. Blessed in some ways. Loves adventure and excitement.

Melody, 11: Insightful, sensitive. Keenly perceptive. Travels frequently. Natural counselor and healer. Reliable, responsible. Dislikes limitations.

Melvin, 30: Family communicator. A free spirit, very adaptable. Communicates skillfully. Intuitive and inspired. Blessed in some ways. Original and unconventional.

Mendel, 8: Patient, tolerant. Original and creative. Opinionated and unconventional. Reliable, responsible. Physical and passionate. Great verbal skills.

Mercedes, 9: Works hard, devoted. A true humanitarian. Gentle, kind, very diligent. Self-expressive, cheerful. Tendency to overindulge. Reliable, responsible. Loves adventure and excitement. Charming and devoted.

Mercer, 8: Patient, tolerant. Original and creative. Intense inner power. Cheerful, optimistic. Physical and passionate. Needs to practice tolerance.

Mercy, 10: Steadfast and determined. Likes change and variety. Diligent, hardworking. Self-expressive, cheerful. Dislikes limitations.

Meredith, 10: Steadfast and determined. Likes change and variety. Diligent, hardworking. Loves adventure and excitement. Reliable, responsible. Blessed in some ways. Dynamic, busy lifestyle. Great judge of character.

Merelis, 9: Works hard, devoted. A true humanitarian. Gentle, kind, very diligent. Loves adventure and excitement. Strong verbal skills. Blessed in some ways. Charming and devoted.

Merle, 8: Patient, tolerant. Original and creative. Intense inner power. Strong verbal skills. Loves adventure and excitement.

Merlin, 8: Patient, tolerant. Original, creative, and unconventional. Intense inner power. Strong verbal skills. Blessed in some ways.

Merrick, 5: Entertains at home. Physical and passionate. Good deed doer. Tendency to lose items. Blessed in some ways. Self-expressive, cheerful. Strong desire to succeed.

Merrie, 5: Entertains at home. Physical and passionate. Good deed doer. Tendency to lose items. Blessed in some ways. A free spirit, very adaptable.

Merrill, 6: Creative entrepreneur. A step ahead of others. Duty-bound, self-sacrificing. Tendency to lose items. Blessed in some ways. Strong verbal skills. Financial ups and downs.

Merritt, 4: Strong physical constitution. Accesses quickly. Gentle, kind, a hard worker. Tendency to lose items. Blessed in some ways. Dynamic, busy lifestyle. Sensitive and easily hurt.

Merry, 7: Must have faith. A free spirit, very adaptable. Gentle, kind, very diligent. Tendency to lose items. Dislikes limitations.

Merton, 4: Strong physical constitution. Accesses quickly. Gentle, kind, a hard worker. Dynamic, busy lifestyle. Natural counselor and healer. Original and opinionated.

Merv, 22: A workaholic, focused. Has big plans and ideas. Gentle, kind, very diligent. Intuitive and inspired.

Mervin, 9: Works hard, devoted. A true humanitarian. Gentle, kind, very diligent. Intuitive and inspired. Blessed in some ways. Original and unconventional.

Mervyn, 7: Must have faith. Not easily fooled. A truth seeker. Intuitive and inspired. Needs a lot of freedom. Original and unconventional.

Meryl, 10: Steadfast and determined. Likes change and variety. Gentle, kind, a hard worker. Dislikes limitations. Strong verbal skills.

Meyer, 30: Family communicator. A free spirit, very adaptable. Dislikes limitations. Loves adventure and excitement. Gentle, kind, a hard worker.

Mia, 5: Entertains at home. Generous, thoughtful. Bright, adventuresome.

Mic, 7: Must have faith. Blessed in some ways. Self-expressive, cheerful.

Micaela, 8: Patient, tolerant. Gives practical gifts. Optimistic, outspoken. Independent, self-motivated. Physical and passionate. Strong verbal skills. Resolute and purposeful.

Micah, 7: Must have faith. Blessed in some ways. Sees the irony in situations. Independent, critical of self and others.

Michael, 6: Creative entrepreneur. Artistic, having good taste. Self-expressive, cheerful. Great judge of character. Independent, critical of self and others. A free spirit, very adaptable. Strong verbal skills.

Michaela, 7: Must have faith. Blessed in some ways. Self-expressive, cheerful. Great judge of character. Independent, critical of self and others. A free spirit, very adaptable. Strong verbal skills. Not easily influenced.

Michel, 5: Entertains at home. Generous, thoughtful. Optimistic, outspoken. Great judge of character. A free spirit, very adaptable. Strong verbal skills.

Michele, 10: Steadfast and determined. Respectful, kind. Self-expressive, cheerful. Great judge of character. A free spirit, very adaptable. Strong verbal skills. Loves adventure and excitement.

Michelle, 4: Strong physical constitution. Teaches kindness. Self-expressive, cheerful. Great judge of character. A free spirit, very adaptable. Strong verbal skills. Loves adventure and excitement. Ups and downs financially.

Mick, 9: Works hard, devoted. Blessed in some ways. Self-expressive, cheerful. Strong desire to succeed.

Mickey, 30: Family communicator. Blessed in some ways. Cheerful, lighthearted. Strong desire to succeed. A free spirit, very adaptable. Dislikes limitations.

Micky, 7: Must have faith. Artistic, having good taste. Self-expressive, cheerful. Strong desire to succeed. Dislikes limitations.

Midori, 5: Entertains at home. Generous, thoughtful. Reliable, responsible. Natural counselor and healer. Gentle, kind, very diligent. Artistic, having good taste.

Miguel, 4: Strong physical constitution. Teaches kindness. Scientific and philosophical. Attractive and charming. A free spirit, very adaptable. Strong verbal skills.

Mika, 7: Must have faith. Artistic, having good taste. Strong desire to succeed. Independent, critical of self and others.

Mike, 20: Domestically social. Emotional, considerate. Diplomatic, tactful. A free spirit, very adaptable.

Mikey, 9: Works hard, devoted. Blessed in some ways. Sees the big picture. A free spirit, very adaptable. Dislikes limitations.

Mikhail, 9: Works hard, devoted. Blessed in some ways. Sees the big picture. Great judge of character. Independent, critical of self and others. Artistic, having good taste. Excellent verbal skills.

Mikko, 5: Entertains at home. Generous, thoughtful. Strong desire to succeed. A bit forceful at times. Natural counselor and healer.

Mildred, 11: Insightful, sensitive. Blessed in some ways. Strong verbal skills. Domestic, responsible. Gentle, kind, a hard worker. A free spirit, very adaptable. Down-to-earth, faithful.

Miles, 22: A workaholic, focused. Blessed in some ways. Strong verbal skills. A free spirit, very adaptable. Charming and devoted.

Milford, 5: Entertains at home. Generous, thoughtful. Strong verbal skills. Self-sacrificing, loving. Natural counselor and healer. Gentle, kind, very diligent. Reliable, responsible.

Millard, 6: Creative entrepreneur. Artistic, having good taste. Travels frequently. Ups and downs financially. Independent, self-motivated. Gentle, kind, a hard worker. Natural problem solver.

Millicent, 7: Must have faith. Needs alone time. Communicates skillfully. Ups and downs financially. Artistic, having good taste. Self-expressive, cheerful. A free spirit, very adaptable. Original and unconventional. Dynamic, busy lifestyle.

Millie, 6: Creative entrepreneur. Artistic, having good taste. Great verbal skills. Ups and downs financially. Blessed in some ways. A free spirit, very adaptable.

Milo, 22: A workaholic, focused. Blessed in some ways. Strong verbal skills. Natural counselor and healer.

Milt, 9: Works hard, devoted. Idealistic, humanitarian. Communicates skillfully. Dynamic, busy lifestyle.

Milton, 11: Insightful, sensitive. Blessed in some ways. Travels frequently. Dynamic, busy lifestyle. Natural counselor and healer. Original and unconventional.

Mimi, 8: Patient, tolerant. Blessed in some ways. Desires financial security. Artistic, having good taste.

Mina, 10: Steadfast and determined. Respectful, kind. Original and unconventional. Independent, critical of self and others.

Minerva, 10: Steadfast and determined. Respectful, kind. Romantic, opinionated. A free spirit, very adaptable. Gentle, kind, very diligent. Intuitive and inspired. Independent, critical of self and others.

Minette, 5: Entertains at home. Generous, thoughtful. Original and unconventional. A free spirit, very adaptable. Dynamic, busy lifestyle. Sensitive and easily hurt. Loves adventure and excitement.

Minna, 6: Creative entrepreneur. Artistic, having good taste. Original and opinionated. Sensual and romantic. Independent, self-motivated.

Minnie, 10: Steadfast and determined. Respectful, kind. Original and unconventional. Romantic, sensual. Artistic, having good taste. A free spirit, very adaptable.

Minoo, 30: Family communicator. Blessed in some ways. Creative, original. Natural counselor and healer. Has musical talent.

Mi:ok, 3: Family communicator. Blessed in some ways. Natural counselor and healer. Strong desire to succeed.

Mira, 5: Entertains at home. Generous, thoughtful. Intense inner power. Bright, adventuresome.

Mirabel, 6: Creative entrepreneur. Artistic, having good taste. Gentle, kind, a hard worker. Pioneer and risk taker. Friendly, but shy. A free spirit, very adaptable. Strong verbal skills.

Miranda, 6: Creative entrepreneur. Artistic, having good taste. Gentle, kind, a hard worker. Independent, critical of self and others. Original and unconventional. Reliable, responsible. Bold, courageous, a bit stubborn.

Miriam, 9: Works hard, devoted. Blessed in some ways. Idealistic, humanitarian. Artistic, having good taste. Helpful, sincere. Desires financial security.

Misael, 5: Entertains at home. Generous, thoughtful. Charming and devoted. Bright, adventuresome. A free spirit, very adaptable. Strong verbal skills.

Missy, 22: A workaholic, focused. Blessed in some ways. Very charismatic. Impulsive and extreme. Needs a lot of freedom.

Mistique, 5: Entertains at home. Generous, thoughtful. Charming and devoted. Dynamic, busy lifestyle. Artistic, having good taste. Attracts wealth. Very lucky. A free spirit, very adaptable.

Misty, 5: Entertains at home. Generous, thoughtful. Charming and devoted. Dynamic, busy lifestyle. Needs a lot of freedom.

Mitch, 8: Patient, tolerant. Blessed in some ways. Dynamic, busy lifestyle. Self-expressive, cheerful. Great judge of character.

Mitchell, 10: Steadfast and determined. Respectful, kind. Dynamic, busy lifestyle. Self-expressive, cheerful. Great judge of character. A free spirit, very adaptable. Strong verbal skills. Financial ups and downs.

Mitzi, 5: Entertains at home. Generous, thoughtful. Dynamic, busy lifestyle. Uses common sense. Artistic, having good taste.

Moe, 6: Creative entrepreneur. Natural counselor and healer. A free spirit, very adaptable.

Mohammad, 5: Entertains at home. Enjoys working. Great judge of character. Independent, self-motivated. Domestic, hardworking. Systematic, organized. Bold, courageous, a bit stubborn. Practical, conservative.

Mohammed, 9: Works hard, devoted. Natural counselor and healer. Great judge of character. Independent, self-motivated. Domestic, hardworking. Systematic, organized. A free spirit, very adaptable. Practical, conservative.

Moira, 11: Insightful, sensitive. Creates group harmony. Blessed in some ways. Gentle, kind, a hard worker. Independent, critical of self and others.

Moises, 8: Patient, tolerant. Competitive in business. Blessed in some ways. Charming and devoted. A free spirit, very adaptable. Many mood swings.

Mollie, 30: Family communicator. Natural counselor and healer. Strong verbal skills. Financial ups and downs. Blessed in some ways. A free spirit, very adaptable.

Molly, 5: Entertains at home. Enjoys working. Communicates skillfully. Financial ups and downs. Needs a lot of freedom.

Mona, 7: Must have faith. Open to opportunities. Creative and original. Independent, critical of self and others.

Monett, 6: Creative entrepreneur. Magnetic personality. Romantic, sensual. A free spirit, very adaptable. Dynamic, busy lifestyle. Sensitive and easily hurt.

Monetta, 7: Must have faith. Open to opportunities. Original and unconventional. A free spirit, very adaptable. Dynamic, busy lifestyle. Sensitive and easily hurt. Independent, critical of self and others.

Monica, 10: Steadfast and determined. Self-sacrificing, devoted. Creative and original. Blessed in some ways. Self-expressive, cheerful. Independent, critical of self and others.

Monika, 6: Creative entrepreneur. Magnetic personality. Original and unconventional. Artistic, having good taste. Strong desire to succeed. Independent, critical of self and others.

Monique, 4: Strong physical constitution. Assumes responsibility. Original and unconventional. Blessed in some ways. Attracts wealth. Very lucky. A free spirit, very adaptable.

Monroe, 8: Patient, tolerant. Competitive in business. Creative and original. Gentle, kind, a hard worker. May have musical abilities. Physical and passionate.

Monte, 22: A workaholic, focused. Creates group harmony. Original and unconventional. Dynamic, busy lifestyle. A free spirit, very adaptable.

Montgomery, 10: Steadfast and determined. Natural counselor and healer. Creative, original. Dynamic, busy lifestyle. Intelligent opportunist. Creates group harmony. Domestically organized. A free spirit, very adaptable. Gentle, kind, a hard worker. Dislikes limitations.

Monty, 6: Creative entrepreneur. Magnetic personality. Original and unconventional. Dynamic, busy lifestyle. Needs a lot of freedom.

Mora, 20: Domestically social. Natural counselor and healer. Gentle, kind, very diligent. Independent, critical of self and others.

Moreen, 7: Must have faith. Open to opportunities. Gentle, kind, a hard worker. A free spirit, very adaptable. Physical and passionate. Original and unconventional.

Morene, 7: (Same as Moreen.)

Morgan, 5: Entertains at home. Enjoys working. Intense inner power. Scientific and philosophical. Bright, adventuresome. Romantic, sensual.

Morley, 7: Must have faith. Open to opportunities. Gentle, kind, a hard worker. Great verbal skills. A free spirit, very adaptable. Dislikes limitations.

Morris, 11: Insightful, sensitive. Creates group harmony. Gentle, kind, very diligent. Tendency to lose items. Blessed in some ways. Charming and devoted.

Mort, 3: Family communicator. Nurturing, loving. Gentle, kind, a hard worker. Dynamic, busy lifestyle.

Morticia, 7: Must have faith. Open to opportunities. Gentle, kind, a hard worker. Dynamic, busy lifestyle. Blessed in some ways. Self-expressive, cheerful. Artistic, having good taste. Not easily influenced.

Mortie, 8: Patient, tolerant. Competitive in business. Intense inner power. Dynamic, busy lifestyle. Blessed in some ways. A free spirit, very adaptable.

Mortimer, 3: Family communicator. Natural counselor and healer. Gentle, kind, very diligent. Dynamic, busy lifestyle. Blessed in some ways. Desires financial security. A free spirit, very adaptable. Tendency to lose items.

Morton, 5: Entertains at home. Enjoys working. Gentle, kind, very diligent. Dynamic, busy lifestyle. Magnetic personality. Romantic, opinionated.

Morty, 10: Steadfast and determined. Self-sacrificing, devoted. Gentle, kind, very diligent. Dynamic, busy lifestyle. Needs a lot of freedom.

Moses, 8: Patient, tolerant. Competitive in business. Charming and devoted. A free spirit, very adaptable. Intense and extreme.

Moshe, 6: Creative entrepreneur. Magnetic personality. Charming and devoted. Great judge of character. A free spirit, very adaptable.

Mu Lan, 7: Must have faith. Stylish and refined. Communicates skillfully. Not easily influenced. Original and unconventional.

Muriel, 6: Creative entrepreneur. Attractive and charming. Gentle, kind, a hard worker. Blessed in some ways. A free spirit, very adaptable. Strong verbal skills.

Murray, 6: Creative entrepreneur. Attractive and charming. Gentle, kind, a hard worker. Intense inner power. Independent, self-motivated. Needs a lot of freedom.

Mustafa, 9: Works hard, devoted. Gracious, well-mannered. Charming and devoted. Dynamic, busy lifestyle. Independent, critical of self and others. Self-sacrificing, loving. Bold, courageous, a bit stubborn.

Mutie, 5: Entertains at home. Attractive and charming. Dynamic, busy lifestyle. Blessed in some ways. A free spirit, very adaptable.

Myer, 7: Must have faith. Refined and stylish. Loves adventure and excitement. Gentle, kind, a hard worker.

Mykola, 5: Entertains at home. Needs a lot of freedom. Strong desire to succeed. Natural counselor and healer. Frequent traveler. Independent, critical of self and others.

Myra, 3: Family communicator. Needs a lot of freedom. Gentle, kind, a hard worker. Aims to please.

Myrna, 8: Patient, tolerant. Strong intuition. Intense inner power. Original and unconventional. Independent, critical of self and others.

Myron, 4: Strong physical constitution. Finds shortcuts. Gentle, kind, very diligent. Natural counselor and healer. Original and unconventional.

Myrtle, 30: Family communicator. Needs a lot of freedom. Gentle, kind, a hard worker. Dynamic, busy lifestyle. Strong verbal skills. Loves adventure and excitement.

Mystique, 3: Family communicator. Needs a lot of freedom. Charming and devoted. Dynamic, busy lifestyle. Blessed in some ways. Attracts wealth. Youthful, attractive. Loves adventure and excitement.

Myung-hee, 8: Patient, tolerant. Strong intuition. Attractive and charming. Original and unconventional. Scientific and philosophical. Great judge of character. Loves adventure and excitement. Needs change.

N

If a name begins with N, has more than one N, or ends with an N, this person is romantic, creative, tends to have many love affairs, and is opinionated and unconventional.

The letter N is the 14th letter of the alphabet. Since $1 + 4 = 5$, the 14th letter has the same vibrational influence as the number 5. The 1 rules beginnings, 4 rules work and family, and 5 rules change. So the N person is beginning work and family and dealing with change. It's difficult to be free when responsible for work and family, but the N person must buckle down to the obligations of work and family while having the desire to be free. The higher-evolved N person will somehow manage to meet these obligations and attain freedom as well. The lesser-evolved will have difficulty handling their obligations and may give in to tendencies of escapism.

An N anywhere in a person's name will make him or her more romantic and sensual. N people usually have many love affairs and often keep a diary. N names are very sentimental and will want to hang on to the mementos of a relationship long after it's over. Although this letter's influence tends to fall in and out of love quickly, when N is in the right relationship, it proves to be the model of happiness. The N is similar to the astrological signs Leo and Aquarius. They are as freedom-oriented and unconventional as an Aquarian, yet as romantic, creative, and subtle as a Leo. Both of these signs are fixed and stubborn, and so is this 5-ruled letter.

N-named people are original and unusual; we often see role reversal with this letter. For example, men stay at home with the kids and women are the head of the household. Often this personality finds itself in careers geared towards the opposite sex. N types are ahead of their time, similar to letters E and W. They like to experiment; they'll wear a shirt inside out, or they'll put peanut butter on lettuce and call it a sandwich. The strange and unusual is their wavelength. The Aquarian side of the N makes some secretly enjoy shocking others; however, most N names are a social delight. They seem to fit in with any crowd, high, low, or in the middle. This letter loves meeting new people almost as much as Ws. They are often forward-looking and interested in the latest fads and gadgets.

This letter is also very opinionated! Dennis Miller, double N commentator and guest speaker on many talk shows, demonstrates his opinion on a regular basis. Pick a topic and he has an opinion. Don't try to change it; the N influence will put on their hats and leave with the same opinions as before. It's a very fixed and stubborn letter.

Names with the 5-ruled letters E, N, and W are in danger of falling victim to drug and alcohol abuse. They tend to overindulge in sensual pleasures, such as food, and other forms of escapism. Similar to E, N wants to experience all five senses: taste, smell, feel, sound, and vision. Life's an adventure with so much to experience! Also similar to the letter E, the letter N's biggest fear is boredom. Similar to E and W , N needs to adopt the attitude, "everything in moderation," or they'll overdo it in some area. Ask Jenny Craig—she has two Ns in her name—she knows all about overindulgence.

The typical N person adapts to the changes life demands of them. Nicole Kidman adapted quickly to single life after being married for many years to the famous Tom Cruise. With two hidden 8s in her name, she will let us know why their marriage ended when she's ready, not before. She's in control, although it's not obvious, since her 8s are hidden. It's no surprise that Nicole is now acting in some movies based on comedy. With a C and an L in her name, she's a natural. Not only are those two letters good with comedy, but they also excel at communication. The film *The Interpreter* showed us her communication abilities. Last but not least, with a power number 4, she's professional. Her power number 4 indicates that she intently studies her roles, as she doesn't want to be made a fool. There's also a bit of natural teacher in her. She could probably home-school her children easily.

Another interesting N person is Noah, of Noah's Ark. His name adds up to a 20 power number. The number 20 means partnership and assistance from God. Interestingly enough he received assistance from

God when pairing up all the animals, male and female. Also, his children had partners. All the pairs sailed off to ensure our future! It's also worth noting that he had a parental O first vowel. This is the most nurturing and duty-bound of all the vowels. Those with names that begin with N, or have an N anywhere, love adventure and excitement. How excited Noah must have been to go on that adventure! God knew what he was doing when he chose a man named Noah for the Ark project.

Nancy Reagan, First Lady and wife of the late Ronald Reagan, also exemplifies her name. With two Ns in her name, no wonder President Reagan wrote so many love letters to Nancy. Double Ns are very romantic. Her name also adds up to a power number 3 which is a natural in the area of communication and writing. With a 3 power number she was cheerful and easygoing, just perfect for a man with so much on his mind. She's been able to communicate easily about her husband through books and shares the love letters from her famous Presidential husband freely. She's proud of the love they shared. It's the power number 3 that keeps her smiling. Nancy has a hidden 6 at the beginning of her name, so she is very nurturing and loving. Most people don't realize this because it's hidden. Only those who really know Nancy understand that she has a lot of love to give.

We have at least three famous men whose names are Neil: Neil Armstrong, astronaut; Neil Diamond, singer/songwriter; and Neil Simon, playwright. The name Neil adds up to a 22 power number. The number 22 is one of the master numbers. Of all the power numbers, 22 seeks worldwide success; it's the "master builder." Each Neil in his own right has become an international success. Also, all of them share the romantic personality of the N. Neil Diamond wrote and sang romantic songs; Neil Simon wrote romantic plays; and while others gazed romantically at the moon, astronaut Neil Armstrong actually walked on it!

As we've seen, N is romantic. Even that great big ape, King Kong, has two Ns in his name. Who'd have thought a giant gorilla could have love interests? Without the Ns he'd have been boring. Even the sound of N seems warm and loving somehow. The shape of this letter looks as though it's ready to take off. It's a ready letter. It likes its freedom and it likes its romance. It's the first letter in the word "New" and just like a 5-ruled letter, N looks forward to experiencing all five senses with adventure and excitement. This letter hates being stuck in a routine for too long. So keep it fresh and new; our N friends will supply the romance.

Some other famous N names are: Nelson Mandela, Nicole Richie, Nolan Ryan, Nicole Brown Simpson, Nicolas Cage, Nancy Travis, Neve Campbell, Nelly, Nick Nolte, Natalie Portman, Nat King Cole, Norah Jones, Nicolaus Copernicus, Nostradamus, Noel Coward, Norman Vincent Peale, Neil Young, Nia Long, Nell Carter, Nick Lachey, Norman Rockwell, Newt Gingrich, and Natalie Wood.

QUICK REFERENCE OF "N" NAMES

Naavah, 20: Socially active. Reads people easily. Bold, courageous, a bit stubborn. Intuitive and inspired. Pioneer and risk taker. Great judge of character.

Nacho, 5: Romantically inclined. Bright, adventuresome. Self-expressive, cheerful. Great judge of character. Natural counselor and healer.

Nader, 6: Puts needs of others first. Pioneer and risk taker. Reliable, responsible. A free spirit, very adaptable. Gentle, kind, hard worker.

Nadia, 20: Socially active. Reads people easily. Practical, conservative. Blessed in some ways. Bold, courageous, a bit stubborn.

Nadine, 11: Intuitive, perceptive, and creative. Reliable, responsible. Blessed in some ways. Romantic, sensual. A free spirit, very adaptable.

Nadya, 9: Unassuming, naive. Helpful, sincere. Reliable, responsible. Needs a lot of freedom. Pioneer and risk taker.

Naeil, 5: Romantically inclined. Bright, adventuresome. A free spirit, very adaptable. Blessed in some ways. Strong verbal skills.

Naida, 20: (Same as Nadia.)

Namaste, 10: Initiates change. Independent, critical of self and others. Domestic, hardworking. Bold, courageous, a bit stubborn. Charming and devoted. Dynamic, busy lifestyle. A free spirit, very adaptable.

Namid, 5: Romantically inclined. Bright, adventuresome. Domestic, hardworking. Blessed in some ways. Reliable, responsible.

Nan, 11: Intuitive, perceptive, and creative. Keenly perceptive. Romantic, sensual.

Nance, 10: Initiates change. Independent, critical of self and others. Romantic, sensual. Self-expressive, cheerful. A free spirit, very adaptable.

Nanci, 5: Romantically inclined. Bright, adventuresome. Self-expressive, cheerful. Blessed in some ways.

Nancy, 3: Young at heart. Aims to please. Romantic, sensual. Self-expressive, cheerful. Needs a lot of freedom.

Nanette, 7: Enjoys the mysteries of life. Not easily influenced. Romantic, sensual. A free spirit, very adaptable. Dynamic, busy lifestyle. Sensitive and easily hurt. Loves adventure and excitement.

Nani, 20: Socially active. Reads people easily. Romantic, sensual. Blessed in some ways.

Naoma, 8: Realistic with money. Resolute and purposeful. Natural counselor and healer. Domestic, hardworking. Bold, courageous, a bit stubborn.

Naomi, 7: Enjoys the mysteries of life. Not easily influenced. Natural counselor and healer. Domestic, hardworking. Blessed in some ways.

Naser, 3: Young at heart. Aims to please. Charming and devoted. Physical and passionate. Gentle, kind, a hard worker.

Nashia, 7: Enjoys the mysteries of life. Not easily influenced. Charming and devoted. Great judge of character. Blessed in some ways. Bold, courageous, a bit stubborn.

Nat, 8: Realistic with money. Resolute and purposeful. Energetic, highly charged.

Natacha, 3: Young at heart. Aims to please. Dynamic, busy lifestyle. Pioneer and risk taker. Cheerful, self-expressive. Great judge of character. Bold, courageous, a bit stubborn.

Natalie, 8: Realistic with money. Resolute and purposeful. Energetic, highly charged. Bold, courageous, a bit stubborn. Strong verbal skills. Blessed in some ways. A free spirit, very adaptable.

Natalya, 20: Socially active. Reads people easily. Dynamic, busy life-style. Bold, courageous, a bit stubborn. Strong verbal skills. Needs a lot of freedom. Pioneer and risk taker.

Natane, 10: Initiates change. Independent, critical of self and others. Dynamic, busy lifestyle. Bold, courageous, a bit stubborn. Original and opinionated. Physical and passionate.

Natasha, 10: Initiates change. Independent, critical of self and others. Dynamic, busy lifestyle. Bold, courageous, a bit stubborn. Charming and devoted. Great judge of character. Pioneer and risk taker.

Nate, 4: Original, but practical. Natural teaching ability. Dynamic, busy lifestyle. A free spirit, very adaptable.

Nathan, 22: Intuitive and creative. Ambitious leader, great vision. Dynamic, busy lifestyle. Great judge of character. Bold, courageous, a bit stubborn. Romantic, sensual.

Nathaniel, 3: Young at heart. Aims to please. Dynamic, busy lifestyle. Great judge of character. Bold, courageous, a bit stubborn. Romantic, sensual. Blessed in some ways. A free spirit, very adaptable. Strong verbal skills.

Neal, 5: Romantically inclined. Perceptive, socially adept. Bright, adventuresome. Strong verbal skills.

Neale, 10: Initiates change. Likes variety. Independent, critical of self and others. Strong verbal skills. Physical and passionate.

Ned, 5: Romantically inclined. Perceptive, socially adept. Domestic, responsible.

Neil, 22: Intuitive and creative. Has big plans and ideas. Blessed in some ways. Great verbal skills.

Nelcy, 5: Romantically inclined. Perceptive, socially adept. Communicates skillfully. Self-expressive, cheerful. Needs a lot of freedom.

Nell, 7: Enjoys the mysteries of life. Not easily fooled. Strong verbal skills. Slow to make decisions.

Nellie, 30: Young at heart. A free spirit, very adaptable. Great verbal skills. Travels frequently. Blessed in some ways. Loves adventure and excitement.

Nelly, 5: Romantically inclined. Perceptive, socially adept. Communicates skillfully. Slow to make decisions. Dislikes limitations.

Nelson, 7: Enjoys the mysteries of life. Not easily fooled. Travels frequently. Charming and devoted. Natural counselor and healer. Romantic, sensual.

Nelva, 9: Unassuming, naive. Enjoys giving gifts. Strong verbal skills. Intuitive and inspired. Helpful, sincere.

Nemo, 20: Socially active. Sound business aptitude. Domestic, hardworking. Natural counselor and healer.

Neo, 7: Enjoys the mysteries of life. Not easily fooled. Open to opportunities.

Neon, 3: Young at heart. A free spirit, very adaptable. Natural counselor and healer. Romantic, sensual.

Nerina, 7: Enjoys the mysteries of life. Not easily fooled. Gentle, kind, a hard worker. Blessed in some ways. Romantic, sensual. Independent, critical of self and others.

Nerine, 11: Intuitive and creative. Keenly perceptive. Gentle, kind, a hard worker. Blessed in some ways. Romantic, sensual. Loves adventure and excitement.

Nerissa, 4: Original, but practical. Accesses quickly. Hardworking, diligent. Blessed in some ways. Charming and devoted. Impulsive and extreme. Independent, critical of self and others.

Nero, 7: Enjoys the mysteries of life. Not easily fooled. Gentle, kind, a hard worker. Natural counselor and healer.

Netta, 6: Puts needs of others first. A step ahead of others. Dynamic, busy lifestyle. Sensitive and easily hurt. Independent, self-motivated.

Neve, 10: Initiates change. Likes variety. Intuitive and inspired. Tendency to overindulge.

Nevil, 8: Realistic with money. Original and creative. Intuitive and inspired. Blessed in some ways. Strong verbal skills.

Neville, 7: Enjoys the mysteries of life. Not easily fooled. Intuitive and inspired. Blessed in some ways. Strong verbal skills. Slow to make decisions. Physical and passionate.

Nevin, 10: Initiates change. Likes variety. Efficient, goal-oriented. Blessed in some ways. Romantic, sensual.

Nevis, 6: Puts needs of others first. A step ahead of others. Intuitive and inspired. Artistic, having good taste. Charming and devoted.

Newman, 7: Enjoys the mysteries of life. Not easily fooled. Likes to meet new people. Domestic, hardworking. Independent, critical of self and others. Romantic, sensual.

Newt, 8: Realistic with money. Original and creative. Likes to meet new people. Dynamic, busy lifestyle.

Newton, 10: Initiates change. Likes variety. Has charisma and charm. Dynamic, busy lifestyle. Natural counselor and healer. Romantic, sensual.

Nia, 6: Puts needs of others first. Artistic, having good taste. Pioneer and risk taker.

Nic, 8: Realistic with money. Gives practical gifts. Optimistic, outspoken.

Nichol, 7: Enjoys the mysteries of life. Needs alone time. Self-expressive, cheerful. Great judge of character. Natural counselor and healer. Strong verbal skills.

Nicholas, 9: Unassuming, naive. Blessed in some ways. Self-expressive, cheerful. Great judge of character. Natural counselor and healer. Strong verbal skills. Helpful, sincere. Charming and devoted.

Nichole, 3: Young at heart. Considerate, understanding. Youthful, outspoken. Great judge of character. Natural counselor and healer. Strong verbal skills. A free spirit, very adaptable.

Nick, 10: Initiates change. Respectful, kind. Self-expressive, cheerful. Strong desire to succeed.

Nicky, 8: Realistic with money. Gives practical gifts. Self-expressive, cheerful. Strong desire to succeed. Needs a lot of freedom.

Nico, 5: Romantically inclined. Generous, thoughtful. Cheerful, light-hearted. Natural counselor and healer.

Nicodemus, 4: Original, but practical. Blessed in some ways. Optimistic, outspoken. Natural counselor and healer. Reliable, responsible. A free spirit, very adaptable. Domestic, hardworking. Attractive and charming. Very devoted.

Nicola, 9: Unassuming, naive. Blessed in some ways. Self-expressive, cheerful. Natural counselor and healer. Strong verbal skills. Independent, critical of self and others.

Nicolas, 10: Initiates change. Respectful, kind. Self-expressive, cheerful. Natural counselor and healer. Strong verbal skills. Independent, critical of self and others. Charming and devoted.

Nicole, 4: Original, but practical. Blessed in some ways. Optimistic, outspoken. Natural counselor and healer. Strong verbal skills. A free spirit, very adaptable.

Nicolette, 4: Original, but practical. Blessed in some ways. Optimistic, outspoken. Natural counselor and healer. Strong verbal skills. A free spirit, very adaptable. Dynamic, busy lifestyle. Sensitive and easily hurt. Loves adventure and excitement.

Nicolle, 7: Enjoys the mysteries of life. Needs alone time. Self-expressive, cheerful. Natural counselor and healer. Communicates skillfully. Ups and downs financially. A free spirit, very adaptable.

Nigel, 11: Intuitive and creative. Emotional, considerate. Scientific and philosophical. A free spirit, very adaptable. Strong verbal skills.

Nika, 8: Realistic with money. Gives practical gifts. Has a powerful presence. Resolute and purposeful.

Niki, 10: Initiates change. Respectful, kind. Strong desire to succeed. Artistic, having good taste.

Nikita, 10: Initiates change. Respectful, kind. Strong desire to succeed. Artistic, having good taste. Dynamic, busy lifestyle. Independent, critical of self and others.

Nikki, 30: Young at heart. Considerate, understanding. Strong desire to succeed. A bit forceful. Artistic, having good taste.

Nikky, 7: Enjoys the mysteries of life. Needs alone time. Multifaceted and disciplined. A bit forceful. Needs a lot of freedom.

Nila, 9: Unassuming, naive. Blessed in some ways. Great verbal skills. Helpful, sincere.

Niles, 5: Romantically inclined. Generous, thoughtful. Communicates skillfully. A free spirit, very adaptable. Charming and devoted.

Nina, 20: Socially active. Emotional, considerate. Romantic, sensual. Reads people easily.

Niro, 11: Intuitive and creative. Emotional and considerate. Gentle, kind, a hard worker. Natural counselor and healer.

Nita, 8: Realistic with money. Gives practical gifts. Dynamic, busy lifestyle. Resolute and purposeful.

Noah, 20: Socially active. Works well with others. Reads people easily. Great judge of character.

Noami, 7: (Same as Naomi.)

Noble, 3: Young at heart. Nurturing, loving. Friendly, but shy. Communicates skillfully. A free spirit, very adaptable.

Noel, 10: Initiates change. Self-sacrificing, devoted. A free spirit, very adaptable. Great verbal skills.

Noela, 20: Socially active. Works well with others. A free spirit, very adaptable. Strong verbal skills. Independent, critical of self and others.

Noelle, 9: Unassuming, naive. Artistic, creative. Physical and passionate. Frequent traveler. Ups and downs financially. Loves adventure and excitement.

Noemi, 11: Intuitive and creative. Creates group harmony. A free spirit, very adaptable. Domestic, hardworking. Blessed in some ways.

Nola, 6: Puts needs of others first. Natural counselor and healer. Strong verbal skills. Pioneer and risk taker.

Nolan, 20: Socially active. Works well with others. Great verbal skills. Reads people easily. Romantic, sensual.

Noland, 6: Puts needs of others first. Magnetic personality. Strong verbal skills. Pioneer and risk taker. Romantic, sensual. Reliable, responsible.

Nomi, 6: Puts needs of others first. Magnetic personality. Domestic, hardworking. Blessed in some ways.

Nona, 8: Realistic with money. Competitive in business. Romantic, sensual. Resolute and purposeful.

Nora, 3: Young at heart. Nurturing, loving. Gentle, kind, a hard worker. Aims to please.

Norah, 11: Intuitive and creative. Creates group harmony. Gentle, kind, a hard worker. Independent, ambitious. Great judge of character.

Norbert, 11: Intuitive and creative. Creates group harmony. Gentle, kind, a hard worker. Friendly, but shy. A free spirit, very adaptable. Tendency to lose items. Dynamic, busy lifestyle.

Noreen, 8: Realistic with money. Competitive in business. Intense inner power. A free spirit, very adaptable. Loves adventure and excitement. Romantic, sensual.

Norene, 8: (Same as Noreen.)

Nori, 11: Intuitive and creative. Creates group harmony. Gentle, kind, a hard worker. Blessed in some ways.

Noriko, 10: Initiates change. Self-sacrificing, devoted. Hardworking, diligent. Blessed in some ways. Strong desire to succeed. Natural counselor and healer.

Norine, 3: Young at heart. Nurturing, loving. Diligent, hardworking. Blessed in some ways. Romantic, sensual. A free spirit, very adaptable.

Norla, 6: Puts needs of others first. Magnetic personality. Sympathetic, kind. Strong verbal skills. Independent, critical of self and others.

Norlina, 11: Intuitive and creative. Creates group harmony. Gentle, kind, a hard worker. Strong verbal skills. Blessed in some ways. Romantic, sensual. Independent, self-motivated.

Norm, 6: Puts needs of others first. Magnetic personality. Sympathetic, kind. Domestic, hardworking.

Norma, 7: Enjoys the mysteries of life. Open to opportunities. Gentle, kind, a hard worker. Systematic, organized. Not easily influenced.

Norman, 30: Young at heart. Nurturing, loving. Diligent, hardworking. Systematic, organized. Aims to please. Romantic, sensual.

Normie, 11: Intuitive and creative. Creates group harmony. Gentle, kind, a hard worker. Systematic, organized. Blessed in some ways. A free spirit, very adaptable.

Norris, 3: Young at heart. Nurturing, loving. Diligent, hardworking. Tendency to lose items. Blessed in some ways. Charming and devoted.

Nort, 22: Intuitive and creative. Creates group harmony. Gentle, kind, a hard worker. Dynamic, busy lifestyle.

Northrop, 7: Enjoys the mysteries of life. Open to opportunities. Gentle, kind, a hard worker. Dynamic, busy lifestyle. Great judge of character. Tendency to lose items. Has musical talent. Intelligent and knowledgeable.

Norton, 6: Puts needs of others first. Magnetic personality. Sympathetic, kind. Dynamic, busy lifestyle. Natural counselor and healer. Romantic, sensual.

Norville, 8: Realistic with money. Competitive in business. Intense inner power. Intuitive and inspired. Blessed in some ways. Great verbal skills. Financial ups and downs. A free spirit, very adaptable.

Nova, 7: Enjoys the mysteries of life. Open to opportunities. Intuitive and inspired. Not easily influenced.

Nubia, 20: Socially active. Attractive and charming. Friendly, but shy. Blessed in some ways. Independent, critical of self and others.

Nubula, 8: Realistic with money. Attractive and charming. Friendly, but shy. Difficulty making decisions. Strong verbal skills. Independent, critical of self and others.

Nuri, 8: Realistic with money. Attractive and charming. Intense inner power. Blessed in some ways.

Nuriel, 7: Enjoys the mysteries of life. Has style and grace. Gentle, kind, a hard worker. Blessed in some ways. A free spirit, very adaptable. Strong verbal skills.

Nyla, 7: Enjoys the mysteries of life. Stylish and refined. Great verbal skills. Not easily influenced.

I f a name begins with O, has O as the first vowel, has more than one O, or ends with an O, this person is a natural counselor and healer, has strong religious convictions, needs someone to love or nurture, and is very emotional.

The letter O is the 15th letter of the alphabet. Since 1 + 5 = 6, the 15th letter has the same vibrational influence as the number 6. The 1 rules beginnings, 5 rules change, and 6 rules love. The O person is beginning to experience change and learning to love. Perhaps they are learning to love in a different way this lifetime. The types of love are manifold. Love encompasses all kinds of emotions, and so does the O-named person.

Similar to the letter F, O is capable of jealousy and can be moody as well. The O person needs to guard against feelings of jealousy and feeling sorry for themselves or brooding for long periods of time. Some Os can be meddling and try to have their way in family quarrels. The O can really put a damper on family dinner hour if upset.

This love-ruled letter is magnetic. It's guided by Venus, the planet of attraction. Joe and Lori may not be considered "good-looking," but people, and even animals, tend to be drawn to them somehow. When someone with an O in his or her name, especially at the beginning or end, enters a room, people notice. Love is not intelligent; it's a feeling, an emotion. Sometimes it's blind, deaf, and dumb, but our O-named friends are here to learn from the lessons of love. O types live to love and love to give. They're service-oriented and best placed among those who need them desperately. They're never too tired to demonstrate what love really is.

Many O types are found in religious settings. After all, "God is Love." God, Lord, and Love all have O as the first vowel. Even the word "morals" has an O first vowel. If people have an O anywhere in their name, they will have more than the average dose of willpower and religious conviction. The typical O person will respect rules and regulations. Unfortunately, there is a downside to this letter. If not taught good moral values while young, they might not respect the rights and property of others when they become adults. Plenty of names in the news reflect the negative side of the O: the Scott Peterson double murder trial; Sharon Osborne allegedly broke into and stole from a star's dressing room; Winona Ryder stole clothes from Saks Fifth Avenue; Tonya Harding hired a hit man to take out one of her competitors in the 1994 Winter Olympics. Unfortunately, O types can be naughty this way.

The typical O is responsible for themselves and will take on the responsibilities of others willingly. Similar to the sixth letter, F, most of them are self-sacrificing and duty-bound. The majority of O names make great parents, counselors, and religious leaders. They are the natural counselors and healers, so they often attract patients to themselves. Since they often willingly burden themselves with service and duty, they may want to carefully choose their mate. The male with an O in his name seems to be attracted to the damsel in distress. The female with an O in her name is often attracted to a mama's boy, or someone whom she can coddle or dote on. Both seem to attract people who have counseling or nurturing needs, which sometimes ends up more of a burden than they bargained for.

The sense of smell is intensified with our O-named friends. For some reason this letter tends to complain of odors more than the other letters. Similar to the letter F, some are allergic to perfumes or can feel sick if they have to endure unpleasant odors for long.

Those with an O anywhere in their name are often musically inclined, which recalls the saying, "Music is love in search of a word." Unfortunately, most Os are too duty-bound to pursue a musical career. Still some of the best in the music field have an O in their name: singers/songwriters Josh Groban, Olivia Newton John, Norah Jones, Roberta Flack, Elton John, Joni Mitchell, Hootie and the Blowfish, Boz Scaggs, Bono, Rod Stewart, Beyonce Knowles, Johnny Cash, Bonnie Raitt, Toby Keith, John Lennon, and Otis Rush are just a few that were able to make a career for themselves with music. Eccentric Ozzy Osborne, violinist Yo-Yo Ma, and musical writer Oscar Hammerstein also fit into this musical category.

O names make excellent gardeners, given their natural nurturing abilities. Children, pets, and gardens are fortunate if an O person is taking care of them. O types have a way of making us feel taken care of when we're in their presence. We can count on the O. If O people are unable to have children of their own, they'll often treat their pets as if they were children. They may put clothes, scarves, or sunglasses on them and take them everywhere. Just as with the character "Mr. Bojangles," when O people lose a pet, they may grieve for many years. If O names don't have pets or children, they may manage large groups of people. They are natural parents and make wonderful bosses. The Bible shows this example with O first-vowel Moses and Noah managing large groups of people. Consequently, O types usually don't like anyone looking over their shoulder. They are responsible and duty-bound, and resent when others don't recognize and respect their authority.

Oprah Winfrey has an empire of people she manages quite well, plus millions of followers. Just as the O dictates, she is emotional and not afraid to show it. She's human, real, and most people can relate to her. Oprah is a natural counselor and healer, guiding complete strangers by the millions over the air waves each week. Wearing her O in the beginning of her name makes her especially magnetic. The hidden 5 at the end of her name shows the enjoyment she receives while giving gifts to others. This same number helps her enjoy meeting new people, but it may keep her from getting married or tied down, as the 5 likes to be free. The P in her name shows us that as much as Oprah likes people, she still needs her privacy. The H as her capstone letter shows her ability to manage over the material world. She is one of the wealthiest women alive. Two hidden 4s at the beginning of her name, plus the 4 power number, gives Oprah the ability to go in and quickly assess a situation. It's the human computer effect; she always does her homework before taking on an assignment. The hidden 4s in Oprah's name also show she's had more hardships than most of us will ever know.

Orlando Bloom not only wears his O up front, but also at the end. His cornerstone and capstone letters are both an O. The name Orlando adds up to a 7 power number which often performs well in the movie industry or in front of a camera. His two favorite cities are London and Los Angeles, which both have the O and L in them. We often feel comfortable in cities that have the same letters as in our own names.

Another interesting and magnetic personality whose name starts with an O is Oliver North. O people are service-oriented and will work tirelessly to perform the task at hand. Oliver has a hidden 9 (O and L add up to 9), plus an I and an R in his name, which are both ruled by the number 9. And his name sums up to a power number 9. All of these 9s indicate that people feel safe with him somehow. They ask him questions because they think he knows the answer. With the 6 and 9 energy in his name, he's a go-with-the-flow type person, not uptight at all. He's a true humanitarian with that much 9. The L gives him an above-average ability to communicate.

Some other famous O names are: Olympia Dukakis, Orson Welles, Ozzy Nelson, Oscar Wilde, Ogden Nash, Ossie Davis, Olivia de Havilland, Oliver Hardy, O. J. Simpson, Oliver Wendell Holmes, Oleta Adams, Orville Wright, Otis Redding, Otto Preminger, and Omar Sharif.

QUICK REFERENCE OF "O" NAMES

Oakley, 6: Magnetic personality. Pioneer and risk taker. Strong desire to succeed. Great verbal skills. A free spirit, very adaptable. Dislikes limitations.

Obadiah, 4: Assumes responsibility. Friendly, but shy. Natural teaching ability. Domestic, responsible. Blessed in some ways. Bold, courageous, a bit stubborn. Great judge of character.

Obayana, 5: Enjoys working. Sparkling, emotional outlook. Bright, adventuresome. Needs a lot of freedom. Bold, courageous, a bit stubborn. Original and unconventional. Pioneer and risk taker.

Oberon, 6: Magnetic personality. Friendly, but shy. A free spirit, very adaptable. Gentle, kind, a hard worker. Natural counselor and healer. Original and unconventional.

Octave, 3: Has creative solutions. Cheerful, lighthearted. Dynamic, busy lifestyle. Aims to please. Intuitive and inspired. A free spirit, very adaptable.

Octavia, 8: Competitive in business. Self-expressive, cheerful. Energetic, highly charged. Resolute and purposeful. Intuitive and inspired. Blessed in some ways. Bold, courageous, a bit stubborn.

Octavio, 4: Assumes responsibility. Self-expressive, cheerful. Dynamic, busy lifestyle. Natural teaching ability. Intuitive and inspired. Blessed in some ways. Natural counselor and healer.

Octavius, 11: Creates group harmony. Self-expressive, cheerful. Dynamic, busy lifestyle. Reads people easily. Intuitive and inspired. Blessed in some ways. Attractive and charming. Loving, devoted.

Odela, 10: Ambitious and innovative. Domestic, down-to-earth. Likes variety and change. Strong verbal skills. Independent, critical of self and others.

Odele, 5: Enjoys working. Reliable, responsible. A free spirit, very adaptable. Strong verbal skills. Physical and passionate.

Odelia, 10: Ambitious and innovative. Domestic, down-to-earth. Likes variety and change. Strong verbal skills. Blessed in some ways. Independent, critical of self and others.

Odell, 3: Has creative solutions. Reliable, responsible. A free spirit, very adaptable. Communicates skillfully. Slow to make decisions.

Odessa, 9: Artistic, creative. Reliable, responsible. A free spirit, very adaptable. Charming and devoted. Impulsive and extreme. Helpful, sincere.

Odetta, 20: Works well with others. Reliable, responsible. Social, entertaining. Dynamic, busy lifestyle. Sensitive and easily hurt. Reads people easily.

Odette, 6: Magnetic personality. Duty-bound, self-sacrificing. A free spirit, very adaptable. Dynamic, busy lifestyle. Sensitive and easily hurt. Loves adventure and excitement.

Odin, 6: Magnetic personality. Duty-bound, self-sacrificing. Blessed in some ways. Original and unconventional.

Ofelia, 30: Has creative solutions. Self-sacrificing, loving. A free spirit, very adaptable. Great verbal skills. Blessed in some ways. Independent, critical of self and others.

Ogden, 9: Artistic, creative. Scientific and philosophical. Reliable, responsible. A free spirit, very adaptable. Original and unconventional.

Ogilvie, 7: Open to opportunities. A thinker, determined. Blessed in some ways. Communicates skillfully. Intuitive and inspired. Artistic, having good taste. A free spirit, very adaptable.

Oglesby, 4: Assumes responsibility. Scientific and philosophical. Strong verbal skills. A free spirit, very adaptable. Charming and devoted. Friendly, but shy. Dislikes limitations.

Ojeda, 8: Competitive in business. Clever and talented. A free spirit, very adaptable. Reliable, responsible. Resolute and purposeful.

Ok-hee, 8: Competitive in business. Has a powerful presence. Great judge of character. A free spirit, very adaptable. Loves adventure and excitement.

Okilani, 8: Competitive in business. Has a powerful presence. Blessed in some ways. Great verbal skills. Independent, critical of self and others. Original and unconventional. Artistic, having good taste.

Oksana, 7: Open to opportunities. Strong desire to succeed. Charming and devoted. Independent, critical of self and others. Original and unconventional. Bold, courageous, a bit stubborn.

Ola, 10: Ambitious and innovative. Communicates skillfully. Bold, courageous, a bit stubborn.

Olaf, 7: Open to opportunities. Strong verbal skills. Bold, courageous, a bit stubborn. Self-sacrificing, loving.

Olavo, 20: Works well with others. Honest and sincere. Reads people easily. Has a strong imagination. Natural counselor and healer.

Oleg, 8: Competitive in business. Strong verbal skills. A free spirit, very adaptable. Scientific and philosophical

Olena, 20: Works well with others. Frequent traveler. Social and entertaining. Original and unconventional. Reads people easily.

Oleta, 8: Competitive in business. Great verbal skills. A free spirit, very adaptable. Dynamic, busy lifestyle. Resolute and purposeful.

Olga, 8: Competitive in business. Great verbal skills. Scientific and philosophical. Resolute and purposeful.

Olin, 5: Enjoys working. Communicates skillfully. Blessed in some ways. Original and unconventional.

Olisa, 20: Works well with others. Strong verbal skills. Blessed in some ways. Charming and devoted. Independent, critical of self and others.

Olive, 9: Artistic, creative. Frequent traveler. Idealistic, humanitarian. Tactful and refined. A free spirit, very adaptable.

Oliver, 9: Artistic, creative. Frequent traveler. Idealistic, humanitarian. Tactful and refined. A free spirit, very adaptable. Gentle, kind, a hard worker.

Olivia, 5: Enjoys working. Communicates skillfully. Blessed in some ways. Intuitive and inspired. Artistic, having good taste. Independent, critical of self and others.

Olivier, 9: Artistic, creative. Frequent traveler. Idealistic, humanitarian. Tactful and refined. Blessed in some ways. A free spirit, very adaptable. Gentle, kind, a hard worker.

Olivine, 5: Enjoys working. Communicates skillfully. Blessed in some ways. Intuitive and inspired. Artistic, having good taste. Original and unconventional. A free spirit, very adaptable.

Ollie, 8: Competitive in business. Great verbal skills. Ups and downs financially. Blessed in some ways. A free spirit, very adaptable.

Olney, 8: Competitive in business. Great verbal skills. Original and unconventional. A free spirit, very adaptable. Dislikes limitations.

Olympia, 10: Ambitious and innovative. Strong verbal skills. Needs a lot of freedom. Domestic, hardworking. Levelheaded. Blessed in some ways. Independent, critical of self and others.

Omar, 20: Works well with others. Domestic, hardworking. Reads people easily. Sensitive, emotional, kind.

Ona, 3: Has creative solutions. Original and unconventional. Aims to please.

Oona, 9: Artistic, creative. Natural counselor and healer. Original and unconventional. Helpful, sincere.

Opal, 8: Competitive in business. Intelligent, knowledgeable. Resolute and purposeful. Great verbal skills.

Opaline, 9: Artistic, creative. Levelheaded. Helpful, sincere. Strong verbal skills. Blessed in some ways. Original and unconventional. A free spirit, very adaptable.

Ophelia, 3: Has creative solutions. Intelligent, knowledgeable. Great judge of character. A free spirit, very adaptable. Strong verbal skills. Blessed in some ways. Aims to please.

Opie, 9: Artistic, creative. Levelheaded. Blessed in some ways. A free spirit, very adaptable.

Opra, 5: Enjoys working. Intelligent, knowledgeable. Gentle, kind, a hard worker. Bright, adventuresome.

Oprah, 4: Assumes responsibility. Intelligent, knowledgeable. Gentle, kind, a hard worker. Natural teaching ability. Great judge of character.

Oracio, 7: Open to opportunities. Diligent, helpful. Independent, self-motivated. Inspiring and creative. Blessed in some ways. Natural counselor and healer.

Oralie, 6: Magnetic personality. Gentle, kind, a hard worker. Pioneer and risk taker. Great verbal skills. Artistic, having good taste. A free spirit, very adaptable.

O-Ren, 7: Open to opportunities. Compassionate and understanding. Not easily fooled. Romantic and opinionated.

Oreste, 10: Ambitious and innovative. Diligent, helpful, kind. Likes change and variety. Charming and devoted. Dynamic, busy lifestyle. Physical and passionate.

Ori, 6: Magnetic personality. Duty-bound, self-sacrificing. Artistic, having good taste.

Oriana, 4: Assumes responsibility. Gentle, kind, a hard worker. Blessed in some ways. Natural teaching ability. Original and unconventional. Bold, courageous, a bit stubborn.

Oribel, 7: Open to opportunities. Compassionate, understanding. Needs alone time. Friendly, but shy. A free spirit, very adaptable. Communicates skillfully.

Oriel, 5: Enjoys working. Good deed doer. Blessed in some ways. A free spirit, very adaptable. Great verbal skills.

Orino, 8: Competitive in business. Intense inner power. Blessed in some ways. Original and creative. Natural counselor and healer.

Orion, 8: (Same as Orino.)

Orlando, 7: Open to opportunities. Compassionate, understanding. Strong verbal skills. Not easily influenced. Original and unconventional. Reliable, responsible. Natural counselor and healer.

Ormond, 7: Open to opportunities. Compassionate, understanding. Domestic, hardworking. May have musical abilities. Original and unconventional. Reliable, responsible.

Orpah, 4: (Same as Oprah.)

Orsen, 8: Competitive in business. Intense inner power. Charming and devoted. A free spirit, very adaptable. Original and unconventional.

Orson, 9: Artistic, creative. Gentle, kind, a hard worker. Charming and devoted. May have musical abilities. Original and unconventional.

Orval, 5: Enjoys working. Good deed doer. Intuitive and inspired. Bright, adventuresome. Strong verbal skills.

Orville, 3: Has creative solutions. Gentle, kind, a hard worker. Intuitive and inspired. Blessed in some ways. Strong verbal skills. Many ups and downs financially. A free spirit, very adaptable.

Os, 7: Open to opportunities. Charming and devoted. Very charismatic.

Osaka, 11: Creates group harmony. Charismatic and charming. Independent, critical of self and others. Strong desire to succeed. Bold, courageous, a bit stubborn.

Osborn, 11: Creates group harmony. Charismatic and charming. Friendly, but shy. Natural counselor and healer. Gentle, kind, a hard worker. Original and unconventional.

Osborne, 7: Open to opportunities. Charming and devoted. Friendly, but shy. May have musical abilities. Gentle, kind, a hard worker. Original and unconventional. A free spirit, very adaptable.

Osbourne, 10: Ambitious and innovative. Charming and devoted. Friendly, but shy. May have musical abilities. Attractive and lucky. Gentle, kind, a hard worker. Original and unconventional. A free spirit, very adaptable.

Oscar, 20: Works well with others. Socially refined. Self-expressive, cheerful. Independent, critical of self and others. Gentle, kind, a hard worker.

Osmond, 8: Competitive in business. Passionate and loving. Domestic, hardworking. May have musical abilities. Original and unconventional. Reliable, responsible.

Osmund, 5: Enjoys working. Extremely charming. Practical, duty-bound. Youthful and appealing. Original and unconventional. Reliable, responsible.

Osvaldo, 7: Open to opportunities. Charming and devoted. Intuitive and inspired. Independent, critical of self and others. Strong verbal skills. Reliable, responsible. May have musical abilities.

Oswald, 20: Works well with others. Socially refined. Likes to meet new people. Reads people easily. Strong verbal skills. Reliable, responsible.

Othello, 6: Magnetic personality. Dynamic, busy lifestyle. Great judge of character. A free spirit, very adaptable. Great verbal skills. Frequent traveler. Natural counselor and healer.

Otis, 9: Artistic, creative. Dynamic, busy lifestyle. Blessed in some ways. Charming and devoted.

Otto, 7: Open to opportunities. Dynamic, busy lifestyle. Sensitive and easily hurt. Natural counselor and healer.

Owen, 3: Has creative solutions. Likes to meet new people. Physical and passionate. Original, opinionated.

Oxford, 10: Ambitious and innovative. Artistic, sensual, perceptive. Self-sacrificing, loving. Natural counselor and healer. Gentle, kind, a hard worker. Reliable, responsible.

Oz, 5: Enjoys working. Uses common sense. Creative and determined.

Ozzie, 9: Artistic, creative. Uses common sense. A great mediator. Blessed in some ways. A free spirit, very adaptable.

Ozzy, 10: Ambitious and innovative. Uses common sense. A great mediator. Needs a lot of freedom.

P

If a name begins with P, has more than one P, or ends with a P, this person is levelheaded, intelligent, knowledgeable, and gives a commanding first impression.

The letter P is the 16th letter of the alphabet. Since $1 + 6 = 7$, the 16th letter has the same vibrational influence as the number 7. The 1 rules beginnings, 6 rules love, and 7 rules faith. The P person is beginning love in some aspect of his or her life, but the sum total is faith or religion, which requires solitude. So the P person desires love but also needs solitude for meditation. Since love can be demanding, the P needs to balance giving love with taking time to meditate or be alone. This is the P's big challenge.

P names show common sense and seem levelheaded, but they can be impatient. P-named people tend to be selfish with their time. The P is usually highly photogenic, similar to G and Y names. That's because these letters are similar to the astrological sign Pisces, the fish, which is ruled by Neptune. This same influence rules images or things that are "not real," as an image of a person is not the same as a real person. Neptune also rules the oceans and tides, so many influenced by the letter P prefer to live by water. As this letter is prone to escapism, the Neptunian influence can be so strong, some of them drink like a fish! So, the same amount of caution should be exercised in regard to drugs and alcohol as their G- and Y-named siblings.

It's possible to be happy in relationships with P names as long as we give them space and time for privacy or solitude. Somehow it recharges their batteries and we're all the better for it. When a breakup occurs, we often have difficulty completely remembering those ruled by P. They're a bit elusive, like a half-remembered song. We can hum the melody, but the lyrics keep slipping away. The memory of them wants to evaporate somehow.

Those with a P anywhere in their name often prefer to work alone. Just stick them in a corner somewhere and they'll be happy. But Ps are not shy—they're honest and can probably tell the boss what's wrong with his new marketing plan. Yes, they are that bold. If a P person goes into acting or some type of stage life, they still want their privacy more than the other letters. Let's just say, P is for privacy! They might be emotional, but tend to have difficulty expressing their feelings. P types, similar to G and Y, sometimes have difficulty giving and receiving affection. This letter is extremely cerebral, and since love is not, the P often has difficulty understanding the emotion of love. P-named people can be stubborn and inflexible and insist on independence. This is another reason why it can be difficult for the P to maintain permanent relationships. The biggest downfall, however, is that this 7-ruled letter, similar to G and Y, can be egotistical. This letter is more enjoyable to be around when it places faith in a higher being. If the P doesn't humble itself to a higher source, it often has an inflated sense of self-importance. As the saying goes, some either worship God or think they are God. Those that bear this faith-based letter seem to be either one or the other.

Paul Newman, Paul McCartney, Paul Simon, and Paul Anka not only share the same first name, but also share the same nameology interpretation. P is a 7 letter and the A is a 1, so there is a hidden 8 in the beginning of each of their names. This means they've had lessons relating to material goods. They may be attracted to taxes, joint finances, or other people's money. Often hidden 8s have a brush with death or lose a meaningful loved one unexpectedly. They secretly like being in control. When we add the hidden 8 to the U, which is a 3, it adds up to a hidden 11. All four of these men have loads of creative inspiration. Then to the 11 we add the last letter L, which is a 3. This adds up to 14, which condenses to a power number 5. All four of these famous men share the love of adventure and excitement. They are adaptable to change. They are natural entertainers. Most importantly, they really need freedom with a power number 5. Yet at the front of their name, similar to a rising sign, is the private P. The first two letters are cerebral; these guys are extremely intelligent. However, the last two letters are ruled by the number 3, so they may be slow to make decisions. The number 3-ruled letters also tend to be lucky. They most likely managed to be in the right place at the right time at critical junctures in their lives. Last, but not least, the numbers 3, 5, and 8 bring financial ups and downs. So these men have no doubt ridden the financial roller coaster a time or two. Not every person named Paul is going to be famous, but there is potential, given the opportunity the name provides.

Phyllis Diller, with all those Ls in her name, is a natural comedian. L is ruled by the number 3, and along with number 5, gives a wonderful stage presence. Also her Ls not only allow her to communicate well, but also to listen well. Still, she has two letters ruled by the number 7, so she really likes her privacy. Her name adds up to a power number 11, which is a master number. She has a very strong desire to succeed in life. The H in her name is the "Hercules" of letters. She is strong, and with the P, that adds up to a hidden 6. She's a nurturer and prefers being her own boss. When we add Y, which is the second 7-ruled letter, 7 + 8 + 7 adds up to another master number, 22! Deep inside of her, hidden, is a desire to be successful on a global scale. We only have two master numbers, 11 and 22. Phyllis has both of them hidden in her name. Still, the center of her name is an L which is ruled by 3, so she strives to communicate and be "out there," while the 7s in her name want her to be alone. She must balance the desire to be alone with the need to be on stage. Ultimately, the H, which desires material wealth, most likely gave her the push she needed to get out there in the public eye, even though she may have preferred to be alone.

How about the name Peter, as in Peter Fonda, Peter Sellers, Peter Boyle, or Peter Gallagher? First, three out of five letters are cerebral, the P and the two Es. The R at the end of their name is gentle, kind, and very hard-working. The T in the middle of their names makes them dynamic, with a busy lifestyle. The first three letters add up to a hidden 5 and with a T in the middle, these guys like to entertain and keep very busy. Sometimes they need to be forced to slow down! With all that 5 energy, they love adventure and excitement. When we add the whole name together we find it has a power number 10. People with power number 10 find themselves either extremely busy, or they personally have nothing going on at all. At times they are in great demand, inspired to counsel others with their assistance from God (coming from the 0 in their 10 power number). At other times, they twiddle their thumbs.

Some more famous P names are: Phil Donahue, Dr. Phil McGraw, Paris Hilton, Penny Marshall, Patrick Stewart, Patty Duke, Petula Clark, Pablo Picasso, Paloma Picasso, Patty Hearst, Paula Abdul, Peter Frampton, Phil Collins, Pat Sajak, Pamela Anderson, Pink, Pearl Bailey, Pat Boone, Pierre Cardin, Patrick Swayze, Pat Benatar, Prince, Perry Como, Paul Hogan, Patrick Henry, Paul Revere, Patricia Arquette, and Patsy Cline.

QUICK REFERENCE OF "P" NAMES

Pablo, 10: Strives for excellence. Independent, critical of self and others. Friendly, but shy. Strong verbal skills. Natural counselor and healer.

Paddy, 5: Maintains a high dream. Bright, adventuresome. Reliable, responsible. Down-to-earth, faithful. Needs a lot of freedom.

Padma, 7: Highly refined intellect. Not easily influenced. Reliable, responsible. Domestic, hardworking. Bold, courageous, a bit stubborn.

Page, 20: Socially refined. Reads people easily. Scientific, philosophical. A free spirit, very adaptable.

Paige, 11: Knowledgeable in many areas. Intuitive, perceptive. Blessed in some ways. Scientific, philosophical. A free spirit, very adaptable.

Paine, 9: Gift for understanding others. Helpful, sincere. Blessed in some ways. Original and unconventional. A free spirit, very adaptable.

Paley, 5: Maintains a high dream. Bright, adventuresome. Communicates skillfully. A free spirit, very adaptable. Dislikes limitations.

Palmer, 11: Knowledgeable in many areas. Intuitive, perceptive. Strong verbal skills. Domestic, hardworking. A free spirit, very adaptable. Gentle, kind, very helpful.

Paloma, 22: Knowledgeable in many areas. Ambitious leader, great vision. Strong verbal skills. Natural counselor and healer. Domestic, hardworking. Bold, courageous, a bit stubborn.

Pam, 3: Optimistic in faith. Aims to please. Domestic, hardworking.

Pamela, 3: Optimistic in faith. Aims to please. Domestic, hardworking. A free spirit, very adaptable. Great verbal skills. Bold, courageous, a bit stubborn.

Pammy, 5: Maintains a high dream. Bright, adventuresome. Domestic, hardworking. Systematic, organized. Needs a lot of freedom.

Pansy, 3: Optimistic in faith. Aims to please. Original and creative. Charming and devoted. Needs a lot of freedom.

Papa, 7: Highly refined intellect. Not easily influenced. Levelheaded. Bold, courageous, a bit stubborn.

Paris, 9: Gift for understanding others. Independent, self-motivated. Gentle, kind, a hard worker. Blessed in some ways. Charming and devoted.

Park, 10: Strives for excellence. Independent, critical of self and others. Gentle, kind, a hard worker. Strong desire to succeed.

Parker, 6: Needs harmony and beauty. Pioneer and risk taker. Duty-bound, self-sacrificing. Strong desire to succeed. A free spirit, very adaptable. Tendency to lose items.

Parnel, 30: Optimistic in faith. Aims to please. Sympathetic, kind. Opinionated, creative. Physical and passionate. Strong verbal skills.

Parnell, 6: Needs harmony and beauty. Pioneer and risk taker. Duty-bound, self-sacrificing. Original and unconventional. A free spirit, very adaptable. Communicates skillfully. Financial ups and downs.

Parrish, 8: Enjoys rivalry and challenge. Resolute and purposeful. Intense inner power. Compassionate, understanding. Blessed in some ways. Charming and devoted. Great judge of character.

Pascal, 7: Levelheaded. Not easily influenced. Charming and devoted. Self-expressive, cheerful. Bold, courageous, a bit stubborn. Communicates skillfully.

Pat, 10: Strives for excellence. Independent, critical of self and others. Takes the initiative.

Pate, 6: Needs harmony and beauty. Pioneer and risk taker. Dynamic, busy lifestyle. A free spirit, very adaptable.

Patience, 10: Strives for excellence. Independent, critical of self and others. Takes the initiative. Blessed in some ways. A free spirit, very adaptable. Original and unconventional. Self-expressive, cheerful. Loves adventure and excitement.

Patrice, 9: Gift for understanding others. Helpful, sincere. Generous to a fault. Gentle, kind, a hard worker. Blessed in some ways. Self-expressive, cheerful. A free spirit, very adaptable.

Patricia, 5: Maintains a high dream. Bright, adventuresome. Energetic, highly charged. Gentle, kind, a hard worker. Blessed in some ways. Self-expressive, cheerful. Artistic, having good taste. Bold, courageous, a bit stubborn.

Patrick, 6: Needs harmony and beauty. Pioneer and risk taker. Dynamic, busy lifestyle. Gentle, kind, a hard worker. Blessed in some ways. Self-expressive, cheerful. Strong desire to succeed.

Patsy, 9: Gift for understanding others. Helpful, sincere. Generous to a fault. Charming and devoted. Needs a lot of freedom.

Patti, 3: Optimistic in faith. Aims to please. Dynamic, busy lifestyle. Sensitive and easily hurt. Blessed in some ways.

Patton, 5: Maintains a high dream. Bright, adventuresome. Energetic, highly charged. Sensitive and easily hurt. Natural counselor and healer. Original and unconventional.

Patty, 10: Strives for excellence. Independent, critical of self and others. Takes the initiative. Sensitive and easily hurt. Needs a lot of freedom.

Paul, 5: Maintains a high dream. Bright, adventuresome. Attractive and charming. Strong verbal skills.

Paula, 6: Needs harmony and beauty. Independent, critical of self and others. Attractive and charming. Strong verbal skills. Bold, courageous, a bit stubborn.

Paulette, 10: Strives for excellence. Independent, critical of self and others. Youthful, appealing. Strong verbal skills. A free spirit, very adaptable. Dynamic, busy lifestyle. Sensitive and easily hurt. Loves adventure and excitement.

Paulina, 11: Knowledgeable in many areas. Intuitive, perceptive. Creative, inspiring. Strong verbal skills. Blessed in some ways. Original and unconventional. Bold, courageous, a bit stubborn.

Pauline, 6: Needs harmony and beauty. Pioneer and risk taker. Attractive and charming. Great verbal skills. Blessed in some ways. Original and unconventional. A free spirit, very adaptable.

Paulo, 20: Socially refined. Reads people easily. Attractive and charming. Communicates skillfully. A natural counselor and healer.

Paxon, 7: Levelheaded. Not easily influenced. Artistic, sensual, perceptive. Natural counselor and healer. Original and unconventional.

Paxton, 9: Gift for understanding others. Helpful, sincere. Artistic, sensual, perceptive. Dynamic, busy lifestyle. Natural counselor and healer. Original and unconventional.

Payne, 7: Levelheaded. Not easily influenced. Needs a lot of freedom. Original and unconventional. A free spirit, very adaptable.

Payton, 10: Strives for excellence. Independent, critical of self and others. Needs a lot of freedom. Dynamic, busy lifestyle. Natural counselor and healer. Original and unconventional.

Peace, 3: Optimistic in faith. A free spirit, very adaptable. Aims to please. Self-expressive, cheerful. Physical and passionate.

Pearce, 30: Optimistic in faith. A free spirit, very adaptable. Aims to please. Gentle, kind, a hard worker. Self-expressive, cheerful. Physical and passionate.

Pearl, 7: Levelheaded. Not easily fooled. Stylish and refined. Gentle, kind, a hard worker. Strong verbal skills.

Pearle, 30: Optimistic in faith. A free spirit, very adaptable. Aims to please. Gentle, kind, a hard worker. Communicates skillfully. Tendency to overindulge.

Pedro, 4: Bit of a homebody. Accesses quickly. Reliable, responsible. Gentle, kind, a hard worker. Natural counselor and healer.

Peg, 10: Strives for excellence. Likes change and variety. Scientific and philosophical.

Peggy, 6: Needs harmony and beauty. A step ahead of others. Scientific and philosophical. Needs solitude. Needs a lot of freedom.

Pembroke, 4: Bit of a homebody. Accesses quickly. Domestic, hardworking. Friendly, but shy. Gentle and kind. Natural counselor and healer. Strong desire to succeed. Loves adventure and excitement.

Penelope, 7: Levelheaded. Not easily fooled. Original and unconventional. Physical and passionate. Strong verbal skills. Natural counselor and healer. Intelligent, knowledgeable. Loves adventure and excitement.

Penley, 5: Maintains a high dream. Physical and passionate. Original and unconventional. Great verbal skills. Likes meeting new people. Needs a lot of freedom.

Penn, 22: Knowledgeable in many areas. Has big plans and ideas. Original and unconventional. Romantic, sensual.

Penny, 11: Knowledgeable in many areas. Keenly perceptive. Original and creative. Romantic, sensual. Needs a lot of freedom.

Penrod, 9: Gift for understanding others. Enjoys giving gifts. Romantic, opinionated. Gentle, kind, a hard worker. Natural counselor and healer. Reliable, responsible.

Peony, 30: Optimistic in faith. A free spirit, very adaptable. Natural counselor and healer. Original and unconventional. Dislikes limitations.

Pepita, 4: Bit of a homebody. Accesses quickly. Levelheaded. Blessed in some ways. Dynamic, busy lifestyle. Natural teaching ability.

Percival, 5: Maintains a high dream. Perceptive, socially adept. Intense inner power. Self-expressive, cheerful. Blessed in some ways. Intuitive and inspired. Bright, adventuresome. Great verbal skills.

Percy, 4: Bit of a homebody. Accesses quickly. Hardworking, kind, diligent. Self-expressive, cheerful. Dislikes limitations.

Peregrine, 7: Levelheaded. Not easily fooled. Spiritually motivated. A free spirit, very adaptable. Needs solitude. Tendency to lose items. Blessed in some ways. Original and unconventional. Loves adventure and excitement.

Peri, 30: Optimistic in faith. A free spirit, very adaptable. Sympathetic, kind. Blessed in some ways.

Perl, 6: Needs harmony and beauty. A step ahead of others. Gentle, kind, a hard worker. Strong verbal skills.

Perla, 7: Levelheaded. Not easily fooled. Spiritually motivated. Great verbal skills. Bold, courageous, a leader.

Perle, 11: Knowledgeable in many areas. Keenly perceptive. Gentle, kind, a hard worker. Travels frequently. Loves adventure and excitement.

Pernell, 10: Strives for excellence. Likes change and variety. Diligent, hardworking. Original and unconventional. Loves adventure and excitement. Strong verbal skills. Frequent traveler.

Perry, 10: Strives for excellence. Likes change and variety. Diligent, hardworking. Tendency to lose items. Needs a lot of freedom.

Pete, 10: Strives for excellence. Likes change and variety. Dynamic, busy lifestyle. Loves adventure and excitement.

Peter, 10: Strives for excellence. Likes change and variety. Dynamic, busy lifestyle. Loves adventure and excitement. Gentle, kind, a hard worker.

Petra, 6: Needs harmony and beauty. A step ahead of others. Dynamic, busy lifestyle. Gentle, kind, a hard worker. Independent, critical of self and others.

Petrina, 11: Knowledgeable in many areas. A free spirit, very adaptable. Dynamic, busy lifestyle. Gentle, kind, a hard worker. Blessed in some ways. Romantic, opinionated. Intuitive, perceptive.

Petula, 3: Optimistic in faith. A free spirit, very adaptable. Dynamic, busy lifestyle. Attractive and charming. Great verbal skills. Aims to please.

Petunia, 5: Maintains a high dream. Perceptive, socially adept. Dynamic, busy lifestyle. Attractive and charming. Original and unconventional. Blessed in some ways. Bright, adventuresome.

Peyton, 5: Maintains a high dream. Perceptive, socially adept. Needs a lot of freedom. Dynamic, busy lifestyle. Natural counselor and healer. Romantic, creative.

Phelan, 11: Knowledgeable in many areas. Self-reliant, successful. Keenly perceptive. Strong verbal skills. Independent, critical of self and others. Original and unconventional.

Phelia, 6: Needs harmony and beauty. Original, creative. A step ahead of others. Great verbal skills. Blessed in some ways. Independent, critical of self and others.

Phelps, 4: Bit of a homebody. Great judge of character. Accesses quickly. Frequent traveler. Levelheaded. Charming and devoted.

Phil, 9: Gift for understanding others. Relies on own judgment. Blessed in some ways. Great verbal skills.

Philbert, 9: Gift for understanding others. Relies on own judgment. Blessed in some ways. Great verbal skills. Friendly, but shy. A free spirit, very adaptable. Gentle, kind, a hard worker. Dynamic, busy lifestyle.

Philip, 7: Levelheaded. Great judge of character. Blessed in some ways. Communicates skillfully. Artistic, having good taste. Overly secretive, distant.

Philippa, 6: Needs harmony and beauty. Original, creative. Blessed in some ways. Strong verbal skills. Artistic, having good taste. Overly secretive, distant. Levelheaded. Not easily influenced.

Phillis, 4: Bit of a homebody. Great judge of character. Blessed in some ways. Great verbal skills. Frequent traveler. Artistic, having good taste. Charming and devoted.

Philo, 6: Needs harmony and beauty. Original, creative. Blessed in some ways. Frequent traveler. Natural counselor and healer.

Philomena, 3: Optimistic in faith. Makes and loses money easily. Blessed in some ways. Strong verbal skills. Natural counselor and healer. Domestic, hardworking. A free spirit, very adaptable. Romantic, creative. Pioneer and risk taker.

Phineas, 9: Gift for understanding others. Relies on own judgment. Blessed in some ways. Romantic, opinionated. A free spirit, very adaptable. Not easily influenced. Charming and devoted.

Phinnaeus, 8: Enjoys rivalry and challenge. Great judge of character. Blessed in some ways. Romantic, sensual. Original, opinionated. Independent, a leader. A free spirit, likes change. Attractive, flirtatious. Charming and devoted.

Phoebe, 6: Needs harmony and beauty. Original, creative. Natural counselor and healer. A free spirit, very adaptable. Friendly, but shy. Tendency to overindulge.

Phoenix, 10: Strives for excellence. Great judge of character. Natural counselor and healer. A free spirit, very adaptable. Original and unconventional. Blessed in some ways. Artistic, sensual, perceptive.

Phylis, 8: Enjoys rivalry and challenge. Great judge of character. Needs a lot of freedom. Strong verbal skills. Blessed in some ways. Charming and devoted.

Phyllis, 11: Knowledgeable in many areas. Self-reliant, successful. Needs a lot of freedom. Communicates skillfully. Frequent traveler. Blessed in some ways. Charming and devoted.

Pia, 8: Enjoys rivalry and challenge. Blessed in some ways. Resolute and purposeful.

Pierce, 8: Enjoys rivalry and challenge. Blessed in some ways. A free spirit, very adaptable. Gentle, kind, a hard worker. Self-expressive, cheerful. Loves adventure and excitement.

Pilar, 11: Knowledgeable in many areas. Artistic, having good taste. Strong verbal skills. Independent, critical of self and others. Gentle, kind, a hard worker.

Piper, 10: Strives for excellence. Creative and artistic. Levelheaded. A free spirit, very adaptable. Gentle, kind, a hard worker.

Pita, 10: Strives for excellence. Creative and artistic. Dynamic, busy lifestyle. Independent, critical of self and others.

Pitney, 8: Enjoys rivalry and challenge. Blessed in some ways. Dynamic, busy lifestyle. Original and unconventional. A free spirit, very adaptable. Dislikes limitations.

Pius, 20: Socially refined. Blessed in some ways. Attractive and flirtatious. Charming and devoted.

Plato, 10: Strives for excellence. Communicates skillfully. Independent, critical of self and others. Dynamic, busy lifestyle. Natural counselor and healer.

Polly, 8: Enjoys rivalry and challenge. Competitive in business. Strong verbal skills. Ups and downs financially. Needs a lot of freedom.

Polo, 22: Knowledgeable in many areas. Natural counselor and healer. Strong verbal skills. Magnetic personality.

Pomeroy, 8: Enjoys rivalry and challenge. Competitive in business. Desires financial security. Loves adventure and excitement. Gentle, kind, a hard worker. Magnetic personality. Needs a lot of freedom.

Poncho, 8: Enjoys rivalry and challenge. Competitive in business. Original and unconventional. Self-expressive, cheerful. Great judge of character. Has musical abilities.

Poppy, 7: Levelheaded. Natural counselor and healer. Intelligent, knowledgeable. A bit secretive. Needs a lot of freedom.

Porsche, 3: Optimistic in faith. Nurturing, loving. Considerate, helpful. Charming and devoted. Self-expressive, cheerful. Great judge of character. A free spirit, very adaptable.

Porter, 3: Optimistic in faith. Nurturing, loving. Considerate, helpful. Dynamic, busy lifestyle. A free spirit, very adaptable. Tendency to lose items.

Portia, 7: Levelheaded. Natural counselor and healer. Gentle, kind, a hard worker. Dynamic, busy lifestyle. Blessed in some ways. Independent, critical of self and others,

Preciosa, 5: Maintains a high dream. Good deed doer. A free spirit, very adaptable. Self-expressive, cheerful. Blessed in some ways. Natural counselor and healer. Charming and devoted. Independent, critical of self and others.

Precious, 7: Levelheaded. Gentle, kind, a hard worker. Not easily fooled. Self-expressive, cheerful. Blessed in some ways. Natural counselor and healer. Youthful, appealing. Charming and devoted.

Prentice, 9: Gift for understanding others. Gentle, kind, a hard worker. A free spirit, very adaptable. Original and unconventional. Dynamic, busy lifestyle. Blessed in some ways. Self-expressive, cheerful. Loves adventure and excitement.

Prescott, 8: Enjoys rivalry and challenge. Intense inner power. Original, creative. Passionate and loving. Self-expressive, cheerful. Natural counselor and healer. Dynamic, busy lifestyle. Sensitive and easily hurt.

Presley, 10: Strives for excellence. Diligent, hardworking. Likes change and variety. Charming and devoted. Strong verbal skills. Loves adventure and excitement. Dislikes limitations.

Preston, 8: Enjoys rivalry and challenge. Intense inner power. Original, creative, and unconventional. Passionate and loving. Dynamic, busy lifestyle. Natural counselor and healer.

Price, 6: Needs harmony and beauty. Duty-bound, self-sacrificing. Artistic, having good taste. Self-expressive, cheerful. A free spirit, very adaptable.

Pricilla, 8: Enjoys rivalry and challenge. Intense inner power. Blessed in some ways. Self-expressive, cheerful. Artistic, having good taste. Communicates skillfully. Ups and downs financially. Resolute and purposeful.

Princess, 4: Bit of a homebody. Gentle, kind, a hard worker. Blessed in some ways. Original and unconventional. Self-expressive, cheerful. A free spirit, very adaptable. Charming and devoted. Impulsive and extreme.

Priscilla, 9: Gift for understanding others. Gentle, kind, a hard worker. Blessed in some ways. Charming and devoted. Self-expressive, cheerful. Artistic, having good taste. Strong verbal skills. Ups and downs financially. Helpful, sincere.

Proctor, 6: Needs harmony and beauty. Duty-bound, self-sacrificing. Natural counselor and healer. Self-expressive and cheerful. Dynamic, busy lifestyle. May have musical abilities. Gentle, kind, a hard worker.

Pru, 10: Strives for excellence. Gentle, kind, a hard worker. Attractive and charming.

Prudence, 5: Maintains a high dream. Good deed doer. Youthful, appealing. Reliable, responsible. A free spirit, very adaptable. Original and unconventional. Self-expressive, cheerful. Physical and passionate.

Prudy, 30: Optimistic in faith. Sympathetic, kind. Attractive and charming. Reliable, responsible. Needs a lot of freedom.

Prunella, 9: Gift for understanding others. Gentle, kind, a hard worker. Attractive and charming. Original and unconventional. A free spirit, very adaptable. Great verbal skills. Frequent traveler. Helpful, sincere.

Pryce, 4: Bit of a homebody. Gentle, kind, a hard worker. Needs a lot of freedom. Self-expressive, cheerful. Loves adventure and excitement.

Pryor, 11: Knowledgeable in many areas. Gentle, kind, a hard worker. Needs a lot of freedom. Natural counselor and healer. Tendency to lose items.

Pulani, 10: Strives for excellence. Attractive and charming. Great verbal skills. Independent, critical of self and others. Original and unconventional. Blessed in some ways.

Punky, 6: Needs harmony and beauty. Creative, inspiring. Original and unconventional. Strong desire to succeed. Needs a lot of freedom.

Purcell, 6: Needs harmony and beauty. Creative, inspiring. Gentle, kind, a hard worker. Self-expressive, cheerful. A step ahead of others. Communicates skillfully. Frequent traveler.

Putnam, 22: Knowledgeable in many areas. Attractive and charming. Dynamic, busy lifestyle. Original and unconventional. Ambitious leader, great vision. Domestic, hardworking.

If a name begins with Q, has more than one Q, or ends with a Q, this person attracts money and wealth, has a natural authority, and has the ability to influence others.

The letter Q is the 17th letter of the alphabet. Since $1 + 7 = 8$, the 17th letter has the same vibrational influence as the number 8, similar to its sibling letters, H and Z. It's more highly evolved than the H, but more youthful than the Z, as the 3-ruled U tends to accompany this letter more often than not. The 1 rules beginnings, 7 rules religion, and 8 rules rewards. So in many ways the Q person is beginning to have faith which will bring rewards. Since Q is ruled by the number 8 vibration, which is Scorpio-like, there can be many changes that occur beyond their control. This depends on the karmic lessons they have brought upon themselves. Although they prefer to be in control, there must be a certain amount of prayer work and faith before the reward comes into play. Still, Qs have a natural authority. Others seem to respect Q automatically, because it is a rare letter, not often seen, and has an intimidating, unpredictable Scorpio-type energy.

Q anywhere in a person's name is seldom seen without the letter U immediately following. This can make the Q person a victim of gossip. U is a communication letter and Q is Scorpio-like with its stinger tail, so the world of media can be pretty cruel to anyone with the QU combination in their name. This also makes the person with these letters outspoken, to say the least. Their tongue can cut like a knife with this combination. And some of the Qs are boring and compulsive talkers. However most with the QU are extremely impressive with a talent for oration. Similar to H and Z, this letter likes to delegate authority and be in control. Similar to its alphabetical siblings H and Z, this letter enjoys rivalry and competition.

Q plus U equal the master number 11, making Queenie a bit high-strung and giving her a strong desire to be successful. Also $1 + 1 = 2$, so the Q and U make a good partnership, since 2 rules partnerships. Rarely is Q seen without its partner U. Q names are rare in and of themselves. The capacity for a high level of creativity results from the rarity of the QU combination. The 8 and 3 combined with a hidden 11 should produce some interesting creations, as seen by our famous Q names below.

In the psychology of sales, when a salesperson asks a question, they are in control. Whoever asks the most questions controls the conversation. This is why children seem to always be in control! The very word "question" starts with a Q, which is ruled by the controlling Scorpio-like 8. Next to a young, attractive, and charming U, really, how can we get mad? This same thinking is what helps the QU person move ahead. The U likes to intellectualize, so they may need time to make decisions. Still, the Q person seems to be able to hold interest and control outcomes, making Q people more sexy, attractive, and charming than others.

In fact, the QU combination is similar to the CH combination, and in fact may be compatible with CH names. I know a young boy named Chris who gets along very well with a boy in his class named Quentin. They probably get along well because their personalities are similar in some ways. They are able to relate to one another because C and U are ruled by the same number 3, and H and Q are ruled by the same number 8. The beginning of their names are compatible.

Quentin Tarantino is a director, actor, and writer. His most familiar films include *Pulp Fiction* and *Kill Bill*. Interestingly enough, he's an Aries, which is the first sun sign of the Zodiac. His first name adds up to a 10 power number; I + 0 = I, an Aries number. Also his nickname, QT, adds up to a 10. The I rules beginnings, which is Aries-like. The 0 rules assistance from God, which means he personally receives assistance from God. The number 0 is an all or nothing influence. It seems everything is happening all at once, or nothing is happening at all. So this very famous director must take advantage of his extremely busy "all" when it's here, before he gets a lot of "nothing" going on. The Q is ruled by number 8, which is materialistic, so, chances are, Quentin is smart about managing his money. The U is a very lucky letter, so he may have been able to cash in on some of that luck. Quentin also has the numbers 3, 5, and 8 in his name, which all tend to be lucky. Also, we associate these numbers with financial ups and downs. Quentin has an intensity 5 in his name with the E and two Ns. During a television interview shortly after the release of the first *Kill Bill* movie, he mentioned, "I wanted this movie to be entertaining…" That would be the intensity 5 in his name. He's not afraid to take chances and be unusual in his delivery. Rock stars often have an intensity 5 in their names. Quentin's name says his personality is freedom-loving, unconventional, charming, sexy, and in control. What a combination!

Another famous Q name is Quincy Jones, producer, director, and composer of music. He wrote television theme music for *Ironside*, *Sanford and Son*, and *The Bill Cosby Show*. He also produced Michael Jackson's first solo album, *Off the Wall*, then teamed up with Jackson again to produce *Thriller*. As discussed earlier, QU names always have a hidden master number 11. The pitfall of the 8 and the 3 is, once again, having financial ups and downs. This aspect of Quincy's name almost put him out of business, if it weren't for the lucky U bringing help in the form of a loan at a critical time in his life. The I right next to his U blesses him in the area of youth. He may have been lucky as a youth, or he might be gifted in working with young people. The I also gives him good taste as well as natural artistic ability, which he demonstrates time and again through his work with music. The Y at the end of his name makes him need a lot of freedom. Quincy adds up to an 8 power number, so he's a survivor. The Scorpio-like 8-ruled letter Q sometimes gives the bearer a brush with death to help them know how truly fortunate they really are.

Quinn Cummings was a child star in the '70s. Because of the youthful U as a first vowel, Q people tend to have something to do with the young. In Quinn's case, she was a child actress. Now an adult with a young child herself, she is known to have invented the "HipHugger," a sling-like baby carrier. With her name adding up to a power number 30, she works with writers to publish short stories online. The number 3 is the number for writers and 0 is assistance from God, so she must be a tremendous help to new writers with her wise and inspired counseling.

Some famous Q names: Queen Latifah, Quentin Tarantino, Quinn Cummings, and Quincy Jones. Another famous person with a Q in his name: Shaquille O'Neal, "Shaq."

QUICK REFERENCE OF "Q" NAMES

Quartus, 9: Highly evolved. Easygoing attitude. Helpful, sincere. Gentle, kind, a hard worker. Dynamic, busy lifestyle. Very lucky. Charming and devoted.

Queena, 9: Highly evolved. Easygoing attitude. A free spirit, very adaptable. Physical and passionate. Original and unconventional. Independent, critical of self and others.

Queenie, 4: Constructive, helpful. Gracious, well-mannered. A free spirit, very adaptable. Physical and passionate. Original and unconventional. Blessed in some ways. Loves adventure and excitement.

Quenby, 30: Direct and outspoken. Youthful, appealing. A free spirit, very adaptable. Original and unconventional. Friendly, but shy. Dislikes limitations.

Quenelle, 10: A strong leader. Attractive and charming. A free spirit, very adaptable. Original and unconventional. Physical and passionate. Strong verbal skills. Frequent traveler. Loves adventure and excitement.

Quenelles, 11: Potential to achieve greatness. Creative, inspiring. A free spirit, very adaptable. Original and unconventional. Physical and passionate. Strong verbal skills. Frequent traveler. Loves adventure and excitement. Charming and devoted.

Quennel, 7: Often misunderstood. Stylish and refined. Not easily fooled. Original and unconventional. Romantic, sensual. Likes change and variety. Great verbal skills.

Quent, 5: Sudden losses and gains. Fun, flirtatious. Physical and passionate. Original and unconventional. Dynamic, busy lifestyle.

Quentin, 10: A strong leader. Attractive and charming. A free spirit, very adaptable. Original and unconventional. Dynamic, busy lifestyle. Blessed in some ways. Romantic, sensual.

Quenton, 7: Often misunderstood. Stylish and refined. Not easily fooled. Original and unconventional. Dynamic, busy lifestyle. Natural counselor and healer. Romantic, sensual.

Questa, 20: Highly developed sense of tact. Social, charming. A free spirit, very adaptable. Many mood swings. Dynamic, busy lifestyle. Independent, critical of self and others.

Queta, 10: A strong leader. Attractive and charming. A free spirit, very adaptable. Dynamic, busy lifestyle. Independent, critical of self and others.

Quigley, 6: Ability to influence others. Idealistic in relationships. Artistic, having good taste. Scientific, philosophical. Great verbal skills. A free spirit, very adaptable. Dislikes limitations.

Quillion, 10: A strong leader. Attractive and charming. Blessed in some ways. Strong verbal skills. Frequent traveler. Artistic, having good taste. Natural counselor and healer. Original and unconventional.

Quinby, 7: Often misunderstood. Stylish and refined. Needs alone time. Original and unconventional. Friendly, but shy. Needs a lot of freedom.

Quincy, 8: A true survivor. Usually very lucky. Blessed in some ways. Original and unconventional. Self-expressive, cheerful. Needs a lot of freedom.

Quinn, 30: Direct and outspoken. Youthful, appealing. Considerate, understanding. Original and unconventional. Romantic, sensual.

Quinsy, 6: Ability to influence others. Idealistic in relationships. Artistic, having good taste. Original and unconventional. Many mood swings. Needs a lot of freedom.

Quint, 9: Highly evolved. Easygoing attitude. Blessed in some ways. Original and unconventional. Dynamic, busy lifestyle.

Quinta, 10: A strong leader. Attractive and charming. Blessed in some ways. Original and unconventional. Dynamic, busy lifestyle. Independent, critical of self and others.

Quintana, 7: Often misunderstood. Stylish and refined. Needs alone time. Original and unconventional. Dynamic, busy lifestyle. Independent, critical of self and others. Romantic, sensual. Bold, courageous, a bit stubborn.

Quintin, 5: Sudden losses and gains. Fun, flirtatious. Generous, thoughtful. Original and unconventional. Dynamic, busy lifestyle. Artistic, having good taste. Romantic, sensual.

Quinton, II: Potential to achieve greatness. Creative, inspiring. Blessed in some ways. Original and unconventional. Dynamic, busy lifestyle. Natural counselor and healer. Romantic, sensual.

Quirita, 5: Sudden losses and gains. Fun, flirtatious. Generous, thoughtful. Gentle, kind, a hard worker. Artistic, having good taste. Dynamic, busy lifestyle. Independent, critical of self and others.

I f a name begins with R, has more than one R, or ends with an R, this person is kind, gentle, and works very hard for the good of the whole, but may need to practice tolerance.

The letter R is the 18th letter of the alphabet. Since 1 + 8 = 9, the 18th letter has the same vibrational influence as the number 9. The 1 rules beginnings, 8 rules rewards, and 9 rules completions. The person whose name begins with R is often beginning to receive rewards and completing a stage of learning in this lifetime. The 1 and 8 combination can produce a bit of a bully. Except for number 4, 1 and 8 are two of the harshest numbers. The number 9 is similar to the astrological sign Sagittarius, which is ruled by the largest planet, Jupiter. Jupiter is more than twice as massive as all the other planets put together! So when a person with an R anywhere in his or her name enters a room, people somehow sense this bigness about them. The R-named person can seem pretty intimidating, even unintentionally. They command respect, and usually get it. Similar to the I, they are blessed more than the rest. They often get away with being a little naughty because even God sometimes looks the other way. Similar to "Christians aren't perfect, just forgiven." Somehow, right or wrong, people will follow them and forgive or over-look their faults. R people are usually gentle, kind, and hardworking. R names, similar to I names, are often placed upon a pedestal. They are at the end of their journey in some aspects of their development, and are given a little more leeway—okay, a lot more leeway. But who's going to argue with them when they've got God on their side?

The toughest task for the R-named individual is to stay balanced and even tempered. Three 3s go into 9, making balance of utmost impor-tance. They tend to overdo things. If the R drinks, they'll binge drink. Again, it's the Jupiter influence. Jupiter is the planet of abundance. The R tends to be overly optimistic or enthusiastic in almost everything, often making promises they can't keep. Still they have this intense inner power that enables them to work hard toward any goal. They'll do their job and everyone else's too. The R person is a humanitarian by nature and will work tirelessly for the good of the whole, without complaining and often without even a thank you. Turning within for meditation or hypnosis can be a wonderful tool for any R-named individual. Prayer also seems to help the R names. If they don't attempt to stay balanced by going within to meditate, they can become very critical and ill-tempered.

When you add 9 to any number, it will condense to the other number. For example: Raymond, R-9, A-1; we add 9 + 1 = 10, which condenses to 1; the 9 is colored by 1. So R is mutable. The letter R is a "go with the flow" letter which is easily influenced by its conjunction letter. The 9 added to any number goes back into itself after condensing. This is why our R-named friends are so diverse. R types can do almost anything the rest of the letters in their name allow them to do. They are heavily influenced by the letter next to it. Our alphabet only has two 9-ruled letters, unlike all the others numbers, which rule three letters. So these two 9-ruled letters are important. Those completing a cycle of learning in this lifetime, usually have an R or I somewhere in their name.

Those whose names begin with R, or have an R anywhere in their name, have a tendency to lose items or be a little forgetful. They're not unlike the absentminded professor. If they lose something, they might look for days, ranting and raving, only to be embarrassed later, finding the object exactly where they left it. R people are great at helping others; they see the big picture, often spreading themselves far and wide for the good of the whole. They could misplace their keys, or forget where they parked the car while out buying a present for a friend, but their hearts are always in the right place.

People whose name begins with RI, as in Rick, or IR, as in Irene, are especially blessed in some ways. Richie Rich, a cartoon character, is an example of the extremely blessed. This is because of the double 9, or intensity 9, in the beginning of his name. Intensity 9 names seem to have an artistic eye for beauty. People tend to look up to them or place them on a pedestal, whether they are right or wrong. These types are especially idealistic, humanitarian, and like to spread themselves thin.

If their name begins with RO, these names often, but not always, have a voice that carries. Some Robs and Roseannes don't need a megaphone to have a crowd hear them. This combination also makes for dynamic orators in the religious field. Robert Schuller, with his Crystal Cathedral, is an excellent example of this type. The RO names often make great singers as well. Usually they excel in providing a service of some kind and are more nurturing, as well as gifted counselors.

Those whose name begins with RA, as in Ralph or Raquel, will be more ambitious and independent. This combination is hard to beat. Actress Raquel Welch is a bit more ambitious because of the Q, which is ruled by the materialistic 8. Also, her name adds up to a power number 11, which encourages desire for success. The Scorpio-like Q in her name next to the attractive and charming U is responsible for her sex appeal.

Talking about sex appeal, another sexy actress is Renee Zellweger. She seems to be a chameleon with the ability to change her looks and personality with every role. That would be the Es in her name. Renee has an intensity 5, causing her to prefer variety, change, and adventure. She may secretly enjoy shocking or surprising others with all that 5 energy in her name. At the very least she's extremely adaptable.

Rex Harrison, an English actor who starred in *The Ghost and Mrs. Muir*, *My Fair Lady*, and a variety of other productions, also seems to like change. Rex adds up to a power number 20, so with him it's all or nothing in terms of partnership and other people. It seems some of his greatest roles involved a partner, which would portray the power number 20: partnership and assistance from God.

Rudy Giuliani, former Mayor of New York City, has the attractive and charming U first vowel. The U gives him an above-average ability to communicate. The D lends him toward being systematic and organized. The Y, well, he needs a lot of freedom. All together his name sums up to a 5 power number. The number 5 rules change; he made a lot of changes for the better in New York City. No city is really safe, and New York City used to have a much higher crime rate before Rudy came along. Rudy changed all that. The

R made him want to work for the good of the whole. He also proved to be gentle, kind, and hardworking during the 9/11 ordeal. Although his term was up as mayor, he stayed on, working late into the nights to help everyone through the turmoil. He wouldn't leave his beloved city when it needed him most. This is typical of an R-named person. They work for the whole, keeping the big picture in mind.

Some other famous R names: Rachel Ray, Ralph Lauren, Rock Hudson, Robin Williams, Richard Gere, Richard Burton, Ron Howard, Rob Reiner, Rachel Hunter, Rod Stewart, Ralph Nader, Roberta Flack, Rob Thomas, Rosie O'Donnell, Roman Polanski, Rita Moreno, Rosa Parks, Richard Chamberlain, Rush Limbaugh, Rob Lowe, R. Kelly, Rosemary Clooney, Richard Nixon, Rita Hayworth, Randolph W. Hearst, Rocky Marciano, Roy Rogers, Robert Wagner, Russell Crowe, Reba McEntire, Ray Charles, Rudolf Nureyev, Reese Witherspoon, Regis Philbin, Roger Moore, Robert Redford, and Richard Dreyfuss.

QUICK REFERENCE OF "R" NAMES

Rabi, 3: Sympathetic, kind. Aims to please. Friendly, but shy. Blessed in some ways.

Race, 9: Humanitarian, idealistic. Helpful, sincere. Self-expressive, cheerful. A free spirit, very adaptable.

Rachael, 30: Sympathetic, kind. Aims to please. Self-expressive, cheerful. Great judge of character. A free spirit, very adaptable. Strong verbal skills.

Rachel, 11: Strives to improve humanity. Intuitive, perceptive. Self-expressive, cheerful. Great judge of character. A free spirit, very adaptable. Communicates skillfully.

Rachelle, 10: Diligent, hardworking. Independent, critical of self and others. Self-expressive, cheerful. Great judge of character. A free spirit, very adaptable. Communicates skillfully. Frequent traveler. Loves adventure and excitement.

Radcliff, 5: Good deed doer. Bright, adventuresome. Reliable, responsible. Optimistic, outspoken. Great verbal skills. Blessed in some ways. Self-sacrificing, loving. High moral standards.

Radcliffe, 10: Diligent, hardworking. Independent, critical of self and others. Reliable, responsible. Self-expressive, cheerful. Strong verbal skills. Blessed in some ways. Self-sacrificing, loving. High moral standards. A free spirit, very adaptable.

Rae, 6: Duty-bound, self-sacrificing. Pioneer and risk taker. A free spirit, very adaptable.

Rafael, 7: Spiritual, a truth seeker. Not easily influenced. Self-sacrificing, loving. Bold, courageous, a bit stubborn. A free spirit, very adaptable. Strong verbal skills.

Rafferty, 9: Humanitarian, idealistic. Helpful, sincere. Self-sacrificing, loving. High moral standards. A free spirit, very adaptable. Tendency to lose items. Dynamic, busy lifestyle. Dislikes limitations.

Rahim, 4: Strong and healthy. Natural teaching ability. Great judge of character. Blessed in some ways. Systematic, organized.

Rain, 6: Duty-bound, self-sacrificing. Pioneer and risk taker. Artistic, having good taste. Creative and opinionated.

Raina, 7: Spiritual, a truth seeker. Not easily influenced. Blessed in some ways. Original and unconventional. Bold, courageous, a bit stubborn.

Raini, 6: Duty-bound, self-sacrificing. Pioneer and risk taker. Blessed in some ways. Original and unconventional. Idealistic and humanitarian.

Raisa, 3: Sympathetic, kind. Aims to please. Blessed in some ways. Charming and devoted. Bold, courageous, a bit stubborn.

Raizel, 8: Uses good judgment. Resolute and purposeful. Blessed in some ways. Uses common sense. A free spirit, very adaptable. Strong verbal skills.

Raleigh, 6: Duty-bound, self-sacrificing. Pioneer and risk taker. Communicates skillfully. A free spirit, very adaptable. Blessed in some ways. Scientific and philosophical. Great judge of character.

Ralph, 10: Diligent, hardworking. Independent, critical of self and others. Strong verbal skills. Intelligent and knowledgeable. Great judge of character.

Ralston, 9: Humanitarian, idealistic. Helpful, sincere. Strong verbal skills. Charming and devoted. Dynamic, busy lifestyle. Natural counselor and healer. Original and unconventional.

Rambert, 5: Good deed doer. Bright, adventuresome. Systematic, organized. Friendly, but shy. A free spirit, very adaptable. Tendency to lose items. Dynamic, busy lifestyle.

Rambo, 22: Strives to improve humanity. Ambitious leader, great vision. Systematic, organized. Friendly, but shy. Natural counselor and healer.

Ramon, 7: Spiritual, a truth seeker. Not easily influenced. Systematic, organized. Natural counselor and healer. Original and unconventional.

Ramona, 8: Uses good judgment. Resolute and purposeful. Systematic, organized. Natural counselor and healer. Original and unconventional. Bold, courageous, a bit stubborn.

Ramsey, 9: Humanitarian, idealistic. Helpful, sincere. Systematic, organized. Charming and devoted. A free spirit, very adaptable. Dislikes limitations.

Randall, 8: Uses good judgment. Resolute and purposeful. Creative, original. Reliable, responsible. Bold, courageous, a bit stubborn. Communicates skillfully. Travels frequently.

Randi, 10: Diligent, hardworking. Independent, critical of self and others. Original and unconventional. Reliable, responsible. Blessed in some ways.

Randie, 6: Duty-bound, self-sacrificing. Pioneer and risk taker. Creative, opinionated. Reliable, responsible. Blessed in some ways. A free spirit, very adaptable.

Randolf, 7: Spiritual, a truth seeker. Not easily influenced. Original and unconventional. Reliable, responsible. Natural counselor and healer. Strong verbal skills. Self-sacrificing, loving.

Randolph, 7: Spiritual, a truth seeker. Not easily influenced. Original and unconventional. Reliable, responsible. Natural counselor and healer. Strong verbal skills. Intelligent, knowledgeable. Great judge of character.

Randy, 8: Uses good judgment. Resolute and purposeful. Creative, original. Reliable, responsible. Needs a lot of freedom.

Ranger, 9: Humanitarian, idealistic. Helpful, sincere. Original and unconventional. Scientific, philosophical. A free spirit, very adaptable. Tendency to lose items.

Rani, 6: Duty-bound, self-sacrificing. Pioneer and risk taker. Creative, opinionated. Artistic, having good taste.

Ranice, 5: Good deed doer. Bright, adventuresome. Romantic, opinionated. Blessed in some ways. Self-expressive, cheerful. A free spirit, very adaptable.

Ranit, 8: Uses good judgment. Resolute and purposeful. Original and unconventional. Blessed in some ways. Dynamic, busy lifestyle.

Ranita, 9: Humanitarian, idealistic. Helpful, sincere. Original and unconventional. Blessed in some ways. Dynamic, busy lifestyle. Bold, courageous, a bit stubborn.

Raoul, 22: Strives to improve humanity. Ambitious leader, great vision. Natural counselor and healer. Attractive and charming. Strong verbal skills.

Raphael, 7: Spiritual, a truth seeker. Not easily influenced. Intelligent, knowledgeable. Great judge of character. Bold, courageous, a bit stubborn. A free spirit, very adaptable. Strong verbal skills.

Raphaela, 8: Uses good judgment. Resolute and purposeful. Intelligent, knowledgeable. Great judge of character. Bold, courageous, a bit stubborn. A free spirit, very adaptable. Strong verbal skills. Pioneer and risk taker.

Raquel, 11: Strives to improve humanity. Intuitive, perceptive. Attracts wealth. Attractive and charming. A free spirit, very adaptable. Strong verbal skills.

Rasha, 20: Sensitive, emotional. Reads people easily. Charming and devoted. Great judge of character. Independent, critical of self and others.

Rashaad, 7: Spiritual, a truth seeker. Not easily influenced. Charming and devoted. Great judge of character. Bold, courageous, a bit stubborn. Pioneer and risk taker. Reliable, responsible.

Rashi, 10: Diligent, hardworking. Independent, critical of self and others. Charming and devoted. Great judge of character. Blessed in some ways.

Rashid, 5:Good deed doer. Bright, adventuresome. Charming and devoted. Great judge of character. Blessed in some ways. Reliable, responsible.

Rashida, 6: Duty-bound, self-sacrificing. Pioneer and risk taker. Charming and devoted. Great judge of character. Blessed in some ways. Reliable, responsible. Bold, courageous, a bit stubborn.

Ravi, 5: Good deed doer. Bright, adventuresome. Intuitive and inspired. Blessed in some ways.

Rawling, 3: Sympathetic, kind. Aims to please. Likes to meet new people. Strong verbal skills. Blessed in some ways. Original and unconventional. Scientific and philosophical.

Ray, 8: Uses good judgment. Resolute and purposeful. Needs a lot of freedom.

Raye, 22: Strives to improve humanity. Ambitious leader, great vision. Needs a lot of freedom. Loves adventure and excitement.

Rayburn, 9: Humanitarian, idealistic. Helpful, sincere. Needs a lot of freedom. Friendly, but shy. Attractive and charming. Can be forgetful. Original and unconventional.

Raymond, 9: Humanitarian, idealistic. Helpful, sincere. Needs a lot of freedom. Systematic, organized. Natural counselor and healer. Original and unconventional. Reliable, responsible.

Rayna, 5: Good deed doer. Bright, adventuresome. Needs a lot of freedom. Romantic, opinionated. Bold, courageous, a bit stubborn.

Rayne, 9: Humanitarian, idealistic. Helpful, sincere. Stylish and refined. Creative and opinionated. Loves adventure and excitement.

Raynor, 10: Diligent, hardworking. Independent, critical of self and others. Needs a lot of freedom. Original and unconventional. Natural counselor and healer. Tendency to lose items.

Read, 10: Diligent, hardworking. Likes change and variety. Independent, critical of self and others. Reliable, responsible.

Reade, 6: Duty-bound, self-sacrificing. A step ahead of others. Pioneer and risk taker. Reliable, responsible. Loves adventure and excitement.

Reagan, 10: Diligent, hardworking. Likes change and variety. Independent, critical of self and others. Scientific and philosophical. Bold, courageous, a bit stubborn. Original and unconventional.

Reah, 5: Good deed doer. Physical and passionate. Resolute and purposeful. Great judge of character.

Reanna, 8: Uses good judgment. Original, creative, and unconventional. Resolute and purposeful. Romantic, sensual. Bold, courageous, a bit stubborn.

Reba, 8: Uses good judgment. Original and creative. Friendly, but shy. Resolute and purposeful.

Rebba, 10: Diligent, hardworking. Likes change and variety. Friendly, but shy. Emotional, sensitive. Independent, critical of self and others.

Rebecca, 10: Diligent, hardworking. Likes change and variety. Friendly, but shy. Likes change and variety. Self-expressive, cheerful. Outgoing, youthful outlook. Independent, critical of self and others.

Rebekah, 5: Good deed doer. Physical and passionate. Friendly, but shy. A free spirit, very adaptable. Strong desire to succeed. Bright, adventuresome. Great judge of character.

Red, 9: Humanitarian, idealistic. Enjoys giving gifts. Reliable, responsible.

Redd, 22: Strives to improve humanity. Has big plans and ideas. Reliable, responsible. Down-to-earth, faithful.

Redford, 7: Spiritual, a truth seeker. Not easily fooled. Reliable, responsible. Self-sacrificing, loving. Natural counselor and healer. May be forgetful.

Redmond, 10: Diligent, hardworking. Likes change and variety. Reliable, responsible. Systematic, organized. Natural counselor and healer. Original and unconventional. Down-to-earth, faithful.

Reece, 9: Humanitarian, idealistic. Enjoys giving gifts. A free spirit, adaptable to change. Self-expressive, cheerful. Loves adventure and excitement.

Reed, 5: Good deed doer. Physical and passionate. A free spirit, adaptable to change. Reliable, responsible.

Reena, 7: Spiritual, a truth seeker. Not easily fooled. Physical and passionate. Original and unconventional. Independent, critical of self and others.

Reeve, 10: Diligent, hardworking. Likes change and variety. Physical and passionate. Intuitive and inspired. Loves adventure and excitement.

Regan, 9: Humanitarian, idealistic. Enjoys giving gifts. Scientific and philosophical. Independent, critical of self and others. Original and unconventional.

Reggie, 6: Duty-bound, self-sacrificing. A step ahead of others. Has willpower and determination. Periodically needs solitude. Blessed in some ways. Loves adventure and excitement.

Regina, 9: Humanitarian, idealistic. Enjoys giving gifts. Scientific and philosophical. Blessed in some ways. Original and unconventional. Independent, critical of self and others.

Reginald, 7: Spiritual, a truth seeker. Not easily fooled. Scientific and philosophical. Blessed in some ways. Original and unconventional. Independent, critical of self and others. Strong verbal skills. Reliable, responsible.

Regis, 4: Strong and healthy. Accesses quickly. Has willpower and determination. Blessed in some ways. Charming and devoted.

Rei, 5: Good deed doer. Physical and passionate. Blessed in some ways.

Reid, 9: Humanitarian, idealistic. Enjoys giving gifts. Artistic, having good taste. Reliable, responsible.

Reiko, 4: Strong and healthy. Accesses quickly. Blessed in some ways. Strong desire to succeed. Natural counselor and healer.

Reina, 11: Strives to improve humanity. Keenly perceptive. Blessed in some ways. Original and unconventional. Independent, critical of self and others.

Remington, 7: Spiritual, a truth seeker. Not easily fooled. Systematic, organized. Blessed in some ways. Original and unconventional. Scientific and philosophical. Dynamic, busy lifestyle. Natural counselor and healer. Romantic, sensual.

Rena, 20: Sensitive, emotional. Social and entertaining. Original and unconventional. Reads people easily.

Renata, 5: Good deed doer. Physical and passionate. Creative and original. Bright, adventuresome. Dynamic, busy lifestyle. Bold, courageous, a bit stubborn.

Renato, 10: Diligent, hardworking. Likes change and variety. Original and unconventional. Independent, critical of self and others. Dynamic, busy lifestyle. Natural counselor and healer.

Rene, 6: Duty-bound, self-sacrificing. A step ahead of others. Creative and opinionated. Loves adventure and excitement.

Renee, 11: Strives to improve humanity. Keenly perceptive. Creative and opinionated. Physical and passionate. Loves adventure and excitement.

Reni, 10: Diligent, hardworking. Likes change and variety. Original and unconventional. Blessed in some ways.

Renita, 4: Strong and healthy. Accesses quickly. Original and unconventional. Blessed in some ways. Dynamic, busy lifestyle. Independent, critical of self and others.

Renne, 11: Strives to improve humanity. Keenly perceptive. Original and unconventional. Romantic, sensual. A free spirit, very adaptable.

Rennie, 11: Strives to improve humanity. Keenly perceptive. Original and unconventional. Romantic, sensual. Blessed in some ways. Physical and passionate.

Reone, 30: Sympathetic, kind. A free spirit, very adaptable. Natural counselor and healer. Creative, opinionated. Physical and passionate.

Reseda, 7: Spiritual, a truth seeker. Not easily fooled. Charming and devoted. A free spirit, very adaptable. Reliable, responsible. Independent, critical of self and others.

Reuben, 11: Strives to improve humanity. Keenly perceptive. Attractive and charming. Friendly, but shy. Physical and passionate. Original and unconventional.

Reva, 10: Diligent, hardworking. Likes change and variety. Intuitive and inspired. Independent, critical of self and others.

Rex, 20: Sensitive, emotional. Social and entertaining. Artistic, sensual, perceptive.

Rexana, 9: Humanitarian, idealistic. Enjoys giving gifts. Artistic, sensual, perceptive. Independent, critical of self and others. Original and unconventional. Bold, courageous, a bit stubborn.

Rexanne, 9: Humanitarian, idealistic. Enjoys giving gifts. Artistic, sensual, perceptive. Independent, critical of self and others. Original and unconventional. Creative, opinionated. A free spirit, adaptable to change.

Rexine, 3: Sympathetic, kind. A free spirit, very adaptable. Artistic, sensual, perceptive. Blessed in some ways. Original and unconventional. Physical and passionate.

Rey, 3: Sympathetic, kind. A free spirit, very adaptable. Dislikes limitations.

Reyla, 7: Spiritual, a truth seeker. Not easily fooled. Needs a lot of freedom. Communicates skillfully.

Reymundo, 7: Spiritual, a truth seeker. Not easily fooled. Needs a lot of freedom. Domestic, hardworking. Attractive and charming. Original and unconventional. Reliable, responsible. Natural counselor and healer.

Reyna, 9: Idealistic, humanitarian. Enjoys giving gifts. Needs a lot of freedom. Original and unconventional. Helpful, sincere

Reynalda, 8: Uses good judgment. Original, creative, and unconventional. Dislikes limitations. Resolute and purposeful. Strong verbal skills. Reliable, responsible. Bold, courageous, a bit stubborn.

Reynard, 4: Strong and healthy. Accesses quickly. Dislikes limitations. Original and unconventional. Resolute and purposeful. Gentle, kind, a hard worker. Natural problem solver.

Rhett, 8: Uses good judgment. Great judge of character. Original and creative. Dynamic, busy lifestyle. Sensitive and easily hurt.

Rhoda, 10: Diligent, hardworking. Self-reliant, successful. Natural counselor and healer. Reliable, responsible. Independent, critical of self and others.

Rhodes, 6: Duty-bound, self-sacrificing. Creative in business. Magnetic personality. Reliable, responsible. A free spirit, very adaptable. Charming and devoted.

Rhodie, 5: Good deed doer. Makes and loses money easily. Natural counselor and healer. Reliable, responsible. Blessed in some ways. A free spirit, very adaptable.

Rhona, 11: Strives to improve humanity. Great judge of character. Creates group harmony. Original and unconventional. Intuitive, perceptive.

Rhonda, 6: Duty-bound, self-sacrificing. Creative in business. Magnetic personality. Original and unconventional. Reliable, responsible. Independent, critical of self and others.

Ricardo, 5: Good deed doer. Generous, thoughtful. Optimistic, outspoken. Bright, adventuresome. Could be forgetful. Reliable, responsible. Natural counselor and healer.

Rich, 11: Strives to improve humanity. Blessed in some ways. Self-expressive, cheerful. Great judge of character.

Richard, 7: Spiritual, a truth seeker. Needs alone time. Self-expressive, cheerful. Great judge of character. Independent, critical of self and others. Could be forgetful. Reliable, responsible.

Richelle, 9: Humanitarian, idealistic. Blessed in some ways. Self-expressive, cheerful. Great judge of character. A free spirit, very adaptable. Strong verbal skills. Frequent traveler. Loves adventure and excitement.

Rick, 5: Good deed doer. Generous, thoughtful. Self-expressive, cheerful. Strong desire to succeed.

Ricky, 30: Sympathetic, kind. Considerate, understanding. Optimistic, outspoken. Strong desire to succeed. Needs a lot of freedom.

Rigo, 4: Strong and healthy. Blessed in some ways. Scientific and philosophical. Natural counselor and healer.

Riki, 11: Strives to improve humanity. Blessed in some ways. Strong desire to succeed. Artistic, having good taste.

Riley, 6: Duty-bound, self-sacrificing,. Artistic, having good taste. Communicates well. Likes change and variety. Needs a lot of freedom.

Rilla, 7: Spiritual, a truth seeker. Needs alone time. Great verbal skills. Frequent traveler. Not easily influenced.

Rina, 6: Duty-bound, self-sacrificing. Artistic, having good taste. Original and unconventional. Pioneer and risk taker.

Rinaldo, 10: Diligent, hardworking. Respectful, kind. Original and unconventional. Independent critical of self and others. Strong verbal skills. Reliable, responsible. Natural counselor and healer.

Riordan, 7: Spiritual, a truth seeker. Needs alone time. Natural counselor and healer. Could be forgetful. Reliable, responsible. Independent, critical of self and others. Original and unconventional.

Ripley, 4: Strong and healthy. Blessed in some ways. Intelligent, knowledgeable. Strong verbal skills. A free spirit, very adaptable. Dislikes limitations.

Risa, 20: Sensitive, emotional. Friendly, considerate. Charming and devoted. Reads people easily.

Rita, 3: Sympathetic, kind. Considerate, understanding. Dynamic, busy lifestyle. Aims to please.

Rito, 8: Uses good judgment. Gives practical gifts. Dynamic, busy lifestyle. Natural counselor and healer.

Riva, 5: Good deed doer. Generous, thoughtful. Intuitive and inspired. Bright, adventuresome.

Roan, 3: Sympathetic, kind. Nurturing, loving. Aims to please. Romantic and creative.

Roana, 22: Strives to improve humanity. Creates group harmony. Independent, self-motivated. Original and unconventional. Bold, courageous, a bit stubborn.

Roanna, 9: Humanitarian, idealistic. Natural counselor and healer. Helpful, sincere. Creative and opinionated. Romantic, sensual. Bold, courageous, a bit stubborn.

Roanne, 4: Strong and healthy. Assumes responsibility. Natural teaching ability. Original and unconventional. Romantic, sensual. A free spirit, very adaptable.

Roark, 9: Humanitarian, idealistic. Artistic, creative. Helpful, sincere. Could be forgetful. Strong desire to succeed.

Roarke, 5: Good deed doer. Enjoys working. Bright, adventuresome. Could be forgetful. Strong desire to succeed. A free spirit, very adaptable.

Rob, 8: Uses good judgment. Competitive in business. Enjoys luxury items.

Robbie, 6: Duty-bound, self-sacrificing. Magnetic personality. Friendly, but shy. Emotional, sensitive. Blessed in some ways. A free spirit, very adaptable.

Robert, 6: Duty-bound, self-sacrificing. Magnetic personality. Friendly, but shy. A free spirit, very adaptable. Could be forgetful. Dynamic, busy lifestyle.

Roberta, 7: Spiritual, a truth seeker. Open to opportunities. Gives moral support. A free spirit, very adaptable. Could be forgetful. Dynamic, busy lifestyle. Not easily influenced.

Robin, 4: Strong and healthy. Assumes responsibility. Friendly, but shy. Blessed in some ways. Original and unconventional.

Robyn, 11: Strives to improve humanity. Creates group harmony. Friendly, but shy. Needs a lot of freedom. Creative and original.

Rocco, 9: Humanitarian, idealistic. Artistic, creative. Self-expressive, cheerful. Outgoing, youthful outlook. Natural counselor and healer.

Rochella, 11: Strives to improve humanity. Creates group harmony. Self-expressive, cheerful. Great judge of character. A free spirit, very adaptable. Great verbal skills. Frequent traveler. Intuitive, perceptive.

Rochelle, 6: Duty-bound, self-sacrificing. Magnetic personality. Optimistic, outspoken. Great judge of character. A free spirit, very adaptable. Strong verbal skills. Frequent traveler. Loves adventure and excitement.

Rochester, 3: Sympathetic, kind. Nurturing, loving. Self-expressive, cheerful. Great judge of character. A free spirit, very adaptable. Charming and devoted. Dynamic, busy lifestyle. Tendency to over-indulge. Could be forgetful.

Rocio, 6: Duty-bound, self-sacrificing. Magnetic personality. Self-expressive, cheerful. Blessed in some ways. Natural counselor and healer.

Rock, 20: Sensitive, emotional. Works well with others. Self-expressive, cheerful. Strong desire to succeed.

Rockley, 8: Uses good judgment. Competitive in business. Self-expressive, cheerful. Strong desire to succeed. Great verbal skills. A free spirit, very adaptable. Dislikes limitations.

Rockwell, 9: Humanitarian, idealistic. Artistic, creative. Optimistic, outspoken. Strong desire to succeed. Likes to meet new people. A free spirit, very adaptable. Great verbal skills. Frequent traveler.

Rod, 10: Diligent, hardworking. Self-sacrificing, devoted. Domestic, practical.

Roderic, 9: Humanitarian, idealistic. Artistic, creative. Reliable, responsible. A free spirit, very adaptable. Could be forgetful. Blessed in some ways. Self-expressive, cheerful.

Roderick, 11: Strives to improve humanity. Creates group harmony. Reliable, responsible. A free spirit, very adaptable. Could be forgetful. Blessed in some ways. Self-expressive, cheerful. Strong desire to succeed.

Rodger, 4: Strong and healthy. Assumes responsibility. Reliable, diligent. Has willpower and determination. A free spirit, very adaptable. Gentle, kind, a hard worker.

Rodney, 9: Humanitarian, idealistic. Artistic, creative. Reliable, responsible. Opinionated, original. Physical and passionate. Needs a lot of freedom.

Rodrick, 6: Duty-bound, self-sacrificing. Magnetic personality. Reliable, responsible. Could be forgetful. Blessed in some ways. Self-expressive, cheerful. Strong desire to succeed.

Rogelio, 9: Humanitarian, idealistic. Artistic, creative. Scientific, philosophical. A free spirit, very adaptable. Strong verbal skills. Blessed in some ways. Natural counselor and healer.

Roger, 9: Humanitarian, idealistic. Artistic, creative. Scientific and philosophical. A free spirit, very adaptable. Could be forgetful.

Rohana, 30: Sympathetic, kind. Nurturing, loving. Great judge of character. Independent, critical of self and others. Original and unconventional. Bold, courageous, a bit stubborn.

Rohelio, 10: Diligent, hardworking. Self-sacrificing, devoted. Great judge of character. A free spirit, very adaptable. Strong verbal skills. Blessed in some ways. May have musical abilities.

Rohit, 7: Spiritual, a truth seeker. Open to opportunities. Great judge of character. Blessed in some ways. Dynamic, busy lifestyle.

Rola, 10: Diligent, hardworking. Self-sacrificing, devoted. Great verbal skills. Independent, critical of self and others.

Roland, 10: Diligent, hardworking. Self-sacrificing, devoted. Great verbal skills. Independent, critical of self and others. Creative and original. Domestic, responsible.

Rolanda, 11: Strives to improve humanity. Creates group harmony. Strong verbal skills. Independent, critical of self and others. Original and unconventional. Reliable, responsible. Bold, courageous, a bit stubborn.

Rolf, 6: Duty-bound, self-sacrificing. Magnetic personality. Strong verbal skills. Has musical abilities.

Rolland, 4: Strong and healthy. Assumes responsibility. Strong verbal skills. Frequent traveler. Independent, critical of self and others. Original and unconventional. Reliable, diligent.

Rollo, 9: Humanitarian, idealistic. Artistic, creative. Strong verbal skills. Frequent traveler. Natural counselor and healer.

Rolls, 22: Strives to improve humanity. Creates group harmony. Strong verbal skills. Frequent traveler. Charming and devoted.

Rolph, 6: Duty-bound, self-sacrificing. Magnetic personality. Strong verbal skills. Intelligent and knowledgeable. Great judge of character.

Roma, 8: Uses good judgment. Competitive in business. Domestic, responsible. Resolute and purposeful.

Romaine, 3: Sympathetic, kind. Nurturing, loving. Systematic, organized. Aims to please. Blessed in some ways. Romantic, creative. A free spirit, very adaptable.

Romala, 3: Sympathetic, kind. Nurturing, loving. Systematic, organized. Aims to please. Communicates skillfully. Bold, courageous, a bit stubborn.

Roman, 7: Spiritual, a truth seeker. Open to opportunities. Systematic, organized. Not easily influenced. Original and unconventional.

Romana, 8: Uses good judgment. Competitive in business. Domestic, responsible. Resolute and purposeful. Original and unconventional. Bold, courageous, a bit stubborn.

Romeo, 30: Sympathetic, kind. Nurturing, loving. Systematic, organized. A free spirit, very adaptable. Natural counselor and healer.

Romulus, 5: Good deed doer. Enjoys working. Creative entrepreneur. Attractive and charming. Strong verbal skills. Very lucky. Intense and extreme.

Ron, 20: Sensitive, emotional. Works well with others. Creative, romantic.

Rona, 3: Sympathetic, kind. Nurturing, loving. Creative, romantic. Independent, critical of self and others.

Ronald, 10: Diligent, hardworking. Self-sacrificing, devoted. Opinionated, romantic. Independent, critical of self and others. Great verbal skills. Reliable, responsible.

Ronalda, 11: Strives to improve humanity. Creates group harmony. Original and unconventional. Intuitive, perceptive. Communicates skillfully. Reliable, responsible. Bold, courageous, a bit stubborn.

Ronan, 8: Uses good judgment. Competitive in business. Creative and original. Resolute and purposeful. Romantic, sensual.

Ronda, 7: Spiritual, a truth seeker. Natural counselor and healer. Original and unconventional. Independent, critical of self and others. Reliable, responsible. Not easily influenced.

Ronit, 4: Strong and healthy. Assumes responsibility. Original and unconventional. Blessed in some ways. Dynamic, busy lifestyle.

Ronnie, 10: Diligent, hardworking. Self-sacrificing, devoted. Original and unconventional. Romantic, sensual. Blessed in some ways. A free spirit, very adaptable.

Ronny, 5: Good deed doer. Enjoys working. Original and unconventional. Romantic, sensual. Needs a lot of freedom.

Ronson, 5: Good deed doer. Enjoys working. Original and unconventional. Charming and devoted. Natural counselor and healer. Romantic, sensual.

Roper, 9: Humanitarian, idealistic. Artistic, creative. Intelligent and knowledgeable. A free spirit, very adaptable. Gentle, kind, a hard worker.

Rorie, 11: Strives to improve humanity. Creates group harmony. Gentle, kind, a hard worker. Blessed in some ways. A free spirit, very adaptable.

Rory, 4: Strong and healthy. Assumes responsibility. Gentle, kind, hardworking. Needs a lot of freedom.

Ros, 7: Spiritual, a truth seeker. Open to opportunities. Stylish and refined.

Rosa, 8: Uses good judgment. Competitive in business. Charming and devoted. Resolute and purposeful.

Rosabel, 9: Humanitarian, idealistic. Artistic, creative. Angelic leanings. Helpful and sincere. Friendly, but shy. A free spirit, very adaptable. Strong verbal skills.

Rosalee, 30: Sympathetic, kind. Nurturing, loving. Gift of gab. Aims to please. Strong verbal skills. A free spirit, very adaptable. Physical and passionate.

Rosaleen, 8: Uses good judgment. Competitive in business. Charming and devoted. Resolute and purposeful. Strong verbal skills. A free spirit, very adaptable. Physical and passionate. Original and unconventional.

Rosales, 8: Uses good judgment. Competitive in business. Charming and devoted. Resolute and purposeful. Strong verbal skills. A free spirit, very adaptable. Intense and extreme.

Rosalie, 7: Spiritual, a truth seeker. Open to opportunities. Stylish and refined. Not easily influenced. Strong verbal skills. Blessed in some ways. A free spirit, very adaptable.

Rosalind, 11: Strives to improve humanity. Creates group harmony. Charming and devoted. Intuitive, perceptive. Strong verbal skills. Blessed in some ways. Original and unconventional. Reliable, responsible.

Rosaline, 3: Sympathetic, kind. Nurturing, loving. Gift of gab. Aims to please. Strong verbal skills. Blessed in some ways. Original and unconventional. A free spirit, very adaptable.

Rosamond, 9: Humanitarian, idealistic. Artistic, creative. Angelic leanings. Helpful, sincere. Systematic, organized. Natural counselor and healer. Original and unconventional. Reliable, responsible.

Rosamund, 6: Duty-bound, self-sacrificing. Magnetic personality. Completely devoted. Pioneer and risk taker. Systematic, organized. Attractive and charming. Creative, original. Reliable, responsible.

Rosana, 5: Good deed doer. Enjoys working. Charming and devoted. Independent, critical of self and others. Original and unconventional. Bold, courageous, a bit stubborn.

Rosanna, 10: Diligent, hardworking. Self-sacrificing. Charming and devoted. Independent, critical of self and others. Original and unconventional. Romantic, sensual. Bold, courageous, a bit stubborn.

Rosario, 5: Good deed doer. Enjoys working. Charming and devoted. Independent, critical of self and others. Gentle, kind, a hard worker. Blessed in some ways. May have musical abilities.

Roscoe, 30: Sympathetic, kind. Nurturing, loving. Gift of gab. Self-expressive, cheerful. May have musical abilities. A free spirit, very adaptable.

Rose, 3: Sympathetic, kind. Nurturing, loving. Gift of gab. A free spirit, very adaptable.

Roseanna, 6: Duty-bound, self-sacrificing. Magnetic personality. Charming and devoted. Physical and passionate. Resolute and purposeful. Creative and opinionated. Original and unconventional. Independent, self-motivated.

Roseanne, 10: Diligent, hardworking. Self-sacrificing. Charming and devoted. A free spirit, very adaptable. Independent, critical of self and others. Original and unconventional. Romantic, sensual. Tendency to overindulge.

Rosel, 6: Duty-bound, self-sacrificing. Magnetic personality. Charming and devoted. A free spirit, very adaptable. Strong verbal skills.

Roselani, 3: Sympathetic, kind. Nurturing, loving. Gift of gab. A free spirit, very adaptable. Strong verbal skills. Aims to please. Original and unconventional. Blessed in some ways.

Rosemarie, 4: Strong and healthy. Assumes responsibilities. Quickly sizes up situations. A free spirit, very adaptable. Systematic, organized. Pioneer and risk taker. May be forgetful. Blessed in some ways. Loves adventure and excitement.

Rosemary, 6: Duty-bound, self-sacrificing. Magnetic personality. Charming and devoted. A free spirit, very adaptable. Systematic, organized. Pioneer and risk taker. May be forgetful. Dislikes limitations.

Rosie, 30: Sympathetic, kind. Nurturing, loving. Gift of gab. Blessed in some ways. A free spirit, very adaptable.

Rosita, 10: Diligent, hardworking. Self-sacrificing, duty-bound. Charming and devoted. Blessed in some ways. Dynamic, busy lifestyle. Independent, critical of self and others.

Roslin, 6: Duty-bound, self-sacrificing. Magnetic personality. Charming and devoted. Strong verbal skills. Blessed in some ways. Original and unconventional.

Roslyn, 4: Strong and healthy. Assumes responsibilities. Quickly sizes up situations. Strong verbal skills. Needs a lot of freedom. Original and unconventional.

Ross, 8: Uses good judgment. Competitive in business. Charming and devoted. Impulsive and extreme.

Rowen, 30: Sympathetic, kind. Nurturing, loving. Likes to meet new people. Physical, passionate. Original, opinionated.

Rowena, 4: Strong and healthy. Assumes responsibilities. Likes to meet new people. A free spirit, very adaptable. Original and unconventional. Natural teaching abilities.

Rox, 3: Sympathetic, kind. Nurturing, loving. Artistic, sensual, perceptive.

Roxane, 5: Good deed doer. Enjoys working. Artistic, sensual, perceptive. Bright, adventuresome. Original and unconventional. A free spirit, very adaptable.

Roxanna, 6: Duty-bound, self-sacrificing. Magnetic personality. Artistic, sensual, perceptive. Pioneer and risk taker. Original and unconventional. Creative, opinionated. Bold, courageous, a bit stubborn.

Roxanne, 10: Diligent, hardworking. Self-sacrificing, devoted. Artistic, sensual, perceptive. Independent, critical of self and others. Original and unconventional. Creative, opinionated. A free spirit, very adaptable.

Roxette, 8: Uses good judgment. Competitive in business. Artistic, sensual, perceptive. A free spirit, very adaptable. Dynamic, busy lifestyle. Sensitive and easily hurt. Tendency to overindulge.

Roxie, 8: Uses good judgment. Competitive in business. Artistic, sensual, perceptive. Blessed in some ways. A free spirit, very adaptable.

Roxy, 10: Diligent, hardworking. Self-sacrificing, devoted. Artistic, sensual, perceptive. Needs a lot of freedom.

Roy, 22: Strives to improve humanity. Creates group harmony. Needs a lot of freedom.

Royce, 30: Sympathetic, kind. Nurturing, loving. Needs a lot of freedom. Self-expressive, cheerful. Loves adventure and excitement.

Roz, 5: Good deed doer. Enjoys working. Uses common sense.

Rozalie, 5: Good deed doer. Enjoys working. Uses common sense. Bright, adventuresome. Strong verbal skills. Blessed in some ways. A free spirit, very adaptable.

Rozalinda, 10: Diligent, hardworking. Self-sacrificing, devoted. Uses common sense. Independent, critical of self and others. Strong verbal skills. Blessed in some ways. Original and unconventional. Reliable, responsible. Bold, courageous, a bit stubborn.

Rozeanne, 8: Uses good judgment. Competitive in business. A great mediator. A free spirit, very adaptable. Resolute and purposeful. Original and unconventional. Romantic, sensual. Loves adventure and excitement.

Rube, 10: Diligent, hardworking. Optimistic and outgoing. Anticipates next move. A free spirit, very adaptable.

Ruben, 6: Duty-bound, self-sacrificing. Idealistic in relationships. Friendly, but shy. A free spirit, very adaptable. Original and unconventional.

Rubentina, 5: Good deed doer. Fun, flirtatious. Friendly, but shy. Physical and passionate. Original and unconventional. Dynamic, busy lifestyle. Blessed in some ways. Romantic, sensual. Bright, adventuresome.

Rubin, 10: Diligent, hardworking. Optimistic and outgoing. Anticipates next move. Blessed in some ways. Creative and opinionated.

Ruby, 3: Sympathetic, kind. Youthful and appealing. Loyal and understanding. Needs a lot of freedom.

Rudolf, 4: Strong and healthy. Gracious, well-mannered. Domestic, hardworking. Natural counselor and healer. Communicates skillfully. Self-sacrificing, loving.

Rudolph, 4: Strong and healthy.. Gracious, well-mannered. Domestic, hardworking. Natural counselor and healer. Communicates skillfully. Intelligent and knowledgeable. Great judge of character.

Rudy, 5: Good deed doer. Fun, flirtatious. Reliable, responsible. Needs a lot of freedom.

Ruel, 20: Sensitive, emotional. Attractive and charming. A free spirit, very adaptable. Strong verbal skills.

Rufina, 6: Duty-bound, self-sacrificing. Idealistic in relationships. Magnetic, charming. Blessed in some ways. Original and unconventional. Independent, critical of self and others.

Rufus, 22: Strives to improve humanity. Creative and inspiring. Self-sacrificing, loving. Attractive and charming. Intense and extreme.

Rumaldo, 30: Sympathetic, kind. Difficulty making decisions. Domestic, hardworking. Pioneer and risk taker. Strong verbal skills. Down-to-earth, faithful. Natural counselor and healer.

Rumer, 30: Sympathetic, kind. Difficulty making decisions. Domestic, hardworking. A free spirit, adaptable to change. Tendency to lose items.

Rumford, 5: Good deed doer. Fun, flirtatious. Systematic, organized. Self-sacrificing, loving. Natural counselor and healer. Tendency to lose items. Reliable, responsible.

Rupert, 8: Uses good judgment. Attractive and charming. Intelligent, knowledgeable. A free spirit, very adaptable. Tendency to lose items. Dynamic, busy lifestyle.

Rush, 3: Sympathetic, kind. Difficulty making decisions. Charming and devoted. Great judge of character.

Russ, 5: Good deed doer. Fun, flirtatious. Charming and devoted. Intense and extreme.

Russell, 7: Spiritual, a truth seeker. Stylish and refined. Charming and devoted. Intense and extreme. A free spirit, very adaptable. Strong verbal skills. Ups and downs financially.

Rust, 6: Duty-bound, self-sacrificing. Idealistic in relationships. Charming and devoted. Dynamic, busy lifestyle.

Rusty, 22: Strives to improve humanity. Creative and inspiring. Charming and devoted. Dynamic, busy lifestyle. Needs a lot of freedom.

Ruta, 6: Duty-bound, self-sacrificing. Idealistic in relationships. Dynamic, busy lifestyle. Independent, critical of self and others.

Ruth, 22: Strives to improve humanity. Creative and inspiring. Dynamic, busy lifestyle. Great judge of character.

Rutherford, 7: Spiritual, a truth seeker. Stylish and refined. Dynamic, busy lifestyle. Great judge of character. A free spirit, adaptable. Could be forgetful. High moral standards. Natural counselor and healer. Needs to practice tolerance. Reliable, responsible.

Rutley, 11: Strives to improve humanity. Attractive and charming. Dynamic, busy lifestyle. Strong verbal skills. A free spirit, very adaptable. Dislikes limitations.

Ry, 7: Spiritual, a truth seeker. Needs a lot of freedom. Influential.

Ryan, 22: Strives to improve humanity. Needs a lot of freedom. Independent, self-motivated. Original and creative.

Ryana, 5: Good deed doer. Needs a lot of freedom. Bright, adventuresome. Original and creative. Bold, courageous, a bit stubborn.

Ryann, 9: Humanitarian, idealistic. Needs a lot of freedom. Helpful, sincere. Original and opinionated. Romantic, sensual.

Ryanna, 10: Diligent, hardworking. Needs a lot of freedom. Independent, critical of self and others. Original and unconventional. Romantic, sensual. Bold, courageous, a bit stubborn.

Ryder, 7: Spiritual, a truth seeker. Needs a lot of freedom. Reliable, responsible. Loves adventure and excitement. Gentle, kind, a hard worker.

$\mathcal{S}$

If a name begins with S, has more than one S, or ends with an S, this person is charming, loving, and devoted; however, they can be impulsive, extreme, and exhibit mood swings.

The letter S is the 19th letter of the alphabet. Since $1 + 9 = 10$ and $1 + 0 = 1$, so the 19th letter has the same vibrational influence as the number 1. The person whose name begins with S is often beginning a new stage of learning as well as completing a stage of learning in this lifetime. The 1 and 9 combination is very dynamic and charismatic. The energy of the 1 makes the S-named person ambitious, competitive, energetic, confident, and self-reliant. Similar to the letters A and J, they are perfectionists and their own worst critic. However, the 1-ruled S is more highly evolved than its siblings A and J. Combining 1 with the 9 vibration gives them angelic "higher love" qualities. They are more broadminded and less prejudiced than most of the other letters. This rare combination can cause others to be jealous of them. They are capable of achievement and somehow blessed more than the rest of us. It just doesn't seem fair that the S person has so much going for them, and they are often good-looking too!

S people are often attractive. S is shaped like a snake, which in Chinese astrology is symbolically defined as charming and seductive. S people are very much like that snake symbol. But there is one flaw in their personality. With the 9 influence, the S person can have a balance problem. They need to take the time to carefully make the right choices. If they had a difficult childhood, it could be the reason they act in extreme ways. Remember the 9 won't be happy unless they can forgive others for past wrongdoings. The inability to let go of the past creates many emotional ups and downs for this charming letter.

Simon Cowell, of *American Idol,* a popular television show, not only gets away with being critical, but actually is in demand because of it. S is ruled by the critical and independent number 1 vibration. It's natural and easy for him to criticize, which the public sees in his role as a judge on *American Idol*. It's not so much his talent to criticize that he's famous for, but his meanness. His nicknames are "Mr. Nasty" and "Judge Dread." Simon's name adds up to a power number 7, which can have a mean streak. Of all the numbers, 7 is capable of being the meanest. Those with power number 7 are truth seekers, which is the quality that most people admire about Simon. Simon's not afraid to say what he feels to be truthful. The M in the center of his name means systematic and organized. He goes in and assesses a situation in a clinical, almost terminator-like fashion. His heart's desire letter, or first vowel, is an I. This influence helps him to get away with murder, if you will. People think he has all the answers and will follow him whether he's right or wrong. The I first vowel also helps him to appreciate art. The O in his name makes him want to be his own boss. Although he can be mean, Simon can also be nurturing and healing. An O anywhere in a name will give the bearer a real need to give love to children, pets, a garden, or to manage a group of people. There is a bit of nurturing and loving "parent" in Simon Cowell.

Hollywood's best-known director, Steven Spielberg, fits his name well. Steven adds up to a 22 power number. The number 22 is a master number, the number for global enterprises. Those with this power number seem to have no limits. This well-known producer, director, and writer has directed films *Saving Private Ryan*, *Schindler's List*, *Jurassic Park*, *Indiana Jones*, *E.T.*, and countless others. He is one of the wealthiest filmmakers in the world. His S shows he is charming and devoted. The T is ruled by the number 2, which is social and partnership-oriented. The T is also dynamic and quite busy all the time. When we add these two letters together they sum up to a hidden 3. Number 3 is the writer and communicator. His hidden talent is the ability to communicate. Adding the 3 to his 5-ruled E reveals a hidden 8. Steven is materialistically motivated. Also 3, 5, and 8 are the luckiest numbers to have for winning the lottery. He seems to ride the financial waves quite well, although he's no doubt had his pitfalls. Steven Spielberg has an intensity 5 in his name; half of the letters in his name are ruled by the number 5. So taking chances are a part of his makeup. He loves adventure and excitement. The number 5 rules change, so he's naturally prepared to make changes and is adaptable and adjustable to life's many ups and downs. Interestingly enough, V is the 22nd letter of the alphabet, giving validation to Steven's global mission in life. Not all Steven's are going to be this talented; however, the potential for greatness exists. This Steven has served his name well.

Sheryl Crow has a nice blend of letters in her first name. None of the numbers repeat themselves; in other words, she has no intensity numbers in her name. This means she doesn't have to repeat her lessons. Furthermore, Sheryl adds up to a 6 power number. Often those with a 6 anywhere in their name are musical as well as magnetic. She ends up getting the message across with an L at the end of her name. Communication is important and often her songs express her rather upbeat way of getting her point across. The S and H are sexually dynamic, as well as her E first vowel. With all this at the beginning of her name, she leaves quite a lasting first impression.

Sean Connery and Sean "P. Diddy" Combs share the same first name and celebrity status. Again we have a sexually attractive E first vowel. Both of these men are charming and devoted with an S in the beginning of their name. The name Sean adds up to a 3 power number. The number 3 is also the number for "temporary." The 3 coupled with an intensity 5, which rules change, explains why Sean Puff Daddy, P. Diddy, Diddy Combs keeps changing his name! Both men have a youthful outlook on life, no matter what their age. They each share the first two letters adding up to a hidden 6. This causes them to want to be their own boss, even if it isn't obvious. They are magnetic and have nurturing abilities. Both are natural counselors and healers. Add to the hidden 6 the I-ruled A and we have a hidden 7. The 7 likes the camera and could explain their ability to look so good on film. They are truth-seekers and value their privacy, although many may not see these qualities, as they are ruled by a hidden number. What better man to have played the sexy James Bond than Sean Connery with an intensity 5 in his first name. The intensity 5 is physical, passionate, and loves adventure and excitement. Interesting that the name James also adds up to a 3 power number. He was perfect for the role, if only "temporary."

Some other famous S names are: Sammy Davis Jr., Sylvester Stallone, Sarah Ferguson, Suze Orman, Salma Hayek, Sarah Jessica Parker, Sean Penn, Sandra Bullock, Sandra Dee, Steven Seagal, Shania Twain, Serena Williams, Samuel L. Jackson, Sting, Sandra Day O'Connor, Sidney Sheldon, Susan B. Anthony, Sally Field, Snoop Dog, Sidney Poitier, Sigmund Freud, Sela Ward, Scarlett Johansson, Samuel Goldwyn, Spiro Agnew, Sonny Bono, Sophia Loren, Shirley Temple, Spencer Tracy, Scott Carpenter, Steven Tyler, Spike Lee, Shirley Jones, Selma Blair, Shirley MacLaine, Stevie Nicks, and Shia LeBeouf.

QUICK REFERENCE OF "S" NAMES

Saba, 5: Extremely charming. Bright, adventuresome. Friendly, but shy. Bold, courageous, a bit stubborn.

Sabina, 10: Needs to be independent. Critical of self and others. Anticipates next move. Blessed in some ways. Original and unconventional. Bold, courageous, a bit stubborn.

Sabine, 5: Extremely charming. Bright, adventuresome. Friendly, but shy. Blessed in some ways. Original and unconventional. A free spirit, very adaptable.

Sabra, 5: Extremely charming. Bright, adventuresome. Friendly, but shy. Gentle, kind, a hard worker. Bold, courageous, a bit stubborn.

Sabrina, 10: Needs to be independent. Critical of self and others. Anticipates next move. Gentle, kind, a hard worker. Blessed in some ways. Original and unconventional. Bold, courageous, a bit stubborn.

Sacha, 5: Extremely charming. Bright, adventuresome. Self-expressive, cheerful. Great judge of character. Bold, courageous, a bit stubborn.

Sadelle, 22: A charismatic person. Ambitious leader, great vision. Reliable, responsible. A free spirit, very adaptable. Great verbal skills. Travels frequently. Physical and passionate.

Sadie, 20: Charming and devoted. Reads people easily. Reliable, responsible. Blessed in some ways. A free spirit, very adaptable.

Sadira, 7: An opportunist. Not easily influenced. Domestic, responsible. Blessed in some ways. Gentle, kind, a hard worker. Bold, courageous, a bit stubborn.

Sadye, 9: Angelic leanings. Helpful, sincere. Reliable, responsible. Needs a lot of freedom. Loves adventure and excitement.

Saeb, 9: Angelic leanings. Helpful, sincere. A free spirit, very adaptable. Friendly, but shy.

Sage, 5: Extremely charming. Bright, adventuresome. Scientific and philosophical. A free spirit, very adaptable.

Sahara, 3: Gift of gab. Aims to please. Great judge of character. Bold, courageous, a bit stubborn. Gentle, kind, a hard worker. Pioneer and risk taker.

Saira, 3: Gift of gab. Aims to please. Blessed in some ways. Gentle, kind, a hard worker. Bold, courageous, a bit stubborn.

Saki, 4: Quickly sizes up situations. Natural teaching ability. Strong desire to succeed. Blessed in some ways.

Sal, 5: Extremely charming. Bright, adventuresome. Communicates skillfully.

Salena, 7: An opportunist. Not easily influenced. Strong verbal skills. A free spirit, very adaptable. Creative and opinionated. Bold, courageous, a bit stubborn.

Sallie, 22: A charismatic person. Ambitious leader, great vision. Strong verbal skills. Frequent traveler. Blessed in some ways. A free spirit, very adaptable.

Sally, 6: Completely devoted. Pioneer and risk taker. Strong verbal skills. Frequent traveler. Needs a lot of freedom.

Salma, 10: Needs to be independent. Critical of self and others. Strong verbal skills. Domestic, hardworking. Great leadership abilities.

Salome, 20: Charming and devoted. Reads people easily. Strong verbal skills. Natural counselor and healer. Domestic and hardworking. A free spirit, very adaptable.

Salvador, 11: A charismatic person. Strong verbal skills. Intuitive and inspired. Bold, courageous, a bit stubborn. Reliable, responsible. Natural counselor and healer. Gentle, kind, a hard worker.

Salvatore, 5: Extremely charming. Bright, adventuresome. Strong verbal skills. Intuitive and inspired. Bold, courageous, a bit stubborn. Reliable, responsible. Natural counselor and healer. Gentle, kind, a hard worker. A free spirit, very adaptable.

Sam, 6: Completely devoted. Pioneer and risk taker. Systematic, organized.

Samantha, 5: Extremely charming. Bright, adventuresome. Domestic, hardworking. Bold, courageous, a bit stubborn. Original and unconventional. Dynamic, busy lifestyle. Great judge of character. Pioneer and risk taker.

Samara, 8: Passionate and loving. Resolute and purposeful. Domestic, hardworking. Bold, courageous, a bit stubborn. Gentle, kind. Pioneer and risk taker.

Sami, 6: Completely devoted. Pioneer and risk taker. Systematic, organized. Blessed in some ways.

Samina, 3: Gift of gab. Aims to please. Domestic, hardworking. Blessed in some ways. Original and unconventional. Bold, courageous, a bit stubborn.

Samira, 7: An opportunist. Not easily influenced. Domestic, hardworking. Blessed in some ways. Gentle, kind. Bold, courageous, a bit stubborn.

Sammie, 6: Completely devoted. Pioneer and risk taker. Systematic, organized. Desires financial security. Blessed in some ways. A free spirit, very adaptable.

Sammy, 8: Passionate and loving. Resolute and purposeful. Domestic, hardworking. Desires financial security. Needs a lot of freedom.

Sampson, 7: An opportunist. Not easily influenced. Domestic, hardworking. Intelligent and knowledgeable. Charming and devoted. Natural counselor and healer. Original and unconventional.

Samson, 6: Completely devoted. Pioneer and risk taker. Systematic, organized. Impulsive and extreme. Natural counselor and healer. Original and unconventional.

Samuel, 8: Passionate and loving. Resolute and purposeful. Domestic, hardworking. Very lucky. A free spirit, very adaptable. Strong verbal skills.

Sancho, 6: Completely devoted. Pioneer and risk taker. Romantic, creative. Self-expressive, cheerful. Great judge of character. Natural counselor and healer.

Sandi, 20: Charming and devoted. Reads people easily. Original and unconventional. Reliable, responsible. Blessed in some ways.

Sandie, 7: An opportunist. Not easily influenced. Original and unconventional. Reliable, responsible. Blessed in some ways. A free spirit, very adaptable.

Sandra, 3: Gift of gab. Aims to please. Romantic, creative. Reliable, responsible. Gentle, kind, a hard worker. Bold, courageous, a bit stubborn.

Sandy, 9: Angelic leanings. Helpful, sincere. Original and unconventional. Reliable, responsible. Needs a lot of freedom.

Sanford, 5: Extremely charming. Bright, adventuresome. Original, opinionated. Self-sacrificing, loving. Natural counselor and healer. Gentle, kind, a hard worker. Reliable, responsible.

Santiago, 5: Extremely charming. Bright, adventuresome. Original and unconventional. Dynamic, busy lifestyle. Blessed in some ways. Bold, courageous, a bit stubborn. Scientific and philosophical. Natural counselor and healer.

Sapphire, 11: A charismatic person. Intuitive, perceptive. Intelligent and knowledgeable. Overly secretive, distant. Great judge of character. Blessed in some ways. Gentle, kind, a hard worker. A free spirit, very adaptable.

Sara, 3: Gift of gab. Aims to please. Gentle, kind, a hard worker. Independent, critical of self and others.

Sarah, 20: Charming and devoted. Reads people easily. Sensitive, emotional. Bold, courageous, a bit stubborn. Great judge of character.

Sargent, 30: Gift of gab. Aims to please. Gentle, kind, a hard worker. Stylish and refined. Physical and passionate. Original, opinionated. Dynamic, busy lifestyle.

Sari, 20: Charming and devoted. Reads people easily. Gentle, kind, a hard worker. Blessed in some ways.

Sarila, 6: Completely devoted. Pioneer and risk taker. Duty-bound, self-sacrificing. Blessed in some ways. Strong verbal skills. Bold, courageous, a bit stubborn.

Sarita, 5: Extremely charming. Bright, adventuresome. Good deed doer. Blessed in some ways. Dynamic, busy lifestyle. Bold, courageous, a bit stubborn.

Sasha, 3: Gift of gab. Aims to please. Impulsive and extreme. Great judge of character. Bold, courageous, a bit stubborn.

Saul, 8: Passionate and loving. Resolute and purposeful. Attractive and charming. Strong verbal skills.

Savanah, 3: Gift of gab. Aims to please. Intuitive and inspired. Bold, courageous, a bit stubborn. Original and unconventional. Pioneer and risk taker. Great judge of character.

Savannah, 8: Passionate and loving. Resolute and purposeful. Intuitive and inspired. Bold, courageous, a bit stubborn. Original and unconventional. Romantic, sensual. Pioneer and risk taker. Great judge of character.

Saverio, 8: Passionate and loving. Resolute and purposeful. Intuitive and inspired. A free spirit, very adaptable. Gentle, kind, a hard worker. Blessed in some ways. Natural counselor and healer.

Scarlet, 6: Completely devoted. Optimistic, outspoken. Pioneer and risk taker. Gentle, kind, a hard worker. Strong verbal skills. A free spirit, very adaptable. Dynamic, busy lifestyle.

Scarlett, 8: Passionate and loving. Optimistic, outspoken. Resolute and purposeful. Intense inner power. Communicates skillfully. A free spirit, very adaptable. Dynamic, busy lifestyle. Sensitive and easily hurt.

Schuyler, 3: Gift of gab. Cheerful, lighthearted. Great judge of character. Attractive and charming. Needs a lot of freedom. Strong verbal skills. A free spirit, very adaptable. Gentle, kind, a hard worker.

Scot, 3: Gift of gab. Cheerful, lighthearted. Natural counselor and healer. Dynamic, busy lifestyle.

Scott, 5: Extremely charming. Optimistic, outspoken. Natural counselor and healer. Dynamic, busy lifestyle. Sensitive and easily hurt.

Scottie, 8: Passionate and loving. Optimistic, outspoken. Natural counselor and healer. Dynamic, busy lifestyle. Sensitive and easily hurt. Blessed in some ways. A free spirit, very adaptable.

Scotty, 3: Gift of gab. Cheerful, lighthearted. Natural counselor and healer. Dynamic, busy lifestyle. Sensitive and easily hurt. Needs a lot of freedom.

Scout, 6: Completely devoted. Optimistic, outspoken. Natural counselor and healer. Attractive, charming. Dynamic, busy lifestyle.

Seamus, 6: Completely devoted. A step ahead of others. Independent, critical of self and others. Domestic, hardworking. Attractive and charming. Loving and passionate.

Sean, 3: Gift of gab. A free spirit, very adaptable. Aims to please. Romantic and creative.

Sebastian, 9: Angelic leanings. A true humanitarian. Friendly, but shy. Independent, critical of self and others. Impulsive and extreme. Dynamic, busy lifestyle. Artistic, having good taste. Bold, courageous, a bit stubborn. Original and unconventional.

Sedgewick, 5: Extremely charming. Physical and passionate. Reliable, responsible. Scientific and philosophical. A free spirit, adaptable to change. Likes to meet new people. Blessed in some ways. Optimistic, outspoken. Strong desire to succeed.

Sedgwick, 9: Angelic leanings. A true humanitarian. Reliable, responsible. Scientific and philosophical. Likes to meet new people. Blessed in some ways. Self-expressive, cheerful. Strong desire to succeed.

Seki, 8: Passionate and loving. Original and creative. Strong desire to succeed. Blessed in some ways.

Sela, 10: Needs to be independent. Likes change and variety. Great verbal skills. Critical of self and others.

Selby, 9: Angelic leanings. A true humanitarian. Strong verbal skills. Friendly, but shy. Dislikes limitations.

Seldon, 6: Completely devoted. A step ahead of others. Communicates well. Creative problem solver. Natural counselor and healer. Original and opinionated.

Selena, 20: Charming and devoted. Social and entertaining. Strong verbal skills. Physical and passionate. Original and unconventional. Reads people easily.

Selma, 5: Extremely charming. Physical and passionate. Strong verbal skills. Domestic, hardworking. Bright, adventuresome.

Serena, 8: Passionate and loving. Original and creative. Gentle, kind, a hard worker. A free spirit, very adaptable. Opinionated and unconventional. Resolute and purposeful.

Serge, 9: Angelic leanings. A true humanitarian. Gentle, kind, a hard worker. Scientific and philosophical. Physical and passionate.

Setareh, 4: Quickly sizes up situations. Enjoys working. Dynamic, busy lifestyle. Independent, critical of self and others. Gentle, kind, diligent. A free spirit, very adaptable. Great judge of character.

Seth, 7: An opportunist. Not easily fooled. Dynamic, busy lifestyle. Great judge of character.

Seton, 10: Needs to be independent. Likes change and variety. Dynamic, busy lifestyle. Natural counselor and healer. Original and unconventional.

Sevag, 9: Angelic leanings. A true humanitarian. Intuitive and inspired. Helpful, sincere. Scientific and philosophical.

Seymour, 8: Passionate and loving. Original and creative. Dislikes limitations. Domestic, hardworking. Natural counselor and healer. Attractive and charming. Intense inner power.

Shaina, 7: An opportunist. Perceptive, psychic. Not easily influenced. Blessed in some ways. Original and unconventional. Bold, courageous, a bit stubborn.

Shana, 7: An opportunist. Perceptive, psychic. Not easily influenced. Original and unconventional. Bold, courageous, a bit stubborn.

Shane, 20: Charming and devoted. Excellent mediator. Reads people easily. Romantic, sensual. A free spirit, very adaptable.

Shania, 7: (Same as Shaina.)

Shannon, 4: Quickly sizes up situations. Great judge of character. Natural teaching ability. Original and unconventional. Romantic, sensual. Natural counselor and healer. Creative, opinionated.

Sharai, 11: A charismatic person. Self-reliant, successful. Intuitive, perceptive. Gentle, kind, a hard worker. Bold, courageous, a bit stubborn. Blessed in some ways.

Shareen, 7: An opportunist. Perceptive, psychic. Not easily influenced. Gentle, kind, a hard worker. A free spirit, very adaptable. Physical and passionate. Creative and opinionated.

Shari, 10: Needs to be independent. Great judge of character. Critical of self and others. Gentle, kind, a hard worker. Blessed in some ways.

Sharletta, 5: Extremely charming. Very passionate. Bright, adventuresome. Gentle, kind, a hard worker. Strong verbal skills. A free spirit, very adaptable. Dynamic, busy lifestyle. Sensitive and easily hurt. Bold, courageous, a bit stubborn.

Sharon, 30: Gift of gab. Makes and loses money easily. Aims to please. Gentle, kind, a hard worker. Natural counselor and healer. Original and unconventional.

Sharyn, 4: Quickly sizes up situations. Great judge of character. Natural teaching ability. Gentle, kind, a hard worker. Needs a lot of freedom. Original and unconventional.

Shaun, 9: Angelic leanings. Enjoys helping others. Hardworking, sincere. Attractive and charming. Creative and original.

Shauna, 10: Needs to be independent. Great judge of character. Critical of self and others. Very lucky. Original and unconventional. Bold, courageous, a bit stubborn.

Shaunti, 11: A charismatic person. Self-reliant, successful. Independent, critical of self and others. Very lucky. Original and unconventional. Dynamic, busy lifestyle. Blessed in some ways.

Shawn, 20: Charming and devoted. Excellent mediator. Reads people easily. Works well with others. Romantic, opinionated.

Shawna, 3: Gift of gab. Makes and loses money easily. Aims to please. Likes to meet new people. Original and unconventional. Bold, courageous, a bit stubborn.

Shawnee, 30: Gift of gab. Makes and loses money easily. Aims to please. Likes to meet new people. Original and unconventional. A free spirit, very adaptable. Tendency to overindulge.

Shawni, 11: A charismatic person. Self-reliant, successful. Intuitive, perceptive. Involved in major activities. Original and unconventional. Blessed in some ways.

Shawnti, 4: Quickly sizes up situations. Great judge of character. Natural teaching ability. Likes to meet new people. Original and unconventional. Dynamic, busy lifestyle. Blessed in some ways.

Shayna, 5: Extremely charming. Very passionate. Bright, adventuresome. Needs a lot of freedom. Original and unconventional. Bold, courageous, a bit stubborn.

Shea, 6: Completely devoted. Creative in business. Physical and passionate. Pioneer and risk taker.

Sheba, 8: Passionate and loving. Great judge of character. Original and creative. Friendly, but shy. Independent, critical of self and others.

Sheena, 7: An opportunist. Perceptive, psychic. Not easily fooled. Physical and passionate. Original and unconventional. Independent, critical of self and others.

Sheila, 9: Angelic leanings. Enjoys helping others. A free spirit, very adaptable. Blessed in some ways. Great verbal skills. Independent, critical of self and others.

Sheilah, 8: Passionate and loving. Great judge of character. Original and creative. Blessed in some ways. Strong verbal skills. Resolute and purposeful. Self-reliant, successful.

Shelby, 8: Passionate and loving. Great judge of character. Original and creative. Strong verbal skills. Friendly, but shy. Dislikes limitations.

Sheldon, 5: Extremely charming. Very passionate. A free spirit, very adaptable. Communicates skillfully. Reliable, responsible. Natural counselor and healer. Original and unconventional.

Shelley, 5: Extremely charming. Very passionate. A free spirit, very adaptable. Communicates skillfully. Many ups and downs financially. Tendency to overindulge. Dislikes limitations.

Shelly, 9: Angelic leanings. Enjoys helping others. A free spirit, very adaptable. Frequent traveler. Ups and downs financially. Dislikes limitations.

Shelton, 30: Gift of gab. Makes and loses money easily. A free spirit, very adaptable. Frequent traveler. Dynamic, busy lifestyle. Natural counselor and healer. Original and unconventional.

Sheri, 5: Extremely charming. Very passionate. A free spirit, very adaptable. Gentle, kind, a hard worker. Blessed in some ways.

Sherif, 11: A charismatic person. Great judge of character. A free spirit, very adaptable. Gentle, kind, a hard worker. Blessed in some ways. Self-sacrificing, loving.

Sherlock, 10: Needs to be independent. Great judge of character. Likes change and variety. Gentle, kind, a hard worker. Frequent traveler. Natural counselor and healer. Self-expressive, cheerful. Strong desire to succeed.

Sherman, 6: Completely devoted. Great judge of character. A step ahead of others. Gentle, kind, a hard worker. Systematic, organized. Independent, critical of self and others. Original and unconventional.

Sherri, 5: Extremely charming. Very passionate. A free spirit, very adaptable. Gentle, kind, a hard worker. Sometimes forgetful. Blessed in some ways.

Sherrill, 11: A charismatic person. Great judge of character. A free spirit, very adaptable. Gentle, kind, a hard worker. Sometimes forgetful. Blessed in some ways. Strong verbal skills. Travels frequently.

Sherry, 3: Gift of gab. Makes and loses money easily. A free spirit, very adaptable. Gentle, kind, a hard worker. Tendency to lose items. Dislikes limitations.

Sherwin, 6: Completely devoted. Creative in business. Physical and passionate. Gentle, kind, a hard worker. Likes to meet new people. Blessed in some ways. Original and opinionated.

Sheryl, 6: Completely devoted. Creative in business. A free spirit, very adaptable. Gentle, kind, a hard worker. Dislikes limitations. Strong verbal skills.

Shia, 10: Needs to be independent. Great judge of character. Blessed in some ways. Ambitious, critical of self and others.

Shifra, 7: An opportunist. Perceptive, psychic. Blessed in some ways. Devoted, loving. Gentle, kind, a hard worker. Not easily influenced.

Shilo, 9: Angelic leanings. Enjoys helping others. Blessed in some ways. Strong verbal skills. Natural counselor and healer.

Shiloh, 8: Passionate and loving. Great judge of character. Blessed in some ways. Strong verbal skills. Natural counselor and healer. Self-reliant, successful.

Shipley, 4: Quickly sizes up situations. Great judge of character. Blessed in some ways. Intelligent and knowledgeable. Strong verbal skills. A free spirit, very adaptable. Dislikes limitations.

Shipuh, 9: Angelic leanings. Enjoys helping others. Blessed in some ways. Intelligent and knowledgeable. Attractive and charming. Self-reliant, successful.

Shirlee, 4: Quickly sizes up situations. Great judge of character. Blessed in some ways. Gentle, kind, a hard worker. Strong verbal skills. A free spirit, very adaptable. Likes change and variety.

Shirleen, 9: Angelic leanings. Enjoys helping others. Blessed in some ways. Gentle, kind, a hard worker. Strong verbal skills. A free spirit, very adaptable. Physical and passionate. Original and unconventional.

Shirlene, 9: (Same as Shirleen.)

Shirley, 6: Completely devoted. Creative in business. Artistic, having good taste. Gentle, kind, a hard worker. Strong verbal skills. A free spirit, very adaptable. Dislikes limitations.

Shizu, 11: A charismatic person. Self-reliant, successful. Blessed in some ways. A good mediator. Attractive and charming.

Sibil, 6: Completely devoted. Artistic, having good taste. Friendly, but shy. Blessed in some ways. Strong verbal skills.

Sibyl, 22: A charismatic person. Idealistic, humanitarian. Friendly, but shy. Needs a lot of freedom. Strong verbal skills.

Sid, 5: Extremely charming. Generous, thoughtful. Domestic, responsible.

Sidney, 4: Quickly sizes up situations. Blessed in some ways. Reliable, responsible. Original and unconventional. A free spirit, very adaptable. Dislikes limitations.

Siegfried, 10: Needs to be independent. Respectful, kind. Likes change and variety. Has willpower and determination. Self-sacrificing, loving. Gentle, kind, a hard worker. Artistic, having good taste. Physical and passionate. Natural authority.

Sigfried, 5: Extremely charming. Generous, thoughtful. Has willpower and determination. Self-sacrificing, loving. Gentle, kind, a hard worker. Artistic, having good taste. Physical and passionate. Natural authority.

Sigmund, 6: Completely devoted. Artistic, having good taste. Scientific and philosophical. Domestic, hardworking. Very lucky. Original and unconventional. Reliable, responsible.

Silas, 6: Completely devoted. Artistic, having good taste. Strong verbal skills. Independent, critical of self and others. Many mood swings.

Silvano, 11: A charismatic person. Blessed in some ways. Frequent traveler. Intuitive and inspired. Independent, critical of self and others. Original and unconventional. Natural counselor and healer.

Silvester, 3: Gift of gab. Considerate, understanding. Communicates skillfully. Intuitive and inspired. Physical and passionate. Charming and devoted. Dynamic, busy lifestyle. Loves freedom and adventure. Gentle, kind, a hard worker.

Silvia, 9: Angelic leanings. Blessed in some ways. Strong verbal skills. Intuitive and inspired. Artistic, having good taste. Helpful, sincere.

Silvio, 5: Extremely charming. Generous, thoughtful. Communicates skillfully. Intuitive and inspired. Artistic, having good taste. Natural counselor and healer.

Sima, 6: Completely devoted. Artistic, having good taste. Domestic, hardworking. Pioneer and risk taker.

Simon, 7: An opportunist. Needs alone time. Systematic, organized. Natural counselor and healer. Creative, opinionated.

Simone, 30: Gift of gab. Considerate, understanding. Domestic, hardworking. Natural counselor and healer. Romantic, sensual. A free spirit, very adaptable.

Sinclair, 4: Quickly sizes up situations. Blessed in some ways. Original and unconventional. Self-expressive, cheerful. Communicates skillfully. Natural teaching ability. Artistic, having good taste. Gentle, kind, a hard worker.

Sisley, 8: Passionate and loving. Blessed in some ways. Charming and devoted. Strong verbal skills. Likes change and variety. Needs a lot of freedom.

Sissy, 10: Needs to be independent. Blessed in some ways. Charming and devoted. Impulsive and extreme. Needs a lot of freedom.

Skelly, 3: Gift of gab. Strong desire to succeed. A free spirit, very adaptable. Excellent verbal skills. Ups and downs financially. Dislikes limitations.

Skip, 10: Needs to be independent. Strong desire to succeed. Respectful, kind. Intelligent and knowledgeable.

Skipp, 8: Passionate and loving. Strong desire to succeed. Blessed in some ways. Intelligent and knowledgeable. Levelheaded.

Sky, 10: Needs to be independent. Strong desire to succeed. Needs a lot of freedom.

Skye, 6: Completely devoted. Strong desire to succeed. Needs a lot of freedom. A step ahead of others.

Skylar, 5: Extremely charming. Strong desire to succeed. Dislikes restrictions. Communicates skillfully. Bright, adventuresome. Gentle, kind, a hard worker.

Skyler, 9: Angelic leanings. Strong desire to succeed. Dislikes restrictions. Communicates skillfully. A free spirit, very adaptable. Gentle, kind, a hard worker.

Slade, 5: Extremely charming. Communicates skillfully. Bright, adventuresome. Reliable, responsible. A free spirit, very adaptable.

Sloan, 7: An opportunist. Strong verbal skills. Natural counselor and healer. Not easily influenced. Original and unconventional.

Sly, 11: A charismatic person. Communicates skillfully. Needs a lot of freedom.

Smedley, 11: A charismatic person. Domestic, hardworking. Keenly perceptive. Reliable, responsible. Strong verbal skills. Physical and passionate. Needs a lot of freedom.

Sofia, 5: Extremely charming. Natural counselor and healer. Self-sacrificing, loving. Blessed in some ways. Independent, critical of self and others.

Sol, 10: Needs to be independent. Self-sacrificing, devoted. Strong verbal skills.

Solomon, 4: Quickly sizes up situations. Assumes responsibility. Strong verbal skills. Natural counselor and healer. Domestic, hardworking. Has musical talent. Original and unconventional.

Sondra, 8: Passionate and loving. Competitive in business. Original and unconventional. Reliable, responsible. Gentle, kind, a hard worker. Resolute and purposeful.

Song, 10: Needs to be independent. Self-sacrificing, devoted. Creative and opinionated. Stylish and refined.

Sonia, 22: A charismatic person. Creates group harmony. Intuitive and creative. Blessed in some ways. Ambitious leader, great vision.

Sonja, 5: Extremely charming. Natural counselor and healer. Original and unconventional. Clever and talented. Bright, adventuresome.

Sonny, 6: Completely devoted. Magnetic personality. Creative, opinionated. Romantic, sensual. Needs a lot of freedom.

Sonya, 20: Charming and devoted. Works well with others. Original and unconventional. Needs a lot of freedom. Reads people easily.

Sophey, 7: An opportunist. Natural counselor and healer. Stylish and refined. Great judge of character. Not easily fooled. Needs a lot of freedom.

Sophia, 5: Extremely charming. Natural counselor and healer. Intelligent and knowledgeable. Great judge of character. Blessed in some ways. Bright, adventuresome.

Sophie, 9: Angelic leanings. Artistic, creative. Levelheaded. Great judge of character. Blessed in some ways. A free spirit, very adaptable.

Sophy, 11: A charismatic person. Creates group harmony. Intelligent and knowledgeable. Great judge of character. Needs a lot of freedom.

Spalding, 10: Needs to be independent. Intelligent and knowledge-able. Bold, courageous, a bit stubborn. Strong verbal skills. Reliable, responsible. Blessed in some ways. Original and unconventional. Scientific and philosophical.

Spangler, 11: A charismatic person. Highly refined intellect. Intuitive, perceptive. Original and unconventional. Scientific and philosophi-cal. Strong verbal skills. A free spirit, very adaptable. Gentle, kind, a hard worker.

Spence, 8: Passionate and loving. Enjoys rivalry and challenge. A free spirit, very adaptable. Original and unconventional. Optimistic, outspoken. Likes change and variety.

Spencer, 8: Passionate and loving. Enjoys rivalry and challenge. A free spirit, very adaptable. Original and unconventional. Optimistic, outspoken. Likes change and variety. Gentle, kind, a hard worker.

Spike, 6: Completely devoted. Intelligent and knowledgeable. Blessed in some ways. Strong desire to succeed. A free spirit, very adaptable.

Spiro, 5: Extremely charming. Intelligent and knowledgeable. Blessed in some ways. Gentle, kind, a hard worker. Natural counselor and healer.

Spring, 11: A charismatic person. Highly refined intellect. Gentle, kind, a hard worker. Blessed in some ways. Creative and original. Scientific and philosophical.

Srila, 5: Extremely charming. Gentle, kind, a hard worker. Blessed in some ways. Strong verbal skills. Independent, critical of self and others.

Stacey, 10: Needs to be independent. Dynamic, busy lifestyle. Criti-cal of self and others. Self-expressive, cheerful. A free spirit, very adaptable. Dislikes limitations.

Stacie, 3: Gift of gab. Dynamic, busy lifestyle. Aims to please. Opti-mistic, outspoken. Blessed in some ways. A free spirit, very adapt-able.

Stacy, 5: Extremely charming. Energetic, highly charged. Bright, adventuresome. Self-expressive, cheerful. Needs a lot of freedom.

Stafford, 8: Passionate and loving. Dynamic, busy lifestyle. Resolute and purposeful. Self-sacrificing, devoted. High moral standards. Natural counselor and healer. Gentle, kind, a hard worker. Reliable, responsible.

Stan, 9: Angelic leanings. Generous to a fault. Helpful, sincere. Original and unconventional.

Standish, 3: Gift of gab. Dynamic, busy lifestyle. Aims to please. Creative, opinionated. Reliable, responsible. Blessed in some ways. Impulsive and extreme. Great judge of character.

Stanford, 7: An opportunist. Dynamic, busy lifestyle. Not easily influenced. Original and unconventional. Self-sacrificing, loving. Natural counselor and healer. Gentle, kind, a hard worker. Reliable, responsible.

Stanislaus, 9: Angelic leanings. Generous to a fault. Helpful, sincere. Original and unconventional. Blessed in some ways. Charming and devoted. Strong verbal skills. Independent, critical of self and others. Attractive, flirtatious. Impulsive and extreme.

Stanley, 6: Completely devoted. Dynamic, busy lifestyle. Pioneer and risk taker. Romantic, opinionated. Strong verbal skills. A free spirit, very adaptable. Needs a lot of freedom.

Starr, 22: A charismatic person. Dynamic, busy lifestyle. Ambitious leader, great vision. Gentle, kind, a hard worker. Intense inner power.

Steadman, 5: Extremely charming. Energetic, highly charged. A free spirit, very adaptable. Bright, adventuresome. Reliable, responsible. Domestic, hardworking. Bold, courageous, a bit stubborn. Romantic, opinionated.

Stefan, 20: Charming and devoted. Dynamic, busy lifestyle. Social, entertaining. Self-sacrificing, loving. Reads people easily. Creative, original.

Stefanie, 7: An opportunist. Perceptive, psychic. Not easily fooled. Self-sacrificing, loving. Independent, critical of self and others. Original and unconventional. Blessed in some ways. Likes change and variety.

Stella, 6: Completely devoted. Dynamic, busy lifestyle. A step ahead of others. Great verbal skills. Frequent traveler. Independent, critical of self and others.

Stephan, 11: A charismatic person. Dynamic, busy lifestyle. Keenly perceptive. Intelligent and knowledgeable. Great judge of character. Independent, critical of self and others. Original and creative.

Stephane, 7: An opportunist. Perceptive, psychic. Not easily fooled. Intelligent and knowledgeable. Great judge of character. Independent, critical of self and others. Original and unconventional. Physical and passionate.

Stephanie, 7: An opportunist. Perceptive, psychic. Not easily fooled. Intelligent and knowledgeable. Great judge of character. Independent, critical of self and others. Original and unconventional. Blessed in some ways. Physical and passionate.

Stephen, 6: Completely devoted. Dynamic, busy lifestyle. A step ahead of others. Intelligent and knowledgeable. Great judge of character. Physical and passionate. Original and unconventional.

Sterling, 5: Extremely charming. Energetic, highly charged. A free spirit, very adaptable. Gentle, kind, a hard worker. Strong verbal skills. Blessed in some ways. Creative, opinionated. Scientific and philosophical.

Steve, 8: Passionate and loving. Dynamic, busy lifestyle. Original, creative. Intuitive and inspired. Loves adventure and excitement.

Steven, 22: A charismatic person. An excellent mediator. Has big plans and ideas. Intuitive and inspired. Physical and passionate. Creative and opinionated.

Stevie, 8: Passionate and loving. Dynamic, busy lifestyle. A free spirit, very adaptable. Intuitive and inspired. Blessed in some ways. Loves adventure and excitement.

Stew, 4: Quickly sizes up situations. Dynamic, busy lifestyle. A free spirit, very adaptable. Likes to meet new people.

Stewart, 7: An opportunist. Perceptive, psychic. Not easily fooled. Likes to meet new people. Independent, critical of self and others. Gentle, kind, a hard worker. Sensitive and easily hurt.

Storm, 22: A charismatic person. An excellent mediator. Creates group harmony. Gentle, kind, a hard worker. Systematic, organized.

Stormy, 11: A charismatic person. An excellent mediator. Creates group harmony. Gentle, kind, a hard worker. Systematic, organized. Needs a lot of freedom.

Story, 7: An opportunist. Dynamic, busy lifestyle. Natural counselor and healer. Gentle, kind, a hard worker. Needs a lot of freedom.

Stu, 6: Completely devoted. Dynamic, busy lifestyle. Attractive and charming.

Stuart, 9: Angelic leanings. Dynamic, busy lifestyle. Attractive and charming. Helpful, sincere. Gentle, kind, a hard worker. Sensitive and easily hurt.

Sue, 9: Angelic leanings. Attractive and charming. A free spirit, very adaptable.

Suke, 11: A charismatic person. Creative and inspiring. Strong desire to succeed. A free spirit, very adaptable.

Suki, 6: Completely devoted. Idealistic in relationships. Strong desire to succeed. Blessed in some ways.

Sullivan, 11: A charismatic person. Creative and inspiring. Great verbal skills. Frequent traveler. Blessed in some ways. Intuitive, inspired, and perceptive. Original and romantic.

Summer, 8: Passionate and loving. Attractive and charming. Domestic, hardworking. Systematic, organized. A free spirit, very adaptable. Intense inner power.

Sunday, 3: Gift of gab. Youthful, appealing. Original, unconventional. Systematic, organized. Independent, self-motivated. Needs a lot of freedom.

Sunita, 3: Gift of gab. Youthful, appealing. Original and unconventional. Blessed in some ways. Dynamic, busy lifestyle. Aims to please.

Sunni, 5: Extremely charming. Attractive and appealing. Original and unconventional. Romantic, sensual. Blessed in some ways.

Sunny, 3: Gift of gab. Youthful, appealing. Original and unconventional. Romantic, sensual. Needs a lot of freedom.

Suri, 22: A charismatic person. Attractive and charming. Gentle, kind, a hard worker. Blessed in some ways.

Susan, 11: A charismatic person. Attractive and charming. Impulsive and extreme. Intuitive, perceptive. Original and romantic.

Susana, 3: Gift of gab. Youthful, appealing. Impulsive and extreme. Aims to please. Original and creative. Bold, courageous, a bit stubborn.

Susanna, 8: Passionate and loving. Attractive and charming. Impulsive and extreme. Resolute and purposeful. Original and unconventional. Romantic, sensual. Bold, courageous, a bit stubborn.

Susannah, 7: An opportunist. Attractive and charming. Impulsive and extreme. Independent, critical of self and others. Original and unconventional. Romantic, sensual. Bold, courageous, a bit stubborn. Great judge of character.

Susanne, 3: Gift of gab. Youthful, appealing. Impulsive and extreme. Aims to please. Original and unconventional. Romantic, sensual. A free spirit, very adaptable.

Suse, 10: Needs to be independent. Optimistic, outgoing. Impulsive and extreme. A free spirit, very adaptable.

Susie, 10: Needs to be independent. Attractive and charming. Impulsive and extreme. Blessed in some ways. A free spirit, very adaptable.

Sutcliff, 6: Completely devoted. Idealistic in relationships. Dynamic, busy lifestyle. Self-expressive, cheerful. Strong verbal skills. Blessed in some ways. Self-sacrificing. Loving. High moral standards.

Suzann, 5: Extremely charming. Attractive and appealing. Has high expectations. Independent, critical of self and others. Original and unconventional. Romantic, sensual.

Suzanna, 6: Completely devoted. Idealistic in relationships. Uses common sense. Independent, critical of self and others. Original and unconventional. Romantic, sensual. Bold, courageous, a bit stubborn.

Suzanne, 10: Needs to be independent. Optimistic, outgoing. Uses common sense. Independent, critical of self and others. Original and unconventional. Romantic, sensual. A free spirit, very adaptable.

Suze, 8: Passionate and loving. Charming and attractive. Has high expectations. A free spirit, very adaptable.

Suzette, 8: Passionate and loving. Attractive and charming. Has great reflexes. A free spirit, very adaptable. Dynamic, busy lifestyle. Sensitive and easily hurt. Loves adventure and excitement.

Suzi, 3: Gift of gab. Youthful, appealing. Uses common sense. Blessed in some ways.

Suzie, 8: Passionate and loving. Attractive and charming. Has great reflexes. Blessed in some ways. A free spirit, very adaptable.

Suzy, 10: Needs to be independent. Attractive and charming. Uses common sense. Needs a lot of freedom.

Sven, 6: Completely devoted. Intuitive and inspired. A step ahead of others. Creative and opinionated.

Sweeney, 6: Completely devoted. Likes to meet new people. A step ahead of others. Tendency to overindulge. Original and unconventional. Physical and passionate. Needs a lot of freedom.

Swen, 7: An opportunist. Likes to meet new people. Not easily fooled. Romantic and sensual.

Sybil, 22: A charismatic person. Dislikes limitations. Friendly, but shy. Blessed in some ways. Great verbal skills.

Sybill, 7: An opportunist. Needs a lot of freedom. Friendly, but shy. Blessed in some ways. Great verbal skills. Frequent traveler.

Syd, 3: Gift of gab. Needs a lot of freedom. Domestic, responsible.

Sydney, 11: Charismatic person. Needs a lot of freedom. Reliable, responsible. Original and creative. Loves adventure and excitement. Highly perceptive.

Sylvester, 10: Needs to be independent. Dislikes limitations. Strong verbal skills. Intuitive and inspired. Loves adventure and excitement. Impulsive and extreme. Dynamic, busy lifestyle. A free spirit, very adaptable. Gentle, kind, a hard worker.

Sylvia, 7: An opportunist. Dislikes limitations. Strong verbal skills. Intuitive and inspired. Blessed in some ways. Not easily influenced.

Sylvie, 11: A charismatic person. Dislikes limitations. Strong verbal skills. Intuitive and inspired. Blessed in some ways. A free spirit, very adaptable.

T

If a name begins with T, has more than one T, or ends with a T, this person is dynamic, social, and has a very busy lifestyle. They need to force themselves to slow down and they can be overly sensitive.

The letter T is the 20th letter of the alphabet. Since $2 + 0 = 2$, the 20th letter has the same vibrational influence as the number 2; it's co-ruled by number 2. The person whose name begins with T is partnership-oriented, and extremely protective of others. The 2 rules partnership and 0 rules assistance from God. Invariably, the T-named person is learning lessons in partnership, and has times in their life when all or nothing is happening with partnerships, other people, or social situations. Consequently, they are either very busy in their social life or with partners, or they have nothing going on at all. Of course, if it were up to them, they'd be constantly busy. This is what makes them so dynamic.

Similar to the number 2, the T-named person seeks peace and harmony and avoids conflict whenever possible. If a T is anywhere in a person's name, they will automatically be more diplomatic and sensitive to the needs of others. They might be interested in psychic phenomena and numerology or other studies that allow them to have a better understanding of people. T-named people are "people" people. Seldom do they enjoy being alone. If it were up to them, they'd always have a mate.

Those with a T anywhere in their name have a hustle-bustle kind of lifestyle. It's difficult for them to slow down. Often, they like to add to their already busy schedule. They will be the first to volunteer when they already have a lot on their plate, and they usually manage to get it all done. T names sometimes need to force themselves to slow down! With all this dynamic energy and sensitivity, they can sometimes react too quickly and make the wrong decisions. Some of their wrong decisions are morally incorrect. This is what gives the reputation "terrible twos" to the number 2-ruled letters. Similar to the tenth letter J, the

20th letter T has an assistance from God number 0, which can often pull them out of predicaments; except for the T, God's assistance usually has something to do with partnerships or social situations. The typical T person is so charming and cuddly, one can't help but overlook their faults. You just have to love them. It's impossible to stay mad when they are being so cute.

T-named people make wonderful partners, but may be a little bewildered about parenthood at first, unless they have some 6-ruled letters in their name. Similar to B names, they tend to become friends with their children later in life. As children, the T-named can get their feelings hurt very easily and will need lots of hugs for healthy emotional development. Next to Bs and Ks, they are among the most affectionate of all the letters.

Similar to the letter B, Ts wrote the book on partnership. T-named people become one of the best, most socially acceptable partners to be with. They'll protect and stand by their partners no matter what. What more could anyone ask for?

Tom Hanks, Tom Cruise, and Tom Jones have more than their first name in common. First of all, because their names start with a T, they have very dynamic and busy lifestyles. Also, they are each social and like to add to their already busy agendas. Because T is a 2 and O is a 6, Toms have a hidden 8 in their name. This number is also materialistic; let's just say they like the finer things in life. An 8 anywhere in a name can give its bearer the attitude, "He who dies with the most toys wins!" Because the 8 is hidden, it's possible that Toms are good at dabbling with stocks or other investments, but prefer to keep it to themselves.

As mentioned in the O section, an O anywhere in a name can lean toward musical abilities, as Tom Jones demonstrates. The T is similar to the letter B. Often these letters cling to ideas long after they have outlived their usefulness. In the case of Tom Jones, this quality is beneficial. It doesn't matter what he sings—his style never changes. He radiates sexuality with that hidden 8 and sings with a robust throaty voice that drives women wild. Still today, after over thirty years of performing, women throw their underwear at him while he's on stage.

Speaking of underwear, Tom Cruise's claim to fame was performing in the movie *Risky Business*, where he played a typical upscale teenager who worried about his grades and upsetting his parents' trust. He met a prostitute and ended up operating a business with her out of his parents' home while they were away. The sex and money fit in perfectly with Tom's hidden 8. Was it a coincidence Tom Cruise was cast so well in the movie *Top Gun?* The name of this movie has the same first two letters in it as Tom's first name. The movie *Top Gun* had death, ruled by 8, and airplanes, which are ruled by 3, as well. Tom adds up to a 3 power number, which among many things rules youthfulness or adolescence, and all forms of transportation (like airplanes), which helped Tom fit perfectly into both roles.

Power number 3 is lucky, as Tom Hanks found out. Tom Hanks's career began when he wasn't cast in a college play, but was invited by the director to go to Cleveland, which is where his career started. He's known for playing conflicted regular guys in movies. The number 3 is the natural comedian and Tom Hanks generally plays characters that make us laugh, even when he's being serious. O first vowels like to be the boss. Power number 3 knows how to communicate, so it's no surprise that Tom Hanks is now directing films as well as acting in them.

Double Ts in a name can create a whirlwind. In a 2003 television interview with double-T Patty Duke, Patty mentions that at one point she had to force herself to slow down. At one time during her life, Patty had too much going on and didn't know how to stop. She's an actress, mother, and political activist for issues such as the ERA (Equal Rights Amendment), AIDS, and nuclear disarmament. T is the 20th letter, so it's an all or nothing letter. Imagine how busy a person would be with two Ts in a name!

Tiger Woods is another dynamic, energetic T person. He's an American professional golfer whose achievements to date rank him among the most successful golfers of all time. He's been golfing since he was old enough to walk. Tiger has a lot of 9s in his name, which blesses him tremendously. He is quite a humanitarian. Tiger adds up to a 5 power number, so he likes his freedom and loves adventure and excitement. The G in the middle of his name is what makes him look so good on camera.

Tina Turner also has been blessed with an I first vowel. However, her name adds up to an 8 power number, so she's sexy and a survivor. Although she loves people, the hidden 7 shows she needs her solitude as well. Dynamic as she is, Tina needs her solitude to commune with God. Also, with the I first vowel, she must forgive those who have hurt her in the past in order to be happy today.

Other famous T names are: Thomas Jefferson, Thomas Edison, Mother Teresa, Ted Danson, Theodore Roosevelt, Tony Danza, Tony Curtis, Tanya Tucker, Troy Donahue, Tyra Banks, Tara Reid, Tommy Lee, Tori Amos, Ted Williams, Tug McGraw, Tracey Ullman, Tommy Hilfiger, Ted Kennedy, Timothy Leary, Tony Bennett, Tyrone Power, Travis Tritt, Tracy Chapman, Tom Green, and Truman Capote.

QUICK REFERENCE OF "T" NAMES

Taber, 10: Takes the initiative. Independent, critical of self and others. Anticipates next move. A free spirit, very adaptable. Gentle, kind, a hard worker.

Tabia, 6: Has business aptitude. Pioneer and risk taker. Friendly, but shy. Blessed in some ways. Bold, courageous, a bit stubborn.

Tabitha, 7: Perceptive, psychic. Not easily influenced. Friendly, but shy. Blessed in some ways. Sensitive and easily hurt. Great judge of character. Bold, courageous, a bit stubborn.

Tabor, 20: Extremely social. Reads people easily. Friendly, but shy. Natural counselor and healer. Gentle, kind, a hard worker.

Tad, 7: Perceptive, psychic. Not easily influenced. Reliable, responsible.

Tae, 8: An excellent mediator. Resolute and purposeful. Physical and passionate.

Tahlia, 6: Has business aptitude. Pioneer and risk taker. Great judge of character. Strong verbal skills. Blessed in some ways. Bold, courageous, a bit stubborn.

Tahnee, 8: An excellent mediator. Resolute and purposeful. Great judge of character. Original and unconventional. Physical and passionate. Loves adventure and excitement.

Tai, 3: Always coming and going. Aims to please. Blessed in some ways.

Taima, 8: An excellent mediator. Resolute and purposeful. Blessed in some ways. Domestic, hardworking. Bold, courageous, a bit stubborn.

Taj, 4: Busy family life. Natural teaching ability. Clever and talented.

Takara, 7: Perceptive, psychic. Not easily influenced. Strong desire to succeed. Bold, courageous, a bit stubborn. Gentle, kind, a hard worker. Pioneer and risk taker.

Talar, 7: Perceptive, psychic. Not easily influenced. Communicates skillfully. Not easily fooled. Gentle, kind, a hard worker.

Talia, 7: Perceptive, psychic. Not easily influenced. Communicates skillfully. Blessed in some ways. Bold, courageous, a bit stubborn.

Tallulah, 6: Has business aptitude. Pioneer and risk taker. Strong verbal skills. Ups and downs financially. Attractive and charming. Frequent traveler. Bold, courageous, a bit stubborn. Great judge of character.

Tally, 7: Perceptive, psychic. Not easily influenced. Strong verbal skills. Ups and downs financially. Needs a lot of freedom.

Talya, 5: Dynamic, busy lifestyle. Bright, adventuresome. Strong verbal skills. Needs a lot of freedom. Bold, courageous, a bit stubborn.

Tamar, 8: An excellent mediator. Resolute and purposeful. Patient, tolerant. Bold, courageous, a bit stubborn. Gentle, kind, a hard worker.

Tamara, 9: Generous to a fault. Helpful, sincere. Desires financial security. Bold, courageous, a bit stubborn. Gentle, kind, a hard worker. Pioneer and risk taker.

Tami, 7: Perceptive, psychic. Not easily influenced. Desires financial security. Blessed in some ways.

Tamica, 20: Needs to slow down. Reads people easily. Down-to-earth, practical. Blessed in some ways. Optimistic, outspoken. Independent, critical of self and others.

Tamilyn, 6: Has business aptitude. Pioneer and risk taker. Creative entrepreneur. Artistic, having good taste. Strong verbal skills. Needs a lot of freedom. Original and unconventional.

Tammi, 20: Extremely social. Reads people easily. Down-to-earth, practical. Domestic, hardworking. Blessed in some ways.

Tammie, 7: Perceptive, psychic. Not easily influenced. Desires financial security. Domestic, hardworking. Blessed in some ways. A free spirit, very adaptable.

Tammy, 8: An excellent mediator. Resolute and purposeful. Patient, tolerant. Domestic, hardworking. Needs a lot of freedom.

Tani, 8: An excellent mediator. Resolute and purposeful. Romantic, sensual. Artistic, having good taste.

Tania, 9: Generous to a fault. Helpful, sincere. Creative and opinionated. Blessed in some ways. Pioneer and risk taker.

Tanisha, 9: Generous to a fault. Helpful, sincere. Creative and opinionated. Blessed in some ways. Charming and devoted. Great judge of character. Bold, courageous, a bit stubborn.

Tanja, 10: Takes the initiative. Independent, critical of self and others. Creative, opinionated. Clever and talented. Bold, courageous, a bit stubborn.

Tanner, 9: Generous to a fault. Helpful, sincere. Original and unconventional. Creative, opinionated. Physical and passionate. Gentle, kind, a hard worker.

Tanya, 7: Perceptive, psychic. Not easily influenced. Original and unconventional. Needs a lot of freedom. Bold, courageous, a bit stubborn.

Tara, 4: Busy family life. Natural teaching ability. Gentle, kind, a hard worker. Bold, courageous, a bit stubborn.

Taralyn, 10: Takes the initiative. Independent, critical of self and others. Gentle, kind, a hard worker. Bold, courageous, a bit stubborn. Strong verbal skills. Needs a lot of freedom. Creative and original.

Tarrah, 30: Always coming and going. Aims to please. Gentle, kind, a hard worker. May be forgetful. Bold, courageous, a bit stubborn. Great judge of character.

Taryn, 6: Has business aptitude. Aims to please. Gentle, kind, a hard worker. Needs a lot of freedom. Creative and original.

Tasha, 4: Busy family life. Natural teaching ability. Charming and devoted. Great judge of character. Bold, courageous, a bit stubborn.

Tashi, 3: Always coming and going. Aims to please. Charming and devoted. Great judge of character. Blessed in some ways.

Tate, 10: Takes the initiative. Independent, critical of self and others. Sensitive and easily hurt. A free spirit, very adaptable.

Tatiana, 3: Always coming and going. Aims to please. Sensitive and easily hurt. Blessed in some ways. Bold, courageous, a bit stubborn. Original and unconventional. Pioneer and risk taker.

Tatum, 3: Always coming and going. Aims to please. Sensitive and easily hurt. Attractive and charming. Domestic, hardworking.

Tavis, 8: An excellent mediator. Resolute and purposeful. Intuitive and inspired. Blessed in some ways. Charming and devoted.

Tawnee, 5: Dynamic, busy lifestyle. Bright, adventuresome. Likes to meet new people. Original and unconventional. A free spirit, very adaptable. Physical and passionate.

Tawni, 22: A force of nature. Ambitious leader, great vision. Likes to meet new people. Original and romantic. Blessed in some ways.

Tawny, 20: Extremely social. Reads people easily. Likes to meet new people. Original and unconventional. Needs a lot of freedom.

Taylor, 10: Takes the initiative. Independent, critical of self and others. Needs a lot of freedom. Strong verbal skills. Natural counselor and healer. Gentle, kind, a hard worker.

Tayna, 7: Perceptive, psychic. Not easily influenced. Needs a lot of freedom. Original and unconventional. Bold, courageous, a bit stubborn.

Teah, 7: Perceptive, psychic. Not easily fooled. Resolute and purposeful. Great judge of character.

Ted, 11: A force of nature. Keenly perceptive. Domestic, responsible.

Teddy, 22: A force of nature. Has big plans and ideas. Reliable, responsible. Workaholic, determined. Needs a lot of freedom.

Teena, 9: Generous to a fault. A free spirit, very adaptable. Physical and passionate. Original and unconventional. Independent, critical of self and others.

Tempestt, 10: Takes the initiative. Likes change and variety. Domestic, hardworking. Intelligent, knowledgeable. Loves adventure and excitement. Charming and devoted. Sensitive and easily hurt. Needs to slow down.

Templeton, 3: Always coming and going. A free spirit, very adaptable. Domestic, hardworking. Intelligent, knowledgeable. Strong verbal skills. Loves adventure and excitement. Sensitive and easily hurt. Natural counselor and healer. Original and unconventional.

Tennyson, 9: Generous to a fault. A free spirit, very adaptable. Original and unconventional. Romantic, sensual. Needs a lot of freedom. Charming and devoted. Natural counselor and healer. Creative, opinionated.

Terence, 7: Perceptive, psychic. Not easily fooled. Gentle, kind, a hard worker. Physical and passionate. Original and unconventional. Self-expressive, cheerful. Loves adventure and excitement.

Teresa, 5: Dynamic, busy lifestyle. Perceptive, socially adept. Gentle, kind, a hard worker. Physical and passionate. Charming and devoted. Bright, adventuresome.

Teri, 7: Perceptive, psychic. Not easily fooled. Gentle, kind, a hard worker. Blessed in some ways.

Terrence, 7: Perceptive, psychic. Not easily fooled. Gentle, kind, a hard worker. Could be forgetful. Physical and passionate. Original and unconventional. Self-expressive, cheerful. Loves adventure and excitement.

Terri, 7: Perceptive, psychic. Not easily fooled. Gentle, kind, a hard worker. Could be forgetful. Blessed in some ways.

Terrill, 4: Busy family life. Accesses quickly. Diligent, hardworking. Could be forgetful. Blessed in some ways. Communicates skillfully. Frequent traveler.

Terry, 5: Dynamic, busy lifestyle. Perceptive, socially adept. Intense inner power. Could be forgetful. Needs a lot of freedom.

Tess, 9: Generous to a fault. A free spirit, very adaptable. Charming and devoted. Impulsive and extreme.

Tessa, 10: Takes the initiative. Likes change and variety. Charming and devoted. Impulsive and extreme. Independent, critical of self and others.

Tessie, 5: Dynamic, busy lifestyle. Perceptive, socially adept. Charming and devoted. Impulsive and extreme. Blessed in some ways. Physical and passionate.

Thad, 6: Has business aptitude. Creative in business. Pioneer and risk taker. Domestic, responsible.

Thaddea, 7: Perceptive, psychic. Great judge of character. Not easily influenced. Reliable, responsible. Workaholic, determined. A free spirit, very adaptable. Bold, courageous, a bit stubborn.

Thaddeus, 10: Takes the initiative. Sometimes a loner. Independent, critical of self and others. Reliable, responsible. Workaholic, determined. A free spirit, very adaptable. Attractive and charming. Very devoted.

Thalia, 6: Has business aptitude. Creative in business. Pioneer and risk taker. Strong verbal skills. Blessed in some ways. Bold, courageous, a bit stubborn.

Thao, 8: An excellent mediator. Enjoys competition. Resolute and purposeful. Natural counselor and healer.

Thatcher, 11: A force of nature. Self-reliant, successful. Independent, critical of self and others. Dynamic, busy lifestyle. Optimistic, outspoken. Great judge of character. A free spirit, very adaptable. Gentle, kind, a hard worker.

Thea, 7: Perceptive, psychic. Great judge of character. A free spirit, very adaptable. Not easily influenced.

Theda, 20: Extremely social. Excellent mediator. A free spirit, very adaptable. Practical, conservative. Reads people easily.

Thelma, 5: Dynamic, busy lifestyle. Very passionate. A free spirit, very adaptable. Strong verbal skills. Domestic, hardworking. Bright, adventuresome.

Theo, 3: Always coming and going. Makes and loses money easily. A free spirit, very adaptable. Natural counselor and healer.

Theodora, 5: Dynamic, busy lifestyle. Very passionate. A free spirit, very adaptable. Natural counselor and healer. Reliable, responsible. Has musical talent. Gentle, kind, a hard worker. Independent, critical of self and others.

Theodore, 9: Generous to a fault. Great judge of character. A free spirit, very adaptable. Natural counselor and healer. Reliable, responsible. Has musical talent. Gentle, kind, a hard worker. Loves adventure and excitement.

Theresa, 4: Busy family life. Relies on own judgment. Accesses quickly. Gentle, kind, a hard worker. Loves adventure and excitement. Charming and devoted. Independent, critical of self and others.

Therese, 8: An excellent mediator. Great judge of character. Original and creative. Gentle, kind, a hard worker. Loves adventure and excitement. Charming and devoted. Physical and passionate.

Thia, 20: Extremely social. Excellent mediator. Blessed in some ways. Reads people easily.

Thomas, 22: A force of nature. Self-reliant, successful. Natural counselor and healer. Domestic, hardworking. Ambitious leader, great vision. Charming and devoted.

Thor, 7: Perceptive, psychic. Great judge of character. Natural counselor and healer. Gentle, kind, a hard worker.

Thurman, 5: Dynamic, busy lifestyle. Very passionate. Attractive and charming. Gentle, kind, a hard worker. Systematic, organized. Bright, adventuresome. Creative, romantic.

Thurston, 9: Generous to a fault. Great judge of character. Attractive and charming. Gentle, kind, a hard worker. Loving and devoted. Sensitive and easily hurt. Natural counselor and healer. Original and unconventional.

Tia, 3: Always coming and going. Considerate, understanding. Aims to please, thoughtful.

Tiah, 20: Extremely social. Emotional, considerate. Reads people easily. An excellent mediator.

Tiana, 9: Generous to a fault. Blessed in some ways. Independent, critical of self and others. Original and unconventional. Bold, courageous, a bit stubborn.

Tiegh, 4: Busy family life. Blessed in some ways. A free spirit, very adaptable. Scientific and philosophical. Great judge of character.

Tifanie, 10: Takes the initiative. Respectful, kind. Self-sacrificing, loving. Independent, critical of self and others. Original and unconventional. Artistic, having good taste. A free spirit, very adaptable.

Tiff, 5: Dynamic, busy lifestyle. Generous, thoughtful. Self-sacrificing, loving. Has musical abilities.

Tiffany, 9: Generous to a fault. Blessed in some ways. Self-sacrificing, loving. Has musical abilities. Independent, critical of self and others. Original and unconventional. Needs a lot of freedom.

Tiffy, 30: Always coming and going. Considerate, understanding. Self-sacrificing, loving. Has musical abilities. Needs a lot of freedom.

Tilden, 10: Takes the initiative. Respectful, kind. Strong verbal skills. Natural authority. Physical and passionate. Original and unconventional.

Tillie, 4: Busy family life. Blessed in some ways. Communicates skillfully. Frequent traveler. Artistic, having good taste. A free spirit, very adaptable.

Tilly, 6: Has business aptitude. Artistic, having good taste. Communicates skillfully. Frequent traveler. Needs a lot of freedom.

Tim, 6: Has business aptitude. Artistic, having good taste. Domestic, hardworking.

Timmy, 8: An excellent mediator. Blessed in some ways. Domestic, hardworking. Systematic, organized. Needs a lot of freedom.

Timothy, 11: A force of nature. Intuitive, perceptive. Domestic, hardworking. Natural counselor and healer. Sensitive and easily hurt. Great judge of character. Needs a lot of freedom.

Tina, 8: An excellent mediator. Blessed in some ways. Original and unconventional. Independent, critical of self and others.

Tiona, 5: Dynamic, busy lifestyle. Generous, thoughtful. Natural counselor and healer. Original and unconventional. Independent, critical of self and others.

Tipper, 3: Always coming and going. Considerate, understanding. Intelligent and knowledgeable. Stylish and refined. A free spirit, very adaptable. Gentle, kind, a hard worker.

Tippi, 7: Perceptive, psychic. Needs alone time. Intelligent and knowledgeable. Stylish and refined. Artistic, having good taste.

Tippie, 3: Always coming and going. Considerate, understanding. Intelligent and knowledgeable. Stylish and refined. Artistic, having good taste. A free spirit, very adaptable.

Titania, 11: A force of nature. Intuitive, perceptive. Sensitive and easily hurt. Reads people easily. Original and unconventional. Artistic, having good taste. Bold, courageous, a bit stubborn.

Titus, 8: An excellent mediator. Blessed in some ways. Dynamic, busy lifestyle. Attractive and charming. Loving and devoted.

Tobe, 6: Has business aptitude. Magnetic personality. Friendly, but shy. A free spirit, very adaptable.

Tobey, 22: A force of nature. Creates group harmony. Friendly, but shy. A free spirit, very adaptable. Dislikes limitations.

Tobi, 10: Takes the initiative. Self-sacrificing, devoted. Anticipates next move. Blessed in some ways.

Tobiah, 10: Takes the initiative. Self-sacrificing, devoted. Anticipates next move. Blessed in some ways. Independent, critical of self and others. Great judge of character.

Tobias, 3: Always coming and going. Nurturing, loving. Loyal and understanding. Blessed in some ways. Aims to please. Charming and devoted.

Tobin, 6: Has business aptitude. Magnetic personality. Friendly, but shy. Blessed in some ways. Original and unconventional.

Toby, 8: An excellent mediator. Competitive in business. Enjoys luxury items. Needs a lot of freedom.

Tod, 3: Always coming and going. Nurturing, loving. Domestic, responsible.

Todd, 7: Perceptive, psychic. Open to opportunities. Reliable, responsible. Workaholic, determined.

Tom, 3: Always coming and going. Nurturing, loving. Domestic, hardworking.

Tomas, 5: Dynamic, busy lifestyle. Enjoys working. Systematic, organized. Independent, critical of self and others. Charming and devoted.

Tomiko, 11: A force of nature. Creates group harmony. Domestic, hardworking. Blessed in some ways. Strong desire to succeed. May have musical abilities.

Tomkin, 10: Takes the initiative. Self-sacrificing, devoted. Domestic, hardworking. Strong desire to succeed. Blessed in some ways. Original and unconventional.

Tommy, 5: Dynamic, busy lifestyle. Enjoys working. Systematic, organized. Domestically social. Needs a lot of freedom.

Toney, 7: Perceptive, psychic. Open to opportunities. Original and unconventional. A free spirit, very adaptable. Dislikes limitations.

Toni, 22: A force of nature. Creates group harmony. Original and unconventional. Blessed in some ways.

Tonia, 5: Dynamic, busy lifestyle. Enjoys working. Romantically inclined. Blessed in some ways. Independent, critical of self and others.

Tonisha, 5: Dynamic, busy lifestyle. Enjoys working. Romantically inclined. Blessed in some ways. Charming and devoted. Great judge of character. Bright, adventuresome.

Tony, 20: Extremely social. Works well with others. Original and unconventional. Needs a lot of freedom.

Tonya, 3: Always coming and going. Nurturing, loving. Young at heart. Needs a lot of freedom. Aims to please.

Topaz, 6: Has business aptitude. Magnetic personality. Intelligent and knowledgeable. Pioneer and risk taker. Uses common sense.

Tor, 8: An excellent mediator. Competitive in business. Gentle, kind, a hard worker.

Torey, 11: A force of nature. Creates group harmony. Intense inner power. Likes change and variety. Needs a lot of freedom.

Tori, 8: An excellent mediator. Competitive in business. Intense inner power. Blessed in some ways.

Torin, 4: Busy family life. Assumes responsibility. Gentle, kind, a hard worker. Blessed in some ways. Original and unconventional.

Torrance, 4: Busy family life. Assumes responsibility. Gentle, kind, a hard worker. Could be forgetful. Independent, critical of self and others. Original and unconventional. Self-expressive, cheerful. A free spirit, very adaptable.

Tory, 6: Has business aptitude. Magnetic personality. Gentle, kind, a hard worker. Needs a lot of freedom.

Toshiro, 5: Dynamic, busy lifestyle. Enjoys working. Charming and devoted. Great judge of character. Blessed in some ways. Gentle, kind, diligent. May have musical abilities.

Tova, 11: A force of nature. Creates group harmony. Intuitive and inspired. Reads people easily.

Tovah, 10: Takes the initiative. Self-sacrificing, devoted. Intuitive and inspired. Independent, critical of self and others. Great judge of character.

Trace, 20: Extremely social. Sensitive, emotional. Reads people easily. Self-expressive, cheerful. A free spirit, very adaptable.

Tracey, 9: Generous to a fault. Humanitarian, idealistic. Helpful, sincere. Optimistic, outspoken. A free spirit, very adaptable. Dislikes limitations.

Traci, 6: Has business aptitude. Duty-bound, self-sacrificing. Pioneer and risk taker. Self-expressive, cheerful. Blessed in some ways.

Tracie, 11: A force of nature. Strives to improve humanity. Intuitive, perceptive. Self-expressive, cheerful. Blessed in some ways. A free spirit, very adaptable.

Tracy, 22: A force of nature. Strives to improve humanity. Ambitious leader, great vision. Self-expressive, cheerful. Needs a lot of freedom.

Travers, 4: Busy family life. Strong and healthy. Natural teaching ability. Intuitive and inspired. A free spirit, very adaptable. Could be forgetful. Charming and devoted.

Travis, 8: An excellent mediator. Uses good judgment. Resolute and purposeful. Intuitive and inspired. Blessed in some ways. Charming and devoted.

Trejo, 5: Dynamic, busy lifestyle. Intense inner power. A free spirit, very adaptable. Clever and talented. A natural counselor and healer.

Trent, 5: Dynamic, busy lifestyle. Intense inner power. Physical and passionate. Original and unconventional. Sensitive and easily hurt.

Trevor, 8: An excellent mediator. Uses good judgment. Original and creative. Intuitive and inspired. Natural counselor and healer. Tendency to lose items.

Trey, 5: Dynamic, busy lifestyle. Intense inner power. A free spirit, very adaptable. Dislikes limitations.

Trianna, 5: Dynamic, busy lifestyle. Intense inner power. Blessed in some ways. Bright, adventuresome. Original and unconventional. Romantic, sensual. Pioneer and risk taker.

Tricia, 6: Has business aptitude. Duty-bound, self-sacrificing. Blessed in some ways. Self-expressive, cheerful. Artistic, having good taste. Pioneer and risk taker.

Trieu, 10: Takes the initiative. Diligent, hardworking. Blessed in some ways. Likes change and variety. Attractive and charming.

Trina, 8: An excellent mediator. Original and creative. Blessed in some ways. Romantic, sensual. Resolute and purposeful.

Trinity, 7: Perceptive, psychic. Spiritually motivated. Blessed in some ways. Original and unconventional. Artistic, having good taste. Dynamic, busy lifestyle. Needs a lot of freedom.

Trish, 11: A force of nature. Strives to improve humanity. Blessed in some ways. Charming and devoted. Great judge of character.

Tristan, 11: A force of nature. Strives to improve humanity. Blessed in some ways. Charming and devoted. Sensitive, easily hurt. Intuitive, perceptive. Original and unconventional.

Trixie, 4: Busy family life. Strong and healthy. Blessed in some ways. Artistic, sensual, perceptive. Idealistic and humanitarian. Accesses quickly.

Troy, 6: Has business aptitude. Duty-bound, self-sacrificing. Natural counselor and healer. Needs a lot of freedom.

Trudie, 5: Dynamic, busy lifestyle. Intense inner power. Attractive and charming. Reliable, responsible. Blessed in some ways. A free spirit, very adaptable.

Trudy, 7: Perceptive, psychic. Spiritually motivated. Attractive and charming. Reliable, responsible. Needs a lot of freedom.

Truman, 6: Has business aptitude. Duty-bound, self-sacrificing. Attractive and charming. Domestic, hardworking. Pioneer and risk taker. Original and unconventional.

Tuck, 10: Takes the initiative. Attractive and charming. Optimistic, outspoken. Strong desire to succeed.

Tucker, 6: Has business aptitude. Idealistic in relationships. Self-expressive, cheerful. Strong desire to succeed. A step ahead of others. Gentle, kind, a hard worker.

Tuesday, 5: Dynamic, busy lifestyle. Attractive and charming. A free spirit, very adaptable. Many mood swings. Reliable, responsible. Independent, critical of self and others. Dislikes limitations.

Tulia, 9: Generous to a fault. Attractive and charming. Strong verbal skills. Blessed in some ways. Helpful, sincere.

Tullia, 3: Always coming and going. Youthful, appealing. Communicates skillfully. Ups and downs financially. Blessed in some ways. Aims to please.

Tully, 9: Generous to a fault. Attractive and charming. Strong verbal skills. Ups and downs financially. Needs a lot of freedom.

Ty, 9: Generous to a fault. Needs a lot of freedom. Very perceptive.

Tyla, 4: Busy family life. Needs a lot of freedom. Strong verbal skills. Natural teaching ability.

Tylena, 5: Dynamic, busy lifestyle. Dislikes limitations. Communicates skillfully. A free spirit, very adaptable. Romantic, sensual. Bright, adventuresome.

Tyler, 8: An excellent mediator. Dislikes limitations. Strong verbal skills. Original, creative. Gentle, kind, a hard worker.

Tyra, 10: Takes the initiative. Needs a lot of freedom. Gentle, kind, a hard worker. Independent, critical of self and others.

Tyrone, 7: Perceptive, psychic. Dislikes limitations. Spiritually motivated. Natural counselor and healer. Romantic, sensual. A free spirit, very adaptable.

Tyrus, 22: A force of nature. Needs a lot of freedom. Strives to improve humanity. Attractive and charming. Loving, devoted.

Tyson, 3: Always coming and going. Needs a lot of freedom. Charming and devoted. Natural counselor and healer. Original and unconventional.

$\mathcal{U}$

If a name begins with U, has U as the first vowel, has more than one U, or ends with a U, this person is attractive, charming, and very lucky, but may have difficulty making decisions and may have financial ups and downs.

The letter U is the 21st letter of the alphabet. Since 2 + 1 = 3, the 21st letter has the same vibrational influence as the number 3. The 2 rules partnership, 1 rules beginnings, and 3 rules balance. People with U in their names must balance their ability to be in a partnership, while at the same time strive for independence.

Similar to the number 3-ruled letters C and L, the U-named individual likes to intellectualize their experiences. This makes it difficult for them to make up their minds. U names need to assess their situations quickly and then be ready to make a commitment to those goals. Unfortunately, selfishness or the inability to make up their minds causes many of their financial problems. What they lack in stability, they make up for in good looks and charm. The U-named person can be quite glamorous and attractive. They easily fit into any social circle. A person with this letter in his or her name could grace the cover of any glamour magazine. The 3 vibrational influence could win a best-dressed contest, unless they were up against an E first vowel. If they didn't win, they would at least come in second place. The U types are bright and witty and a welcome addition to any social event.

The best qualities of the U-named individual are the ability to bounce back from financial and physical setbacks. They have creativity, strong communication skills, and the luck of being in the right place at the right time. The U's charming, sunny, openhearted manner is another one of their greatest attributes. The worst qualities of U people are frivolity, superficiality, and they can be dramatic. They may scatter their energies and give in to escapist tendencies. Sometimes they can be very selfish. But, all in all, this letter is a positive one.

The letter U is one of the shortest name sections because not many names begin with the letter U. Still, a U anywhere in a name will give the bearer a more attractive and charming quality. They will have a natural ability to communicate socially with others. Most find the U names youthful, easygoing, and cheerful for the most part. Although this letter finds itself going through many financial ups and downs, it is one of the luckiest letters in the alphabet to have in a name.

Ulysses S. Grant, 18th President of the United States, exemplified his U letter with many financial ups and downs throughout his entire life. Similar to the letters L and C, U tends to be very lucky. Ulysses had a U and an L in his name, so he was very lucky. He spent many years on the battlefield without serious injury. His claim to fame was when he forced Robert E. Lee to surrender, ending the four-year bloody Civil War. He became an overnight success and international hero. Even the Queen of England wanted to meet him. Ulysses' two presidential terms are best remembered for financial scandals among members of his party and administration. He went bankrupt when he put his money into an investment firm that stole their investors' money. Ulysses turned to writing his memoirs to support his family. The letter U is ruled by the number 3, which lends skill in the area of writing. His name also added up to a 3 power number. His books became a success, but unfortunately his health gave out and he never lived to see the profits. It's too bad he waited so long to write, or he may not have died bankrupt.

Most people with names that begin with U or have a U first vowel are attractive and charming, just as our beautiful actress Ursula Andress. She is most remembered for her appearance as a Bond Girl in *Dr. No.* This number 3-ruled U is a letter of communication, so it's no surprise that Ursula, with two Us in her name, speaks fluent English, French, Italian, German, and Swiss-German! Her name adds up to a 20 power number, so it seems she is either very busy with partnerships and social situations, or has nothing going on at all romantically or socially. It's an all or nothing power number.

Another interesting U name is the ever popular Uma Thurman of the *Kill Bill* movies. Uma's an attractive and charming six-foot-tall model-turned-actress. Her father, Robert Thurman, was the first westerner to become a Tibetan Buddhist monk. Uma was named for a Hindu goddess. Her mother was a Swedish model. She is very easygoing and has a cheerful attitude about life. This is one of the best traits of the U. They are pleasant to be around and go with the flow. The M in the middle of Uma's name gives her domestic tendencies. She probably loves being at home and doesn't mind doing the household chores and errands. M is a 4-ruled letter and rules work and family. She no doubt loves the whole family scene. Her name adds up to an 8 power number, so she is a survivor and will achieve financial rewards in this lifetime. Also the number 8 is often associated with death, so *Kill Bill* was a natural attraction for her. She's strong with an 8 power number, healthy and resilient with a U first letter, down-to-earth with an M in the middle, and a perfectionist with an A at the end of her name. No doubt we'll be seeing a great deal more of Uma in future films. She's talented, strong, and easy on the eyes.

The United States of America, more commonly called USA, is also a U name. Although many call the USA, "America," technically it's the United States of America. The USA is considered lucky by most other countries. Also U is a youthful letter and USA is one of the youngest countries on the continent. Some of the USA's most important resources are in the areas of communication and transportation—both qualities of the 3-ruled letter U. The USA has a difficult time making decisions, taking forever to pass bills through Congress and intellectualizing the whole process, another common U trait. The USA has a Gemini rising, which is a youthful, adolescent personality. We are young, misunderstood, and think we know everything, rather similar to teenagers. Other countries who have been around longer probably find us irritating.

Interesting fact: Mount Rushmore, with its U first vowel, is notable for the fact that in its fourteen years of construction there was never a serious accident. Never underestimate the luck of the U.

Famous names that begin with U are: Uma Thurman, Usher, Ursula Andress, Ulysses S. Grant, Uri Geller, and Upton Sinclair. Famous names with U first vowels: Humphrey Bogart, Julius Caesar, Jules Verne, Dustin Hoffman, Rudolph Valentino, Julie Andrews, Audrey Hepburn, Julia Roberts, Lucille Ball, and Suzanne Somers.

QUICK REFERENCE OF "U" NAMES

Udel, 6: Idealistic in relationships. Creative problem solver. A step ahead of others. Strong verbal skills.

Udele, 20: Social and charming. Practical, conservative. A free spirit, very adaptable. Strong verbal skills. Physical and passionate.

Udell, 9: Go with the flow. Reliable, responsible. A free spirit, very adaptable. Communicates skillfully. Ups and downs financially.

Udo, 4: Socially organized. Down-to-earth, faithful. Natural counselor and healer.

Ukiah, 5: Ups and downs financially. Strong desire to succeed. Blessed in some ways. Bright, adventuresome. Great judge of character.

Ula, 7: Has style and grace. Intellectually sound. Independent, critical of self and others.

Ulani, 3: Youthful, appealing. Slow to make decisions. Aims to please. Creative, romantic. Blessed in some ways.

Ullah, 9: Go with the flow. Great verbal skills. Ups and downs financially. Helpful, sincere. Great judge of character.

Ulna, 3: Youthful, appealing. Slow to make decisions. Original and romantic. Aims to please.

Ulric, 9: Go with the flow. Great verbal skills. Humanitarian, idealistic. Blessed in some ways. Self-expressive, cheerful.

Ulrich, 8: Usually very lucky. Strong verbal skills. Uses good judgment. Blessed in some ways. Self-expressive, cheerful. Great judge of character.

Ulrick, 11: Creative and inspiring. Travels frequently. Gentle, kind, a hard worker. Artistic, having good taste. Self-expressive, cheerful. Sensitive and diplomatic.

Ultima, 22: Creative and inspiring. Travels frequently. Dynamic, busy lifestyle. Blessed in some ways. Domestic, hardworking. Ambitious leader, great vision.

Ultimo, 9: Go with the flow. Great verbal skills. Dynamic, busy lifestyle. Blessed in some ways. Domestic, hardworking. Natural counselor and healer.

Ulysses, 3: Youthful, appealing. Slow to make decisions. Dislikes restrictions. Loving, devoted. Impulsive and extreme. A free spirit, very adaptable. Needs to be independent.

Uma, 8: Usually very lucky. Domestic, hardworking. Resolute and purposeful.

Umeko, 20: Social and charming. Domestic, hardworking. A free spirit, very adaptable. Strong desire to succeed. Natural counselor and healer.

Umi, 7: Has style and grace. Domestic, hardworking. Blessed in some ways.

Una, 9: Go with the flow. Original and unconventional. Helpful, sincere.

Upton, 5: Ups and downs financially. Intelligent and knowledgeable. Dynamic, busy lifestyle. Natural counselor and healer. Romantic, opinionated.

Urania, 10: Optimistic and outgoing. Gentle, kind, a hard worker. Independent, critical of self and others. Original and unconventional. Blessed in some ways. Bold, courageous, a bit stubborn.

Urban, 20: Social and charming. Sensitive, emotional. Friendly, but shy. Independent, critical of self and others. Original and unconventional.

Urea, 9: Go with the flow. Humanitarian, idealistic. A free spirit, very adaptable. Independent, critical of self and others.

Uri, 3: Youthful, appealing. Sympathetic, kind. Friendly, considerate.

Uria, 22: Creative and inspiring. Strives to improve humanity. Blessed in some ways. Independent, critical of self and others.

Uriah, 30: Youthful, appealing. Sympathetic, kind. Friendly, considerate. Independent, critical of self and others. Great judge of character.

Urias, 5: Ups and downs financially. Good deed doer. Blessed in some ways. Independent, critical of self and others. Impulsive and extreme.

Uric, 6: Idealistic in relationships. Duty-bound, self-sacrificing. Artistic, having good taste. Self-expressive, cheerful.

Uriel, 11: Creative and inspiring. Strives to improve humanity. Blessed in some ways. A free spirit, very adaptable. Strong verbal skills.

Ursala, 9: Go with the flow. Humanitarian, idealistic. Angelic leanings. Independent, critical of self and others. Strong verbal skills. Bold, courageous, a bit stubborn.

Ursei, 9: Go with the flow. Humanitarian, idealistic. Angelic leanings. A free spirit, very adaptable. Blessed in some ways.

Ursina, 10: Optimistic and outgoing. Diligent, hardworking. Charming and devoted. Blessed in some ways. Original and unconventional. Independent, critical of self and others.

Ursine, 5: Ups and downs financially. Good deed doer. Charming and devoted. Blessed in some ways. Original and unconventional. Physical and passionate.

Ursula, 20: Social and charming. Sensitive, emotional. Impulsive and extreme. Difficulty making decisions. Strong verbal skills. Reads people easily.

Ursuline, 11: Creative and inspiring. Strives to improve humanity. Very charismatic. Attractive, flirtatious, slightly scattered. Strong verbal skills. Blessed in some ways. Original, opinionated. Physical and passionate.

Usher, 8: Usually very lucky. Charming and devoted. Great judge of character. Physical and passionate. Gentle, kind, a hard worker.

Uziel, 10: Optimistic and outgoing. Uses common sense. Blessed in some ways. Likes change and variety. Strong verbal skills.

Uzoma, 22: Creative and inspiring. Uses common sense. Natural counselor and healer. Reliable, responsible. Ambitious leader, great vision.

$\mathcal{V}$

If a name begins with V, has more than one V, or ends with a V, this person is successful, sincere, loyal, and dependable; however, they can also be overly possessive, unpredictable, and eccentric.

The letter V is the 22nd letter of the alphabet. The number 22 is one of the master numbers. We have only two master numbers, 11 and 22. The number 22 is often referred to as the "master builder." It is the most successful of all the numbers. This 22nd letter must serve the world in a practical way. Since $2 + 2 = 4$, people with this letter in their name will experience lessons in partnership, twice over from the double 2s. The 4 vibrational influence will bring lessons in work and family. Partnership, partnership, work, and family. These people will be quite hard workers, down-to-earth, and practical in most respects. This does not mean they will have two partners or two marriages. The double emphasis on partners means dealing with the outside world in a social way. In a big way! They will be Capricorn-like, or goal-oriented, and possess the ability to manifest considerable plans and ideas. With a V anywhere in their name, they may feel pressure to accomplish something worthwhile on a grand scale. The pressure comes from within; they will be harder on themselves than anyone else could ever be. V is for Victory! They should be efficient goal setters. At the very least, they will be as hardworking as a 4-ruled letter.

The V produces inspiring and prophetic individuals; however, their imaginations can be so strong that it sometimes interferes with their judgment. Also, the V can be too possessive in romantic relationships. On a positive note, similar to the letters D and M, this letter has the ability to be faithful. Somehow cheating on a partner goes against their grain. They are sincere, not flirtatious, and tend to dislike flamboyant, superficial personalities. Anyone with a V in his or her name has the ability to accomplish great tasks. Most are domestic, down-to-earth, and feel a strong need to be financially secure. Similar to D and M, the sound of rustling currency is soothing to their nerves.

V is also like D and M in that people with this letter in their names are able to enter a situation, look around, and quickly assess their surroundings. They don't want to look like fools, so they will do their homework before deciding to take on a project. This letter is like "The Terminator"—not much gets past them, they notice everything! V people make excellent teachers and usually end up in some type of professional field. Also, as a rule, V names don't usually get along with superficial people. They can see right through them. Although V is ruled by the same number that rules D and M, this letter is more highly evolved; it's worldly and prominent. Only those who are truly up to the task can wear it.

Viggo Mortensen of *The Lord of the Rings,* who also had a part in the movie *Witness,* fits his name quite well. The V is world-wide and so is Viggo. As a child he and his family traveled to other countries because of his father's work. He has a serious yet sad look in his eyes. His first vowel I added to his first letter V sums up to a hidden 4, so he's had to endure some hardships. The I influences him to not feel happy unless he's able to forgive others who have hurt him in the past. This serious sadness look helped him in *The Lord of the Rings.* His two 7-ruled Gs in the middle of his name indicate the very center of his being. He is a private, introspective person. As it turns out, besides being an actor, he is also an accomplished poet, photographer, and painter. G is very stylish, but Viggo wears his style on the inside. He has an intensity number 7, which makes him a truth seeker. It also helps him to look good on camera. Furthermore, he is a nurturer and healer with a 6-ruled O at the end of his name. His name also adds up to a power number 6. All this means he has to have someone to love. Viggo almost turned down the role for *The Lord of the Rings* because he wanted to spend time with his ten-year-old son. Fortunately his son was knowledgeable about the series and enthusiastically convinced his father to take the role. The O and power number 6 make for a good parent; he's duty-bound, nurturing, loving, and caring. With that much love-ruled 6 in his name, he is highly magnetic.

Another well-known actress and singer is Vanessa Williams. The V added to her first vowel, A, sums up to a hidden 5. She loves adventure and excitement. She also has an intensity 1 in her name as she has four letters ruled by the number 1, two As and two Ss. She is a perfectionist and works very hard to maintain her high status. Vanessa was the first black Miss America. The number 1 means leader, pioneer, and risk taker. Vanessa is driven to accomplish great things with an intensity 1 in her name. She was born to pave the way for others. As it turns out, her name adds up to a 9 power number. She's a humanitarian and blessed in some ways. Often those with a 9 power number are blessed; others can be jealous of this. With two Ss she is even more broadminded and less prejudiced than most of the other letters, giving her higher angelic qualities.

Val Kilmer also seems to have the perfect name for himself. He has a hidden 5 in the beginning of his name, as the 4-ruled V and the 1-ruled A add up to a 5. This means he loves adventure and excitement. The hidden 5 may be the reason he has the ability to play very diverse characters. Val was in blockbuster films *Top Gun, Batman Forever,* and *The Prince of Egypt.* He has three letters in his first name, so he is a good communicator. Also, his name adds up to an 8 power number, so he's a survivor, enjoys the finer things in life, and is very sexy. The A first vowel makes him very critical of himself and others, so he most likely researches each movie script. Last but not least, the L gives him a cheerful, youthful, and easygoing attitude. With an L at the end of his name, it may be difficult for him to make decisions at times; however, once he's made up his mind, he sticks with it. The L also gives him strong verbal skills. With three letters in his name and an L at the end, he's probably a little "car happy." Also if he finds himself lucky, it's the L that should receive the credit. Next to C and U, L is one of the luckiest letters to have in a name.

More famous people whose names begin with V are: Vincent Price, Valentino, Valerie Bertinelli, Venus Williams, Veronica Lake, Vladimir Horowitz, Valerie Harper, Vivien Leigh, Vincent van Gogh, Vladimir Putin, Van Morrison, Vanna White, Victoria Principal, Vikki Carr, Voltaire, and Vanessa Redgrave.

QUICK REFERENCE OF "V" NAMES

Vaclav, 7: A brilliant mind. Not easily influenced. Self-expressive, cheerful. Communicates skillfully. Bold, courageous, a bit stubborn. Overly possessive.

Vadin, 5: Eccentric or unpredictable. Bright, adventuresome. Reliable, responsible. Blessed in some ways. Romantic, opinionated.

Val, 8: Efficient, wants to see results. Resolute and purposeful. Strong verbal skills.

Vala, 9: Has big plans and ideas. Helpful, sincere. Frequent traveler. Bold, courageous, a bit stubborn.

Valda, 4: Honest and sincere. Natural teaching abilities. Great verbal skills. Reliable, responsible. Bold, courageous, a bit stubborn.

Valdemar, 4: Honest and sincere. Natural teaching abilities. Great verbal skills. Reliable, responsible. A free spirit, very adaptable. Domestic, hardworking. Bold, courageous, a bit stubborn. Diligent, helpful.

Vale, 4: Honest and sincere. Natural teaching abilities. Frequent traveler. A free spirit, very adaptable.

Valente, 7: A brilliant mind. Not easily influenced. Communicates skillfully. A free spirit, very adaptable. Original and unconventional. Dynamic, busy lifestyle. Physical and passionate.

Valentina, 8: Efficient, wants to see results. Resolute and purposeful. Strong verbal skills. A free spirit, very adaptable. Original and unconventional. Dynamic, busy lifestyle. Blessed in some ways. Romantic, sensual. Independent, critical of self and others.

Valentine, 3: Inspired and prophetic. Aims to please. Communicates skillfully. A free spirit, very adaptable. Original and unconventional. Dynamic, busy lifestyle. Blessed in some ways. Romantic, sensual. Tendency to overindulge.

Valerie, 9: Has big plans and ideas. Helpful, sincere. Frequent traveler. A free spirit, very adaptable. Gentle, kind, a hard worker. Blessed in some ways. Physical and passionate.

Valery, 11: Great potential. Intuitive, perceptive. Strong verbal skills. A free spirit, very adaptable. Gentle, kind, a hard worker. Dislikes limitations.

Valetta, 9: Has big plans and ideas. Helpful, sincere. Frequent traveler. A free spirit, very adaptable. Dynamic, busy lifestyle. Sensitive and easily hurt. Bold, courageous, a bit stubborn.

Valiant, 7: A brilliant mind. Not easily influenced. Strong verbal skills. Blessed in some ways. Bold, courageous, a bit stubborn. Original and unconventional. Dynamic, busy lifestyle.

Van, 10: Self-reliant, a natural leader. Independent, critical of self and others. Original and unconventional.

Vance, 9: Has big plans and ideas. Helpful, sincere. Romantic, opinionated. Self-expressive, cheerful. A free spirit, very adaptable.

Vanessa, 9: Has big plans and ideas. Helpful, sincere. Romantic, opinionated. A free spirit, very adaptable. Charming and devoted. Impulsive and extreme. Bold, courageous, a bit stubborn.

Vanna, 7: A brilliant mind. Not easily influenced. Original and unconventional. Romantic, sensual. Bold, courageous, a bit stubborn.

Vaughan, 11: Great potential. Intuitive, perceptive. Attractive and charming. Scientific and philosophical. Great judge of character. Bold, courageous, a bit stubborn. Original and unconventional.

Vaughn, 10: Self-reliant, a natural leader. Independent, critical of self and others. Attractive and charming. Scientific and philosophical. Great judge of character. Original and unconventional.

Veda, 5: Eccentric or unpredictable. Physical and passionate. Reliable, responsible. Bright, adventuresome.

Vega, 8: Efficient, wants to see results. Original and creative. Scientific and philosophical. Resolute and purposeful.

Vegas, 9: Has big plans and ideas. Enjoys giving gifts. Stylish and refined. Helpful, sincere. Charming and devoted.

Vela, 4: Honest and sincere. Accesses quickly. Great verbal skills. Natural teaching ability.

Velda, 8: Efficient, wants to see results. Original and creative. Strong verbal skills. Reliable, responsible. Resolute and purposeful.

Velma, 8: Efficient, wants to see results. Original and creative. Strong verbal skills. Domestic, hardworking. Resolute and purposeful.

Velvet, 5: Eccentric or unpredictable. Physical and passionate. Great verbal skills. Overly possessive. Loves adventure and excitement. Dynamic, busy lifestyle.

Venus, 9: Has big plans and ideas. Enjoys giving gifts. Romantic, opinionated. Attractive and charming. Loving, devoted.

Vera, 10: Self-reliant, a natural leader. Likes change and variety. Diligent, hardworking. Independent, critical of self and others.

Vergil, 10: Self-reliant, a natural leader. Likes change and variety. Diligent, hardworking. Scientific, philosophical. Blessed in some ways. Communicates skillfully.

Verlyn, 6: Responsible and trustworthy. A step ahead of others. Duty-bound, self-sacrificing. Strong verbal skills. Needs a lot of freedom. Romantic, opinionated.

Vern, 5: Eccentric or unpredictable. Physical and passionate. Gentle, kind, a hard worker. Original and unconventional.

Verna, 6: Responsible and trustworthy. A free spirit, very adaptable. Duty-bound, self-sacrificing. Original and unconventional. Pioneer and risk taker.

Verne, 10: Self-reliant, a natural leader. Likes change and variety. Diligent, hardworking. Original and unconventional. Physical and passionate.

Vernita, 8: Efficient, wants to see results. Physical and passionate. Intense inner power. Original, creative. Blessed in some ways. Dynamic, busy lifestyle. Resolute and purposeful.

Vernon, 7: A brilliant mind. Not easily fooled. Gentle, kind, a hard worker. Creative, original. Natural counselor and healer. Romantic, sensual.

Veronica, 6: Responsible and trustworthy. A step ahead of others. Duty-bound, self-sacrificing. Natural counselor and healer. Original and unconventional. Blessed in some ways. Self-expressive, cheerful. Independent, critical of self and others.

Veronique, 9: Has big plans and ideas. Enjoys giving gifts. Gentle, kind, a hard worker. Natural counselor and healer. Original and unconventional. Blessed in some ways. Attracts wealth. Attractive and charming. Tendency to overindulge.

Vespera, 5: Eccentric or unpredictable. Physical and passionate. Charming and devoted. Intelligent and knowledgeable. Loves adventure and excitement. Gentle, kind, a hard worker. Independent, critical of self and others.

Vi, 4: Honest and sincere. Teaches kindness. Hardworking, organized.

Vic, 7: A brilliant mind. Needs alone time. Self-expressive, cheerful.

Vichy, 4: Honest and sincere. Blessed in some ways. Self-expressive, cheerful. Great judge of character. Needs a lot of freedom.

Vick, 9: Has big plans and ideas. Blessed in some ways. Self-expressive, cheerful. Strong desire to succeed.

Vicki, 9: Has big plans and ideas. Blessed in some ways. Self-expressive, cheerful. Strong desire to succeed. Blessed in some ways.

Vickie, 5: Eccentric or unpredictable. Blessed in some ways. Optimistic, outspoken. Strong desire to succeed. A free spirit, very adaptable.

Vicky, 7: A brilliant mind. Needs alone time. Self-expressive, cheerful. Strong desire to succeed. Needs a lot of freedom.

Victor, 6: Responsible and trustworthy. Artistic, having good taste. Self-expressive, cheerful. Dynamic, busy lifestyle. Natural counselor and healer. Gentle, kind, a hard worker.

Victoria, 7: A brilliant mind. Needs alone time. Self-expressive, cheerful. Dynamic, busy lifestyle. Natural counselor and healer. Gentle, kind, a hard worker. Artistic, having good taste. Not easily influenced.

Vida, 9: Has big plans and ideas. Blessed in some ways. Reliable, responsible. Independent, critical of self and others.

Vidal, 3: Inspired and prophetic. Considerate, understanding. Optimistic, outspoken. Pioneer and risk taker. Frequent traveler.

Viggo, 6: Responsible and trustworthy. Artistic, having good taste. Scientific and philosophical. Extremely intelligent. Natural counselor and healer.

Viktor, 5: Eccentric or unpredictable. Blessed in some ways. Strong desire to succeed. Dynamic, busy lifestyle. Natural counselor and healer. Gentle, kind, a hard worker.

Vin, 9: Has big plans and ideas. Blessed in some ways. Original and unconventional.

Vince, 8: Efficient, wants to see results. Gives practical gifts. Romantic, sensual. Self-expressive, cheerful. Original and creative.

Vincent, 6: Responsible and trustworthy. Artistic, having good taste. Original and unconventional. Self-expressive, cheerful. A step ahead of others. Romantic, sensual. Dynamic, busy lifestyle.

Vincente, 11: Great potential. Intuitive, perceptive. Original and unconventional. Self-expressive, cheerful. A free spirit, very adaptable. Romantic, sensual. Dynamic, busy lifestyle. Loves adventure and excitement.

Vincenzo, 9: Has big plans and ideas. Blessed in some ways. Original and unconventional. Self-expressive, cheerful. A free spirit, very adaptable. Romantic, sensual. Uses common sense. Natural counselor and healer.

Vinnie, 10: Self-reliant, a natural leader. Respectful, kind. Creative, opinionated. Romantic, sensual. Artistic, having good taste. Likes variety and change.

Vinny, 30: Inspired and prophetic. Considerate, understanding. Original and unconventional. Romantic, sensual. Needs a lot of freedom.

Viola, 5: Eccentric or unpredictable. Generous, thoughtful. Natural counselor and healer. Strong verbal skills. Bright, adventuresome.

Violet, 11: Great potential. Intuitive, perceptive. Natural counselor and healer. Strong verbal skills. A free spirit, very adaptable. Dynamic, busy lifestyle.

Virg, 11: Great potential. Intuitive, perceptive. Gentle, kind, a hard worker. Scientific, and philosophical.

Virgie, 7: A brilliant mind. Blessed in some ways. Spiritually motivated. Stylish and refined. Artistic, having good taste. Not easily fooled.

Virgil, 5: Eccentric or unpredictable. Generous, thoughtful. Good deed doer. Scientific and philosophical. Artistic, having good taste. Communicates skillfully.

Virgilio, 11: Great potential. Intuitive, perceptive. Gentle, kind, a hard worker. Scientific, philosophical. Artistic, having good taste. Strong verbal skills. Blessed in some ways. Natural counselor and healer.

Virginia, 8: Efficient, wants to see results. Gives practical gifts. Uses good judgment. Scientific, philosophical. Artistic, having good taste. Original, creative. Blessed in some ways. Resolute, purposeful.

Virgy, 9: Has big plans and ideas. Blessed in some ways. Gentle, kind, a hard worker. Scientific and philosophical. Needs a lot of freedom.

Visolela, 5: Eccentric or unpredictable. Generous, thoughtful. Charming and devoted. Natural counselor and healer. Strong verbal skills. A free spirit, very adaptable. Frequent traveler. Bright, adventuresome.

Vita, 7: A brilliant mind. Needs alone time. Dynamic, busy lifestyle. Not easily influenced.

Vito, 3: Inspired and prophetic. Considerate, understanding. Dynamic, busy lifestyle. Natural counselor and healer.

Vittorio, 11: Great potential. Blessed in some ways. Dynamic, busy lifestyle. Sensitive and easily hurt. Natural counselor and healer. Gentle, kind, a hard worker. Artistic, having good taste. Musically talented.

Viv, 8: Efficient, wants to see results. Blessed in some ways. Has a strong imagination.

Vivian, 5: Eccentric or unpredictable. Generous, thoughtful. Has a strong imagination. Artistic, having good taste. Bright, adventuresome. Creative, opinionated.

Vivica, 30: Inspired and prophetic. Considerate, understanding. Has a strong imagination. Artistic, having good taste. Self-expressive, cheerful. Pioneer and risk taker.

Vivien, 9: Has big plans and ideas. Blessed in some ways. Has a strong imagination. Artistic, having good taste. A free spirit, very adaptable. Creative, opinionated.

Vivienne, 10: Self-reliant, a natural leader. Respectful, kind. Has a strong imagination. Artistic, having good taste. A free spirit, very adaptable. Original and unconventional. Romantic, sensual. Tendency to overindulge.

Vlad, 3: Inspired and prophetic. Great verbal skills. Aims to please. Domestic, responsible.

Vladamir, 8: Efficient, wants to see results. Strong verbal skills. Resolute and purposeful. Reliable, responsible. Bold, courageous, a bit stubborn. Desires financial security. Blessed in some ways. Gentle, kind, a hard worker.

Vladimir, 7: A brilliant mind. Communicates skillfully. Not easily influenced. Domestic, responsible. Artistic, having good taste. Desires financial security. Blessed in some ways. Gentle, kind, a hard worker.

Voleta, 3: Inspired and prophetic. Natural counselor and healer. Frequent traveler. A free spirit, very adaptable. Dynamic, busy lifestyle. Aims to please.

Volta, 7: A brilliant mind. Open to opportunities. Strong verbal skills. Dynamic, busy lifestyle. Independent, critical of self and others.

Von, 6: Responsible and trustworthy. Natural counselor and healer. Creative and original.

Vonn, 20: Tactful and refined. Natural counselor and healer. Original and unconventional. Romantic, sensual.

Vonnie, 7: A brilliant mind. Open to opportunities. Creative, opinionated. Romantic, sensual. Blessed in some ways. A free spirit, very adaptable.

Vonny, 9: Has big plans and ideas. Natural counselor and healer. Original and unconventional. Romantic, sensual. Needs a lot of freedom.

$$\mathcal{W}$$

If a name begins with W, has more than one W, or ends with a W, this person likes to meet new people, has charisma, can be superficial, is creative, and needs change.

The letter W is the 23rd letter of the alphabet. Since 2 + 3 = 5, the person with a W influence will experience partnership, balance, and changing circumstances. They will be very social, adept in conversation, and prefer variety and change. Since 5 influences the W, this person loves adventure and excitement. The number 5 rules entertainment, so you can count on the W person to keep you entertained.

Names that begin with W are able to express themselves quite well and seem to have a strong sense of purpose. Just the thought of travel and freedom to roam excites them. W is the last 5-ruled letter of the alphabet, and so is more highly evolved than the E and N. Sometimes this influence can be quite opinionated and stubborn. If they remain patient and stay on target with their goals, they could achieve greatness.

Whitney Houston is an American pop and R&B singer, actress, film producer, record producer, songwriter, and former fashion model. Whitney is "The Most Awarded Female Artist of All Time" according to the Guinness Book of World Records. She loves meeting new people, as her W first letter indicates. The W, N, and E give her an intensity 5, which means that overindulgence could be her worst enemy. With a 5 power number, she really needs to put the reins on herself at times. Change happens to people with that much 5 in their name. The H makes her a survivor. She is strong and capable of anything she puts her mind to. Also, she is blessed with an I first vowel. Then there's a very dynamic, yet vulnerable, T in the middle of her name. Deep down inside she craves partnership, but it's an "all or nothing" letter. The Y makes her need a lot of freedom.

The negative side of the W is a tendency to cut corners or procrastinate. Some names with a W can be superficial. However, the average W person is a social delight, extremely bright, loves meeting new people, and is highly adaptable to change.

If a name begins with WA, the person will be very intelligent, opinionated, stubborn, and critical of themselves and others. Also, he or she will excel at managing, owning, and operating a business. If his or her name begins with WE, that person will be intelligent, look and smell good, and will be adventuresome and freedom-oriented, but might need to be careful of overindulgence. If the person's name begins with WI, he or she will be a humanitarian, as well as artistic and blessed in some ways, but they may need to let go of the past. If his or her name begins with WO, that person will be self-sacrificing and responsible. He or she would make an excellent counselor. If a name begins with WU, that person will be more charming and social, and will possess great communication skills.

This letter likes freedom. Similar to E and N, W types are romantic and love adventure.

Winona Ryder, the actress who starred in the movies *Mr. Deeds*, *Beetle Juice*, *Dracula*, and *Edward Scissorhands*, easily adapts to each different role. The W and two Ns give her an intensity 5. This influence is in part responsible for the diversity in her roles. She can't be stereotyped with all that 5 influence. Intensity 5 names are very romantic and love adventure and excitement. Also, just as their 5-ruled siblings, E and N, W types must guard against overindulgence. 5 is the intensity number that enjoys surprising or even shocking others. Winona likes to meet new people, as indicated by the W in the front of her name. With an I first vowel, others tend to follow her whether she's right or wrong. And similar to I first vowel Tina Turner, she won't be truly happy unless she forgives those in her past who have hurt her. She has a 4 power number; this number doesn't want to look like a fool, so no doubt she studies hard before she agrees to accept a role. With an O in her name, she may desire children someday. However, with all that freedom-loving 5, parenthood may take some adjustment at first. If Winona does have children, she will be good at teaching them due to her 4 power number.

Back in 1879, Wyatt Earp was best known for his role in the famous gunfight at the O.K. Corral in Tombstone, Arizona. He was a peace officer who grew up in the American West. Interestingly enough, his name adds up to an 8 power number, and the letters O and K also add up to an 8. As history tells us, three of Clanton's men were shot to death while Doc Holliday and Wyatt were trying to make an arrest. Ike Clanton and Billy Claiborne ran away from the fight, unharmed. Both McLaurys and Billy Clanton were killed. They were viewed by Wyatt and Doc as cattle rustlers, thieves, and murderers. The number 8 is the number for death. Even though Wyatt liked meeting new people, with a Y as his first vowel, if he didn't like someone, they knew it. Y is the truth seeker and it can't feign liking someone. The 8 power number enjoys rivalry and competition, and also rules death. Wyatt seemed to fit perfectly in his historical role at the O.K. Corral.

Another interesting W person is the late Walt Disney. His name adds up to a master number 11. Those with 11 power numbers have a strong desire to achieve something worthwhile. He liked meeting new people, with a W up front. He was critical of himself and others with an A first vowel. The L helped him to communicate well and the T gave him a very dynamic, social, busy lifestyle. What he achieved in the creation of Disneyland and cartoon characters like Mickey Mouse and Donald Duck lives on all over the world. The number 11 is the "lightning rod" of great ideas, as Walt demonstrated. It's been said Walt frequently asked people what they thought of a new idea; if he received an overwhelming "No," he would get started immediately on making it work. This is the reversal or topsy-turvy way of the W's thinking. Walt's name added up to the inspired lightning rod of power numbers. He truly was a genius.

Wayne Brady of *The Wayne Brady Show* also loves meeting new people. This famous person exemplifies the versatility of the letter W, as some say he is a master of comedy. He seems to be a genius in the area of "improv." He has a power number 5 and an intensity 5, so along with the others, he must be careful of overindulgence. All those 5s give him the ability to get out there and be onstage. He likes variety and most likely loves surprising or shocking others with so much 5 influence in his name. Humor without offense is his trademark in the world of comedy.

Austrian-born Wolfgang Puck, famous chef-restaurateur, began training at fourteen years of age. He developed his cooking skills at several three-star French restaurants. His creativity shows up in his name with the 6-ruled O and F and the 3-ruled L. Numbers 3, 6, and 9 are highly creative. These letters in the beginning of his name gave Wolfgang an early start in his career. The W and N give him the ability to be unusual; he likes change and variety. The end of his name, the two Gs, A, and N are all ruled by cerebral numbers. This man is extremely intelligent. His name adds up to a power number 4; he does his homework first before each presentation. Also 4 power numbers make excellent teachers. With the W in the beginning, he loves freedom and adventure, but he's smart about it.

Some other famous people whose names start with W are: Walter Matthau, Winston Churchill, Warren Beatty, Woody Allen, Will Ferrell, Walter Cronkite, Wayne Newton, Willie Mays, Wolfgang Amadeus Mozart, William Shakespeare, Will Smith, Walt Whitman, Whoopi Goldberg, W. C. Fields, Wilford Brimley, and Willie Nelson.

QUICK REFERENCE OF "W" NAMES

Wade, 6: Has charisma and charm. Pioneer and risk taker. Domestic, down-to-earth. A free spirit, very adaptable.

Wadell, 3: Expressive and outgoing. Aims to please. Reliable, responsible. A free spirit, very adaptable. Communicates skillfully. Frequent traveler.

Wadsworth, 5: Likes to meet new people. Bright, adventuresome. Domestic, responsible. Charming and devoted. Creative and determined. Natural counselor and healer. Gentle, kind, a hard worker. Dynamic, busy lifestyle. Great judge of character.

Wagner, 5: Likes to meet new people. Bright, adventuresome. Scientific and philosophical. Original and unconventional. Physical and passionate. Gentle, kind, a hard worker.

Wain, 20: Works well with others. Reads people easily. Blessed in some ways. Creative, opinionated.

Waine, 7: Strong sense of purpose. Not easily influenced. Blessed in some ways. Original and unconventional. A free spirit, very adaptable.

Waldemar, 5: Likes to meet new people. Bright, adventuresome. Great verbal skills. Reliable, responsible. A free spirit, very adaptable. Domestic, hardworking. Bold, courageous, a bit stubborn. Diligent, helpful.

Walden, 5: Likes to meet new people. Bright, adventuresome. Great verbal skills. Reliable, responsible. Physical and passionate. Original and unconventional.

Waldimar, 9: Enjoys helping others. Hardworking, sincere. Frequent traveler. Reliable, responsible. Blessed in some ways. Domestic, down-to-earth. Bold, courageous, a bit stubborn. Diligent, helpful.

Waldo, 10: Implements original ideas. Independent, critical of self and others. Communicates skillfully. Domestic, responsible. Natural counselor and healer.

Walker, 7: Strong sense of purpose. Not easily influenced. Communicates skillfully. Strong desire to succeed. A free spirit, very adaptable. Gentle, kind, a hard worker.

Wallace, 3: Expressive and outgoing. Aims to please. Strong verbal skills. Frequent traveler. Bold, courageous, a bit stubborn. Self-expressive, cheerful. A free spirit, very adaptable.

Wallie, 8: Highly creative, needs change. Resolute and purposeful. Great verbal skills. Frequent traveler. Blessed in some ways. Physical and passionate.

Wallis, 22: Involved in major activities. Ambitious leader, great vision. Communicates skillfully. Travels frequently. Blessed in some ways. Charming and devoted.

Wally, 10: Implements original ideas. Independent, critical of self and others. Strong verbal skills. Frequent traveler. Needs a lot of freedom.

Walsh, 9: Enjoys helping others. Hardworking, sincere. Great verbal skills. Charming and devoted. Great judge of character.

Walt, 11: Involved in major activities. Intuitive, perceptive. Communicates skillfully. Dynamic, busy lifestyle.

Walter, 7: Strong sense of purpose. Not easily influenced. Communicates skillfully. Dynamic, busy lifestyle. A free spirit, very adaptable. Gentle, kind, a hard worker.

Wanda, 7: Strong sense of purpose. Not easily influenced. Original and unconventional. Reliable, responsible. Bold, courageous, a bit stubborn.

Wanetta, 3: Expressive and outgoing. Aims to please. Romantic and creative. A free spirit, very adaptable. Dynamic, busy lifestyle. Sensitive and easily hurt. Bold, courageous, a bit stubborn.

Ward, 10: Implements original ideas. Independent, critical of self and others. Gentle, kind, a hard worker. Domestic, down-to-earth.

Warner, 7: Strong sense of purpose. Not easily influenced. Gentle, kind, a hard worker. Original and unconventional. Physical and passionate. Tendency to lose items.

Warren, 7: Strong sense of purpose. Not easily influenced. Gentle, kind, a hard worker. Tendency to lose items. Physical and passionate. Creative and opinionated.

Wasfi, 22: Involved in major activities. Ambitious leader, great vision. Charming and devoted. Self-sacrificing, loving. Blessed in some ways.

Wassef, 10: Implements original ideas. Independent, critical of self and others. Charming and devoted. Impulsive and extreme. Loves adventure and excitement. Self-sacrificing, loving.

Wauneta, 22: Involved in major activities. Ambitious leader, great vision. Attractive and charming. Original and creative. Physical and passionate. Dynamic, busy lifestyle. Bold, courageous, a bit stubborn.

Waverly, 7: Strong sense of purpose. Not easily influenced. Intuitive and inspired. A free spirit, very adaptable. Gentle, kind, a hard worker. Strong verbal skills. Dislikes limitations.

Wayland, 3: Expressive and outgoing. Aims to please. Needs a lot of freedom. Communicates skillfully. Bold, courageous, a bit stubborn. Creative and opinionated. Domestic, responsible.

Wayne, 5: Likes to meet new people. Bright, adventuresome. Needs a lot of freedom. Creative and opinionated. Physical and passionate.

Webster, 11: Involved in major activities. Keenly perceptive. Friendly, but shy. Charming and devoted. Dynamic, busy lifestyle. Loves adventure and excitement. Gentle, kind, a hard worker.

Wendel, 9: Enjoys helping others. Generous humanitarian. Original and unconventional. Systematic, organized. Physical and passionate. Great verbal skills.

Wendell, 30: Expressive and outgoing. A free spirit, very adaptable. Romantic, sensual. Reliable, responsible. Tendency to overindulge. Great verbal skills. Frequent traveler.

Wendy, 8: Highly creative, needs change. Relies on own judgment. Original and romantic. Domestic, responsible. Dislikes limitations.

Wenona, 9: Enjoys helping others. Generous humanitarian. Original and unconventional. Natural counselor and healer. Romantic, sensual. Independent, self-motivated.

Wenonah, 8: Highly creative, needs change. Relies on own judgment. Original and unconventional. Natural counselor and healer. Romantic, sensual. Resolute and purposeful. Great judge of character.

Wenses, 22: Involved in major activities. Has big plans and ideas. Original and unconventional. Charming and devoted. Physical and passionate. Impulsive and extreme.

Werner, 11: Involved in major activities. Keenly perceptive. Gentle, kind, a hard worker. Romantic and sensual. Loves adventure and excitement. Tendency to lose items.

Wes, 11: Involved in major activities. Keenly perceptive. A charismatic person.

Wescott, 6: Has charisma and charm. A step ahead of others. Charming and devoted. Self-expressive, cheerful. Natural counselor and healer. Dynamic, busy lifestyle. Sensitive and easily hurt.

Wesley, 8: Highly creative, needs change. Relies on own judgment. Passionate and loving. Frequent traveler. Loves adventure and excitement. Dislikes limitations.

Wesly, 3: Expressive and outgoing. A free spirit, very adaptable. Charming and devoted. Communicates skillfully. Dislikes limitations.

Weston, 6: Has charisma. A step ahead of others. Charming and devoted. Dynamic, busy lifestyle. Natural counselor and healer. Original and unconventional.

Wheaton, 11: Involved in major activities. Great judge of character. Keenly perceptive. Independent, self-motivated. Dynamic, busy lifestyle. Natural counselor and healer. Original and unconventional.

Whitley, 3: Expressive and outgoing. Great judge of character. Blessed in some ways. Dynamic, busy lifestyle. Communicates skillfully. A free spirit, very adaptable. Dislikes limitations.

Whitney, 5: Likes to meet new people. Relies on own judgment. Blessed in some ways. Dynamic, busy lifestyle. Original and unconventional. A free spirit, very adaptable. Dislikes limitations.

Wilbur, 4: Able to teach. Blessed in some ways. Strong verbal skills. Friendly, but shy. Attractive and charming. Gentle, kind, a hard worker.

Wilda, 22: Involved in major activities. Idealistic, humanitarian. Great verbal skills. Domestic, down-to-earth. Ambitious leader, great vision.

Wiley, 11: Involved in major activities. Blessed in some ways. Strong verbal skills. Physical and passionate. Needs a lot of freedom.

Wilford, 6: Has charisma and charm. Artistic, having good taste. Communicates skillfully. Self-sacrificing, loving. Natural counselor and healer. Gentle, kind, a hard worker. Systematic, organized.

Wilfred, 5: Likes to meet new people. Generous, thoughtful. Strong verbal skills. Self-sacrificing, devoted. Gentle, kind, a hard worker. A free spirit, very adaptable. Reliable, responsible.

Wilfreda, 6: Has charisma and charm. Artistic, having good taste. Communicates skillfully. Self-sacrificing, loving. Gentle, kind, a hard worker. A free spirit, very adaptable. Reliable, responsible. Pioneer, risk taker.

Wilhelmina, 7: Strong sense of purpose. Blessed in some ways. Strong verbal skills. Great judge of character. A free spirit, very adaptable. Frequent traveler. Domestic, hard worker. Artistic, having good taste. Original and unconventional. Not easily influenced.

Will, 20: Works well with others. Blessed in some ways. Strong verbal skills. Frequent traveler.

Willa, 3: Expressive and outgoing. Considerate, understanding. Communicates skillfully. Ups and downs financially. Pioneer and risk taker.

Willette, 7: Strong sense of purpose. Needs alone time. Great verbal skills. Frequent traveler. A free spirit, very adaptable. Dynamic, busy lifestyle. Sensitive and easily hurt. Physical and passionate.

William, 7: Strong sense of purpose. Needs alone time. Great verbal skills. Frequent traveler. Artistic, having good taste. Not easily influenced. Domestic, hardworking.

Willie, 7: Strong sense of purpose. Needs alone time. Great verbal skills. Frequent traveler. Artistic, having good taste. A free spirit, very adaptable.

Willis, 30: Expressive and outgoing. Considerate, understanding. Strong verbal skills. Ups and downs financially. Artistic, having good taste. Charming and devoted.

Willow, 4: Able to teach. Blessed in some ways. Communicates skillfully. Ups and downs financially. Natural counselor and healer. Can be superficial.

Willy, 9: Enjoys helping others. Blessed in some ways. Strong verbal skills. Frequent traveler. Needs a lot of freedom.

Wilma, 22: Involved in major activities. Idealistic, humanitarian. Communicates skillfully. Domestic, hardworking. Independent, self-motivated.

Wilona, 11: Involved in major activities. Blessed in some ways. Strong verbal skills. Natural counselor and healer. Original and unconventional. Intuitive, perceptive.

Wilson, 11: Involved in major activities. Blessed in some ways. Strong verbal skills. Charming and devoted. Natural counselor and healer. Original and unconventional.

Win, 10: Implements original ideas. Respectful, kind. Creative and opinionated.

Windy, 30: Expressive and outgoing. Considerate, understanding. Romantic, original. Reliable, responsible. Needs a lot of freedom.

Winfield, 10: Implements original ideas. Respectful, kind. Original and unconventional. Self-sacrificing, loving. Artistic, having good taste. A free spirit, very adaptable. Strong verbal skills. Reliable, responsible.

Winfred, 7: Strong sense of purpose. Needs alone time. Creative, opinionated. Self-sacrificing, loving. Gentle, kind, a hard worker. Physical and passionate. Reliable, responsible.

Wingate, 7: Strong sense of purpose. Needs alone time. Original and unconventional. Scientific and philosophical. Not easily influenced. Dynamic, busy lifestyle. A free spirit, very adaptable.

Winifred, 7: Strong sense of purpose. Needs alone time. Creative, opinionated. Artistic, having good taste. Self-sacrificing, loving. Gentle, kind, a hard worker. Physical and passionate. Reliable, responsible.

Winnie, 11: Involved in major activities. Blessed in some ways. Original and unconventional. Romantic, sensual. Artistic, having good taste. A free spirit, very adaptable.

Winny, 4: Able to teach. Blessed in some ways. Creative, original. Romantic, sensual. Needs a lot of freedom.

Winona, 4: Able to teach. Blessed in some ways. Original and unconventional. Natural counselor and healer. Romantic, sensual. Independent, critical of self and others.

Winslow, 7: Strong sense of purpose. Needs alone time. Original and unconventional. Charming and devoted. Strong verbal skills. Natural counselor and healer. Can be superficial.

Winston, 6: Has charisma. Artistic, having good taste. Creative, opinionated. Charming and devoted. Dynamic, busy lifestyle. Natural counselor and healer. Romantic, sensual.

Winthrop, 6: Has charisma and charm. Artistic, having good taste. Creative, opinionated. Dynamic, busy lifestyle. Great judge of character. Gentle, kind, a hard worker. Natural counselor and healer. Intelligent, levelheaded.

Winton, 5: Likes to meet new people. Generous, thoughtful. Original and unconventional. Dynamic, busy lifestyle. Natural counselor and healer. Romantic, sensual.

Wladimir, 8: Highly creative, needs change. Communicates skillfully. Resolute and purposeful. Reliable, responsible. Blessed in some ways. Systematic, organized. Artistic, having good taste. Gentle, kind, a hard worker.

Wolf, 20: Works well with others. Natural counselor and healer. Strong verbal skills. Self-sacrificing, loving.

Wolfe, 7: Strong sense of purpose. Open to opportunities. Strong verbal skills. Self-sacrificing, loving. A free spirit, very adaptable.

Wolfgang, 4: Able to teach. Assumes responsibility. Great verbal skills. Self-sacrificing, loving. Scientific and philosophical. Resolute and purposeful. Original and unconventional. Extremely intelligent.

Wood, 3: Expressive and outgoing. Nurturing, loving. Natural counselor and healer. Reliable, responsible.

Woodie, 8: Highly creative, needs change. Competitive in business. Nurturing, loving. Reliable, responsible. Blessed in some ways. A free spirit, very adaptable.

Woodrow, 5: Likes to meet new people. Enjoys working. Natural counselor and healer. Domestic, responsible. Gentle, kind, diligent. Very magnetic. Creative and determined.

Woods, 22: Involved in major activities. Creates group harmony. Natural counselor and healer. Down-to-earth, practical. Charming and devoted.

Woody, 10: Implements original ideas. Self-sacrificing, devoted. Nurturing, loving. Reliable, responsible. Needs a lot of freedom.

Wyatt, 8: Highly creative, needs change. Strong intuition, perceptive. Resolute and purposeful. Dynamic, busy lifestyle. Sensitive and easily hurt.

Wylie, 11: Involved in major activities. Dislikes limitations. Strong verbal skills. Blessed in some ways. A free spirit, very adaptable.

Wyllie, 5: Likes to meet new people. Dislikes limitations. Communicates skillfully. Ups and downs financially. Blessed in some ways. A free spirit, very adaptable.

Wyne, 22: Involved in major activities. Finds shortcuts. Romantic, sensual. A free spirit, very adaptable.

Wynn, 22: Involved in major activities. Finds shortcuts. Original, opinionated. Romantic, sensual.

Wynne, 9: Enjoys helping others. Keeps intelligent company. Opinionated, creative. Romantic, sensual. A free spirit, very adaptable.

Wynona, I I: Involved in major activities. Needs a lot of freedom. Original and unconventional. Natural counselor and healer. Romantic, sensual. Intuitive, perceptive.

Wyome, 9: Enjoys helping others. Highly creative. Natural counselor and healer. Domestic, hardworking. A free spirit, very adaptable.

Wyomia, 5: Likes to meet new people. Needs a lot of freedom. Natural counselor and healer. Domestic, hardworking. Blessed in some ways. Independent, critical of self and others.

$$\mathcal{X}$$

If a name begins with X, has more than one X, or ends with an X, this person is very artistic, sensual, responsive, and perceptive. This is a more highly evolved 6-ruled letter of love with more mature lessons involved than the other 6-ruled letters.

The letter X is the 24th letter of the alphabet. Since $2 + 4 = 6$, the person with an X in his or her name will experience partnership, work, and family, which sum up to love. The X sounds ideal and complete; however, they can also be as temperamental as the other 6-ruled letters. Furthermore, the X seems to have an addictive personality, as it is a more highly-evolved magnetic letter.

X names are influenced by the number 6 vibration, so they need to love and nurture someone. Similar to their F and O siblings, they have a natural gift with gardens, flowers, pets, and children. Also they seem to have natural parenting skills and are among the most responsible of letters.

Although X people seem blessed with an abundance of artistic talent and creativity, they must guard against the temptation to acquire beautiful objects by morally improper means. Their other downfall is that they can be meddlesome, thinking they must have their own way in a disagreement. Similar to letters F and O, they can be jealous, moody, temperamental, and too bossy, especially if they have an O elsewhere in their first name or a 6 power number. This being the case, they will be highly magnetic.

Also similar to the O vibration, X seems to have musical abilities. When learning the alphabet, most of us learned the word "xylophone," which is a musical instrument, as our first X word. Xylophones come in all shapes and sizes and colors. So do our X-named friends, who are both rare and extraordinaire! If they are able to spend time cultivating their abilities, they can be quite extraordinary. Unfortunately, because they are so duty-bound, as the 6 vibration of love requires, they often put their musical talents aside to take care of loved ones. This letter is service-oriented and often will work late hours to ensure there is food on the table.

People who were taught good moral values, who also bear an X in their name, will manage to uphold their ideals in marriage, work, and family. They are natural parents and employers. People tend to rely on them as they are most responsible and trustworthy. Similar to the O, there can be religious leanings. The typical X has a high regard for honesty and justice. It's a warm and colorful letter, exploding with the emotion of love!

Xavier Cugat, a conductor remembered for his highly-commercial approach to pop music, is a perfect example of an X type personality. He made his mark as one of the pioneers of Latin American dance music. During his eight-decade career, Xavier helped popularize the tango, cha-cha, mambo, and rumba. Despite being criticized for his middle-of-the-road approach, Xavier remained committed to his commercialized sound. He later explained, "I would rather play 'Chiquita Banana' and have my swimming pool than play Bach and starve." This is the duty-bound part of the X. He did what it took to take care of his loved ones. On the surface, this letter seems exotic, but in reality, it's quite practical and businesslike. X is also all about love, as it is ruled by the 6 vibration, which rules love. Even the word "sex," which has an X in it, is also referred to as "making love." Xavier's fourth wife was beautiful Latin entertainer, Charo, who still appears on many talk shows. Xavier was known to have beautiful women consistently featured in his band.

The word "sex" is magnetic because of its X. It has been said time and again, "Sex sells." This 6-ruled letter of love means business. It's one of the business-type letters and seems to do well in the area of service. People are magnetically drawn to this letter, so it's not a bad idea to use it in advertising. Dos Equis, the brand of beer whose name translates as "two Xs," understands the advertising power of sex when they use beautiful, sexy women in their commercials. It draws attention and people remember the message.

Although she's not real, Xena, Warrior Princess, wears her X up front. This character is sexy, magnetic, and strong. Her name adds up to an 8 power number giving her name Herculean strength. The intensity 5 in her name makes her a bit unique and unusual. With all that 5 and 8 energy, coupled with the magnetic X first letter, one cannot help but associate her with sex appeal. She's a free spirit and loves variety and change. The A at the end of her name makes her independent, bold, and courageous. Xena is a perfectionist with a bully in her head always pushing her to be the best she can be. She can be critical of herself with an A at the end of her name, and doesn't seem to realize how capable she really is—another quality of the A in her name.

The pop music performer, Sting, wrote the song "Roxanne" while still with the band The Police. This song is really all about a woman who exhibits the negative side of the X in her name. She is a "lady of the night" or, in other words, a prostitute. Often the X will lead to sexual overindulgences. As the song goes, "Roxanne, you don't have to put on the red light, you don't have to sell your body to the night." Sometimes the X seems to have no morals. This woman, Roxanne, must not have been taught good moral values, or else she wouldn't have behaved this way. This is the down side of the X—"not caring if it's wrong or right." She had an intensity 6 in her name with an O first vowel. R first names are quite bold and sometimes intimidating. All those 5-ruled letters at the end of her name also give way to an overindulgence in sex. So, Sting really had the right name for a song like this.

Famous names that begin with X are: Xavier Cugat, Xuxa (a Brazilian actress), and X. J. Kennedy (a writer and poet).

QUICK REFERENCE OF "X" NAMES

Xandra, 8: Perceptive and responsive. Resolute and purposeful. Original and unconventional. Reliable, responsible. Gentle, kind, a hard worker. Bold, courageous, a bit stubborn.

Xanthe, 9: Nurturing and giving. Helpful, sincere. Original and unconventional. Dynamic, busy lifestyle. Great judge of character. A free spirit, very adaptable.

Xarah, 7: Learns quickly and easily. Not easily influenced. Gentle, kind, a hard worker. Bold, courageous, a bit stubborn. Great judge of character.

Xasha, 8: Perceptive and responsive. Resolute and purposeful. Charming and devoted. Great judge of character. Bold, courageous, a bit stubborn.

Xavier, 7: Learns quickly and easily. Self-motivated and independent. Intuitive and inspired. Blessed in some ways. A free spirit, very adaptable. Gentle, kind, a hard worker.

Xaviera, 8: Perceptive and responsive. Resolute and purposeful. Intuitive and inspired. Blessed in some ways. A free spirit, very adaptable. Gentle, kind, a hard worker. Bold, courageous, a bit stubborn.

Xena, 8: Perceptive and responsive. Original and creative. Romantic and sensual. Bold, courageous, a bit stubborn.

Xenia, 8: Perceptive and responsive. Original and creative. Romantic and sensual. Blessed in some ways. Resolute and purposeful.

Xenias, 9: Nurturing and giving. Generous, thoughtful. Opinionated, creative. Artistic, having good taste. Helpful, sincere. Charming and devoted.

Xenon, 9: Nurturing and giving. Generous, thoughtful. Original and unconventional. Natural counselor and healer. Creative, opinionated.

Xenos, 5: Sensual and loves excitement. Perceptive, socially adept. Original and unconventional. Natural counselor and healer. Charming and devoted.

Xerxes, 5: Sensual and loves excitement. Perceptive, socially adept. Gentle, kind, a hard worker. Prone to sexual indulgences. Loves adventure and excitement. Charming and devoted.

Xiao, 22: Highly creative and ambitious. Blessed in some ways. Great leadership skills. Magnetic personality.

Xiaomin, 4: Domestic, responsible. Blessed in some ways. Intelligent leader. Natural counselor and healer. Systematic, organized. Artistic, having good taste. Original, opinionated.

Xiaoping, 5: Sensual and loves excitement. Blessed in some ways. Self-motivated and independent. Natural counselor and healer. Intelligent and knowledgeable. Artistic, having good taste. Romantic, physical. Stylish and refined.

Xina, 3: Has an addictive personality. Blessed in some ways. Original and unconventional. Independent, critical of self and others.

Xing, 9: Nurturing and giving. Artistic, having good taste. Original and opinionated. Stylish and refined.

Xiomara, 9: Nurturing and giving. Artistic, having good taste. Natural counselor and healer. Systematic, organized. Independent, critical of self and others. Gentle, kind, a hard worker. Pioneer and risk taker.

Xochitl, 10: Artistic, sensual, perceptive. Self-sacrificing, devoted. Optimistic, outspoken. Great judge of character. Blessed in some ways. Dynamic, busy lifestyle. Communicates skillfully.

Xu, 9: Nurturing and giving. Attractive and charming. Easygoing.

Xuyen, 8: Perceptive and responsive. Attractive and charming. Dislikes limitations. Original and creative. Romantic, sensual.

Xylia, 8: Perceptive and responsive. Needs a lot of freedom. Communicates skillfully. Blessed in some ways. Resolute and purposeful.

Xylon, 9: Nurturing and giving. Needs a lot of freedom. Slow to make decisions. Natural counselor and healer. Romantic, original.

Y

If a name begins with Y, has Y as the first vowel, has more than one Y, or ends with a Y, this person is honest, loves freedom, is a truth seeker, and may be psychic or have excellent intuition.

The letter Y is the 25th letter of the alphabet. Since $2 + 5 = 7$, the person with a Y influence will experience partnership and change. This person will need to have faith in order to be happy. They will be partnership-oriented, but with the 5 and 7, they need a certain amount of freedom. Also, the 7 brings solitude and lessons in faith. The Y individual usually desires partnership, but may want to sleep in separate beds. In some cases, he or she may even want to live in separate houses!

Y names are strongly influenced by the number 7 vibration. Similar to letters G and P they can be very Pisces or Neptune-like. They'll tend to be secretive, photogenic, philosophical, or spiritual, needing solitude or more sleep than most. Some people with Y in their names give in to complaining or whining over nothing. Y is the whiner of letters. Drug or alcohol addiction is a possibility with this letter, as with the letters G and P. This letter likes to escape reality more often than most.

If a Y is anywhere in a person's name, that person will need to demonstrate his or her faith more than other names. In other words, their faith will be tested more than names without it. Time for reflection, meditation, and solitude will be needed. The 7 vibration casts off a spiritual, dream-like connotation. The bearer of a name with Y in it must strive to be realistic as much as possible.

People with Ys in their name are truth seekers. They're philosophical and scientific. These people will spend much of their time searching for answers to the questions their fine minds have. This is why so many of them make great scientists, researchers, educators, and philosophers. On the same note, they can be quite put out if they discover someone has been lying to them. We do not want to get on this letter's bad side. They cannot pretend to like someone they do not like. It's a truthful letter and to pretend is to be dishonest. If this person doesn't like you, you know it. The Y person will close their steel-trap mind and those he or she does not approve of will not gain entry. This letter does not feel the pressure to be socially graceful.

The shape of the letter Y almost resembles a pitch fork without the middle prong. Interesting that it's so similar to King Triton's weapon of choice, the trident. As King Triton rules the oceans and tides with trident in hand, our Neptunian friends rule their own lives, so don't try to tell them what to do. This letter needs a lot of freedom and dislikes restrictions. They can be fiercely independent and are the heartbreaker of letters. The Y-named can move far away from home, disappointing family and friends. Just as water runs through our fingers, we cannot hold onto a Y-named person. They ride their own wave to wherever it leads them.

This letter in a name can also deceive or confuse others. A woman with this letter seems to be the damsel in distress, sometimes not even able to open her own jar of pickles. She'll let you help her, but remember, she's not completely helpless. If you smother her too much she'll pull the disappearing act. All of a sudden she'll find a new job or have some reason to not be around anymore. Although the truth is important to her, she's good at circumventing it if in danger of losing her freedom. Actually, her freedom is pretty innocent. As mentioned before, she is into the truth. So allowing her to be free is a good thing. This also holds true for men with a Y in their name.

Y-named people of both sexes are extremely intelligent and often have strong convictions. This is also one of the more masculine, or positive letters. It's most compatible with those having odd-numbered ruling letters in their name. Vowels such as A and E and letters ruled by 1 and 5 tend to get along with this letter quite well, mostly because of the intelligence factor. Our Neptunian friends are similar to the dolphin that swims in our oceans. They are extremely intelligent, and seem friendly, but dolphins can kill sharks. Just remember to watch out!

Y names are dreamy yet realistic. They are spiritual yet scientific, a paradox that can only work for this rare first name letter. Maybe that's why it's mostly found at the end of a name, just as it's at the end of the alphabet. It's a dreamy, intelligent letter fit for the dreamy intelligent people of this planet.

Some with a Y in their name have a difficult time making up their mind. They tend to vacillate, perhaps because Y is generally considered both a vowel and a consonant. Y is one of the few letters that can be used both ways. Even the shape of this letter splits off in two directions. A person with this letter in their name may go back and forth while trying to make a decision as they look at both sides.

This letter is ruled by the number 7 which usually looks pretty good on camera. Although most of them enjoy moments of solitude, given the opportunity, some can grace the cover of magazines and even go on to television and movies. Still, they could pull the disappearing act if not allowed privacy.

Similar to the letters G and P, Y can have quite an ego. Y is a very spiritual letter, and needs to recognize God or some other spiritual force as a superior being, greater than themselves. If not, they'll wear everyone out with constant bragging and boasting. The Y person is much more pleasant to be around when his or her ego is intact. The average person with Y in his or her name is happier when attending regular religious services or doing prayer work routinely. It's a letter here to learn about faith in God. People with a Y in the beginning, end, or as a first vowel in their name won't truly be happy unless they have faith. Having faith is one of their major lessons in this lifetime.

On April 12, 1961, Russian astronaut Yuri Gagarin made history by being the first human to orbit the earth. At about 10:15 a.m., just after Gagarin began to pass over Africa, the autopilot turned around his spacecraft, Vostok I, and fired the retrorocket, which would take Vostok I out of orbit. This was a very suspenseful time for Yuri Gagarin and mission control. Luckily the retrorocket worked correctly and Vostok I came out of orbit. Those with a U first vowel are often very lucky. Yuri's power number added up to a 10. With the beginning plus assistance from God power number and the luck of his U, Yuri made history that day. Yuri's capstone letter, an I, also blessed him. But it was his Y that got him into the space program initially, as Y types are scientific and have a strong desire to find the answers to questions their fine minds have. Yuri was described by his teachers in Moscow as intelligent and hardworking. Y-named people are extremely intelligent, and Rs work very hard. Yuri lived on the positive side of his name.

Yehudi Menuhin, the American violinist and conductor, had one of the longest and most distinguished careers of any violinist of the twentieth century. Yehudi was born in New York of Russian-Jewish parents who were recent immigrants to America. By the age of seven his performance of Mendelssohn's *Violin Concerto* found him instant fame. As a teenager he toured throughout the world and was considered one of the greats long before his twentieth birthday. Yehudi's first two letters indicate intelligence. Moreover, he had an H, which is competitive and the survivor of letters. His U made him easy to get along with. The D gave him determination. Yehudi's I blessed him; it gave him an appreciation for art. His power number 9, plus his capstone letter I, helped him overcome one of the biggest forgiveness issues of his time. During World War II he performed for inmates of Bergen-Belsen concentration camp after its liberation in April 1945. Then he returned to Germany in 1947 as an act of reconciliation, becoming the first Jewish musician to return to Germany following the Holocaust. Y-named people can be very spiritual. Yehudi's Y, coupled with the world-wise 9 energy in his name, made him truly remarkable.

Other famous Y names are: Yo-Yo Ma, Yanni, Yogi Berra, Yoko Ono, Yves Saint-Laurent, Yvonne Zima, Yao Ming, Yasmine Bleeth, Yul Brynner, Yves Montand, Yasser Arafat, Yakov Smirnoff, and Yvonne De Carlo.

QUICK REFERENCE OF "Y" NAMES

Yale, 7: Refined and stylish. Not easily influenced. Strong verbal skills. Loves adventure and excitement.

Yancy, 5: Keeps intelligent company. Bright, adventuresome. Original and unconventional. Self-expressive, cheerful. Highly perceptive.

Yao, 5: Keeps intelligent company. Bright, adventuresome. Creative, nurturing, and loving.

Yardley, 9: Tremendously talented. Helpful, sincere. Gentle, kind, a hard worker. Reliable, responsible. Strong verbal skills. Likes change and variety. Needs a lot of freedom.

Yasmeena, 11: Strong quest for truth and knowledge. Intuitive, perceptive. Charming and devoted. Domestic, hardworking. Loves adventure and excitement. Tendency to overindulge. Original and unconventional. Independent, critical of self and others.

Yasmin, 9: Tremendously talented. Helpful, sincere. Charming and devoted. Domestic, hardworking. Blessed in some ways. Original and unconventional.

Yasmina, 10: Intelligent, a wise leader. Independent, critical of self and others. Charming and devoted. Domestic, hardworking. Blessed in some ways. Original and unconventional. Bold, courageous, a bit stubborn.

Yasmine, 5: Keeps intelligent company. Bright, adventuresome. Charming and devoted. Domestic, hardworking. Blessed in some ways. Original and unconventional. Loves adventure and excitement.

Yates, 7: Refined and stylish. Not easily influenced. Dynamic, busy lifestyle. Loves adventure and excitement. Charming and devoted.

Ychoaya, 6: Ambitious, responsible. Self-expressive, cheerful. Great judge of character. Natural counselor and healer. Independent, critical of self and others. Needs a lot of freedom. Pioneer and risk taker.

Yedda, 3: Slow to make decisions. A free spirit, very adaptable. Reliable, responsible. Down:to:earth, faithful. Independent, critical of self and others.

Yehuda, 10: Intelligent, a wise leader. Likes change and variety. Great judge of character. Attractive and charming. Reliable, responsible. Independent, critical of self and others.

Yehudah, 9: Tremendously talented. Enjoys giving gifts. Great judge of character. Attractive and charming. Reliable, responsible. Independent, critical of self and others. Many financial ups and downs.

Yehudi, 9: Tremendously talented. Enjoys giving gifts. Great judge of character. Attractive and charming. Reliable, responsible. Blessed in some ways.

Yelena, 8: Strong intuition, just knows things. Original, creative, and unconventional. Strong verbal skills. Tendency to overindulge. Independent, critical of self and others.

Yeoman, 10: Intelligent, a wise leader. Likes change and variety. Natural counselor and healer. Domestic, hardworking. Independent, critical of self and others. Original and unconventional.

Yesenia, 6: Ambitious, responsible. A step ahead of others. Charming and devoted. Tendency to overindulge. Original and unconventional. Blessed in some ways. Independent, critical of self and others.

Yetta, 8: Strong intuition, just knows things. Original and creative. Dynamic, busy lifestyle. Sensitive and easily hurt. Independent, critical of self and others.

Yoanna, 7: Refined and stylish. Open to opportunities. Independent, critical of self and others. Original and unconventional. Romantic, sensual. Bold, courageous, a bit stubborn.

Yogi, 11: Strong quest for truth and knowledge. Creates group harmony. Scientific and philosophical. Blessed in some ways.

Yohei, 8: Strong intuition, just knows things. Competitive in business. Self-reliant, successful. Physical and passionate. Artistic, having good taste.

Yokio, 30: Slow to make decisions. Nurturing, loving. Strong desire to succeed. Blessed in some ways. May have musical abilities.

Yoko, 3: Slow to make decisions. Nurturing, loving. Strong desire to succeed. May have musical abilities.

Yolanda, 9: Tremendously talented. Artistic, creative. Strong verbal skills. Independent, critical of self and others. Original and unconventional. Reliable, responsible. Bold, courageous, a bit stubborn.

Yolande, 4: Finds shortcuts. Assumes responsibility. Strong verbal skills. Independent, critical of self and others. Original and unconventional. Reliable, diligent. Loves adventure and excitement.

Yolie, 30: Slow to make decisions. Nurturing, loving. Strong verbal skills. Blessed in some ways. Loves adventure and excitement.

York, 6: Ambitious, responsible. Magnetic personality. Gentle, kind, a hard worker. Strong desire to succeed.

Yorke, 11: Strong quest for truth and knowledge. Creates group harmony. Gentle, kind, a hard worker. Strong desire to succeed. Loves adventure and excitement.

Yosef, 7: Refined and stylish. Open to opportunities. Charming and devoted. Loves adventure and excitement. Self-sacrificing, loving.

Yoshi, 4: Finds shortcuts. Assumes responsibility. Charming and devoted. Great judge of character. Blessed in some ways.

Yoshino, 6: Ambitious, responsible. Magnetic personality. Charming and devoted. Great judge of character. Blessed in some ways. Original and unconventional. May have musical abilities.

Yosi, 5: Keeps intelligent company. Enjoys working. Charming and devoted. Blessed in some ways.

Young:hee, 7: Refined and stylish. Open to opportunities. Attractive and charming. Original and unconventional. Scientific and philosophical. Great judge of character. Loves adventure and excitement. Tendency to overindulge.

Young:ho, 6: Ambitious, responsible. Magnetic personality. Attractive and charming. Original and unconventional. Scientific and philosophical. Great judge of character. May have musical abilities.

Young:wook, 11: Strong quest for truth and knowledge. Creates group harmony. Attractive and charming. Original and unconventional. Scientific and philosophical. Likes to meet new people. Good parental skills. May have musical abilities. Strong desire to succeed.

Yovel, 7: Refined and stylish. Open to opportunities. Intuitive and inspired. A free spirit, very adaptable. Strong verbal skills.

Ynez, 7: Refined and stylish. Original and unconventional. Physical and passionate. Uses common sense.

Yuki, 3: Slow to make decisions. Attractive and charming. Strong desire to succeed. Blessed in some ways.

Yukiko, 11: Strong quest for truth and knowledge. Attractive and charming. Strong desire to succeed. Blessed in some ways. A bit forceful at times. Natural counselor and healer.

Yul, 4: Finds shortcuts. Slow to make decisions. Communicates skillfully.

Yule, 9: Tremendously talented. Attractive and charming. Strong verbal skills. Loves adventure and excitement.

Yuri, 10: Intelligent, a wise leader. Attractive and charming. Gentle, kind, a hard worker. Blessed in some ways.

Yuriko, 9: Tremendously talented. Attractive and charming. Gentle, kind, a hard worker. Blessed in some ways. Strong desire to succeed. Natural counselor and healer.

Yves, 8: Strong intuition, just knows things. Intuitive and inspired. Loves adventure and excitement. Charming and devoted.

Yvet, 9: Tremendously talented. Intuitive and inspired. Loves adventure and excitement. Dynamic, busy lifestyle.

Yvette, 7: Refined and stylish. Intuitive and inspired. Loves adventure and excitement. Dynamic, busy lifestyle. Sensitive and easily hurt. Tendency to overindulge.

Yvon, 22: Strong quest for truth and knowledge. Intuitive and inspired. Natural counselor and healer. Original and unconventional.

Yvonne, 5: Keeps intelligent company. Intuitive and inspired. Natural counselor and healer. Original and opinionated. Romantic, sensual. Loves adventure and excitement.

I f a name begins with Z, has more than one Z, or ends with a Z, this person has high expectations, looks at the bright side of life, and has good physical and mental reflexes. This is a more highly-evolved 8 vibrational letter.

The letter Z is the 26th letter of the alphabet. Since $2 + 6 = 8$, the person with a Z influence will experience partnership, love, and rewards. They will be partnership-oriented, responsible toward loved ones, and a master over material goods. This letter is somewhat business-like. Similar to the signs Capricorn and Scorpio, the Z personality will reach whatever goals they set. They will move slowly and stubbornly toward their desired destination, regardless of obstacles.

Z names are influenced by the number 8 vibration which also rules Scorpio. Somehow the bearer of the Z will receive rewards of past actions from this or another lifetime. Z is karmically charged and very powerful, similar to H and Q. If their power is misused, it can boomerang back disastrously. If used for selfish reasons, the karmic 8 vibration can quickly result in a negative consequence.

The sharpness of the Z's mental abilities can be attributed to Z being more highly-evolved than its other 8-ruled siblings, H and Q. Those with a Z anywhere in their name have a natural ability to mediate. They are a plus in an emergency that requires a quick response. Higher-evolved Z names show compassion, common sense, and understanding. The lesser-evolved still have material lessons to learn and may have past karmic debts to resolve.

If the Z is accompanied by an A, they will be more independent, ambitious, and critical. If accompanied by an E, they will be physical and passionate and will be easily adaptable to change. If accompanied by an I, they will be more blessed, artistic, and humanitarian by nature. If accompanied by an O, they will be self-sacrificing, responsible, and service-oriented. If accompanied by a U, they will be more charming and attractive, but they'll have many financial ups and downs.

The Z names seem to have a deeper understanding of people, which is why they make such good mediators. This end of the rainbow letter just seems to know things. Z names have a habit of looking at the bright side of life. They have high expectations. Motivational speaker and writer Zig Zigler often says, "If you help enough people get what they want, eventually, you will get what you want." This kind of thinking is typical of a Z personality. This clearly demonstrates the law of give and take, or better still, give and you shall receive. Zig has a G in his name and so he is prone to thinking philosophically about life. The Z in his name makes him want material success, but the I and G make him a humanitarian with a philosophical approach. His name sums up to a power number 6. This number gives him magnetic appeal and an aptitude for business. People are drawn to him and he has a very large following of admirers. The power number 6 is love, which he gladly gives out for a fee; this is the material side of the Z. This side helps him with sales-training seminars which inspire, empower, and motivate. Zig is an example of a successful Z person.

Zorro, the Fox, was created in 1919 by the writer Johnston McCulley for his serialized novel, *The Curse of Capistrano*. Although he is a fictional character, Zorro's name fits him perfectly. Zorro is a romantic hero who fights against injustice in Spanish California's Pueblo de Los Angeles. In the story, Zorro wears a mask so no one will recognize him, for he is the son of a well-known diplomat. His father was forced to go back to Spain because of the corrupt government. He is a sort of Robin Hood who takes from the rich and gives to the poor. He leaves the famous sword mark of a Z slashed on the door of his victims. Z is ruled by the number 8 which is Scorpio-like. This type of influence is prone to encounters with death, joint finances, taxes, insurance, and goods of the dead, so Zorro is properly named to handle these matters in the story. He has an intensity 6 and 9 in his name. The 6 makes him magnetic and the 9 makes him a humanitarian, not necessarily concerned with material wealth. There is much energy to acquire material wealth with the

Z; however, Zorro's double Rs make him want to give the money back! Plus, the two love-ruled Os made for quite a romantic tale. Altogether his name adds up to a power number 11, which is a master number. Zorro desires success; even if he is a fictional character, his name gives a very accurate description of his personality.

Another famous person whose name begins with Z is Zora Neale Hurston. She was a novelist, folklorist, and anthropologist in the late 1920s. She was the prototypical authority on black culture from the Harlem Renaissance. She led the way for black writers. Her best novels investigated voodoo practices in black communities in Florida, New Orleans, and the Caribbean. Interestingly, the practice of voodoo would fall under the influence of Scorpio, which coincidently rules the letter Z of the 8 vibration. Zora was born on January 7th in 1891. January is ruled by the number 1—if we add her birthday of 7 that adds up to an 8 attitude number. Often the letters of our names resonate the numbers of our birthdays. At any rate, Zora wrote about occult practices little-known to the rest of America at that time. The cornerstone, or first letter of her name, shows bravery. The Z loves a challenge and will not back down from the fiercest opposition. The A at the end of her name makes her a pioneer and risk taker. A-named people are bold and courageous. The R in her name shows she was gentle, kind, and hardworking. Most importantly, she had an O first vowel ruled by the 6 vibration. She also had a 6 power number. Those with the 6 influence are creative and want to be their own boss. They are all about service and taking care of others. This combination made her very much a leader, a pioneer, and a strong person who could nurture and take care of others. Unfortunately, like so many ruled by the 8 vibration, she had financial ups and downs. Sadly, she died in poverty. Similar to letters H and Q, Z has material lessons to learn. The Z person must learn to manage material goods. It's a hard lesson.

Other famous Z names are: Ziggy Marley, Zero Mostel, Zsa Zsa Gabor, Zubin Mehta, Zane Grey, Zac Hanson, Ziyi Zhang, Zeppo Marx, Zachery Ty Bryan, ZZ Top, Zena Grey, and Zoe Saldana.

QUICK REFERENCE OF "Z" NAMES

Zac, 3: A tendency to see the bright side. Aims to please. Self-expressive, cheerful.

Zach, 20: Compassionate and kind. Reads people easily. Self-expressive, cheerful. Great judge of character.

Zachariah, 3: A tendency to see the bright side. Aims to please. Self-expressive, cheerful. Great judge of character. Bold, courageous, a bit stubborn. Gentle, kind, a hard worker. Blessed in some ways. Pioneer and risk taker. Self-reliant, successful.

Zacharias, 5: Has high expectations. Bright, adventuresome. Optimistic, outspoken. Great judge of character. Bold, courageous, a bit stubborn. Gentle, kind, a hard worker. Blessed in some ways. Pioneer and risk taker. Charming and devoted.

Zachary, 10: Has a good deal of common sense. Independent, critical of self and others. Self-expressive, cheerful. Great judge of character. Bold, courageous, a bit stubborn. Gentle, kind, a hard worker. Needs a lot of freedom.

Zachery, 5: Has high expectations. Bright, adventuresome. Optimistic, outspoken. Makes and loses money easily. Physical and passionate. Intense inner power. Needs a lot of freedom.

Zack, 5: Has high expectations. Bright, adventuresome. Optimistic, outspoken. Strong desire to succeed.

Zada, 5: Has high expectations. Bright, adventuresome. Reliable, responsible. Bold, courageous, a bit stubborn.

Zahara, 10: Has a good deal of common sense. Independent, critical of self and others. Great judge of character. Pioneer and risk taker. Gentle, kind, a hard worker. Bold, courageous, a bit stubborn.

Zaida, 5: Has high expectations. Bright, adventuresome. Blessed in some ways. Reliable, responsible. Bold, courageous, a bit stubborn.

Zaire, 5: Has high expectations. Bright, adventuresome. Blessed in some ways. Gentle, kind, a hard worker. A free spirit, very adaptable.

Zandra, 10: Has a good deal of common sense. Independent, critical of self and others. Original and unconventional. Reliable, responsible. Gentle, kind, a hard worker. Bold, courageous, a bit stubborn.

Zane, 10: Has a good deal of common sense. Independent, critical of self and others. Original and unconventional. A free spirit, very adaptable.

Zanna, 20: Mediates opposing parties. Reads people easily. Original and unconventional. Romantic, sensual. Bold, courageous, a bit stubborn.

Zara, 10: Has a good deal of common sense. Independent, critical of self and others. Gentle, kind, a hard worker. Bold, courageous, a bit stubborn.

Zared, 9: Desires to help the masses. Hardworking, sincere. Gentle, kind, diligent. A free spirit, very adaptable. Reliable, responsible.

Zarek, 7: Prone to flashes of inspiration. Not easily influenced. Gentle, kind, a hard worker. A free spirit, very adaptable. Strong desire to succeed.

Zea, 5: Has high expectations. Physical and passionate. Bright, adventuresome.

Zeb, 6: Obeys rules and guidelines. A step ahead of others. Friendly, but shy.

Zebada, 3: A tendency to see the bright side. A free spirit, very adaptable. Friendly, but shy. Aims to please. Reliable, responsible. Bold, courageous, a bit stubborn.

Zebadiah, 11: Able to achieve greatness. Keenly perceptive. Friendly, but shy. Independent, self-motivated. Reliable, responsible. Blessed in some ways. Bold, courageous, a bit stubborn. Great judge of character.

Zebe, 20: Mediates opposing parties. Social and entertaining. Friendly, but shy. Physical, passionate.

Zebedee, 7: Prone to flashes of inspiration. Not easily fooled. Friendly, but shy. Physical and passionate. Reliable, responsible. Loves adventure and excitement. Great entertainer.

Zebrina, 3: A tendency to see the bright side. A free spirit, very adaptable. Friendly, but shy. Gentle, kind, a hard worker. Blessed in some ways. Original and unconventional. Aims to please.

Zebulon, 5: Has high expectations. Perceptive, socially adept. Friendly, but shy. Attractive and charming. Strong verbal skills. Natural counselor and healer. Romantic, opinionated.

Zechariah, 7: Prone to flashes of inspiration. Not easily fooled. Optimistic, outspoken. Great judge of character. Bold, courageous, a bit stubborn. Gentle, kind, a hard worker. Blessed in some ways. Pioneer and risk taker. Self-reliant, successful.

Zedekiah, 6: Obeys rules and guidelines. A step ahead of others. Reliable, responsible. Loves adventure and excitement. Strong desire to succeed. Blessed in some ways. Pioneer and risk taker. Great judge of character.

Zee, 9: Desires to help the masses. Generous, giving. A free spirit, adaptable to change.

Zeeman, 10: Has a good deal of common sense. Enjoys change and variety. Loves adventure and excitement. Domestic, hardworking. Independent, critical of self and others. Romantic, sensual.

Zeke, 20: Mediates opposing parties. Social and entertaining. Strong desire to succeed. Loves adventure and excitement.

Zelda, 3: A tendency to see the bright side. A free spirit, very adaptable. Communicates skillfully. Reliable, responsible. Aims to please.

Zelig, 5: Has high expectations. Perceptive, socially adept. Great verbal skills. Blessed in some ways. Scientific and philosophical.

Zelotes, 30: A tendency to see the bright side. A free spirit, very adaptable. Communicates skillfully. Natural counselor and healer. Dynamic, busy lifestyle. Loves adventure and excitement. Charming, devoted.

Zena, 10: Has a good deal of common sense. Likes change and variety. Romantic, opinionated. Independent, critical of self and others.

Zenas, 20: Mediates opposing parties. Social and entertaining. Creative, original. Independent, critical of self and others. Charming and devoted.

Zenobia, 9: Desires to help the masses. Generous, giving. Creative, opinionated. Natural counselor and healer. Friendly, but shy. Blessed in some ways. Not easily influenced.

Zenon, 11: Able to achieve greatness. Keenly perceptive. Opinionated, creative. Natural counselor and healer. Romantic, sensual.

Zenos, 7: Prone to flashes of inspiration. Not easily fooled. Original and unconventional. Natural counselor and healer. Charming and devoted.

Zeph, 10: Has a good deal of common sense. Likes change and variety. Levelheaded. Great judge of character.

Zephaniah, 7: Prone to flashes of inspiration. Not easily fooled. Levelheaded. Great judge of character. Resolute and purposeful. Original and unconventional. Blessed in some ways. Bold, courageous, a bit stubborn. Self-reliant, successful.

Zerlena, 9: Desires to help the masses. Generous, giving. Gentle, kind, a hard worker. Strong verbal skills. Physical and passionate. Original and unconventional. A natural authority.

Zeta, 7: Prone to flashes of inspiration. Not easily fooled. Dynamic, busy lifestyle. Independent, critical of self and others.

Zeus, 8: Responds quickly, great reflexes. Original and creative. A great mediator. Charming and devoted.

Zhane, 9: Desires to help the masses. Great judge of character. Hardworking, generous. Original and creative. A free spirit, very adaptable.

Zinnia, 10: Has a good deal of common sense. Respectful, kind. Original and unconventional. Romantic, sensual. Artistic, having good taste. Independent, critical of self and others.

Zion, 10: Has a good deal of common sense. Respectful, kind. Natural counselor and healer. Original and unconventional.

Zipporah, 10: Has a good deal of common sense. Respectful, considerate. Intelligent and knowledgeable. Overly secretive, distant. Natural counselor and healer. Gentle, kind, a hard worker. Independent, critical of self and others. Great judge of character.

Zita, 20: Mediates opposing parties. Blessed in some ways. Dynamic, busy lifestyle. Independent, critical of self and others.

Ziv, 3: A tendency to see the bright side. Considerate, understanding. Intuitive and inspired.

Zivan, 9: Desires to help the masses. Blessed in some ways. Intuitive and inspired. Independent, critical of self and others. Original and unconventional.

Zivon, 5: Has high expectations. Generous, thoughtful. Intuitive and inspired. Natural counselor and healer. Original and unconventional.

Zizi, 7: Prone to flashes of inspiration. Needs alone time. A great mediator. Artistic, having good taste.

Zoe, 10: Has a good deal of common sense. Self-sacrificing, devoted. A free spirit, very adaptable.

Zoey, 8: Responds quickly, great reflexes. Competitive in business. Original, creative. Dislikes limitations.

Zoie, 10: Has a good deal of common sense. Self-sacrificing, devoted. Blessed in some ways. A free spirit, very adaptable.

Zola, 9: Desires to help the masses. Artistic, creative. Strong verbal skills. Independent, critical of self and others.

Zoltan, 7: Prone to flashes of inspiration. Open to opportunities. Communicates skillfully. Dynamic, busy lifestyle. Not easily influenced. Sensual and romantic.

Zona, 20: Mediates opposing parties. Works well with others. Romantic, opinionated. Reads people easily.

Zora, 6: Obeys rules and guidelines. Magnetic personality. Gentle, kind, a hard worker. Pioneer and risk taker.

Zorina, 11: Able to achieve greatness. Responsible for others. Intense inner power. Artistic, having good taste. Creative, opinionated. Intuitive, perceptive.

Zuly, 3: A tendency to see the bright side. Attractive and charming. Strong verbal skills. Needs a lot of freedom.

Zuri, 11: Able to achieve greatness. Attractive and charming. Gentle, kind, a hard worker. Blessed in some ways.

Zuriel, 10: Has a good deal of common sense. Attractive and charming. Gentle, kind, a hard worker. Blessed in some ways. A free spirit, very adaptable. Communicates skillfully.

ABOUT THE AUTHOR

A student of Astrology for almost forty years, Norma J. Watts is called upon daily for readings and advice. After studying people from all cultures and backgrounds, Norma developed Nameology to understand our true selves and find our purpose. Using Numerology as a guideline, Nameology has been tested in Norma's workplace by vacationers from all over the world for the last seven years. Norma was a regular on a popular talk radio show on KCBQ in the '80s.